The Bible Speaks Today

Series editors: Alec Motyer (OT)
John Stott (NT)
Derek Tidball (Bible Themes)

The Message of
Heaven and Hell

The Bible Speaks Today: Bible Themes series

The Message of the Living God
His glory, his people, his world
Peter Lewis

The Message of the Resurrection
Christ is risen!
Paul Beasley-Murray

The Message of the Cross
Wisdom unsearchable, love indestructible
Derek Tidball

The Message of Salvation
By God's grace, for God's glory
Philip Ryken

The Message of Creation
Encountering the Lord of the universe
David Wilkinson

The Message of Heaven and Hell
Grace and destiny
Bruce Milne

Titles in preparation

The Message of Prayer
Timothy Chester

The Message of Mission
Howard Peskett and Vinoth Ramachandra

The Message of Heaven and Hell

Grace and destiny

Bruce Milne

Formerly Senior Minister, First Baptist Church,
Vancouver, Canada

Inter-Varsity Press

Inter-Varsity Press
38 De Montfort Street, Leicester LE1 7GP, England
Email: ivp@uccf.org.uk
Website: www.ivpbooks.com

First published 2002

British Library Cataloguing in Publication Data
A catalogue record for this book is available from the British Library.

ISBN 0–85111–276–5

Set in Stempel Garamond
Typeset in Great Britain by Servis Filmsetting Ltd, Manchester
Printed and bound in Great Britain by Creative Print and Design (Wales), Ebbw Vale

Inter-Varsity Press is the publishing division of the Universities and Colleges Christian Fellowship (formerly the Inter-Varsity Fellowship), a student movement linking Christian Unions in universities and colleges throughout Great Britain, and a member movement of the International Fellowship of Evangelical Students. For more information about local and national activities write to UCCF, 38 De Montfort Street, Leicester LE1 7GP, email us at email@uccf.org.uk or visit the UCCF website at www.uccf.org.uk

To

First Baptist Church, Vancouver, Canada

In thanksgiving for seventeen exciting and fulfilling years
1984–2001

Contents

Part Three
Destiny declared: heaven and hell in the rest of the New Testament

General preface

THE BIBLE SPEAKS TODAY describes three series of expositions, based on the books of the Old and New Testaments, and on Bible themes that run through the whole of Scripture. Each series is characterized by a threefold ideal:

- to expound the biblical text with accuracy
- to relate it to contemporary life, and
- to be readable.

These books are, therefore, not 'commentaries', for the commentary seeks rather to elucidate the text than to apply it, and tends to be a work rather of reference than of literature. Nor, on the other hand, do they contain the kind of 'sermons' which attempt to be contemporary and readable without taking Scripture seriously enough.

The contributors to The Bible Speaks Today series are all united in their convictions that God still speaks through what he has spoken, and that nothing is more necessary for the life, health and growth of Christians than that they should hear what the Spirit is saying to them through his ancient – yet ever modern – Word.

ALEC MOTYER
JOHN STOTT
DEREK TIDBALL
Series editors

Preface

'People are destined once to die . . .' observes the writer of Hebrews (9:27 NIVI), and few statements in the Bible are as little open to challenge. Despite medical advances in the quest for the prolongation of life, the fact remains that life is limited, even for those in the favoured, Western world. Simply put, neither you nor I will be alive a hundred years from now. Most of us appear able, at least on the surface, to cope with our impending demise with relative equanimity, due in large part to our domination by the materialistic mind-set of our culture.

Even Christians, who ostensibly are committed to the thought of a life of glory beyond death, generally give that prospect relatively little attention. Only too often the 'this life is all I have' mentality seeps its way through. Our ears no longer catch 'the distant triumph song'. We lose sight of the heavenly Jerusalem, and as a result the indescribable glories of the life to come, which were the consistent inspiration of Christians of earlier ages, drop from consciousness.[1] That is a serious situation from the perspective of the New Testament, because Christianity, as reflected in these foundational documents, is consistently orientated towards its heavenly hope, as Harry Blamires noted: 'A prime mark of the Christian mind is that it cultivates the eternal perspective . . . it looks beyond this life to another one. It is supernaturally orientated and brings to bear upon earthly considerations the fact of heaven and the fact of hell.'[2]

The last century witnessed a wholesale attempt on the part of many theologians and Christian spokespeople to represent the Christian faith as an essentially this-worldly religion, and to eliminate its other-worldly concerns as either a symptom of immaturity, or a deliberate evasion of immediate responsibility. The verdict on

---

[1] It is striking in this regard that arguably the last major work on the heavenly life was that of Richard Baxter, *The Saints' Everlasting Rest*, written in 1650.
[2] H. Blamires, *The Christian Mind* (SPCK, 1963), p. 67.

this attempt may now be registered – it has failed abysmally! To eliminate the heavenly hope is to make Christianity something it never was in the Scriptures in general, and in the mind of Jesus and the apostles in particular. In other words, it means severing the connection between the faith we profess today and that of its biblical founders; which, as Gresham Machen showed years ago, means effectively relinquishing our claim to the name Christianity.[3]

The diminution of our other-worldy focus is therefore a perilous development, and one which arguably has contributed to all manner of sicknesses among the churches, particularly in the Western world; features such as the superficializing of worship, the loss of a whole-hearted pursuit of Christian holiness, the neglect of prayer, a diminished zeal for evangelism and world evangelization, and the undue reliance on natural solutions, such as management technique, 'relevant' presentation styles and counselling therapies, in furthering the work of the churches. It would of course be a massive oversimplification to lay all these ills at the door of a loss of the eternal perspective. The relationship is in any case two-way in that the presence of some of these features contributes to the loss of the heavenly dimension, as well as being an explanation of it. Nor are these features altogether novel, as even a casual reading of the history of Christianity, to say nothing of the New Testament, would uncover. And of course, happily, there are many other more positive realities in the present-day church (often met at their richest in the developing world) which give a balancing and altogether healthier picture. However, when these caveats are duly entered, on any reckoning the need for the perspective represented by this book is widespread and clamant.

Just to reassert the fact of our future destinies will not be sufficient in itself. Our deepest need, as these earlier remarks have attempted to highlight, is for the rehabilitation of an entire biblical world view within which these long-held convictions have their necessary place. At the deepest level we are confronting the pervasive need for spiritual revival and renewal which haunts the globe as we move forward in a new millennium. In the final analysis nothing less than the gracious, sovereign and transforming work of God the Holy Spirit can bring about that recovered awareness of spiritual reality which will, as one of its blessed fruits, produce a new sense of our eternal destinies, and a fresh, liberating recognition of the supreme joys and fulfilments of the life of heaven.

In the continuing deferral of that divine visitation, we may at least attempt to demonstrate that the fact of heaven and the fact of hell are

---

[3] J. G. Machen, *Christianity and Liberalism* (Victory, 1923).

not a divine afterthought, arbitrary footnotes to the biblical story. These destinies are intrinsic to all that the Bible teaches about God and humanity, and hence a clear-sighted embracing of this area of Christian doctrine is part and parcel of what it means to have the mind of Christ and to live as a responsible and God-honouring Christian believer.

A further preliminary comment is in order. This particular area of Christian belief has experienced a certain resurgence of interest recently due to debates, especially in the UK and other English-speaking countries, around the ideas of conditional immortality (the view that immortal life beyond death is not natural to humans but possessed only by those to whom God will graciously grant it, post mortem) and annihilationism (the view that the wicked at some point after their death will experience a final extinction of life). Despite the hesitations of believers of earlier centuries concerning these views, are either of them, or an amalgam of the two, a valid understanding of the relevant biblical texts? Can a Bible-loving Christian embrace annihilationism in some form, and hence hold that the fate of the wicked lies in their being subject to ultimate destruction rather than endless retribution, as in the traditional understanding?

This debate will naturally be referred to at points in what follows, most directly in chapter 8. The treatment will necessarily be less extensive than this issue ultimately warrants (which is not to say that I do not have a personal view of this issue, as I will, in a hopefully irenic spirit, make clear). The final resolution of this particular debate, however, is not the primary aim of this book, hence the reader who at this point turns directly to chapter 8 in order to identify my position, and on that basis decides whether or not to read this volume, needs to face some important questions.

The area of biblical doctrine addressed in these pages is so important that a difference of view on a specific issue does not reduce, far less exhaust, the critical need for every Christian to return to this area again and again, in order to muse over, pray through and passionately proclaim the realities it embraces. To be deterred from further concern about the awesome terrors of hell and the overwhelming glories of heaven because of a difference of view on the former's duration is to be, quite simply, in a parlous spiritual condition.

In keeping with the previously established parameters of this series of volumes, the specific aim will be to uncover what the Bible teaches by examining a selection of the primary biblical passages which throw light on our future existence. This prescribed limitation implies that those wishing to probe the more philosophical and speculative dimensions of heaven and hell will not find their interests met within these pages. What does Scripture teach about heaven? What does it teach about hell? These will be the dominating concerns.

In responding to these questions, rather than dealing with hell first and then turning to heaven, the general order within Scripture will be followed, allowing these two human destinies to attain a mutual clarity through the developing biblical story. Even to fulfil this programme proved not quite as straightforward as it may sound. Unlike many of the other volumes in this series, the biblical passages in question only rarely have the overarching theme of the volume, in this case human destiny, as their only – or even primary – focus.[4] This meant repeatedly facing the question of how much to include of the other subjects and themes present in the passages under examination so that the treatment remained responsibly expository. On the whole I have attempted to be guided by the principle 'such as is necessary to allow the teaching on human destiny in this passage to be properly contextualized'.

As we set out on this journey towards a recovered emphasis on the eternal it is important to proceed in a properly optimistic and hopeful spirit. The life to come is, as we will see, a biblical 'fact of life'. The eternal God assures us unambiguously, and repeatedly, that he will meet us all in eternity. As God the Lord he is abundantly able to restore a recognition of this truth through his Spirit whenever and however he may please. He has many allies, as Robert Browning noted more than a century ago in 'Bishop Blougram's Apology'. Just as we are settling into our this-wordly slumbers:

> Just when we are safest, there's a sunset-touch,
> A fancy from a flower-bell, some one's death . . .

Or, as we might now add, a terrorist outrage. Something breaks into our lives that cries out against our materialistic complacency. The great questions of existence rise up once again. What is life? Where is it going? What about death, and the beyond? The sun of conviction breaks through the clouds of our chronic unbelief, and in that instant we know with a deeply rooted certainty that we are more than dust, that life is larger than the boundaries of this terrestrial existence, and

---

[4] That fact is demonstrated by noting that in a systematic theological 'text' the major loci of Christian doctrine do not include 'heaven and hell' as a distinct section, these subjects being treated rather as a subsection of 'the last things', technically known as eschatology. See for example W. Grudem, *Systematic Theology* (IVP, 1994); M. J. Erickson, *Christian Theology* (Baker, 1983); L. Berkhof, *Systematic Theology* (Banner of Truth, 1959); or, at a more basic level, the author's *Know the Truth* (IVP, rev. 1998).

that our death will not in fact be the end of us, but merely the end of the beginning. In other words, we wake up to the fact of human destiny; which, for the Bible, means waking up to the fact of heaven and the fact of hell. My prayer is simply that the God who made us in time for eternity will be pleased to do that through the scriptural texts and stories which we will consider below.

My debt continues to grow to my wife Valerie for her unfailing encouragement, not least throughout the process of creating this manuscript. My appreciation is also extended to all who contributed by reading all or parts of this text and making helpful recommendations for its improvement. In particular in that regard I have appreciated the encouragement of the series editor, Derek Tidball. I have dedicated the book to the congregation of First Baptist Church, Vancouver, where it was my privilege, for seventeen hugely demanding and exciting years, to proclaim the unsearchable riches of Christ.

BRUCE MILNE
Vancouver
Easter, 2002

A note on meanings

Before we launch into this exposition a clarification is required on meanings. Heaven and hell are the subject of regular, often light-hearted comment in our culture generally, much of which is not conducted with an eye to careful theological distinction. 'Hell' suffers less from this, having in general retained its basic biblical meaning of the post-mortem fate of those rejected at the last judgment.

In the Old Testament the Hebrew word for the abode of the dead, *Sheol*, is used fairly indiscriminately of both the righteous and unrighteous. The sense of a punitive realm for the unrighteous develops through the Old Testament period in association with the valley of Himmon south of Jerusalem, a place of child sacrifice in periods of pagan apostasy, and later the city's public incinerator. By New Testament times the Greek term *Hades* was used of the realm of the dead, with some distinction being drawn between the lot of the righteous and that of the unrighteous (as, for example, in Luke 16:23). *Gehenna*, from the earlier 'Himmon', is the usual New Testament word for hell.

'Heaven' carries a variety of meanings in popular usage, a situation complicated by the fact that the Bible itself uses 'heaven' in several distinguishable ways. It first appears as the 'extraterrestrial' creation, i.e. that part of creation which is distinguishable from the earth (Gen. 1:1, 'God created the heavens and the earth'). It can refer to the special abode of God (as in the Lord's Prayer, 'Our Father in heaven', Matt. 6:9). This usage is the commonest occurrence of heaven in both Old and New Testaments (cf. 1 Kgs. 8:30; Ps. 2:4; Heb. 1:3). It can at times refer simply to the sky above (John 17:1, 'Jesus . . . looked towards heaven').

Today 'heaven' is commonly used by Christians to refer to the present location of deceased believers (Eph. 3:15), though the Bible tends to use phrases other than 'heaven' when referring to this: 'paradise' (Luke 23:43), 'Abraham's side' (Luke 16:22), 'under the altar'

15

(Rev. 6:9), or simply 'with Christ' (Phil. 1:23; cf. chapter 9 below which deals with this 'intermediate state').

Since this volume is about human destiny, the eternal future, we will use 'heaven' to refer to the 'new heaven and earth' (Is. 65:17; 66:22; Rev. 21:1), the fullness of God's kingdom, which will appear and commence at the glorious return of Christ. Used in this sense, heaven, as the eternal abode of the redeemed after the last judgment, is the counterpart to hell, the eternal abode of the unredeemed after the last judgment.

Abbreviations

AV	Authorized Version
CD	Church Dogmatics
IBD	Illustrated Bible Dictionary
ISBE	International Standard Bible Encyclopedia
LXX	Septuagint (Greek Old Testament)
NBD	New Bible Dictionary
NCB	New Century Bible
NIC	New International Commentary
NIV	New International Version
NIVI	New International Version Inclusive Language Edition
NJB	New Jerusalem Bible
NLB	New Living Bible
NLT	New Living Translation
NTS	*New Testament Studies*
REB	Revised English Bible
RSV	Revised Standard Version
SJT	*Scottish Journal of Theology*
TB	Tyndale Bulletin
TDNT	Theological Dictionary of the New Testament
TZ	*Theologische Zeitschrift*
WBC	Word Biblical Commentary
ZNW	*Zeitschrift für neutestamentliche Wissenschaft*

Bibliography

Anderson, H., *Mark* (Oliphants, 1976).
A Scholastic Miscellany: Anselm to Ockham, Library of Christian Classics, vol. X (Westminster, 1956).
Baldwin, J. G., *Daniel* (IVP, 1978).
Bankham, R. J., *Jude, 2 Peter* (WBC, 1983).
Barth, K., *The Doctrine of Creation*, Church Dogmatics III, 1 and 2 (T. and T. Clark, 1958).
——, *The Christian Life*, Church Dogmatics IV, 4, fragments (T. and T. Clark, 1980).
Baxter, R., *The Saints' Everlasting Rest* (Wesleyan-Methodist Book Room, n.d.).
Beasley-Murray, G. R., *The Resurrection of Jesus Christ* (Oliphants, 1964).
——, *The Book of Revelation* (Eerdmans, 1974).
——, *Jesus and the Kingdom of God* (Eerdmans, 1986).
Berkouwer, G. C., *The Return of Christ* (Eerdmans, 1972).
Best, E., *1 Peter*, NCB (Eerdmans, 1971).
Blamires, H., *The Christian Mind* (SPCK, 1963).
*Blanchard, J., *Whatever Happened to Hell?* (Evangelical Press, 1993).
Blocher, H., *In the Beginning* (IVP, 1984).
Boettner, L., *Immortality* (Presbyterian and Reformed, 1956).
*Bonda, J., *The One Purpose of God: An Answer to the Problem of Eternal Punishment* (Eerdmans, 1993).
Bonhoeffer, D., *Creation and Fall* (SCM, 1959).
Bray, G., 'Hell: Eternal Punishment or Total Annihilation?', *Evangel*, 10.2 (Summer 1992).
Brown, R., *The Gospel According to John*, vol. 2 (Doubleday, 1966).
Bruce, F. F., *The Book of Acts* (Marshall, Morgan and Scott, 1954).
——, *1 & 2 Corinthians* (Eerdmans, 1971).
——, *The Epistle of Paul to the Romans* (Tyndale, 1973).
Brunner, E., *The Mediator* (Lutterworth, 1934).
——, *The Christian Doctrine of God* (Lutterworth, 1949).

——, *Our Faith* (SCM, 1949).

Caird, G. B., *The Revelation of St John the Divine* (Harper, 1966).

Calvin, J., *The First Epistle of Paul to the Corinthians* (Saint Andrew, 1960).

——, *Epistles of Paul the Apostle to the Romans and to the Thessalonians* (Saint Andrew, 1961).

——, *Institutes of the Christian Religion*, Library of Christian Classics, vols XX and XXI (Westminster, 1961).

——, *The Epistle of Paul the Apostle to the Hebrews, and the First and Second Epistles of St Peter* (Saint Andrew, 1963).

——, *The Second Epistle of Paul the Apostle to the Corinthians and the Epistles to Timothy, Titus and Philemon* (Saint Andrew, 1964).

——, *A Harmony of the Gospels Matthew, Mark and Luke* (Eerdmans, 1980).

*Cameron, N. M. de S. (ed.), *Universalism and the Doctrine of Hell* (Paternoster, 1991).

Carson, D. A., *The Gospel According to John* (IVP, 1991).

*——, *The Gagging of God: Christianity Confronts Pluralism* (Zondervan, 1996).

Charles, R. H., *A Critical and Exegetical Commentary on the Revelation of St John* (T. and T. Clark, 1920).

Clines, D., 'The Image of God in Man', TB 19 (1968).

Clowney, E., *The Message of 1 Peter* (IVP, 1988).

Colwell, J. (ed.), *Called to One Hope* (Paternoster, 2000).

Conze, F. (tr.), *The Buddhist Scriptures* (Penguin, 1959).

Craigie, P. C., *Commentary on Psalms 1 – 50* (Word, 1983).

Cranfield, C. E. B., *The First Epistle of Peter* (SCM, 1950).

——, *The Gospel According to St Mark* (Cambridge University Press, 1959).

——, *The Epistle to the Romans*, vol. 1 (T. and T. Clark, 1975).

*Crockett, W. (ed.), *Four Views on Hell* (Zondervan, 1992).

Dawood, N. J. (trans.), *The Koran* (Penguin, 1990).

Denney, J., *St Paul's Epistle to the Romans*, Expositor's Greek Testament, vol. II (Hodder and Stoughton, 1901).

——, *The Death of Christ* (Hodder and Stoughton, 1903).

——, *Factors of Faith in Immortality* (Hodder and Stoughton, 1910).

——, *The Second Epistle to the Corinthians* (Hodder and Stoughton, 1916).

*Dowsett, D., *God, That's Not Fair!* (OMF, 1998).

Dunn, J. G., *Romans* (Word, 1988).

Eichrodt, W., *Theology of the Old Testament*, 2 vols (SCM, 1967).

Ellis, E. E., *The Gospel of Luke* (Eerdmans, 1974).

*Evangelical Alliance Commission on Truth and Unity, *The Nature of Hell* (Acute, 2000).

Fee, G. D., *The First Epistle to the Corinthians*, NIC (Eerdmans, 1987).

*Fernando, A., *Crucial Questions About Hell* (Kingsway, 1999).

France, R. T., *Matthew* (IVP, 1985).

*Fudge, E. W., *The Fire that Consumes: The Biblical Case for Conditional Immortality* (rev. ed., Paternoster, 1994).

Geldenhuys, N., *Commentary on the Gospel of Luke* (Marshall, 1950).

Green, E. M. B., *The Second Epistle General of Peter and the General Epistle of Jude* (Tyndale, 1958).

Grenz, S., *Created for Community* (Bridgepoint, 1996).

——, *The Social God and the Relational Self* (Westminster John Knox, 2001).

Grudem, W., *1 Peter* (IVP, 1988).

Harris, M. J., *Raised Immortal* (Eerdmans, 1983).

Hiebert, E. D., *First Peter* (Moody, 1984).

Hill, D., *Matthew* (Oliphants, 1972).

Hodge, C., *An Exposition of the First Epistle to the Corinthians* (Banner of Truth, 1958).

*Hoekema, A. A., *The Bible and the Future* (Paternoster, 1978).

Hooker, M. *The Gospel According to St Mark* (Black, 1991).

Hoskyns, E. C., *The Fourth Gospel* (Faber, 1947).

Hughes, P. E., *Paul's Second Epistle to the Corinthians* (Marshall, Morgan and Scott, 1962).

——, *The Book of the Revelation* (IVP, 1990).

Hunter, A. M., *The Gospel According to St Mark* (SCM, 1948).

——, *Interpreting the Parables* (SCM, 1960).

Jeremias, J., *The Parables of Jesus*, rev. ed. (SCM, 1972).

——, *New Testament Theology*, vol. 1 (SCM, 1971).

Kelly, J. N. D., *A Commentary on the Epistles of Peter and Jude* (Black, 1979).

Kidner, D., *Genesis* (Tyndale, 1967).

——, *Psalms 1–72* (IVP, 1973).

Kreeft, P., *Everything You Ever Wanted to Know about Heaven ... but Never Dreamed of Asking* (Ignatius, 1990).

Kunneth, W., *The Theology of the Resurrection* (SCM, 1965).

Ladd, G. E., *A Commentary on the Revelation* (Eerdmans, 1972).

Leupold, H. C., *Exposition of Genesis* (Baker, 1942).

——, *Exposition of the Psalms* (Baker, 1969).

——, *Exposition of Daniel* (Baker, 1969).

Lewis, C. S., *Mere Christianity* (Macmillan, 1943).

——, *Miracles* (Fontana, 1960).

——, *The Problem of Pain* (Macmillan, 1962).

——, *The Four Loves* (Fontana, 1963).

——, *The Great Divorce* (Fontana, 1972).
Lloyd-Jones, D. M., *Expository Sermons on 2 Peter* (Banner of Truth, 1983).
MacArthur, J. F., *The Glory of Heaven* (Crossway, 1996).
Machen, J. G., *Christianity and Liberalism* (Victory, 1923).
Marshall, I. H., *The Gospel of Luke* (Paternoster, 1978).
——, *The Acts of the Apostles* (IVP, 1980).
Martin, R. P., *Mark* (John Knox, 1981).
McCullough, D. W., *The Trivialisation of God* (Navpress, 1955).
McNeile, A. H., *The Gospel According to St Matthew* (Macmillan, 1971).
Milne, B., *The End of the World* (Kingsway, 1979).
Morris, L., *The Apostolic Preaching of the Cross* (Tyndale, 1955).
——, *The First Epistle of Paul to the Corinthians* (Tyndale, 1958).
——, *The Biblical Doctrine of Judgment* (Tyndale, 1961).
——, *Apocalyptic* (IVP, 1972).
——, *Luke* (IVP, 1974).
——, *The Book of Revelation* (IVP, 1987).
——, *The Gospel According to Matthew* (IVP, 1992).
——, *The Cross in the New Testament* (Paternoster, 1965).
Moule, C. F. D., *The Origin of Christology* (Cambridge University Press, 1977).
Moule, H. G. C., *The Epistle of Paul the Apostle to the Romans* (Cambridge University Press, 1903).
Murray, I. H., *The Puritan Hope* (Banner of Truth, 1971).
Murray, J., *The Epistle to the Romans*, vol. 1 (Eerdmans, 1986).
Neill, S., *Crises of Belief* (Hodder and Stoughton, 1984).
Newbigin, L., *The Light Has Come* (Eerdmans, 1982).
Niebuhr, R., *The Nature and Destiny of Man*, 2 vols (Nisbet, 1941, 1943).
Nineham, D. E., *The Gospel of Saint Mark* (Penguin, 1963).
Nygren, A. N., *Commentary on Romans* (Fortress, 1949).
Packer, J. I., 'What did the cross achieve?', TB 25 (1974).
*——, *The Problem of Eternal Punishment* (Orthos, 1990).
*Pawson, D., *The Road to Hell* (Hodder and Stoughton, 1992).
Peterson, E., *Reversed Thunder* (Harper, 1988).
Pinnock, C., 'Fire, then Nothing', *Christianity Today* (20th March 1987).
Plummer, A., *The Gospel According to S. Luke* (T. and T. Clark, 1922).
Prior, D., *The Message of First Corinthians* (IVP, 1985).
von Rad, G., *Genesis* (SCM, 1963).
Robertson, A. and A. Plummer, *A Critical and Exegetical Commentary on the First Epistle of Paul to the Corinthians* (T. and T. Clark, 1973).

Rowley, H. H., *The Faith of Israel* (SCM, 1956).
Schweitzer, E. S., *The Good News According to Mark* (SPCK, 1971).
Smith, W. M., *The Biblical Doctrine of Heaven* (Moody, 1968).
Spurgeon, C. H., *The Treasury of David*, vols. I and III (London, 1872).
Stewart, J. S., *Heralds of God* (Hodder and Stoughton, 1946).
——, *A Faith to Proclaim* (Hodder and Stoughton, 1953).
Stibbs, A., *The First Epistle General of Peter* (Tyndale, 1959).
——, *God's Church* (IVP, 1959).
Stott, J. R. W., *The Message of Acts* (IVP, 1990).
——, *The Contemporary Christian* (IVP, 1992).
——, *The Message of Romans* (IVP, 1994).
*Stott, J. R. W., and D. L. Edwards, *Essentials: A Liberal-Evangelical Dialogue* (Hodder and Stoughton, 1988).
Swete, H. B., *The Gospel According to S. Mark* (Macmillan, 1898).
Tasker, R. V. G., *The Gospel According to St Matthew* (Tyndale, 1961).
Temple, W., *Readings in John's Gospel* (Macmillan, 1961).
Torrance, T. F., *The Apocalypse Today* (Jas. Clarke, 1960).
——, *Space, Time and Resurrection* (Handsel, 1976).
Travis, S. H., *Christian Hope and the Future of Man* (IVP, 1980).
Wallace, R. S., *The Lord is King: The Message of Daniel* (IVP, 1979).
Waltke, B. K., *Genesis* (Zondervan, 2001).
Weiser, A., *The Psalms* (SCM, 1962).
*Wenham, J. W., *The Goodness of God* (IVP, 1974).
Willcox, M., *I Saw Heaven Opened* (IVP, 1975).
Williams, C. S. C., *A Commentary on the Acts of the Apostles* (Black, 1964).
*Wright, N., *The Radical Evangelical* (SPCK, 1996).

Titles marked with an asterisk are particularly relevant to the debate in chapter 8.

Part One
The dawning of destiny: heaven and hell in the Old Testament

Introduction

Why not just skip the Old Testament?

This is a book about human destiny. Its specific aim is to examine, through the lens of a few primary passages, what the Bible teaches about heaven and hell. Its orientation is therefore towards the eternal future, purporting to explore that 'undiscovered country' which no reader of these pages has yet entered, far less returned from; the country labelled 'the afterlife'. This being the case, the starting point of the book may come as a surprise – the Old Testament and, indeed, the opening words of the first chapter of the book of Genesis! Surely we ought to be getting to grips right away with the real stuff. What does Jesus teach about hell? What about the descriptions of heaven in the book of Revelation?

The starting point

In due time we will of course grapple with these central New Testament passages, but we cannot begin there. Without apology we need to start where the Bible starts – with its opening section, the Old Testament, and with its opening words – and for at least three reasons.

First, this is where all the New Testament contributors to our understanding of human destiny began, John, the author of Revelation, quite explicitly so: 'In the beginning was the Word' (John 1:1) is a clear allusion to Genesis 1:1. While the fullest and clearest teachings about the afterlife do certainly come from the lips of Jesus and the apostles in the New Testament, every last one of them was nurtured on the Old Testament. It was in effect the religious and spiritual womb within which their understanding of human destiny was conceived and nurtured. To understand them we need to enter their world, and that means the world of the Old Testament.

Granted an Old Testament starting point, however, need we begin as far back as the first words of the Bible and the story of creation? That brings us to the second reason for starting where we do. Our whole understanding of the future life, and our personal destiny in particular, is fundamentally determined by what we believe about God, the kind of God he is, and the particular relationships we understand him to sustain with the world and its peoples.

By the nature of the case, death will conclude all that we may do to influence our personal destiny; heaven and hell really are completely out of our control. From the point of our last breath onwards God's contribution is one hundred per cent; everything. So in a real sense, when we set out to explore the Bible's teaching about the afterlife we are setting out on an exploration of God. Who God is, and who he will be, is the supreme determinant of our destiny.

In this matter we find ourselves in a position not unlike that of a defendant facing an impending trial. One of the crucial facts which will concern the defendant in preparation for the proceedings, as the counsel will not fail to point out, is the identity of the judge. Who will be trying the case? The answer to that will probably go a significant way towards determining the verdict. So in our anticipation of the last judgment few things are as important as the character and the values of our Judge. Since the Bible's opening words are crucial for understanding God and his values, we need to make them our first port of call.

Third, there is an intrinsic relationship between the beginning and the end of the world. The primary reason is that it is the same God who acts at the beginning as will act at the end. And because God is inherently self-consistent, 'the Father of the heavenly lights, who does not change like shifting shadows' (Jas. 1:17), what he does in creation is a major clue to what he will do at the consummation.

The relationship between the beginning and the end, however, is even more profound than a matter of the consistency of God. The prophet Isaiah hears God say, 'I am the first and I am the last' (Is. 48:12), in anticipation of the claim of the exalted Jesus, 'I am the First and the Last. I am the Living One; I was dead, and behold I am alive for ever and ever! And I hold the keys of death and Hades' (Rev. 1:17–18). The same writer can report, 'I make known the end from the beginning, from ancient times, what is still to come. I say: My purpose will stand, and I will do all that I please' (Is. 46:10). The God who acts to create does so as the expression of an eternal purpose which will reach its conclusion at the end of the ages. Hence the creative acts of God need to be understood as the beginning of a series of divine actions, which stage by stage implement the glorious, age-long plan of God until it reaches its climax in the events surrounding our destiny. The end is therefore in a profound sense present in, and anticipated by, the beginning. To use Kidner's powerful phrase, 'the beginning is pregnant with the end'.[1]

It is the intrinsic relationship of these two 'moments' within the one divine purpose that Peter expresses in his second letter: 'By God's word the heavens existed and the earth was formed out of water . . . by the same word the present heavens and earth are reserved for fire, being kept for the day of judgment' (2 Pet. 3:5, 7).

These three reasons combine in this conclusion: to reach the end we need to begin at the beginning.

A waste of time?

There is a deeper question to be faced before we can begin to expound 'the Old Testament's teaching on the afterlife'. It is not merely that beginning with the Old Testament appears to look in the wrong direction (backwards instead of forwards). What if there is nothing there to see?

This is a serious issue for some. E. F. Sutcliffe, for example, can write:

> There has been a tendency to take it for granted that, like our-selves, Abraham, Moses and David, and the other great men of God of the Old Testament looked forward (!) to a judgment of their lives by God after death with a consequent apportionment of reward or punishment. But an attentive reading of the Old Testament shows that this is a mistaken notion and that for many centuries the religious life of the patriarchs and the people of Israel was based exclusively on God's government of the world during the course of men's pilgrimage on the earth.[2]

Sheol the shadow

In support of this rather bleak conclusion, attention is commonly directed to the main Hebrew term for the abode of humans after death, *Sheol*. Its etymology is disputed; but many scholars favour a root meaning such as 'the desolate realm', or 'the un-world'.[3]

Hence Jacob, on hearing the report of Joseph's presumed death, responds, 'in mourning will I go down to the grave [Heb. *Sheol*] to my son' (Gen. 37:35). Or, as another example, there is the vivid

[1] D. Kidner, *Genesis* (Tyndale, 1967), p. 43.
[2] E. F. Sutcliffe, *Scripture*, ii, 1947, p. 94. Cited H. H. Rowley, *The Faith of Israel* (SCM, 1956), p. 153, fn. 5.
[3] See L. Kohler, TZ II, 1946, pp. 71f; cf. B. Waltke, *Genesis* (Zondervan, 2001), p. 505.

picture drawn in Isaiah 14 where the denizens of *Sheol* taunt the oppressor of the nations as he joins them in the world of the dead: 'The grave below [Heb. *Sheol*] is all astir to meet you at your coming; it arouses the spirits of the departed to greet you . . . They will all respond, they will say to you, "You also have become weak, as we are; you have become like us"' (vv. 9:10). Thus life in *Sheol* appears as a shadowy existence where the boisterous vigour of everyday life is stilled. Furthermore, there appears in general to be no clear distinction in *Sheol* between the lot and location of the righteous and that of the wicked (Ps. 89:48; Eccles. 9:10).[4]

Those in *Sheol* are cut off from knowledge of life here: 'If his sons are honoured, he does not know it' (Job 14:21); 'the dead know nothing' (Eccles. 9:5). More soberingly it appears at one or two points that the dead in *Sheol* are in some sense separated from God: 'It is not the dead who praise the LORD, those who go down to silence' (Ps. 115:17); '. . . the slain who lie in the grave, whom you remember no more' (Ps. 88:5), though it should probably be noted that this latter sombre prospect occurs in a dirge psalm where the writer is reflecting a current mood of deep despair.

The overall impression of *Sheol* as something of an 'un-place' certainly finds support in the Old Testament. There is not much here, it would seem, to enrich our understanding of heaven and its joys, or of hell and its miseries.[5]

On the other hand . . .

There are two further factors to be addressed. When we survey the landscape of the Old Testament with an eye which can look back across that landscape from the mountain range of New Testament fulfilment, a rather different picture emerges. Indeed, as we attempt to demonstrate in the following chapters, it is not at all invalid to talk about the Old Testament's contribution to the Bible's understanding of human destiny.

First, we note that alongside the testimony to the admittedly shadowy life of *Sheol*, there are pointers to a distinct sense of the

---

[4] In fairness, however, in many of the references it is the fate of the wicked which is especially linked to their 'going down to *Sheol*' (cf. Ps. 9:17; 49:14; Ezek. 32:27; Amos 9:2).

[5] H. C. Leupold wrote, '*Sheol* is pictured as a huge, restless monster standing with its mouth wide open, ready to swallow all the children of men as they are swept along toward it' (*Exposition of the Psalms* [Baker, 1969], p. 151). R. A. Mason wrote, 'No-one can claim that passing from life here on earth to existence in *Sheol* was ever spoken of as good news' ('Life before and after death in the Old Testament', in *Called to One Hope*, ed. J. Colwell [Paternoster Press, 2000], p. 69).

continuing presence of the deceased in or around the place of burial. Hence the variations on the phrase 'being gathered to one's fathers' (cf. Gen. 25:8; Deut. 32:50; 1 Kgs. 2:10; 2 Chr. 17:11).[6]

Concerning the relationship between these two different visions of the abode of the departed, Eichrodt observes, 'The idea of *Sheol* . . . was manifestly never able to efface entirely belief in the presence of the dead in the grave, and this for the quite simple reason that the latter had appearance on its side.'[7]

Common to both these ways of thinking of the dead was the belief that what survived was not simply a *part* of the person (in contrast to the Greek notion of the survival of the soul), but rather a shadowy image of the *whole* person. It is 'my soul' (Heb. *nepeš*) which continues to exist after death – 'I' (cf. Ps. 16:10; 30:4; Prov. 23:14).

Second, while this might seem only a meagre advance on *Sheol*'s pale and attenuated prospect, there is another reality which goes a considerable way towards explaining the delay in the development of a more comprehensive view of human destiny during much of the Old Testament period. This was the ever-present threat of ancestor worship, a kind of cult of the dead, with its associated spiritualistic rites. Forms of this primitive religious tradition were widely practised among the nations which surrounded Israel through much of her history. These superstitions, and the occult practices which often accompanied them, were anathema for a people who claimed God as the sole Creator, and their covenant partner, before whom there could be no other gods and who alone presided over the realms of the living and the dead. Thus necromancy is resolutely proscribed in the law (cf. Lev. 19:26; Deut. 18:10; 1 Sam. 15:23; 2 Kgs. 17:17).

This is not to say that Israel was never tempted to betray these bedrock convictions. Isaiah 65:3–4, for example, refers to those 'who continually provoke me to my very face . . . who sit among the graves and spend their nights keeping secret vigil'. However, it can be generally asserted that Israel's experience of God as the sovereign Lord, who was met, and whose mighty deeds were encountered, *on the plane of history* and within the horizons of *this* world, effectively negated speculation concerning the abode of the dead, and disallowed any attempt to establish a meaningful link with it.

> It was the shattering experience of God's will to rule which shut the gates of the kingdom of the dead, and proscribed any dealings with the departed. Yahweh's claim to exclusive lordship covered

---

[6] Hence the importance for that reason of the actual place of burial (2 Sam. 19:37; Gen. 47:29–30).

[7] W. Eichrodt, *Theology of the Old Testament*, vol. 2 (SCM, 1967), p. 213.

not only alien gods but also those subterranean powers which might offer their help to men. In this way his sovereignty was deliberately concentrated on this world; it was on this earth that God's Kingdom was to be set up.[8]

More evidence

There is, however, more to the case for an authentic Old Testament anticipation of the New Testament's revelation of human destiny than the two specific points just made. There are at least four further important ways in which the Old Testament anticipated later developments. It is these which will claim our attention in the following chapters. They are the kind of considerations which stand behind the careful conclusion of H. H. Rowley:

> The beginnings of [New Testament] belief in the resurrection are to be found here in the Old Testament . . . While the differences between the two Testaments are not to be ignored or minimised . . . the contrast is not quite so strong as is [commonly] supposed, and the seeds of every side of New Testament thought [concerning the life to come] are to be found here.[9]

What are these 'seeds'?

1. In the Bible's opening chapters we are handed the foundational moral and spiritual building blocks for its subsequent construction of human destiny. We learn who God is and what he purposes, and who we are and what is expected of us. In other words, these opening scenes of the human drama establish the conceptual value grid in terms of which the realities of human responsibility and accountability on the one hand, and conclusive divine judgment on the other, become credible, even inevitable. Indeed, it is not too much to claim that it is only as these fundamentals of the Bible's world view are embraced by our minds that its teaching on heaven and hell is ever likely to command the support of our imagination and conscience. We will address these 'building blocks' in the first two chapters.
2. The second 'seed' was for some Old Testament believers the experience of a degree of intimacy with God, so certain and so deep that the thought of any destructive intrusion upon that relationship, whether during their earthly lives or whatever might lie

---

[8] ibid., p. 221.
[9] Rowley, *The Faith of Israel*, p. 153.

beyond them, seemed simply incredible. The God who had drawn so very near in the course of life would surely not forsake them in the face of death. This will be our concern in chapter 3.

3. Israel's experience of the monarchy, particularly under David and Solomon, provided a critical model which was to influence profoundly the New Testament anticipation of a future, heavenly reign of God. This kingdom, established through the instrumentality of the messianic King, would culminate God's historic purposes and stretch on endlessly into the future. This aspect, which will concern us in chapter 4, became in turn the mould for Christian anticipations of heaven.

4. In the apocalyptic sections[10] which lie towards the end of the Old Testament, there are several direct references to human destiny beyond death, couched in certain specific concepts and images. These would be reassembled in the New Testament as the inspired pictures of the termination of history and the forms of human existence beyond it. We will address this aspect in chapter 5.

Summary

The Old Testament is the correct place to begin this book. Despite its sparsity of direct afterlife teaching it lays the basis for the later, fuller New Testament exposition of human destiny. In particular it provides:

1. The fundamental moral and spiritual perspectives for understanding and affirming heaven and hell.
2. Expressions of intimate relationship with God which in the New Testament is a primary basis for the hope of personal survival of death.
3. The experience of monarchy which shaped New Testament thinking about the final triumph of God.
4. Apocalyptic writing which asserts the fact of human survival, whether in heaven or hell, and also provides some of the key images used by the New Testament in describing them.

---

[10]'Apocalyptic' is the name given to a loosely defined group of Jewish writings dating mostly from the last two centuries BC and the first century AD. Claiming to be 'revelations' (the literal meaning of apocalypse), i.e. God-given visions, they are characterized by the free use of symbolism, a pessimism concerning present history, and vivid accounts of future events beyond the limits of the present historic process. Cf. 'Apocalypse', L. Morris; IBD, I, p. 73.

Genesis 1:1–5, 26–27; 2:14
1. Meeting the Judge and the defendant

> On the whole I do not find Christians, outside the catacombs, suf-
> ficiently sensible of the conditions. Does anyone have even the
> foggiest idea of what sort of power we so blithely invoke? Or, as
> I suspect, does no-one believe a word of it? . . . It is madness to
> wear ladies' straw hats and velvet hats to church, we should all be
> wearing crash helmets. Ushers should issue life preservers and
> signal flares; they should lash us to our pews. For the sleeping god
> may awake some day and take offense, or the waking god may
> draw us out to a place from which we can never return.
>
> (Annie Dillard, *Teaching a Stone to Talk*)

Belief in an afterlife remains high in most parts of the world, but
there is much less willingness today to envisage the post-mortem
experience in traditional Christian terms. The thought of a final
judgment leading to an eternal destiny in either heaven or hell is
widely dismissed.

The roots of this modern revisionism are diverse, as we noted
earlier, but in general the classical biblical imagery, while regularly
honoured in popular humour – everyone has a story or two about St
Peter and the pearly gates – is rejected as virtually surreal, a fantastic
scenario with no solid connection to everyday experience.

In the opening two chapters (as throughout the book) we will
attempt to reconnect with the traditional concepts, particularly that of
the last judgment, by showing how integral this idea is to the Bible's
revelation of God the Creator, and of humanity as his creature. In
other words, we will aim to meet the Judge and the defendant, and in
the process have our first glimpse of both heaven and hell.

'In the beginning God created the heavens and the earth' (Gen. 1:1).
These are, according to one writer's estimate, 'the most tremendous

words ever penned'.[1] They are replete with implications for the nature of God – the God in whose hands our destiny rests. There are at least three significant implications as far as eternal destiny is concerned.

1. God is personal

The first thing we need to clarify is this: who is this God who created everything? That he is a God of unimaginable power is clear, and will be explored below. Above all, however, the God we meet in Genesis 1:1, as on every page of Scripture, is a personal being, a God for whom relationships with other persons is supremely important. Where do we find that in this opening passage of the Bible?

We begin with the word for 'God' in all of these opening verses, *'elōhîm* (1:1, 2, 3, etc.). This is the commonest word for the Deity in the Old Testament, occuring some 2,570 times. It is derived from a root found in Arabic meaning 'to fear' or 'to reverence'. Its form is plural. While we dare not build too much on this, *'elōhîm* can helpfully be referred to as a 'potential plural, indicating the wealth of the potentialities of the divine being'.[2] Here is witness to a certain 'fullness' and 'richness' in the being of God.

God's Spirit

With this thought we move to the following verses in Genesis 1, where the inspired author develops the creative action of God. Two agencies are mentioned, *God's Spirit* ('the Spirit of God was hovering over the waters' [v. 2]), and his *word* ('And God said, "Let there be light," and there was light' [v. 3]).

The word translated 'Spirit', *rûaḥ*, is the usual Hebrew word for wind. On every other occasion in the Old Testament when this word is linked to *'elōhîm*, as here, it carries an explicit divine reference and is translated 'Spirit of God'. This is further confirmed by the verb referring to the action of the *rûaḥ*, 'hovering', which speaks of an animate agent rather than an inanimate force. Its only other Old Testament usage is graphic: 'like an eagle that stirs up its nest and hovers over its young' (Deut. 32:11).

Blocher thoughtfully reminds us of the coming of the Spirit upon Jesus at his baptism in the form of a dove (Matt. 3:16) with the suggestion, vindicated indeed by the events that flowed from it in the

---

[1] Quoted by Herschel H. Hobbs, *The Origin of All Things: Studies in Genesis* (Word, 1975), p. 9.
[2] H. C. Leupold, *Exposition of Genesis*, vol. 1 (Baker, 1942), p. 43.

mission of Jesus, of the initiation there at the Jordan of a veritable new creation.[3]

God's Word

The creative acts of God are next referred to as the product of the *words of God*: 'And God said, "Let there be . . ." and there was . . .' (v. 3; so also vv. 6–7, 9, 11, 14–15, 20, 24, 26). This creation by divine fiat, which the New Testament echoes (Heb. 11:3; 2 Pet. 3:5), proclaims the 'perfect mastery of God over every event'.[4] God's uttered wish is entirely sufficient for the perfect fulfilment of that desire. God is utterly in control and masters all that he has brought into being.

C. S. Lewis, in his children's story *The Magician's Nephew*, imagines the creation of the world through God's word by picturing a great lion, his Christ-figure Aslan, singing into the formless void and bringing forth the earth in its new-made beauty and richness.[5] Lewis has solid biblical support for this identification. John calls Jesus the 'Word' of God (John 1:1), the Word who 'became flesh' (1:14), the one through whom 'all things were made' (John 1:3). Paul testifies similarly. 'For by him all things were created: things in heaven and on earth . . . all things were created by him and for him. He is before all things, and in him all things hold together' (Col. 1:16–17; cf. Heb. 1:1–3).[6]

Trinity?

Not surprisingly, when this material relating to the Spirit and the Word is surveyed there is an instinct to discern a trinitarian reference in the creation account. 'The Fathers were right when they saw glimpses of the whole mystery of the Trinity in . . . Genesis 1.'[7] So Genesis 1 is only incidentally concerned with almighty power. It is more profoundly concerned with a multipersonal God of glorious relational fullness.

[3] D. J. A. Clines, after an extended examination of the various proposals as to the plural in 1:26, suggests that it is best understood as an address to the Spirit, who has of course already appeared in verse 2. Cf. Clines, 'The Image of God in Man', TB 19 (1968), pp. 53–103.
[4] H. Blocher, *In the Beginning* (IVP, 1984), p. 67.
[5] C. S. Lewis, *The Magician's Nephew* (Collins, 1980), pp. 93–96.
[6] The road that lies from the 'God said' of Genesis 1 to the finally developed creation Christology of these New Testament passages probably runs through Proverbs 8, where the Wisdom of God is declared to be the instrument of God's creative work: 'I was there when he set the heavens in place, when he marked out the horizon on the face of the deep . . . when he marked out the foundations of the earth. Then I was the craftsman at his side' (Prov. 8:27, 29–30).
[7] K. Barth, *The Doctrine of Creation*, CD III, 1 (T. and T. Clark, 1958), p. 116.

We can identify another pointer in the same direction in the second account of creation which immediately follows in Genesis 2:4 – 3:24. Here the Hebrew word for God is *Yahweh 'ᵉlōhîm*.[8] This additional title, *Yahweh,* is explained in Exodus 3:14 as 'I AM', which goes beyond 'I exist' and means rather 'I am actively present'. The context is crucial, God sending Moses to bring his people out of Egyptian bondage, the paradigm Old Testament expression of God as the Redeemer of his people. *Yahweh* is often referred to as a 'covenant' name for God. This is because it arises in connection with God's express purpose to enter into a solemn engagement (covenant) with people – Israel in the Old Testament (lit. Old Covenant), and the church in the New Testament. Again the Trinity is implicitly present; the one who created 'in the beginning', in the past, is the one who comes in Jesus Christ and the Spirit to redeem in the present and future.

So it becomes clear that creation is not for a moment to be viewed as an end in itself. Creation occurs with a view to covenant. The personal God creates human partners 'in his image' (Gen. 1:26) in the anticipation that he can enter into a relationship with them. The created order is formed as a context within which this relationship can be expressed.

Now of course it takes the revelation of the whole Bible to establish God's Trinity fully, just as it takes the whole Bible to unfold the full terms of God's intention to relate himself to his human creatures. The full story will take in the fact of our sinful rebellion against him, and his incredible mercy and love in taking the implications of our sin upon himself in Jesus Christ, the eternal Son of God, the second person of the Trinity. It will also encompass the ministry of the Holy Spirit in generating the very life of God within the dark, unformed hearts of believers (cf. Gen. 1:2). All of that, however, is already present in anticipation in the opening words of the Bible, because the God of Genesis 1:1, 'In the beginning God created the heavens and the earth . . .', is identical with the God of John 3:16, for 'God so loved the world that he gave his one and only Son. . .'

Who, then, is the God of Genesis 1? He is not simply an almighty power but a living, personal God who seeks relationship with his creatures. He is none other than the fully personal God whom we meet in the rest of the Bible, the very same God who exists eternally within the mystery of the eternal love of the three persons of the Godhead, and who seeks a fellowship of love with us, his human creatures.

---

[8] Cf. 'When the LORD God [*Yahweh ᵛlōhîm*] made the earth and the heavens . . .'; so also 2:5, 7, 8, etc.

Our destiny

What does this say about our relationship with God after death, our future destiny? We can establish immediately that, since God exists in and for relationship, he will always treat our relationship to him with the utmost seriousness. This will clearly be the primary issue when we appear before him after death. Whether or not we get to know God and serve him, whether or not we respond to his gracious invitation to know and love him with all of our being, and to love one another, become issues of supreme importance.

God's relational nature carries a further pointer to the life beyond. God, who is love, made us for love. In his incredible love he went to the cross to make it possible for us to come home to his arms.

Yet even when we make that journey back to God, our relationship with him in this world is never perfect. We are pilgrims on a journey as far as our knowing and loving God is concerned. We are thankful to be truly his children. We are thankful for every sense of his love in our lives, and for those limited responses we are enabled from time to time to make to him. But the final destination, loving God with all our heart and mind and strength, is never attainable here. The beating, throbbing heart of God invites our exploration, but so much remains unvisited during our lives on planet earth. That is why we need heaven, as an order of things where relationships are perfected, as a place where we will love God in a manner which is an appropriate response to his eternal love for us.

2. God is powerful

'In the beginning God created the heavens and the earth.' The Bible here asserts an absolute beginning to the universe. It refers to a unique, sovereign, primal act of God which brought all things into existence out of non-existence. While creation is not *first of all* about God's sovereign power, it is *also* about God's power. As Bruce Waltke notes, 'God's creation reveals his immeasurable power and might, his bewildering imagination and wisdom, his immortality and transcendence, ultimately leaving the finite mortal in mystery.'[9]

Mystery

The mention of mystery is very apt in this connection, for in one sense creation brings our minds to an impasse. 'We cannot speak of

[9] B. Waltke, *Genesis* (Zondervan, 2001), p. 59.

the beginning. Where the beginning begins, there our thinking stops
. . . thinking pounds itself to pieces on the beginning.'[10]

'Out of nothing'

More specifically, addressing the 'immeasurable power and might'
which the act of creation reflects, we note that the text in Genesis 1:1
is asserting that God brought everything into being out of a 'previous' non-being by his unaided word of power. There was nothing but
the Trinity, then there was the triune God plus everything that exists.
The technical phrase for this is *creatio ex nihilo*, literally, 'creation out
of nothing'. The phrase itself does not occur in the Bible, but is clearly
enough implied both here in Genesis 1:1 and also at other places in
Scripture (cf. Heb. 11:3; Rom. 4:17; 1 Cor. 1:28; John 1:3; Ps. 33:6).

The verb used here for create, *bārā'*, points in the same direction.
It is used in the Old Testament exclusively with reference to God's
action (cf. Gen. 1:21, 27; 2:3, 4). Sometimes God reshapes formerly
existing things (Gen. 2:1–4; Is. 65:18), but at other times he brings
suddenly into being (Is. 48:3, 7). The stress is consistently on the
newness of the product, and on God as the Creator. While *bārā'* does
not require the idea of creation *ex nihilo*, it nevertheless actually
'contains . . . the idea since it is never connected with any statement
of the material [from which the world was created]'.[11]

Creation, then, is an act which supremely demonstrates the unlimited freedom and majesty of God. 'God was under no constraint, no
obligation, no necessity to create. That he chose to do so was purely
a sovereign act on his part, caused by nothing outside himself, determined by nothing but his own good pleasure.'[12] There is none other
than he; he and he alone is God, as Isaiah never wearies of declaring.
'I am the first and I am the last; apart from me there is no God' (Is.
44:6). 'I am the LORD, and there is no other; apart from me there is
no God' (Is. 45:5).

The Creator-Redeemer God of the Bible is therefore exalted and
apart from all other beings. We cannot mention them in a common
grouping with him or put God into a series where there are others
ranged alongside him. God alone is God.

Self-existent

Another way of saying this is to assert that God alone is self-existent.
Everything else in the universe, whether we think of material realities

[10] D. Bonhoeffer, *Creation and Fall* (SCM, 1959), pp. 25, 27.
[11] G. von Rad, *Genesis* (SCM, 1963), p. 47.
[12] A. W. Pink, *The Attributes of God* (Baker, 1988), p. 2.

or spiritual realities, has this in common – it was made. It came into existence out of non-existence. 'There was when it was not', to adapt a phrase from early Christological debates. Hence all things are in principle eternally and irreducibly contingent; they are dependent on something beyond themselves for their existence. They depend on God. 'For from him and through him and to him are all things' (Rom. 11:36). There is only one exception, God himself. He alone of all things exists by virtue of himself. He 'is not served by human hands, as if he needed anything, because he himself gives all life and breath and everything else' (Acts 17:25 NIVI). Hence for the writer of Genesis God, and God alone, is the Creator of all things, and hence he is the one with whom we have to do at the conclusion of our lives.

Adoration

What do these words at the entrance hall of the Bible teach us about the God into whose hands we will fall in death? What do they tell us about our Judge? Clearly they call for a deep self-abasement of ourselves before his awesome majesty, and highlight our obligation to offer him an adoring, submissive worship. Truly, 'Great is the LORD and most worthy of praise' (Ps. 96:4).

One of the more impressive statements of this awesomeness of God is expressed in the words of the Larger Catechism of the Westminster Confession of Faith, drawn up in 1647 as an instructional tool for those who 'have made some proficiency in the knowledge of the grounds of religion'. To the question 'What is God?' the following response is to be mastered: 'God is a Spirit, in and of himself infinite in being, glory, blessedness, and perfection, all-sufficient, eternal, unchangeable, incomprehensible, every-where present, almighty, knowing all things, most wise, most holy, most just, most merciful and gracious, long-suffering, and abundant in goodness and truth.' In the light of that we do well to pause and reflect on the attitudes towards our Creator and future Judge which often characterize our Christian congregations. Donald McCullough makes the application perceptively.

> Visit a church on a Sunday morning – almost any will do – and you will likely find a congregation comfortably relating to a deity who fits nicely within precise doctrinal positions, or who lends almighty support to social crusades, or who conforms to individual spiritual experiences. But you will not find much awe, or sense of mystery . . . Unaccustomed as we are to mystery, we expect nothing even similar to Abraham's falling on his face, Moses

hiding in terror, Isaiah's crying out, 'Woe is me!' or Saul's being knocked flat. We are more like those described in a novel by Charles Williams who prefer 'their religion taken mild – a pious hope, a devout ejaculation, a general, sympathetic sense of a kindly universe – but nothing upsetting or bewildering, no agony, no darkness, no uncreated light'.[13]

Fearing God

The common biblical word for the appropriate attitude before our great Creator is 'fear'. 'Let all the earth fear the LORD; let all the people of the world revere him. For he spoke, and it came to be; he commanded, and it stood firm' (Ps. 33:8–9).

Jesus reiterates the necessity for this attitude of godly fear in Luke 12:5: 'Fear him who . . . has power to throw you into hell. Yes, I tell you, fear him.' Fear here is the equivalent of awesome respect rather than a craven cringing. We should especially note the grounds of this fear: that God the Creator is the one who will take us into his hands at the end and will himself, with no other to constrain him, determine our eternal destiny, whether in heaven or hell. The metaphor is vivid. 'Throw', or 'cast', conveys our utter helplessness before God's sovereign power. In other words, for Jesus our fear of God is grounded not simply in looking back to our creation but also in looking forward to our destination.

James has a similar insight in a passage with a modern resonance. 'Now listen, you who say, "Today or tomorrow we will go to this or that city, spend a year there, carry on business and make money." Why, you do not even know what will happen tomorrow. What is your life? You are a mist that appears for a little while and then vanishes' (Jas. 4:13–14). The entrepreneur stands exposed. We are masters of our lives, so we imagine. We identify the market opportunity, the critical places to do business, and how long to spend at each centre in order to make the sales and gain the profit. We are clever. We have the know-how. We are our own little gods. And all the time we live *only by God's power and permission*.

In contrast to God's power and greatness, we are a 'mist', a passing, insubstantial puff. Accordingly, the proper attitude which recognizes the reality of who God is, is expressed in James's words: 'Instead, you ought to say, "If it is the Lord's will, we will live and do this or that." As it is, you boast and brag. All such boasting is evil' (4:15–16).

[13] Donald McCullough, *The Trivialisation of God: The Dangerous Illusion of a Manageable Deity* (Navpress, 1995), pp. 13, 18.

'One who is able'

It is all the more striking in that earlier James gives us the theological basis for this perspective: 'There is only one Lawgiver and Judge, the one who is able to save and destroy' (4:12). The majesty of the Creator is the majesty of the Judge. The one who 'spoke and it came to pass', who said, 'Let there be . . . and there was' (Gen. 1:3), is the identical one who is 'the Judge . . . able to save and destroy'. Peter warns similarly, 'Since you call on a Father who judges each person's work impartially, live your lives as strangers here in reverent fear' (1 Pet. 1:17 NIVI). The anticipation of the coming judgment, our 'appearing' before him to receive his judgment on our work, is the ground for a 'reverent fear'.

Peter's equation of the Creator and Judge with the 'Father' is important. It is worth underlining again that the fear which is appropriate to our attitude to our Creator is not a cringing, craven business. The one who made us and into whose hands we will fall at the end for our assignment to either heaven or hell is 'Father', which Jesus taught us to understand in childlike terms of trust and endearment – 'Abba', 'our own dear Father' (Luke 11:2, 11–13; Rom. 8:14–17; Gal. 4:6). The Apostles' Creed catches the balance appropriately: 'I believe in God, the *Father Almighty*. . .' The 'Almighty' *is* part of it. The sheer, overwhelming power and sovereignty of God revealed in creation is the ground for a proper reverence before him, recognizing the awesomeness of the one with whom we have to do, and consequently the seriousness of our appearing before him at the last. Again, creation in the beginning anticipates accounting at the end.

3. God is present

The fact of God's creation of us as described in Genesis 1 has a further dimension. True, it makes clear that God is intrinsically relational, and further that he is overwhelmingly powerful, and that we are obligated thereby to 'fear' him.

At arm's length

Nonetheless, our proud, rebellious hearts regularly refuse to be impressed by God's greatness revealed in creation. We move on with our lives virtually ignoring him. God is probably somewhere out there, and great no doubt, but he is not involved with my life day by day, unless I choose to invite him to be. This widespread viewpoint is based on the unexamined assumption that in running our lives we are able to detach ourselves from God. Maybe God was somehow involved in my coming into existence, and maybe I will meet him at the end of my life. But until then, between my creation and my expiration, I am the one who calls the shots and is in control.

This way of thinking, which is the basic world view of untold multitudes, completely fails to take account of what 'creation' means. It is actually totally untenable by the terms of Genesis 1:1.

The use of *bārā'* (v. 26, 'make') with respect to the creation of the human species announces that we are the products of God's direct, interventive action. We emerge, not in any final sense as a result of our own energies or effort, nor as the product of some staggeringly complex, impersonal and arbitrary chemical process, such as is claimed by materialistic accounts of human origins. Whatever may have been the means by which God brought forth humankind on this planet, we only truly comprehend our existence when we confess with the sacred text that humanity has appeared by the act of God, made 'out of nothing' by his word and action, shaped 'from the dust of the ground', and given 'the breath of life' by the express will of the Creator (Gen. 2:7). 'From him and . . . to him are all things' (Rom. 11:36), including all the 'things' which pertain to our life and its destiny. We are dependent!

Leaning on God

This unqualified dependence upon God is powerfully portrayed in two important New Testament passages which refer to the continuation of the creative process. In Colossians 1:16–17, Paul declares that 'all things were created by him [Jesus Christ, the Son of God the Father] and for him. He is before all things, and in him all things hold together.' Christ is here viewed as the agent of creation, the one through whom God acted when he brought the world into existence. Crucially, in addition, Christ as the creating Word of God is the means by which 'all things hold together' (Gk. *synestēken*, 'stand together').

The writer to the Hebrews has a similar statement which makes the same connection. 'In these last days he [God] has spoken to us by his Son . . . through whom he made the universe. The Son is the radiance of God's glory and the exact representation of his being, sustaining [Gk. *pherōn*, 'carrying' or 'upholding'] all things by his powerful word' (Heb. 1:2–3).

Both these passages assert that the act of creation leads necessarily to a further continuous activity on the part of God, that of 'holding

41

all things together' (Colossians), or of 'carrying (or upholding) all things' (Hebrews).

Some such activity of God is actually inevitable once we grasp what the Bible means in its opening words, 'In the beginning God created the heavens and the earth.' If this means that all things were brought into existence 'out of nothing' by God's action, they possess no inherent power of self-sustenance. Only God exists by virtue of his own power. All other things lack self-existence. They have only what we could term 'God-existence'. That is, they continue to exist only because their existence is continually willed by God. In Christological terms, they are 'held together' or 'upheld' by Christ, the Everlasting Word of God. Thus the unique, primary act of creating necessitates a further unbroken act of *sustaining*. To put the point more metaphorically, the universe has been drawn into existence out of the 'pit' or 'abyss' of non-existence, hence it hangs eternally over that pit into which it will collapse again (and all things other than God will cease to be) if God should for even a moment cease his affirming of the universe. Everything depends continually and utterly upon God.

Applying this personally means that each one of us is utterly and continually dependent upon God. As part of a cosmos which has been called into existence out of non-existence solely by God's word of command, 'Let there be', we continue in existence only by God's upholding word, and consequently we are totally dependent upon God for our lives.

Further, it should be clear from our exposition of the meaning of the creation account in Genesis 1 that this dependence admits no exception, nor permits any qualification. There is no area of our lives, no department of our being, no element of our make-up, no feature of our circumstances, which lies outside, or which can exist for a moment apart from, God's upholding power. We, and all of our life – past, present and future; body, mind and spirit; physical, mental and spiritual; conscious, unconscious and subconscious; individual and social; in infancy, youth, maturity and retiral years; and whatever other divisions and distinctions we may wish to draw – *all* of us in *all* things are *altogether* dependent upon God.

The Bible puts this another way by reminding us that we are a mere breath. Daniel's remonstration with Belshazzar at his pride and idolatry is eloquent in this connection. 'You praised the gods of silver and gold, of bronze, iron, wood and stone, which cannot see or hear or understand. But you did not honour the God *who holds in his hand your life* [lit. 'breath'] *and all your ways*' (Dan. 5:23, my italics; cf. Job 12:9; Ps. 104:29; 146:4; Acts 17:25).

God inescapable

Since we all depend upon God in this radical manner 'godlessness' is, in a strict sense, a patent impossibility. As Emil Brunner put it, 'Without God there would be absolutely nothing at all, without God a man could know nothing. Knowledge is possible only because God is. The question about God is only possible because God already stands behind the question.'[14] Atheism, the state of mind which corresponds to a denial of God, is of course a theoretical possibility and indeed the confessed world view of many modern people. The taproots of atheism are various. We can note as factors which promote atheism the deep, dark enigma of evil and, for some, the experience of stark, personal tragedy. Scripture, which talks of the folly of atheism – 'The fool says in his heart, "There is no God"' (Ps. 14:1) – would link all such denial in some degree with our sinful rebellion against God (cf. 2 Pet. 2:1; Luke 19:14). For Scripture atheism is finally a wilful ignorance, a form of rebellion against the true knowledge of God. Karl Barth has some trenchant comments in this regard.

> The most interesting thing . . . about theoretical atheism . . . is its belligerent character. It constantly breaks out in polemics. If God were absolutely unknown to the world, if the world were as ungodly as it is supposed to be according to atheistic confession, why does it need such a confession? The fact . . . that it has to fight God so excitedly . . . tells us plainly that in some way, and not just superficially, it finds itself unsettled, pressured, and threatened by the objective knowledge of God . . . The world simply cannot be absolutely godless, as it would like to be. The ambivalence of its opposition to God betrays itself in the violence with which it asserts it.[15]

Standing on nothing!

From the perspective of the biblical doctrine of creation theoretical atheism is in fact, finally considered, an astonishing position. Indeed, if the issues here were not so serious, we could almost view it as ridiculous to the point of amusement. Consider the condition of the atheist. Were it not for the God he denies, he would not exist. He is utterly dependent upon the God he denies to draw the breath

[14] E. Brunner, *Our Faith* (SCM, 1949), p. 14.
[15] K. Barth, *The Christian Life*, CD IV, 4, fragments, tr. G. W. Bromily (Eerdmans, 1980), pp. 128–129.

which he expels in asserting, 'There is no God.' He is utterly dependent upon God for that sentence to have rational meaning. The
atheist needs God for the sense of identity which permits him to be
the same person who both thinks the thought, 'There is no God',
and utters the sentence. He depends upon God for the reality of the
human culture and society within which he lives, and in the context
of which he makes his denial of God. He depends upon God for the
parents who birthed him and sustained him. One could go on endlessly, but the point is made. The atheist is, in the end, rather like a
man who stands on a bridge over a vast chasm and shouts at the top
of his lungs, 'There are no such things as bridges!' How fortunate
for him that he is mistaken. We need God to deny God.

This inescapable presence of God applies across the board.
Whatever the theoretical position we adopt, we adopt it in dependence on God. Whatever idol we try to substitute for the true and
living God of the Bible, we only erect that idol and worship it with
the help and enablement of God.

Yet, on all these roads which lead us away from God, he is there,
and only because of his power and enablement do these roads exist
for us and we exist for these roads. God is inescapable. We cannot
evade or avoid him. That was the discovery of the psalmist, memorably recorded in Psalm 139:7–12.

> Where can I flee from your presence?
> If I go up to the heavens, you are there;
> if I make my bed in the depths [*Sheol*], you are there.
> If I rise on the wings of the dawn,
> if I settle on the far side of the sea,
>   even there . . . your right hand will hold me fast.
> If I say, 'Surely the darkness will hide me . . .'
> even the darkness will not be dark to you.

The application of this truth is pervasive as far as our relationship to
God is concerned, for few things will so humble us and bring us to
our knees before our Maker than the realization of our utter and
unrelievable dependence. 'Come, let us bow down in worship, let us
kneel before the LORD our Maker' (Ps. 95:6).

It is also pervasive as far as the thought of our future judgment is
concerned. That we are accountable before God follows inevitably.
Whether we have chosen to embrace or to ignore him makes no difference in the end. The Judge is here right now; we exist before, with
and by him, and sooner or later we shall meet him.

4. We are responsible

So far we have learned three crucial truths about God the Creator, all of which coalesce in the fact of human responsibility. First, the God of creation is personal, constructing an environment within which he can relate in love to his human creature. As relationship with us is fundamental to God, so relationship with God is fundamental to us. Second, the God of creation is overwhelmingly great and therefore claims our respect and worship. Third, the God of creation is our sustainer through whom, and hence before whom, we exist at every moment. On all these grounds we are accountable to him.

A holy God

We begin this section on responsibility by recalling who our Creator is. We noted earlier that the creation accounts reveal a loving, personal God who seeks relationship with us. 'God is love' (1 John 4:16). We need now to fill out that definition with the words recorded earlier in John's letter, 'God is light' (1 John 1:5). We can bring these two fundamentals of God's nature together by affirming, 'God is holy love.' The root of 'holy' (Heb. qāḏôš) is most probably that of separation. God has a specific character, reflecting an eternal commitment on his part. In being who he is, God implacably separates himself from that which he is not. Thus, for example, he is good and hence separates himself eternally from all that is evil. He is true and hence separates himself eternally from all falsehood. He is loving and hence separates himself eternally from all lovelessness. He is merciful and hence separates himself eternally from all unmercifulness.

Now, because we are the creatures, made in the image of such a God (Gen. 1:26–27), we are obligated. We are called to conform to God, summoned to side with him by separating ourselves from all that denies and opposes him. Our being his creatures means that he says to us, 'Be holy, because I am holy' (Lev. 11:44, 45; 19:2; 20:7; 1 Pet. 1:16). Human existence is therefore inescapably moral, a matter of right and wrong, and the endless choices which this entails. Human life is responsible.

Talking about trees

Both creation accounts emphasize this fact. The presentation of creation in Genesis 1:26–27 is immediately followed by the divine direction, 'Be fruitful and increase in number; fill the earth and subdue it. Rule over the fish . . . the birds . . . and over every living creature'

(1:28). Humanity is given a task and becomes accountable for the performance of it. Similarly, in the second presentation in Genesis we read, 'The LORD God took the man and put him in the Garden of Eden to work it and take care of it' (2:15). Then comes the further supremely significant direction, 'You are free to eat from any tree in the garden; but you must not eat from the tree of the knowledge of good and evil, for when you eat of it you will surely die' (2:16–17).

What is the meaning of this choice, and of this special tree? Many expositors have seen here the challenge to leave moral decisions, the determining of what is right and wrong (and hence the determining of our lives and destinies), entirely in the hands of God. By refusing to eat of this tree humanity remains the true child of God, dependent on him for the choices of his life and hence honouring God by affirming him as the one who alone has the prerogative to decide for humanity in his life. By submitting to God's command, humanity expresses identification with God in holiness, by saying 'no' to all that is opposed to God.

> To transgress the Word of the Lord means to do good or evil after one's own will. But this is something which must not be done because it is God who must decide concerning good and evil, commanding the one and prohibiting the other . . . By choosing and deciding for himself he must now become the fountain of life himself. But he is unable to be the fountain of life himself. Hence he can only forfeit his life and die.[16]

Human beings, by contrast, must depend on a revelation from the only one who knows good and evil (cf. Prov. 30:1–6), 'but humanity's temptation is to seize this prerogative independently from God'.[17]

Creatureliness means responsibility. In other words, life is not ours to use as we please, to indulge, direct or invest in whatever ways may appeal to us. The creatorhood of God means that life is not ours at all. It is not a possession to consume, it is a gift to invest. Life is not ours. We receive it moment by moment from the hand of God, and are accordingly totally accountable to him for how we live it. Paul's question to the Corinthians is pertinent. 'What do you have that you did not receive?' (1 Cor. 4:7). Addressed to the proud 'super-spirituals' in the congregation in Corinth, it focuses the simple implication of our creation: everything is gift.

[16] Barth, CD III, 1, p. 287. Cf. also Bruce Waltke, 'The tree represents knowledge and power appropriate only to God [Gen. 3:3, 5, 22]', Waltke, *Genesis*, p. 86.
[17] Waltke, ibid, p. 86.

Accounting

The parables of Jesus make this point in several places. In Luke 19:1–27 a nobleman on his way to being crowned gives his servant sums of money to be 'put to work' during his absence. In Luke 20:9–16 the owner of a vineyard asks his tenants for fruit from the vineyard which he owns. In Matthew 25:31–45 a king reflects on the service which his servants have given to him during his (apparent) absence. In each case there is an ownership which is entrusted. Such is our situation with respect to life. God owns 'our' lives. He makes us a gift, which is life itself. We are totally accountable for what we do with it year after year, day after day, hour after hour, minute after minute.

Thus in these parables there is a day of reckoning. The king comes back to discover what has been done with his money (Luke 19:12), the owner of the vineyard comes to confront the rebellious tenants and repay them for their failure to send the owner his harvest (Luke 20:16), the Son of Man 'comes in his glory' to exercise judgment in terms of how he has been served (Matt. 25:31). Life is a stewardship; the Creator has made it available to us. It is his, and we are to use it for him. On this basis the biblical insistence on God's judgment is completely at home. Granted human responsibility, judgment is an inevitability. Accordingly, the God of the Bible is emphatically a God who judges.

Where is your brother?

On what grounds does God judge? What are the specific obligations laid upon us by the fact of our creation by this God of holy love? Jesus identified two – to love God and to love our neighbour (Matt. 22:37–40), a summary neatly caught by the two questions posed in the opening chapters of Genesis: 'Where are you?' (3:9), the question to Adam and Eve in the Garden, and 'Where is your brother?' (4:4), the question put to Cain after his murder of Abel.

We have already exposed something of the meaning of the first question. God asks where we are in relation to him and his call to be like him, to be holy. The second question, which touches the 'second great commandment' (Matt. 22:38), can be traced also to the heart of the story of creation in the words of Genesis 1:27, 'So God created people in his own image; God patterned them after himself; male and female he created them' (NLT).

The image of God

It would appear from this text that the image of God is not so much a particular attribute or set of attributes which we can possess as a condition within which we may exist, a condition exemplified by the loving reciprocity of Adam and Eve in their marital union, 'the two shall become one'. Stanley Grenz makes this connection as follows: 'The three members of the Trinity are "person" precisely because they are persons-in-relationship; that is, their personal identities emerge out of their reciprocal relation . . . [hence] the Creator's intention that humans be the representation of the divine reality means that the goal of human existence is to be persons-in-community.'[18]

Our being called to 'image' such a God carries huge implications for us as his creatures, for the summons to 'mirror', i.e. to represent him in the world, is the summons also to find ourselves in loving others. The fact of our creation by God in his image implies our being created with the responsibility to reflect the nature of God, not only by separating ourselves from all that stands against him and threatens our own fulfilment (i.e. by being holy), but also by living as persons-in-community, by living a life *for others*.

Thus we encounter the command of God, which represents our accountability to him, both in the question 'Where are you (in relation to me)?' and in the question 'Where is your brother?' The former meets us in the struggles with our conscience as it summons us to be holy (which of course includes the call to turn from hatred and selfishness and to show love). The latter meets us when our conscience is aroused towards our responsibility for others.

Again God is inescapable. Everyone has heard his voice, if not in terms of direct sense of him and his claim, then certainly in the obligations of community, whether in family or in the multiple associations which form the social mesh of our lives every day. We are responsible, and therefore future judgment is both necessary and inevitable.

'Where is God now?'

There is an arrestingly modern feel to the second command of God, touching as it does what Philip Yancey calls 'the central question of

---

[18] S. Grenz, *The Social God and the Relational Self* (Westminster, John Knox, 2001), p. 332. See this text passim, and especially chapter 8; see also his *Created for Community* (Bridgepoint, 1996). 'Man is created not "in" God's image, since God has no image of his own, but "as" God's image, or rather "to be" God's image, that is to deputise in the created order for the transcendent God who remains outside the world order . . . he is representative rather than representation' (Clines, TB 19 [1968], p. 100). The meaning of the image of God has been debated over the centuries. For a very able recent survey see chapter 4 of Grenz, *The Social God and the Relational Self*.

the modern era: "where is God now?" The modern answer from the likes of Nietzsche, Freud, Mark, Camus and Beckett is that he has abandoned us.'[19] That is, he is the absent God. Jesus anticipates this situation in a number of parables, most memorably that of the sheep and the goats (Matt. 25:31–45).[20] Here we note that the king who has been absent reappears and brings his subjects to judgment on the basis of how they have behaved towards those who are 'brothers'. Suddenly the subjects are faced with the overwhelming fact that, despite his apparent absence, the king has all the while been present in their midst in his representatives, especially the needy and the marginalized, the hungry, the thirsty, the homeless, the sick and the imprisoned (Matt. 25:44–45).

Many moderns do not believe in God. 'Where is he?' they ask. And seemingly they get no answer. Accordingly, the notion that they are in some way accountable to him is dismissed out of hand: 'How can your God bring us to judgment when he has apparently abandoned the world and left us insufficient evidence of his reality?' To all such, the truths of the early chapters of Genesis, enlivened by the creative imagination of Jesus, is devastating in its import. He *is* here, and *we are accountable*. In the person of my needy neighbour, the King, my Creator, is present in person. There will be no lack of material for the Judge on judgment day. The books which will be opened will be of encyclopedic proportions. We contribute to them every passing hour in our responses to the King's representatives all around us.

The two questions in Genesis, and their counterpart in the two commandments cited by Jesus, unite in the fact of human responsibility. Accordingly, the Creator appears regularly throughout Scripture with the title of Judge.

God the Judge

In the Old Testament he is 'the judge of all the earth' (Gen. 18:25), 'the LORD, the judge' (Judg. 11:27; cf. Ps. 50:6); the 'righteous judge' (Ps. 7:11), the one to whom judgment 'belongs' (Deut. 1:17). All nations will come to be judged (1 Sam. 2:10; Eccles. 3:17; Ps. 96:10, 13; 98:9; 110:6; Is. 2:4). Judgment is seen as finally expressed in connection with the coming 'day of the LORD' (cf. Joel 2:1; Amos 5:18; 8:9; Obad. 15; Zeph. 1:7, 14; Mal. 4:1).

In the New Testament the stress on judgment, and future judgment in particular, is no less sustained. Judgment is again seen as

---

[19] P. Yancey, *The Jesus I Never Knew* (Zondervan, 1995), p. 232.

[20] Though some would argue that this is less of a parable than a pre-vision of the last judgment; see discussion in chapter 6.

proper of God's essence. He is 'God, the judge of all' (Heb. 12:23).
He is 'the Father who judges each person's work impartially' (1 Pet.
1:17 NIVI); the one 'who judges justly' (2:23); the God 'just in . . .
judgments' (Rev. 16:5). Again the notion of a coming, climatic judgment resounds. 'This [assessment of human behaviour and motives]
will take place on the day when God will judge men's secrets through
Jesus Christ' (Rom. 2:16; cf. 2 Thess. 1:9–10; 1 John 4:17). Again the
universal nature of the judgment is asserted. He will 'judge the living
and the dead' (2 Tim. 4:1; Heb. 2:3; 1 Pet. 4:5). The judgment is all-
inclusive also in terms of embracing the whole person, 'men's secrets'
(Rom. 2:16), 'every purpose of the heart' (1 Cor. 4:5; cf. Mark 4:22;
Luke 12:2f.), and 'every careless word' (Matt. 12:36).

Due to our moral shortcomings we necessarily view judgment,
particularly that which awaits us after death, in negative terms. We
are threatened by it. In itself, however, judgment is perfectly neutral.
It is only the exposure of performance to evaluation. Not all the
Bible's judgments are negative. In Jesus' parables noted earlier, the
majority of those who appeared before the king were commended.
Nor can we forget Paul's reference to the time when 'the Lord comes
[who] will bring to light what is hidden in darkness and will expose
the motives of men's hearts' (1 Cor. 4:5). The outcome is most
encouraging: 'At that time each will receive his praise from God'
(v. 5b). Indeed, if what is of authentic worth in our lives is in the end
the work of God in and through us, then there is a sense in which the
day of judgment can be nothing other than a day of praise.

Underlying this universal future judgment is universal present
accountability, and underlying that again the great truth of Genesis
1 – universal creation by God. Because life is from him, it is lived
with reference to him, hence personal moral responsibility is irrefutable. 'We must all appear before the judgment seat of Christ, that
everyone may receive what is due them for the things done while in
the body, whether good or bad' (2 Cor. 5:10 NIVI).

'The ever-beating waves . . .'

This awareness of our responsibility to God our Creator is impossible to erase from our lives. Even when we consciously turn away
from God in denial of his reality, it still forces itself to the surface in
the form of the uneasy conscience which underlies and drives so
much human behaviour. We can call as witnesses two contributors
who are combined in their rejection of traditional Christian
convictions.

Arthur Koestler expresses it movingly in his autobiographical
Arrow in the Dark.

This latent apprehension, the awareness of guilt and impending punishment, seemed to be always present, like the rhythmic beat of the surf at night along the shore. While there are voices under the open window and laughter on the pier one is apt to forget it, but when the laughter dies away and the voices are stilled, the muffled thunder swells up again and one realises that it has always been present, and that the waves will never stop beating against the stones of the pier.[21]

As a further witness we can cite the poignant confession of humanist Marghanita Laski, 'What I envy most about you Christians is your sense of forgiveness; I have nobody to forgive me.'[22] We are all accountable for our lives, we all need to experience forgiveness, and deep within we know that to be true.

First things, last things

Thus the first things call for the last things. The Creator is necessarily also the Judge. The gift of life necessarily leads to us accounting for our lives before him. The days of creation lead inexorably to the day of judgment. The journey of our lives set in motion by creation moves irresistibly onwards towards its terminus in heaven or hell.

The call of a Lover

It is important in conclusion to revisit what we have learned from Genesis concerning the character of God the Creator. God, as we saw, is 'holy love', and as his creatures we are obligated to represent that in our lives. This makes life a responsible business, and carries the inevitable implication of our facing God's judgment. The danger of so stating things is that it can fuel a misleading, negative impression of God, which both dishonours him and discourages us. We must not lose sight of the fact that the call to love and honour God, and to love our neighbour, is a call to find life in the fullness with which God created it for us. It is true that God separates himself from all that stands opposed to him; true also that he calls us in turn to separate ourselves similarly and identify with him in goodness, truth, faithfulness, love, kindness and all his other glorious attributes. But this call is the call of *a Lover*. It is precisely because he loves us that he summons us to conform to him. Everything he shuns, and commands us to shun also, is deeply inimical to our well-being. To

[21] A. Koestler, *Arrow in the Dark* (Macmillan, 1952), p. 82.
[22] Cited J. R. W. Stott, *The Contemporary Christian* (IVP, 1992), p. 48.

51

disobey him is to turn to destruction (as we shall see in the next chapter). Conversely to conform to him, to be holy as he is holy, is the prescription for true and endless happiness. 'To be holy is to be happy . . . there is no joy like that of holiness.'[23]

Being responsible therefore has this significant positive implication. Being responsible, we are able to choose to side with God, and hence enter into that life in its fullness for which we were created. The pricks of conscience are the lures of God's love. The bliss that Adam and Eve knew in the Garden before sin's intrusion is the bliss to which God calls us in the command to be good and to obey him.

In the final glory of his love, as we shall explore in following chapters, when we refused his loving summons he did not abandon us. At infinite cost to himself, he made it possible for us to hear his voice once more and to follow him, back into the Garden of his embrace, and there taste again the bliss of being like him in the surpassing joys and fulfilments of endless, holy love.

Summary

God is the Creator. This has three pointers to the issues of future destiny.

1. His creation is with a view to relationship in love. Our being truly related to him thus becomes fundamental. In so far as true relationship with him is not realizable here, it points to its realization hereafter.
2. His creation shows him to be of overwhelming majesty, obligating us to fear and honour him.
3. His creation means his sustaining presence in all things in our lives.

These three implications of creation imply our irreducible moral responsibility; we are obligated to love God and our neighbour. That requires our being judged, particularly so at the end of our lives. These truths make heaven and hell both congruent and inevitable.

[23] R. M. McCheyne, *Memoir and Remains of Rev. Robert Murray McCheyne*, Rev. Andrew A. Bonar (Oliphant, Anderson & Ferrier, n.d.), pp. 169, 277.

Genesis 2:16–17; 3:1–24
2. The wages of sin

> Now I am going alone . . . Every torment I have afflicted, every sin
> I have committed, every wrong I have done, I carry the conse-
> quences with me. Strange that I came with nothing into the world,
> and now go away with this stupendous caravan of sin.
>
> (Anita Desai, *Clear Light of Day*)

In this second chapter we move on to consider the human creature
God has brought into existence. In particular we will focus on the
fall, that event which in some senses is the first stop on a journey
whose terminal destinations are heaven and hell. Bavinck aptly
refers to the fall as 'the silent hypothesis of the whole biblical doctrine of sin and redemption'.[1] For the Bible, eternal judgment is
consequentially related to the reality of human sin, and human sin
traces its roots back to this happening, vividly described in Genesis
3. Correspondingly, the reality of heaven represents the final stage
of a process of redemption by which humanity is restored to that
status before God which was forfeited in that same primal act of
disobedience. So once again we need to look back in order to
look ahead.

1. The fact of the fall

We begin by stating unambiguously that the fall took place as an
actual space-time event at the dawn of history. The reasons for so
arguing will become explicit as we proceed.

To assert the 'eventness' of the fall does not mean to ignore its
uniqueness. Indeed, the way in which Scripture traces the whole

---

[1] H. Bavinck, 'The Fall', ISBE, II, p. 1092.

53

history of human evil back to this primal transgression (Rom. 5:12f.) already establishes its specialness.

Language limits

This uniqueness can be indicated from another perspective by noting that for Adam and Eve everything prior to this event took place in an order of things to which we have no direct access, i.e. the paradisal condition before the coming of sin. Consequently, while God is able sovereignly to inform us concerning that paradisal order, the categories he employs in his revelation must necessarily be couched in language which has arisen from our experience on this side of the fall, the only language we know; the language of angels would not serve us! Accordingly, some 'stretching' of language is inevitable. The presence of symbolic elements in the account of the pre-fall order is therefore inherently probable. The two trees in the middle of the garden, the character of the snake, the removal and shaping of Adam's rib, may arguably be examples of figurative elements.[2]

However, 'the presence of symbolic elements in the text in no way contradicts the historicity of its central meaning.'[3] Here as elsewhere our hermeneutic requires to be informed by the 'analogy of faith', the light thrown upon a passage by other biblical passages.

Scripture's witness

Scripture has its own inspired interpretation of the fall, and that interpretation is consistently in terms of its having been a space-time event. One might turn to Job 31:33; Ecclesiastes 7:39; Isaiah 43:27; Ezekiel 28:15; Hosea 6:7; 2 Corinthians 11:3; Romans 5:12–20 and 1 Timothy 2:14. We can add further references to Adam as a historic figure in Genesis 4:1; Deuteronomy 32:8; 1 Chronicles 1:1; Luke 3:38; 1 Corinthians 11:8f.; 15:22f. and Jude 14. References to a historic primal manifestation of evil come in John 8:41–44; Revelation 12:9; 20:2. On any account this is a considerable array of biblical testimony, and it goes a long way to refute the notion that there is virtually no use made of the fall story in the rest of Scripture.[4] Against that we can perhaps set the words of H. Bavinck quoted earlier in

[2] B. Waltke, *Genesis* (Zondervan, 2001), pp. 73–78; H. Blocher, *In the Beginning* (IVP, 1984), pp. 50–59. Following Blocher, Waltke observes, 'We can describe the creation account (Genesis 3) as an artistic, literary interpretation' (*Genesis*, p. 78).
[3] Blocher, ibid., p. 155.
[4] Cf. G. von Rad, 'No prophet, psalm or narrator makes any recognisable reference to the story of the fall' (*Genesis* [SCM, 1963], p. 98).

this chapter, or note the view of G. Wingren: 'Every verse in the New Testament has as its background the chapters in Genesis on creation and the fall.'[5]

Particularly important is Paul's use of the story in Romans 5:12–20, where the fall is understood in equipoise to the crucifixion. The historicity of the one calls for the historicity of the other. Indeed, the whole argument hangs on the crucial influence of the 'one sin' (v. 16), the 'one trespass' (v. 18), being counteracted by the 'one act of righteousness . . . which brings life for all people' (v. 18 NIV). It is extremely difficult to interpret this passage faithfully if we allege a different degree of reality in the acts of the two men concerned.

Finally, at the exegetical level we note the use of the creation story made by Jesus in Matthew 19:3–8. In the phrase 'it was not this way from [in] the beginning' (v. 8) Jesus is noting that a crucial, historic change has taken place in the relationship between humanity and God, from how things were 'in the beginning' to how they subsequently became, from a prior moral condition to a new moral condition. It is a desperate exegetical recourse to argue that he is not appealing to the fall story, which was commonplace among his listeners, hence Jesus here implicitly attaches his dominical authority to a history-based understanding of the narrative in Genesis 3.

Mything the truth?

The alternative view of the passage is to classify it as a 'myth'. This category is notoriously difficult to pin down.[6] The 'mythical' approach usually affirms the special power of the story to throw light on the tragedy of human existence and the realities of temptation and guilt, but it denies any historical core to the story in Genesis 3. There are three basic reasons cited: (a) the meaning of 'Adam' in Hebrew (*'ādām*) as a collective term for humankind; (b) the presence of certain parallels in the Genesis story to other mythologies of the Ancient Near East concerning the beginning of evil; (c) the alleged difficulties in squaring such an event with the findings of science.

None of these is a conclusive refutation. The collective meaning of 'Adam' is actually a biblical conviction. In Romans 5:12 he is viewed as both a discrete individual and the 'father' of the race. On

---

[5] G. Wingren, *Creation and Law* (Oliver and Boyd, 1961), p. 7, citing H. Odeberg.

[6] One investigation identified twelve distinguishable meanings for 'myth'; cf. W. Rogerson, in Waltke (*Genesis*, p. 74, fn. 77).

examination, the alleged cultural parallels are in fact strictly limited and crucially different, both in the general temper of the stories,[7] and in at least one important specific element, as we will note below. The claimed scientific difficulties are inconclusive. Blocher observes, 'The data are fragmentary and the gaps enormous. [Even] supposing one nevertheless accepts the current evolutionary sketch, nothing is easier than slipping in a "miraculous parenthesis". If we admit there are revealed reasons for doing so nothing in the observable phenomena today rules it out absolutely.'[8]

Granted the 'eventness' of the fall, however, what has that to do with our future prospects, and with human destiny in particular? There are two points of contact, as we shall see below.

God and evil

First, the hope of heaven is of the arrival of a new era in human existence in which evil, the devil and sin no longer exist. It is the anticipation of a sinless human order. But this prospect is only possible if we can draw a clear distinction between God and his creation (including humanity) on the one hand, and evil, sin and the devil on the other.

The fall expresses and secures that critical distinction. The Genesis account, in clear contrast to the other Ancient Near Eastern accounts of the emergence of sin and evil, draws a clear line between God and evil, enabling us to affirm both the utter goodness of the Creator *and* the fact of human guilt.[9]

By contrast, in the creation account in Babylonian mythology, evil is part of the created stuff of the universe, and hence endemic to humanity as creature. In these tragic myths there is of necessity a malignancy hidden in the creator himself which accounts for a flawed and therefore evil-inclined creation.

Similar ideas resurface today in Eastern religion generally and in Hinduism and Buddhism in particular. In these traditions there is no real separation between God and evil. Because they lack a doctrine of creation 'out of nothing', evil is viewed as part of what 'is'. Since there is no clear distinction between God and what 'is', evil has

---

[7] Cf. von Rad, 'The reticence, indeed soberness and calm of the biblical story, is especially noticeable in contrast with the arrogant and harsh colours in the myths of other peoples' (*Genesis*, p. 97).

[8] Blocher, *In the Beginning*, pp. 158–159.

[9] Cf. Paul Ricoeur, 'The etiological myth of Adam is the most extreme attempt to separate the origin of evil from the origin of the good; its intention is to set up a radical origin of evil distinct from the more primordial origin of the goodness of things' (*The Symbolism of Evil* [New York, 1967], p. 233).

consequently to be accommodated and placated by acceptance. So, in Hinduism, there is no escape from the rule of fate, karma rules all. *Qué sera, sera* – 'Whatever will be, will be.'[10] In Buddhist thought 'salvation' lies in coming to terms with this, in a heroic act of self-conquest by which all desire is extinguished.[11]

Not surprisingly, in all these ways of relating God and the world there is no real equivalent to the hope of heaven. There can be no sinless world in the future, because God and evil are not in principle finally separable.

The entire ethical monotheism which lies at the core of the Bible's witness, and at the heart of which lies the assurance of God's complete conquest of all his foes in a new righteous order, is predicated upon the fact that 'in the beginning . . . sin entered the world through one man, and death through sin'. The fact of the fall in Eden anticipates the facts of the fall of 'Babylon' (Rev. 18) and the fall 'out of heaven' of the New Jerusalem (Rev. 21 – 22).

A historic salvation

The 'eventness' of the fall affects the shape of human destiny in a second way. We noted above the way in which for Paul the event of the fall is the counterpoint for the glorious event of God's salvation in Jesus Christ. The idea of human solidarity and the resulting spread of the effects of the fall to all humanity expressed in the genealogies of Scripture are further extrapolations from the historical figures of Adam and Eve and their primal act of disobedience. Yet it is on the assumption of that human solidarity in sin that the glorious, benign and universal counter-effect of Jesus' atonement is proclaimed in the New Testament. He is the Second or Last Adam, undoing *for the entire race* the malignant influence *upon the race* of the first Adam (Rom. 5:12ff.; 1 Cor. 15:22f.). Introduce a differential in the degree of historicity involved in the two figures, and the force of these basic New Testament categories evaporates.

The historicity of these happenings is part of a larger historic drama which embraces the whole sweep of God's purposes from the creation to the final arrival of the kingdom. It is as we view the world

[10] Cf. 'The law of Karma tells us that as in the physical world, in the mental and moral world also there is law. The world is an ordered cosmos . . . the universe is ethically sound' (S. Rhadhakrishnan, *The Bramha Sutra* [Oxford, 1960], cited S. Neill, *Crises of Belief* [Hodder and Stoughton, 1984], pp. 122–123).

[11] The third of the 'Four Holy (Aryan) Truths' of the Buddha reads, 'The complete stopping of that craving [desire] the withdrawal from it, the renouncing of it, throwing it back, liberation from it, non-attachment to it' (*The Buddhist Scriptures*, tr. E. Conze [Penguin, 1959], p. 187).

through the lens of that series of events that the blurred meaning of life begins to assume a focus.

The Bible unfolds them generation by generation. We read of the event of God's good act of creation, the tragic event of the fall, the historic covenant with Abraham and his posterity, the redemption of Israel from its enslavement in Egypt, the coming of Jesus Christ into our space-time order 'in the fullness of time', his life of active and passive obedience to all the will of God, his historic death on the cross, his space-time resurrection 'on the third day', the coming of the Spirit 'when the Day of Pentecost was fully come', and our moment of response (rebirth) to the gospel of grace: Christ's glorious future, appearing on the 'day of the Lord', that day 'in which he will judge the world in righteousness', and the emergence of the age-long Sabbath day (Heb. 4:9–11) of God's everlasting presence among his glorified people in heaven.

The attempt to dehistoricize the fall inevitably results in a relativizing of the historical character, not just of the crucifixion but also of the entire story of salvation, which is the central theme of the Bible. Hence the basis of salvation, or whatever that comes to mean, lies not in the dramatic, historic interventions of God, but finally in the inherent character and qualities of the human person as God's creature. Relativize sin, and you relativize salvation.

Thus these redemptive events are bound together in a unique solidarity, like the links in a chain or the pearls on a necklace. To look back to the fall is to look forward to the judgment. The event in the Garden of Eden demands the event in the garden of the New Jerusalem (Rev. 22:1f.). The presently barred tree of life (Gen. 3:22), symbolizing sin's curse upon the world, anticipates the heavenly tree of life which brings about 'the healing of the nations' (Rev. 22:2; cf. 2:7) in a place where the curse is 'no more' (Rev. 22:3). Those who have 'fallen' to the depths must yet rise 'to the highest place'.

2. The fount of the fall

A second, crucial feature of the account is the source of the temptation which brought humanity down. Genesis 3:1 expresses it, 'Now the serpent was more crafty than any of the wild animals the LORD God had made.' The serpent then proceeds to address the woman, Eve. 'Did God really say, "You must not eat from any tree in the garden"?' Eve explains that the prohibition only applies to one of the trees, that of the knowledge of good and evil 'in the middle of the garden', eating the fruit of which will bring about their death (v. 3). The serpent challenges this, 'You will not surely die' (v. 4), and informs her that in fact, to eat of that tree will have the effect that 'your eyes will be opened, and you will be like God, knowing good and evil' (v. 5). What are we to make of this?

Unmasking the enemy

The Bible's own commentary gives us our starting point. In Revelation 12:9 we meet the serpent again. 'The great dragon was hurled down – that ancient serpent called the devil, or Satan, who leads the whole world astray. He was hurled to the earth, and his angels with him.' Revelation 20:2 refers to 'the dragon, that ancient serpent, who is the devil, or Satan'. Paul has a similar interpretation. After referring to 'the serpent's cunning' which 'deceived' Eve, he refers to how 'Satan himself masquerades as an angel of light' (2 Cor. 11:3, 14). We can also note Luke 10:18f., where Jesus appears to echo Genesis 3 as he speaks of having seen 'Satan fall like lightning from heaven. I have given you authority to trample on snakes and scorpions and to overcome all the power of the enemy.'

Thus, most clearly for the Revelation passages, but in the others by implication, Eve's dialogue partner in the garden is none other than Satan himself, the devil, the great enemy of God and his people. We cannot ignore the comment made earlier about the presence of figurative elements in the story. Most helpful at this point is Paul's reference to Satan masquerading as 'an angel of light'.

To debate how literally he encountered Eve in a serpent form in the Garden runs into the danger of allowing the devil to deflect us from the main thrust of this story, which is to unveil our enemy before our eyes and to alert us to his impressive, sinister power. It suits the devil's purpose very well to have us consistently imagine him encased in the body of a mere creature, especially one which slinks around on the ground and which, for many Western people at least, is not an everyday threat to life and well-being. The specific form Satan chose to assume in Eden was that which, arising from his observation of Eve, was best suited to exploit her personal vulnerability. The success of his 'masquerade' is indicated by the degree to which he was able to attract Eve's total attention and to command her respect; she is patently immensely impressed by the 'serpent', and that is surely the primary point to grasp (cf. John 12:31; 14:30; Eph. 6:12; 1 Pet. 5:8).

Sin is not for ever

The reference to Satan has the effect of establishing a distance between God's good creation and the hideous reality of evil in all its forms. The existence of the devil, and his coming to Adam and Eve to enlist them in his rebellion against the good Creator, means that the origin of sin and evil lies outside ourselves. Jude 6 refers to this pre-temporal rebellion. 'The angels . . . did not keep their positions of authority but abandoned their own home' (cf. 2 Pet. 2:4).

Of course, in one sense that only pushes the searching question of the origin of evil a step further back, and we are still faced with an irreducible mystery at this point. But it is an important step, for it establishes the actual existence of a true and full human life and society (Gen. 1:27 – 2:25) to which evil has not contributed and from which evil is (as yet) a stranger. Here is a valuable biblical precursor of the life of heaven. Humanity can exist in its fullest terms without sin! And, since the devil and his angels will be banished eternally from that heavenly order of the fulfilled kingdom of God (cf. Jude 6b; Rev. 20:7–10), that future realm will be secure from any threat in a way the first perfected creation obviously was not.

The devil's doom

One other point of connection with human destiny which needs to be noted in considering the reality of the devil is the fact that his rebellion is such as to hold out no prospect of escape from judgment. Thus 2 Peter 2:4 actually refers to the fallen angels as already in hell. 'If God did not spare angels when they sinned, but sent them to hell . . . to be held for judgment . . .' Jude 6 describes these wretched beings as 'kept in darkness, bound with everlasting chains for judgment on the great Day'. Jesus speaks of hell as 'the eternal fire prepared for the devil and his angels' (Matt. 25:41), anticipating the irrevocable execution of God's judgment described in the vivid terms of Revelation 20:10: 'And the devil, who deceived them, was thrown into the lake of burning sulphur . . . They will be tormented day and night for ever and ever.'

The solemn implication of this is drawn out by Peter: 'The Lord knows how to . . . hold the unrighteous for the day of judgment' (2 Pet. 2:9). Against the ill-founded optimism of universalism, with its dream of the total reconciliation of the creatures of God, stands the awesome moral fact that evil must be brought to judgment, and where the evil concerned has come to dominate a moral agent to the point where repentance is no longer a serious possibility, that agent – in this case Satan (and his minions) – will be brought to final and everlasting punitive judgment. That this same fate awaits human moral agents who have arrived at the same degree of settled impenitence is the clear witness of every one of these passages just cited (cf. Matt. 25:41; 2 Pet. 2:1–3, 10–22; Jude 7–16; Rev. 20:7–9, 15).

One final implication for God's future purposes from the fact of 'that ancient serpent' is that God's final triumph will inevitably involve a reversal of the 'victory' of the devil in the Garden, and the removal and destruction of the entire demonic anti-kingdom of darkness. In maintaining and affirming his majestic sovereignty, God must needs deal with the devil. This is already explicit in the *proto-evangelium* in the Garden, to which we will return below. 'He [the offspring of the woman] will crush your head' (Gen. 3:15).

Jesus the Victor

It is in these terms that the coming of Jesus is represented at repeated points in the Gospels (cf. Matt. 4:1–11; 8:28–32; 10:1, 8; 12:22–29, 43–45; 13:19, 39; 16:23; 17:14–21; 25:41; John 8:42–47; 12:31; 13:27; 14:30). So the later New Testament can represent Jesus' triumph in terms of a victory over Satan. 'Having disarmed the powers and authorities, he made a public spectacle of them, triumphing over them by the cross' (Col. 2:15). 'He too shared in their humanity so that by his death he might destroy him who holds the power of death – that is, the devil . . .' (Heb. 2:14). 'The reason the Son of God appeared was to destroy the devil's work' (1 John 3:8). Through this conquest Satan's work is undone and the Garden is restored to humankind (Rev. 22:1–5).

Here is the ground of our assurance of the coming of the heavenly order: God must be Lord. His name must be vindicated and all his mighty deeds brought to a glorious consummation. 'He must reign until he has put all his enemies under his feet' (1 Cor. 15:25). Among those thus subjected is the devil and all his works. 'He must reign' means that he surely will!

3. The form of the fall

What was the essence of the primal sin?

The best approach is arguably by way of the Bible's own inspired commentary on the fall. Paul draws attention in two places to the cunning and deception involved (2 Cor. 11:3; 1 Tim. 2:14), but no amount of stress on the devil's role can eliminate the element of culpability as far as Adam and Eve were concerned. God himself indicates that by his rejoinder, 'Have you eaten from the tree from which I commanded you not to eat?' (Gen. 3:11). The known command, 'You must not eat from the tree of the knowledge of good and evil' (2:17), had been disobeyed. Similarly, in the principal biblical comment on the Genesis 3 story Paul identifies the sin as 'breaking a command' (Rom. 5:14), 'trespass', which implies stepping over a known boundary (5:15, 18), and 'disobedience' (5:19). The first sin had at its root the element which is common to all sinning, that of resistance to, and rebellion against, the known will of God.

Explaining the inexplicable

Why did first Eve, and then Adam, follow this course? Bonhoeffer appropriately comments, 'Nothing in the nature of humankind or of creation or of the serpent can be uncovered as a basis on which to explain this event. No theory . . . is able to comprehend the fact that the deed was done . . . If we could answer the question *why* then we would not be sinners.'[12]

Acknowledging the force of Bonhoeffer's observation, we may nonetheless attempt some explanation.

Covetousness

First we can identify the desire for the fruit which the text notes. 'When the woman saw that the fruit of the tree was good for food and pleasing to the eye, and also desirable for gaining wisdom, she took some and ate it' (Gen. 3:6). Here is covetousness, the self-centred, self-gratifying desire for an inappropriate object. But that desire only had its force in Eve's (and Adam's) case because, prior to the awakening of the desire, there had taken place during the course of her conversation with Satan a carefully plotted demolition of Eve's previously held assumptions concerning the character and intentions of God.

A new theology?

In so far as we are able to locate a 'cause' for the mysterious eruption of sin in our race, it can thus be identified in that conversation as recorded in Genesis 3:1–5. The reason the tempter succeeded in overthrowing Eve, and Adam, and hence our entire race, lay in his ability to make credible a false understanding of God. It was on the back of a new theology that sin entered and conquered our world. In a quite strict sense, therefore, the root of sin is bad theology – getting it wrong about God. Satan succeeded in creating in Eve's mind a doubt concerning God in at least nine regards, offering her a different way of understanding God at each of these points.

---

[12] D. Bonhoeffer, *Creation and Fall* (SCM, 1959), pp. 119–120.

1. *God's words are not necessarily true.* 'Did God really say . . .?' (v. 1) 'You will not surely die' (despite the fact that God says you will) (v. 4).
2. Closely related to no. 1, and from the same texts, *God's words are not authoritative*; they can be disobeyed with impunity.
3. *God is inappropriately strict.* '. . . from any tree' (v. 1). This is wrong, and a calumny on God's loving provision, but Eve catches the tone of it and when she refutes the slur in verse 2 she adds her own exaggeration of God's prohibition, 'you must not [even] touch it'.
4. Closely allied to no. 3: *God is repressive.* 'God knows that when you eat of it your eyes will be opened . . .' (v. 5); i.e. God is deliberately, and for no good reason, keeping you from what would be to your considerable advantage.
5. *God does not really tell you the whole story*; he keeps you in the dark about things which you have a right to know (v. 5 again).
6. *God's claim to care for you*, which you have believed up to this point, *is false.* He is keeping you back from your true freedom and fulfilment. He only appears to care about you, but in reality he does not (v. 5).
7. *God is actually selfish*, concerned for himself and jealous for his own position and powers at the expense of yours (v. 5).
8. *The real fulfilment of your life*, your true maturity, *lies not in submitting to God at all, but in assuming God's role for yourselves*, determining for yourselves where right and wrong actually lie, and which values you will live by (v. 5).
9. *God's judgment is a myth.* He will not, despite what he may have said, bring judgment on you if you disobey him (v. 4).

Eve is invited to revise her convictions about God. She is to question:

• the reliability and seriousness of his revelation (vv. 1, 2);
• the genuineness of his love and care (vv. 3, 4, 5, 6, 7);
• the extent of his sovereignty (v. 8);
• the inevitability of his judgment (v. 9).

Once the serpent had succeeded in getting her to make these revisions, the actual act of disobedience was nearly a foregone conclusion.

The denial of judgment

These truths have huge implications for every one of us. We particularly note the final one. The denial of judgment lies near to the heart of the fall. But we need to consider the source of the denial – Satan. The notion that God will not judge evil and sin is unveiled in this crucial biblical passage as nothing other than a lie straight from hell itself. However specious the arguments of the universalists may be, and with whatever degree of concern for humanity they may be motivated, the view that future judgment is an erroneous and out-dated myth which can now be thankfully ignored needs to be seen for what it is – an error of the most sinister origin, a slur upon the integrity of God's words to us, and a repetition of the demonic denial of his character as the faithful God.

The fact of hell is highly unpalatable to our human sensitivities and its proclaimed eternal duration a heavy cross to our intellect, but its dismissal is far more problematic. It means the rejection of God's word, and hence the dismissal of his revealed character. It is nothing less than a repetition of the primal sin – a rejection of God himself.

4. The effects of the fall

The final aspect which needs to concern us is what happened as a result of the fall. What are the implications of human fallenness? What did it mean for Adam and Eve to 'die'? What does it mean for us? Is there any hope in the face of this all-encompassing human tragedy?

Death through sin?

The first thing to note is that the judgment passed upon Adam and Eve was not immediate physical dissolution. Clearly they did not die on the spot following their act of collaborated rebellion against God. One may contrast their fate with that of another hapless biblical couple, Ananias and Sapphira, in Acts 5:1–11. That couple's sin of deception against the Lord, when they connived to misrepresent the extent of their offering, was immediately judged by their 'falling down and dying'. In this sense Adam and Eve 'survived', but inevitably the prescription of God's command in due time came into effect: 'When you eat [of the fruit of the tree] you will surely die' (Gen. 2:17).

The New Testament commentary on the passage confirms this verdict. 'Sin entered the world through one man, and death through sin . . . death reigned from the time of Adam . . . by the trespass of the one man, death reigned' (Rom. 5:12, 14, 17). Also in 1 Corinthians 15:22 we read, 'As in Adam all die. . .'

So?

What then happened to Adam and Eve as a result of the fall? We can identify a variety of results. The first noted by the scriptural account is *shame*. 'Then the eyes of both of them were opened, and they realised that they were naked; so they sewed fig leaves together and made coverings for themselves' (Gen. 3:7). A second result was *a craven fear of God*. 'They hid from the LORD God among the trees of the garden' (3:8). A third was *the replacement of mutual trust by mutual accusation*, with its resulting social conflict. 'The woman you put here with me – she gave me some fruit from the tree' (3:12). This is repeated by the woman in her turn: 'The serpent deceived me, and I ate' (3:13). A fourth effect, which may be discerned within the third, was *self-excusing*, and the attempt to evade personal responsibility for a sinful act.

Further effects are identified by God's pronouncement of the curse. In the case of the woman, this means the pain of childbearing and being subject to domination by her husband (3:16). In the case of the man, it means a life of arduous toil exerted on a medium, the earth, which will become relatively resistant to his efforts and will yield its fruit only at considerable physical cost (3:17–19).

To all this, however, God adds the crucial further curse: 'Dust you are and to dust you will return' (3:19). This represents a clear allusion to physical dissolution in death. Thus the pronouncement of death due to sin will be fulfilled in due time. The fundamental element is therein confirmed: 'Sin entered the world . . . and death through sin', for 'the wages of sin is death' (Rom. 5:12; 6:23). We read in Genesis 5:5, 'Altogether Adam lived 930 years, and then he died.' The judgment of God was delayed, but it was sure. From this point the Bible consistently views death as a usurper, an alien which reduces us to the animal level. We are 'like the beasts that perish' (Ps. 49:12). '[Human] fate is like that of the animals . . . As one dies, so dies the other' (Eccles. 3:19).

Banishment

The inner meaning and the ultimate spiritual tragedy of Adam's and Eve's revolt appear at the conclusion of the account in Genesis 3: 'So the LORD God banished him from the Garden of Eden' and 'placed . . . cherubim and a flaming sword flashing back and forth to guard the way to the tree of life' (3:23–24). Thus the presence of God to which Adam and Eve had enjoyed constant and delighted access is now withdrawn from them, and that very presence becomes a threat to them.

A good death?

This causal link between sin and death carries the further implication that had Adam and Eve remained faithful to God's command they would not have died. Of course, in some senses this is a strictly academic question, since in fact they did disobey and hence came under the power of death.

Luther imagines what might have been.

> Adam, if he had not sinned would yet have lived a corporeal life, a life which would have needed meat, drink and rest; a life which would have grown, increased and generated until God would have translated him to that spiritual life in which he would have lived without natural animality, if I may so express it . . . And yet would have been a man with body and bones, and not pure spirit as angels are.[13]

More recently John Stott speculates on the possibilities in the event of death having been averted.

> Perhaps God would have translated [Adam and Eve] like Enoch and Elijah, without the necessity of death. Perhaps he would have 'changed' them 'in a flash, the twinkling of an eye' like those believers who will be alive when Jesus comes (I Cor. 15:51f). Perhaps too we should think of the transfiguration of Jesus in this light. His face shone, his clothing became dazzling white, and his body translucent like the resurrection body he would later have. Because he had no sin, he did not need to die. He could have stepped straight into heaven without dying. But he deliberately came back in order of his own free and loving will to die for us.[14]

This view has been challenged on the grounds that it fails to recognize the force of 1 Timothy 6:16, '[God] alone is immortal.' It is also argued that the identification of sin with death tends to erode a sense of the fundamental goodness of creation, and tends to a Hellenistic rather than biblical understanding of the relationship between finitude and evil. By contrast, it is contended, we should think of the natural order including its cycles of birth, growth and death as part of God's good purpose for our world, and hence for humanity within it.[15]

---

[13] M. Luther, *Commentary on Genesis*, III, 5, 7; cited R. Niebuhr, *The Nature and Destiny of Man, vol. I, Human Nature* (Nisbet, 1941), p. 188.

[14] J. R. W. Stott, *The Message of Romans* (IVP, 1994), p. 166.

[15] See R. Niebuhr, *The Nature and Destiny of Man*, pp. 178–189; K. Barth, *The Doctrine of Creation*, CD III, 1 (T. and T. Clark, 1958), pp. 366ff.

There can be no hesitation in affirming that all life, and hence all prospect of life after death, resides in the eternally fruitful power of the Creator. For any other being to aspire to possess 'naturally' such limitless life as is implied by 'immortality' would impugn the unique self-existence of God. Thus all life, both before and after death, derives from God alone. In the final analysis none but he can be the source of life, whether mortality (mortal life) or immortality (life beyond death). But that does not preclude the possibility of God having created a being to whom he has granted life which is endless. In other words, the text in 1 Timothy 6:16 can be fully honoured without it telling against human immortality. Further, the linkage of death and sin, which has appealed to Christian thinkers in every generation as the plain teaching of Scripture, need not imply an identification of finitude with evil. It simply recognizes that all life is from God and that God assigns to each its proper form. Much is inherently finite, and that is 'good' if so appointed by God. Human beings, however, are uniquely appointed as divine 'imagers' and hence, if God so wills it, created immortal in reflection of one of the primary attributes of the Creator.

The service which the above questioning of 'natural immortality' renders is the reminder that the biblical goal of human life, and hence the biblical form of human destiny, is not the mere prolongation of physical existence. Rather it is all that the Bible, and the New Testament in particular, implies by 'resurrection'. We will defer our exposition of that reality until its appropriate place in the New Testament section of this book. Because of the fall our immortality is overshadowed by the multiple effects of the incursion of sin and evil into God's good world. We may retain our immortal natures, but they are expressed within an order marked by futility, threatened by human selfishness and brutality, and overshadowed by death. We live in a world that has gone wrong in a quite fundamental and pervasive manner. Thus we can identify with Francis Schaeffer's comment that, as a Christian, 'as I look about me I know I live in an abnormal world'.[16]

Our true destiny lies beyond this present order. The primal sin of humanity, with its introduction of a new fallen order as the context of human life on earth, in its way is a pointer to, and even an argument for, the life of heaven. And, not surprisingly, there are indications of hope even within Genesis 3.

The warning note

Before finally coming to that, we do well to stand back from the story of the fall and note the warning which it represents. It is a

[16] F. A. Schaeffer, *Genesis in Space and Time* (IVP, 1972), p. 97.

wake-up call if ever there was one. The consequences of this event are terrible indeed – in particular the radical breakdown of humanity's relationship with the Creator, symbolized poignantly by the banishment from the Garden and the imposition of the flaming sword.

It simply will not do to dismiss this as a piece of interesting, primitive story-telling which has no relevance for our advanced times. For this *is* the story also of our times, and of each of our lives. We have each identified with the tempter's enticement. We too have accepted the satanic 'new theology' and believed the lies about God. We too have snatched at the illusory autonomy of a supposed equality with God, and thereby tasted the forbidden fruit. We are sinners living in a world 'outside the Garden'.

The implications for us are similarly serious – breakdown in relationship with God, banishment from his presence, the threat of his just wrath.[17] This is not the only point in the biblical record where the awfulness of sin stands revealed. Even clearer is the future judgment which it entails: in the case of the impenitent, an eternity in hell. Clearest of all is what it does to the blessed, holy Son of God as we see him impaled upon the cross. The solemnity of our condition as sinners is clear in this passage and needs to be underlined, for we have an incurable tendency to excuse ourselves, or to treat sin as significant only to the degree that it prejudices our happiness. We domesticate sin by reducing it to the human factors involved. We fail to consider its primary nature, as wrongdoing directed against God. Herein lies the true terror of sin, and of the hell to which it can bring us.

The heavy weight

Back in the eleventh century Anselm raised the same issue in his dialogue with Boso: 'You have not yet considered what a heavy weight sin is.'[18] Anselm recognizes sin for what it is in its God-ward implications – it is an offence against God's honour. What it does to God is infinitely more to the point than the relative discomfort it may produce in ourselves. Since it is measurable finally only in terms of God, and since God is by definition the Infinite One, sin's effects are correspondingly infinite. Consequently, the result of having

---

[17] Cf. E. Brunner, *The Christian Doctrine of God* (Lutterworth, 1949), p. 162. 'This is the Divine Wrath, the outworking of the Divine Glory upon those who refuse to give Him glory; the outworking of the Holiness of God against him who irreverently, godlessly, does not acknowledge Him.'

[18] *A Scholastic Miscellany: Anselm to Ockham*, Library of Christian Classics, vol. X (Westminster, 1956), p. 138.

sinned follows – we are rendered helpless as far as rectifying our relationship with God is concerned, since we are completely unable to make an infinite restitution. The best that we can do is to render to God a complete and entire obedience for the remainder of our lives.[19] But even if we were conceivably capable of doing that (an impossibility in practice), since that entire obedience is what we owe him during the remainder of our lives in any event, such obedience, even if attainable, would do nothing to reduce our liability. So, with relentless logic, we are driven to face Anselm's searching conclusion: 'What then will become of you? How are you going to be saved?'[20]

'What then will become of you?'

Thankfully, there is an answer to that question, though one which by the nature of the case only God himself can provide: salvation as a *divine* possibility; salvation by sheer miracle, as utter and eternal *grace*.

This passage in Genesis points us to it at three points, for the story of the fall is not only, as Milton famously discerned, of 'paradise lost', but also of 'paradise regained'. It is the story of sin and expulsion, but also of grace and restoration.

Signs of salvation

The first salvation pointer is God's gracious provision of 'garments' for the hapless pair (Gen. 3:21). The earlier unashamed nakedness (2:25) had given place to a futile attempt to alleviate their fall-engendered sense of physical dis-ease (3:7). Now, however, the Lord himself provides for them. There can be no return to the unsullied openness of their former relationship, but that does not mean they are abandoned to overwhelming shame. God, in pity for his creatures, covers Adam and Eve and so gives them a means of continuing in their mutual relationship with freedom and dignity. Here is hope: God does not abandon his sinning creatures. He will continue to be their God. The fall cannot at this point be undone; there is no return to the unashamed nudity of paradise. Sin cannot be ignored, but it can be *covered*. It is not difficult to see in this action a small, yet not insignificant, anticipation of God's later provision of a moral and spiritual covering with the 'garments of salvation' (Is. 61:10), a robe of spotless righteousness, the perfect rectitude of the Last

[19] ibid., pp. 136–137.
[20] ibid., p. 137.

Adam, the first Adam's son, and Saviour (Luke 3:37; 1 Cor. 15:45; cf. Zech. 3:4f.; Luke 15:22; Gal. 3:27).

A second pointer to salvation is the name of the woman, Eve, which means 'living' (3:20). In the very face of the death which their act of disobedience has engendered, Adam prophetically declares his wife 'the mother of all the living'. In other words, the significance of God's words to Adam and Eve has dawned on Adam. The prospect before them, albeit by way of a journey through immense suffering, hardship, toil and eventual physical dissolution ('dust you are and to dust you shall return' [3:19]), remains a prospect of life, not death.[21]

Third, and most substantial, is the *proto-evangelium*. 'I will put enmity between you and the woman, and between your offspring and hers; he will crush your head, and you will strike his heel' (3:15). We note that God himself takes the initiative in this promise of final victory over the serpent's offspring. The tragedy of the fall is not the final action in the conflict. There is more to come, a 'more' in which the sorry outcome of the temptation in the Garden will be dramatically and gloriously reversed. The tempter will once again be encountered in a natural setting, this time of a desert, and there will be resisted and vanquished by one who bears our full humanity (Matt. 4:1–11). In this future victory, God himself will take the initiative. It will in effect be *his* action, although his instrument will be the humanity which has broken faith with him, the seed of the woman. 'God here announces a battle of champions.'[22]

A costly salvation

Two other critical features of this future triumph are emphasized. First, it will involve *significant cost* – 'You will strike his heel.' Blocher notes the fact that both Hebrew verbs in the text use the same word, and hence probably ought to be translated in parallel, as 'he will bruise your head and you will bruise his heel'.[23] This underlines that the effects are similar in both cases; death will be involved mutually. The distinction lies in the effect of the two assaults. The 'heel' of the seed of the woman implies a genuine wound, but one which will permit recovery. The 'head' of the seed of the serpent implies an irreversibly destructive blow. It is not difficult to see here a divinely inspired foretelling of that awful deed at the heart of the gospel, wherein Emmanuel, the son of Adam, was mortally

---

[21] Cf. Waltke, who refers to Adam's naming of Eve as 'a ray of hope' (*Genesis*, p. 95).

[22] ibid., p. 94. See also on the 'champion' motif, W. Lane, *Hebrews: a Call to Commitment* (Hendrikson, 1998), pp. 47–54.

[23] Blocher, *In the Beginning*, p. 194.

'wounded' on the cross, but thereby effected an eternal expulsion of 'the prince of this world' (John 12:31).

Thus even in the numbing aftermath of humanity's saddest hour, God promises a new day of hope. '[Adam] having been expelled from the garden went forth, under the power of death, and yet a child of God.'[24] The battle has been lost, but the war will yet be won. The full terms of that victory remain future, and will do so throughout the course of recorded history. It is therefore from beyond the historical process that we look for the final confrontation and the imposition of the final triumph, the inbreaking of the heavenly order in the coming of 'a Saviour from there, the Lord Jesus Christ' (Phil. 3:20). Both in general terms of the demand for the ultimate vindication of the Creator, and in the specific terms of his promise in the biblical record, the fallenness of the world demands the heavenly order. The journey begun in Eden must end in 'a new heaven and a new earth, the home of righteousness' (2 Pet. 3:13).

Inevitable judgment

Second, however, the other terminus also comes into focus in the events of Genesis 3 as, at the very origins of our existence as humans, we are brought face to face with *the realities of judgment.* It is 'the first doctrine to be denied',[25] and one of the first to be experienced. God has defined himself as a moral God. By virtue of who he is, he is the normative form of goodness. The universe which he creates accordingly is never a simple physical or psychical entity; it is value-laden, a moral universe. Hence the creature which he calls into existence and makes in his image, which he calls to know and commune with him, is a moral being and the relationships such a being expresses at every level of life are moral relationships. As irreducibly moral beings, we are constantly faced with the summons to obey God, to choose him as our God, the Lord of our life and hence the determiner of our values. But that choice implies a preference, a choice not to disobey him, a choice not to go the way of rebellion, the way of the tempter. Since God is inescapably present in every moment, and since God is always God and cannot cease to be who he is, eternally distinguishing between light and darkness, good and evil, this choice, with its attendant threat of judgment, is the silent context of every moment and every motion of our lives.

It is precisely here, however, at this point when the judgment falls upon Adam and Eve, that the heart of God is most wonderfully

---

[24] E. J. Young, *Exposition of Genesis 3: A Study* (Banner of Truth, 1966), p. 161.
[25] D. Kidner, *Genesis* (Tyndale, 1967), p. 68.

opened. The judgment is accompanied by the promise! The seed of the woman will be struck on the heel by the serpent, but the seed of the woman will triumph over the tempter. The wounding will serve the ultimate victory, and in that promise there is the hope of salvation for Adam and Eve, and for every last one of their offspring, in every age, and in every place. Salvation and judgment, leading finally to heaven and hell: these are the twin themes of Genesis 3.

Summary

Our responsibility to honour and obey God by loving him and our neighbour has not been fulfilled. By the fall, at the dawn of human history, humanity set itself on a course of disobedience leading to judgment.

All people everywhere are affected by that event, which we re-enact every time we sin. Accordingly, we have all forfeited the bliss of God's presence and have become exposed to the sword of his wrath.

God is endlessly gracious: on the heels of the fall comes the first promise of salvation. Though hell is inevitable, the heavenly restoration of paradise is also assured.

Psalm 16
3. The path of life

Live in Christ, die in Christ, and the flesh need not fear death.
(John Knox)

There are few passages in the Old Testament which have had greater
influence in the development of the hope of an afterlife than this
beautiful psalm. Both Peter at Pentecost (Acts 2:25–31) and Paul in
Pisidian Antioch (Acts 13:35) make reference to it, specifically its
anticipation of the resurrection of the Messiah Jesus. In all probability it was prominent among the Old Testament passages to which
Jesus referred (Luke 24:44) in support of his claim to having 'fulfilled' the Old Testament, generally in his ministry and particularly
in his resurrection (John 20:9; Luke 24:44; 1 Cor. 15:4).

This psalm has attracted great attention over the centuries for at
least two reasons. People have been drawn both to its moving reflection of deepest intimacy with God, and to its audacious confidence
of resurrection in the face of the inescapable dissolution of death.

David is the claimed author, and there appears no reason seriously
to question this identification. Only someone 'after God's own
heart' (cf. 1 Sam. 13:14; 16:7), could compose such an intimate
expression of authentic communion with God.

1. The seedbed of heavenly hope (vv. 1–2, 5–8)

David addresses God as one in whom he has come to take refuge
(v. 1). Verse 5 speaks of God having 'made my lot secure', and verse
8 celebrates the blessing of God's continual presence: 'Because he is
at my right hand, I shall not be shaken.' Clearly some dark experience of danger lies behind this psalm. While the precise identification is not offered, as it is with respect to some other psalms (e.g. 18,

34, 51), it would not be difficult to place it during the long years of Saul's reign when David was in daily danger for his life, or on the occasion of one of the periodic threats to his life and future which occurred during his own fairly turbulent reign. The absence of precise identification happily allows us greater latitude in applying it to our own threatening circumstances.

What matters most

Whatever its details, this crisis experience has had a significant effect on the psalmist. It has forced him to reflect on his ultimate values and clarify what truly matters for him. His conclusion is that God himself is his supreme treasure. 'You are my Lord; apart from you I have no good thing' (v. 2). Faced with the real prospect of forfeiting everything else, including his very life, David is brought face to face with the only thing that is ultimately important – God himself, and being loved and held by him. Nothing which is not intimately related to that highest loyalty is truly 'good' for him.

He illustrates this conclusion of his self-inventory, which his experience of crisis has prompted, with two pictures.

'My cup . . .'

First, God is the one who provides his 'cup' (v. 5). In a dry, desert-studded land where the traveller even to this day is constantly threatened with dehydration, the cup symbolized the refreshing, renewing gift of life. Not surprisingly, Jesus was alert to the force of this image in talking with the woman of Samaria (John 4:4–26): 'If you knew the gift of God and who it is that asks you for a drink, you would have asked him and he would have given you living water . . . whoever drinks the water I give him will never thirst. Indeed, the water I give him will become in him a spring of water welling up to eternal life' (vv. 10, 14). In his relationship with God the psalmist discovers the true refreshment and satisfaction of his life.

'. . . and my portion'

Second, God is his 'portion' (v. 5), or 'inheritance' (v. 6). This echoes the period when the land of Israel was divided among the tribes at the conclusion of their war of conquest. For each the 'boundary lines' were drawn, and each received their 'chosen portion'. It was different for Aaron and his tribal successors. As the priestly tribe whose responsibilities were henceforth to be the care and maintenance of the tabernacle, and later the temple, they received no geographical territory as their 'lot'. 'You will have no inheritance in their land [i.e. the land of the other tribes], nor will you have any share among them' (Num. 18:20). Rather, 'I am your share and your inheritance among the Israelites.'

It is possible that there is a hint of the historical background at this point. In 1 Samuel 26:19f., when David confronts Saul after sparing his life, he expresses the effects of the constant pursuit of Saul's soldiers. 'They have now driven me from my share in the LORD's inheritance and have said, "Go, serve other gods."' During the long years of his exile as a fugitive, David has been forced effectively to forfeit his family and tribal inheritance in the land of Israel, and to find his inheritance in foreign lands, under the aegis of foreign, pagan gods. But David has refused to compromise his faith or lose touch with the earlier, happier days when he walked in freedom and rejoiced with those who said, 'Let us go to the house of the LORD' (Ps. 122:1). In this psalm he shares the harvest of these years of material deprivation, when life again and again hung by a thread: he has discovered his true inheritance, the Lord himself, a 'delightful inheritance', and one which has brought him ultimate security (vv. 6, 8).

Crisis contribution

Here is a precious fruit of crises in our experience. When everything seems likely to be lost to us, we are able to discern what we ultimately possess, the Lord himself.

It is interesting in this connection that the single introductory reference in the title of the psalm is a *miktām*. The meaning is uncertain, but one early rabbinical interpretation links the word to the Hebrew for 'gold'; thus this is 'a golden psalm'. Spurgeon seizes on this possibility in entitling his exposition of Psalm 16 'The Psalm of the Precious Secret'.[1] How often the children of God have learned in the crucible of trial a new and hitherto unreached degree of intimacy with their God – the discovery that in the end he is all we can ever need.

This calls to mind Abraham, who, at the time of his call by God in Genesis 12, was faced with giving up all of his past, and then in Genesis 22, in the summons to sacrifice Isaac the son of promise, was faced with giving up all of his future. Abraham thus became a man without either a past or a future; all he had left was the God to whom he clung in the present. No wonder Abraham is the great biblical model of the man or woman of faith (Rom. 4:16; cf. 4:1–25). Such is the heart of faith in every generation.

[1] C. H. Spurgeon, *The Treasury of David*, vol. I (London, 1872), p. 216.

F. W. Robertson, one of the nineteenth century's outstanding preachers, speaks out of a time of intense personal suffering and loneliness not unlike the experience underlying Psalm 16:

> I am alone, lonelier than ever, sympathised with by none, because I sympathise too much with all . . . My experience is closing into this, that I turn with disgust from everything to Christ. I think I get glimpses into his mind, and I am sure that I love him more and more . . . a sublime feeling of a Presence comes about me at times which makes inward solitariness a trifle to talk about.[2]

Corrie ten Boom is known around the globe for the courage and faith with which she faced and triumphed over the horrors of the Ravensbruck concentration camp during the Second World War. Her heroic demonstration, with her sister Betsie, that 'there is no pit so deep but God is not deeper still' has been an inspiration to millions all over the world in the years since.

Less well known is that, following an initial stroke in 1978, she spent the last five years of her life as an invalid, unable to exercise any public ministry and, for much of that period, unable even to speak. Yet in this world of enforced silence she maintained the same radiant confidence in God that had characterized and energized her to that moment.

Reflecting on the lessons of her life during these years, her daily nurse-companion Pamela Rosewell comments,

> In common with a large part of the western world, I had set great store by strength and achievement. A sense of satisfaction was gained by having a goal and employing all faculties, strength, and input from others in order to reach that goal . . . But what happens when a person becomes old, frail, brain-damaged, and in some ways apparently useless?

In Corrie ten Boom she encountered a faith which was not dependent on these outward props for its validity, a faith which reached to God himself behind, and finally irrespective of, these common criteria of success and fulfilment. 'She was living for God. I could see no difference in the attitude of the weak and silent Tante Corrie to that of the strong speaker whom I had joined three years earlier. She served him then; she was serving him now.'[3]

---

[2] *Life and Letters of F. W. Robertson*, II, p. 99, cited in W. E. Sangster, *He Is Able* (Wyvern, 1958), p. 40.
[3] Pamela Rosewell, *The Five Silent Years of Corrie Ten Boom* (Zondervan, 1986), pp. 154, 156.

2. The context of heavenly hope (vv. 3–4)

This little section in the middle of the psalm is simply an implication of that intense spirit of devotion to God which has grown out of the psalmist's sense of crisis.

In the communion of the saints

Although David's relationship with God at the personal level is the heart of this whole composition, it is not finally a solitary religion which he espouses. This accords entirely with the forms of faith which the Scriptures exemplify. Israel in the Old Testament and the church in the New Testament represent the fundamentally social context in which faith is planted and developed. For the Bible, loving God is never separable from loving God's people. 'If anyone says, "I love God," yet hates his brother, he is a liar. For anyone who does not love his brother, whom he has seen, cannot love God, whom he has not seen . . . Whoever loves God must also love his brother' (1 John 4:20–21).

In Lloyd Douglas's novel *The Big Fisherman,* a Roman named Melchius receives his friend Voldi's impression of Jesus: 'On first sight of him I was a bit disappointed. He is not a heroic figure, but the man has a compelling voice. I can't describe it, or the effect of it. It is a unifying voice that converts a great crowd of mutually dis-trustful strangers into a tight little group of blood relatives.'[4] The words are, of course, entirely fictitious, but the estimate of Jesus they express has solid historical support. To know him personally is to find oneself set within a great family of sisters and brothers (Eph. 3:15).

Thus for the psalmist the delighted recognition that 'apart from you [Lord] I have no good thing' (v. 2) leads on naturally to speak-ing of 'the saints who are in the land . . . the glorious ones in whom is all my delight' (v. 3). Glorying in God will make us for ever the heart-companions of those who share that single-minded goal. Not that David's companions during his years in exile were the 'fairest in the land' by the standards of the social elite in Jerusalem – 1 Samuel 22:2 describes the company who gathered to David at the cave of Adullam as 'those who were in distress or in debt or discontented'. But out of that motley crew David shaped a core of followers who were prepared to risk life for him and his claim to the throne of Israel. From that unpretentious seed there was to flower an army and an administration which became the envy of the surrounding

---

[4] Cited John N. Gladstone, *All Saints and All Sorts* (Lancelot Press, 1982), p. 30.

peoples, and whose deeds of renown echoed throughout the land (cf. 2 Sam. 23:8–38).

We can recall similarly Paul's description of the congregation at Corinth huddled in the shadow of that great Greek metropolis: 'Brothers, think of what you were when you were called. Not many of you were wise by human standards; not many were influential; not many were of noble birth' (1 Cor. 1:26). Nonetheless, they were God's people, rescued in some cases from the very garbage heap of that dissolute society (cf. 1 Cor. 6:9–11), and, in Christ, men and women made new, 'saints' in whom Paul had learned to delight (cf. 2 Cor. 7:4).

The gate of heaven

It is no different as we gather today in worship and fellowship. And it is there, in the gathered community of the people of God, that the hope of heaven is rekindled and burns with new intensity. For we come together 'to the heavenly Jerusalem, the city of the living God . . . to thousands upon thousands of angels in joyful assembly, to the church of the firstborn, whose names are written in heaven . . . to God, the judge of all people, to the spirits of the just made perfect' (Heb. 12:22–23 NIVI).

This connection of spiritual community and heavenly anticipation is expressed by the two New Testament sacraments, baptism and the Lord's Supper. In baptism the profound linkage with Jesus' resurrection which the rite establishes (Rom. 6:1–11; cf. Col. 1:12) inevitably anticipates the coming day of his parousia (Col. 3:1–4). 'The day of baptism presses forward and calls for the day of the Lord . . . the sacramental dying and rising with Christ imperatively demands the bodily resurrection with Christ at his *parousia*.'[5] It is no different with respect to the Lord's Supper, which is celebrated 'until he comes' (1 Cor. 11:26), and has traditionally echoed with the cry of '*Maranatha*!' ('Even so, come Lord Jesus!') (1 Cor. 16:22).

In this psalm David anticipates this unique experience of community, and in the final stanza links it, in anticipation of this New Testament witness, to our heavenly hope.

3. The flowering of heavenly hope (vv. 9–11)

In the final section of the psalm David pushes the implications of his experience of God's deliverance to the ultimate, and most audacious,

[5] R. Schnackenberg, *Baptism in the Thought of St Paul* (Oxford, 1964), p. 199.

limit. 'Therefore . . . my body also will rest secure, because you will not abandon me to the grave, nor will you let your Holy One see decay' (vv. 9–10). The word for 'grave', *Sheol,* is (as we noted in chapter 1) the basic Old Testament term for the place to which the dead were thought to pass. Craigie summarizes the beliefs surrounding *Sheol* (Gk. *Hades*):

> The state of the dead is not differentiated with respect to good and evil persons; there is no clear distinction here between heaven and hell. *Sheol* was conceived as a kind of underworld . . . In *Sheol* persons were believed to exist in a form of semi-life, at rest, yet not in joy, for they had not the fullness of life which made possible the richness of relationship with the living God. Death was thus to be dreaded.[6]

Some commentators confine the range of David's hope here to the thought that David will in future experience God delivering him from life-threatening dangers. While the language may well include such hopes, however, its scope exceeds these circumstantial expectations. What David asserts, through the inspiration of the Holy Spirit, are two further astonishing truths.

'Where, O grave, is your victory?'

First, despite his own experience of human mortality encountered in the multitudes of his contemporaries and the countless hosts of his predecessors, there is, David dares to assert, a power in the world of which he has been given personal token in his recent deliverance, which is not subject to the dominion of death. *Sheol* is not God; *Sheol* is at the mercy of God. 'You will not abandon me to *Sheol*' (v. 10). The last word in death, and in his own inevitable future death in particular, does not lie with the power of human mortality and the insatiable fangs of *Sheol.* God is Lord of death.

For sheer audacity of conviction this rivals Job's celebrated claim, 'I know that my Redeemer lives, and that in the end he will stand upon the earth. And after my skin has been destroyed, yet in my flesh I will see God; I myself will see him . . . I, and not another' (Job 19:25–26).

'The writer [of Psalm 16] does not express the thought that he hopes merely to escape from death, but rather the bolder thought that death shall never get dominion over him. Never did faith wax

---

[6] P. Craigie, *Commentary on Psalms 1–50* (Word, 1983), p. 93; cf. Job 17:13–16; Ps. 6:5; Eccles. 9:5, 10; Is. 14:10f.

bolder in dealing with this problem. It ranks on a par with Romans 8:31ff.'[7]

'See the conquering hero comes!'

Second, the ultimate subject of this daring assertion, 'nor will you let your Holy One see decay' (v. 10), is none other than the psalmist's hoped-for Saviour, the Messiah of Israel, Jesus Christ. So Peter was to claim in the course of his Pentecost sermon, 'David . . . was a prophet . . . Seeing what was ahead, he spoke of the resurrection of the Christ, that he was not abandoned to the grave, nor did his body see decay' (Acts 2:24–32, esp. 30, 31).

Likewise Paul, in his address in the synagogue in Pisidian Antioch, said, 'The fact that God raised [Jesus] from the dead, never to decay, is stated in these words . . . "You will not let your Holy One see decay"' (Acts 13:34–35). And Jesus himself said, 'Everything must be fulfilled that is written about me in the Law of Moses, the Prophets and the Psalms' (Luke 24:44; cf. 1 Cor. 15:4; John 20:9).

Suddenly the range of this psalm reaches out into the eternal future and embraces not only the psalmist's own personal destiny, but also the glory of the resurrection of Jesus, and hence beyond that to the return of the Son of Man and the resurrection of the dead of all the ages. In its final reference this simple song, drawn from the worship of God's people centuries ago, embraces the final destinies of every man, woman and child in the entire universe. It also therefore embraces ours. Here in the heart of the Old Testament we encounter an unshakeable conviction of the hope of heaven.

We can finally note the profound connection between the two primary elements in this psalm, David's sense of the intimacy of God's presence and care in the circumstances of his life here, and David's hope of life after death. That hope is conveyed with great beauty and impressiveness in the final verse. 'You have made known to me the path of life; you will fill me with joy in your presence, with eternal pleasures at your right hand' (v. 11).

'Eternal pleasures at your right hand'

'The path of life' is an elemental image of the believer's life with God in the present, a 'walk' down the path of life, day after day. But it moves on almost imperceptibly beyond that, echoing the experience of Enoch, who 'walked with God . . . and God took him away' (Gen.

---

[7] H. C. Leupold, *Exposition of the Psalms* (Baker, 1969), pp. 152, 153.

5:24). At the end of the journey lie the 'eternal pleasures' of life with God on the other side of death.

Here is one of the clearest expressions of biblical hope. It indicates complete satisfaction; 'pleasures', 'joys' (the Hebrew is plural) and 'fullness' all indicate a complete satisfaction of desire. It indicates endless diversity, 'joy in your presence'. Who God is, is complemented by what God gives – 'pleasures at/from your right hand'. It indicates unimaginable intimacy: 'in your presence' is literally 'in your Face'. That is surely heaven's highest delight and final exhilaration, to be 'face to face with God' (Rev. 22:4), to look into that Face of endless, unfathomable love, to gaze upon him who is the Desire of all the ages and the Beloved of all the orders of creation, to see 'him whom our soul loves'. 'We shall see him' (1 John 3:2). It is enough!

'O Love that will not let me go'

It remains to draw to the surface the important relationship between the two primary themes of the psalm. On the one hand, here is a high-water mark in the Old Testament experience of personal union with God. It links with other such expressions in the Psalter (cf. Pss. 63:21–28; 73:1–8; 84:1–12). On the other hand, here is a remarkable Old Testament expression of hope that life with God continues after death.

In a profound sense, the former is the basis of the latter. The awareness of the personal love of God, born in the midst of the history of God's faithful dealings with Israel, focused generation by generation in the covenant, renewed through the experience of worship, deepened and purified through the repeated deliverances of God from life-threatening trials, here stretches forward to touch its ultimate horizon. The God who has assured the psalmist of his personal care and love has proved himself worthy of trust in the face of death. There, too, he will not fail. There, too, he will be proved Lord. There, too, his love will triumph. He will not abandon to the grave. The 'path of life' leads on, and on for ever, before the Face of Everlasting Love.

The presence of God, his unfailing companionship through all the vicissitudes of life, becomes the bedrock of his hope, not only for all that lies in wait for him in this life, but in all that must follow it. For it finally becomes unthinkable to him that the God who has proved so faithful now could ever let him arrive at the point of his pilgrimage where he says he is now leaving him to fend for himself.[8]

---

[8] R. A. Mason, 'Life before and after death in the Old Testament', in *Called to One Hope*, ed. J. Colwell (Paternoster Press, 2000), pp. 78–79.

It is this linkage which in its way anticipates Paul's argument in Romans 8:31–39, albeit immeasurably enriched and deepened by the fires of Calvary, that a love which 'did not spare his own Son' is one from which 'nothing can separate us' in time or eternity. As James Denney expresses it, 'The experience of God's love in life, a providential and redeeming love, of which man was as sure as he was of his life itself, is the primary and the ultimate factor in the faith of immortality.'[9] Upon this bedrock conviction this great psalm rests its hope of life everlasting.

Summary

In the face of some specific threat to his life the psalmist clings to God, whom he experiences in the context of the worshipping community. Here he renews his confidence that the God who has been with him and has sustained him through his earthly life will not leave him in the moment of death. Rather, there awaits him beyond the grave a life in which he will experience even more of God and his joyful presence.

[9] J. Denney, *Factors of Faith in Immortality* (Hodder and Stoughton, 1910), p. 59.

Psalm 72
4. Long may he live!

> Tomorrow's history has already been written . . . at the name of
> Jesus every knee will bow.
>
> (Paul E. Kauffman)

Another important Old Testament contribution to the development
of conviction concerning human destiny in the New Testament is
Israel's experience of the monarchy. It was as the final fulfilment of
the kingdom of God that the New Testament writers understood the
hope of heaven, and that concept was in turn significantly impacted
by the fortunes of Israel during the golden age in the reigns of David
and Solomon.

According to the ancient divisions, which go back at least to the
Septuagint (i.e. the second to the third century BC), Psalm 72 concludes the second book of the Psalter. A more significant issue for
our purpose is the question of the messianic application of these
verses. Do we have a basis for interpreting this ancient song as the
vehicle of a dream of the future heavenly reign of Jesus the Lord?

The New Testament does not make a direct connection, though
tantalizingly the Risen Jesus is reported telling the disciples,
'"Everything must be fulfilled that is written about me in the . . .
Psalms." Then he opened their minds so they could understand the
Scriptures' (Luke 24:44–45). There certainly could have been no
inappropriateness in his having referred to Psalm 72, as we will see –
the more so in that there are close parallels to the terms of this psalm
recorded in Isaiah 11:1–9 and echoes in Isaiah 60 – 62.[1]

---

[1] Cf. the stress on righteousness in vv. 1, 3, 7 with Is. 11:4, 5 and Is. 60:17; 61:3,
10–11; justice in v. 1 with Is. 61:8; judging in v. 2 with Is. 11:2; ministering to the
poor, needy and afflicted in vv. 4, 11, 12 with Is. 11:4; the universal scope of the
kingdom in vv. 8–11 with Is. 11:9, 10 and 60:3; the perpetuity of the kingdom in
vv. 5, 17–18 with Is. 60:19–20; and the tribute brought by the nations in v. 10 with

Quite apart from direct New Testament authorization, however, the transcendent splendours of the kingdom and its king described in Psalm 72 make it clear that no earthly monarch, whether Solomon or David or any other, could match the description.

In addition there is Jewish support for a messianic reading of the psalm. The Targum, the Aramaic version of the Old Testament, adds the word 'Messiah' in verse 1 to 'the King'. There are also rabbinic allusions.[2]

Accordingly, we may echo without reservation the judgment of Spurgeon, 'Jesus is here, beyond all doubt, in the glory of his reign, both as he now is, and as he shall be revealed in his latter-day glory.'[3]

What can we learn here about the life of heaven? The first and most obvious point is that we are to anticipate a kingdom presided over by a unique and perfect ruler. There are numerous New Testament examples of this metaphor, especially in the teaching of Jesus. His parables in particular have a number of sayings along these lines, 'The kingdom of God is a like a king who . . .' The parables of the marriage feast (Matt. 22:1–10), the wedding garment (Matt. 22:11–13), the sheep and the goats (Matt. 25:31–45) and the pounds (Luke 19:12–27) make the clearest use of this identification. Also to be noted are the parables of the divided kingdom (Mark 3:24–26 – by way of contrast with the true unified kingdom?), the strong man (Mark 3:27), the unmerciful servant (Matt. 18:23–25) and the warring king (Luke 14:31f.).

More generally, the whole notion of the kingdom of God itself carries this metaphor in its womb. The kingdom calls for a King; Jesus as the Anointed One of God is the instrument of its coming and hence the Lord of the kingdom (Mark 1:15; Matt. 4:23; 9:35; Luke 4:43; 8:1; 17:20, etc.). One can also note the way in which the crucifixion is presented in terms of the rejection of Jesus' claim to be the messianic ruler: 'Are you the Christ . . . ?' 'I am . . .' (Mark 14:61–62); 'Are you the king of the Jews?' 'Yes, it is as you say' (Mark 15:2; cf. John 18:33); 'Here is your king' (John 19:14). 'Pilate had a notice prepared and fastened to the cross. It read: JESUS OF NAZARETH, THE KING OF THE JEWS' (John 19:19).

The later New Testament echoes this claim, 'saying that there is another king, one called Jesus' (Acts 17:7). 'I saw heaven standing open and there before me was a white horse, whose rider is called

---

Is. 60:5, 10, 11–14 and 62:2. For passages with explicit messianic reference see Matt. 2:23; Acts 13:23; Heb. 7:14; John 7:24; Eph. 6:17; Rev. 5:5; 22:16; Luke 4:16–21; 7:22; 17:8–9; Matt. 5:4, etc.

[2] Cf. D. Kidner, *Psalms 1 – 72* (IVP, 1973), p. 257, fn. 3.

[3] C. H. Spurgeon, *The Treasury of David*, vol. III (London, 1872), p. 316.

Faithful and True . . . he is dressed in a robe dipped in blood, and his name is the Word of God . . . On his robe and on his thigh he has this name written: KING OF KINGS AND LORD OF LORDS' (Rev. 19:11, 13, 16). The link in this last reference between the titles of King and Lord is significant. In a profound sense, every reference to Jesus as Lord carries a similar implication of kingly authority.

In accordance with this thread of testimony we note that the vision of the New Jerusalem has as one of its central features, 'The throne of God and of the Lamb will be in the city' (Rev. 22:3).

Thus the presentation of the Messiah's reign in Psalm 72 sweeps us forward to the terms of his eternal reign. Here we anticipate the life of heaven. We can identify five features of his reign and, as we will see, each is directly anticipatory of the heavenly reign of Jesus Christ.

1. Integrity (vv. 1–4)

The twin qualities of the Messiah's reign are identified as 'justice' (Heb. *mišpāṭ*) and 'righteousness' (Heb. *ṣᵉḏāqâ*). These are nearly equivalents in Old Testament usage.

A righteous reign

The origin of 'righteousness' is probably an Arab root meaning straightness, hence the meaning of conformity to a norm. Righteousness is elsewhere prominent in the qualities embodied in the messianic King (cf. Is. 11:3b–5; 62:1; 32:1–20; Jer. 23:5–6). The Servant of the Lord is especially endowed with righteousness (cf. Is. 42:1f.). God is the source of this quality, and it is therefore prayed for with reference to those who exercise rule (v. 1). It is expressed in terms of delivering fair and impartial judgments (cf. Ex. 33:3, 6; 19:14, 35; Deut. 1:17; 16:18–20). A particular feature of the divine righteousness, and hence of that which reflects his divine kingship, is that of a 'bias in favour of the helpless'.[4] So in our psalm, 'He will judge . . . your afflicted ones with justice . . . He will defend the afflicted among the people and save the children of the needy' (vv. 2, 4).

Elsewhere we find God's righteousness expressed in terms of his taking action on behalf of his people to achieve their deliverance, and hence he is 'a righteous God and a Saviour' (Is. 45:21). David discovered the graciousness of the divine justice in Psalm 51, traditionally composed out of the agony of his sin and guilt over Bathsheba's rape

---

[4] N. H. Snaith, *The Distinctive Ideas of the Old Testament* (Epworth, 1944), p. 68.

and Uriah's murder. 'Save me from bloodguilt, O God, the God who saves me, and my tongue will sing of your righteousness' (Ps. 51:14). Righteousness here is the equivalent of pardoning mercy. The reference to saving the 'children' in verse 4 is particularly vivid since they represent the helpless *par excellence*.

'*Tsedeq* certainly stands for the establishment of justice in the land . . . but important as [that] is it is but half the truth . . . It is "in part" the truth because God's will is wider than justice. He has a particular regard for the helpless ones of earth to rescue them from the clutches of those that are stronger than they.'[5] Both these aspects of the integrity of the reign of the Messiah will find their expression in the heavenly kingdom over which he will reign. It will be as no other a place of utter righteousness, where God's will is done in every regard. Heaven is a holy place, 'a new heaven and a new earth, the home of righteousness' (2 Pet. 3:13), a 'holy city' where 'nothing impure will ever enter . . . nor . . . anyone who does what is shameful or deceitful [or] who loves and practises falsehood' (Rev. 21:27; 22:15).

Specifically it will be a place where justice is done and where complete impartiality reigns. Thus all its citizens will live in the constant, open scrutiny of God's holy presence. Sin will be no more, and that old, corrupt nature which is its source and seedbed. Made 'like him', we will be able at every moment to submit to his righteous gaze, and we will be able to utter the very words of the King himself: 'Which of you convicts me of sin?' (John 8:46 RSV). Gone will be that need to hide ourselves which consumed Adam and Eve in the Garden of Eden (Gen. 3:8). Heaven is a place where pretence is never needed; where we will live in freedom from fear of judgment; where we will never need to pretend or assume an unreal posture or claim an inappropriate credit. It will be a place where we can live for the first time in all our lives in freedom from judgment – the judgment of others and the self-judgments which in this life so regularly cripple and enslave us. We will live in the freedom of the judgment of God. We will have accepted his just judgment on our lives, be utterly one with him who is the embodied righteousness of God, and be renewed in the image of the Righteous One. We will be righteous and will pursue righteousness. We will at last, and for ever, 'do justly . . . love mercy, and . . . walk humbly with [our] God' (Mic. 6:8 AV).

Equality

We will also experience the freedom of God's righteous impartiality. In heaven there is no distinction between those who are

---

[5] ibid., pp. 69–70.

favoured more and those who are favoured less. There God's love in its infinity will be the portion of each and none will be able to exalt themselves over any other, nor will any have reason to feel less valued. The differences which distinguish will never be differences in our perceived value or dignity. Each child of God will recognize him- or herself as an infinitely beloved child of God. All need to compete, or to exalt ourselves, or to put others down will have been eliminated. All will know themselves as 'the disciple whom Jesus loves'.

Underlying all will be that further sense of the divine righteousness as God's acting for the needy. In heaven, as never before, we will be aware of the fathomless depth of our need, our utter and unqualifiable poverty, our eternal and immeasurable dependence. There, as never before, 'the needy will be saved' (v. 13), and will go on and on being saved, through the endless aeons of eternity.

2. Perpetuity (vv. 5, 7)

A second feature of the Messiah's kingdom is its limitless duration. 'He will endure as long as the sun, as long as the moon, through all generations' (v. 5). 'In his days . . . prosperity will abound till the moon is no more' (v. 7). Hence the anticipation of the prayers of verse 15, 'Long may he live!', and verse 17, 'May his name endure for ever'.

The psalmist here employs the imagery of a reign coterminous with the sun and moon. The observation that in fact they will not 'endure for ever' is beside the point (cf. Is. 13:10; 34:4; Mark 13:24–25). As Jeremiah 33:20 and Psalm 89:29 indicate, they were thought of as synonymous with eternity.

This dimension finds further echo in other messianic passages. The rejoicing 'ransomed of the LORD' in Isaiah's vision 'will enter Zion with singing' and 'everlasting joy will crown their heads' (35:10). In the 'new heavens and new earth' time will no longer be measured by present earthly standards. 'Never again will there be . . . an infant who lives but a few days, or an old man who does not live out his years; he who dies at a hundred will be thought a mere youth; he who fails to reach a hundred will be considered accursed' (Is. 65:20).

The reference to dying here is not to be applied literally; it is simply a symbol for complete fulfilment unthreatened by the curtailments of present circumstances. Hence, in more general terms, 'As the new heavens and the new earth that I make will endure before me . . . so will your name and your descendants endure' (Is. 66:22).

In Daniel's visions, the kingdom of 'the God of heaven' (Dan. 2:44) 'will never be destroyed, nor will it be left to another people. It will crush all those kingdoms and bring them to an end, but it will itself endure for ever.' Again, the 'one like a son of man' (Dan. 7:13) is described in these terms: 'His dominion is an everlasting dominion that will not pass away, and his kingdom is one that will never be destroyed' (Dan. 7:14).

'And he shall reign for ever and ever'

This awesome dimension of the promised messianic kingdom finds its fulfilment in the kingdom established by the Lord Jesus Christ. In Mark 13:31 he contrasts the temporariness of 'heaven and earth' with the permanence of his words, which 'will never pass away' (cf. Matt. 24:35). The Lord's Prayer ends in some, admittedly lesser, manuscripts with 'yours is the kingdom for ever and ever' (Matt. 6:13).

More substantially, also in the Sermon on the Mount, Jesus speaks of the security of the heavenly treasures which are impervious to the corrupting forces of 'moth and rust' (Matt. 6:20), secure from the ravages of time. The way of salvation is 'the road . . . to life' (Matt. 7:14), arguably eternal life, life without limitation. In Matthew 12:32 Jesus contrasts the present age with 'the age to come', the age of the endless kingdom of God. And in Matthew 25:46 the parable of the sheep and the goats ends with the assignment to 'eternal life' and 'eternal punishment'. Paul's expectation of the state of things after the return of the Lord is couched in 1 Thessalonians 4:17 in terms of being 'with the Lord for ever'. The book of Revelation has several references to the eternity of the kingdom of Christ. In the imperious words in 1:17–18 the one like 'a son of man' declares, 'I am the First and the Last. I am the Living One; I was dead, and behold I am alive for ever and ever!' Revelation 11:15 records the 'loud voices in heaven' proclaiming, 'The kingdom of the world has become the kingdom of our Lord and of his Christ, and he will reign for ever and ever.' The great final vision of the life of heaven in 22:4–5 concludes with this triumphant perspective: 'They will see his face, and his name will be on their foreheads . . . And they will reign for ever and ever.'

The indestructible

Today, not least in the West, we inhabit a world where impermanence has become a fundamental feature of life. This was famously documented in Alvin Toffler's best-seller *Future Shock*, in which he

introduced the concept of 'the throw-away society'.[6] Toffler illustrates this trend from a number of fields. 'We face a rising flood of
throw-away items, impermanent architecture, mobile and modular
products, rented goods and commodities designed for almost instant
death.' He also comments:

> Anti-materialists tend to deride the importance of 'things'. Yet
> things are highly significant not merely because of their functional
> utility, but also because of their psychological impact. We develop
> relationships with things. Things affect our sense of continuity
> and discontinuity. They play a role in the structure of situations
> and the foreshortening of our relationships with things accelerates
> the pace of life.[7]

In such an ephemeral atmosphere, how desperately we need the
reminder that 'we are receiving a kingdom that cannot be shaken'
(Heb. 12:28), a kingdom which will last for ever and hence will be
impervious to the chances and changes which increasingly characterize the world around us.

In bad times . . .

A recognition of the perpetuity of the kingdom also helps us handle
the opposition and rejection which Scripture assures us will face
those who seek to live faithfully in this present order. Jesus asserted
this quite directly. '"No servant is greater than his master." If they
persecuted me, they will persecute you also' (John 15:20).

> Our great honour lies in being just what Jesus was and is. To be
> accepted by those who accept him, rejected by those who reject
> him, loved by those who loved him, hated by everyone that hates
> him. What greater glory can come to any person? We can afford
> to follow him to failure. Faith dares to fail. The resurrection and
> the judgment will demonstrate before all worlds who won and
> who lost. We can wait.[8]

. . . and sad times

The perpetuity of the kingdom of Christ is also of immense comfort
in the face of the tragic and heartbreaking impermanence of earthly

[6] A. Toffler, *Future Shock* (Pan, 1970), pp. 54–72, etc.
[7] ibid., pp. 74, 55.
[8] A. W. Tozer, *Born After Midnight* (Christian Publications, 1959), p. 59.

relationships. Jesus' tears at the tomb of Lazarus are eloquent in this regard. Death severs the closest and dearest of ties, and none of us can live a lifetime without experiencing death's 'dull, cold ear'. In this darkness the light of the endless prospect of Christ's reign shines with glorious hope and promise. 'We do not want you to be ignorant about those who fall asleep, or to grieve like the rest, who have no hope. We believe that Jesus died and rose again and so we believe that . . . the dead in Christ will rise . . . And so we will be with the Lord for ever' (1 Thess. 4:13, 14, 16, 17 NIVI).

3. Universality (vv. 8, 9, 10, 11)

This further, wonderful dimension of the Messiah's reign is all the more impressive in an age of globalism. For modern people the thought of universal control and influence has become a realistic possibility as never before in human history.

'Only one earth'

In the moving words of Sultan Bin Salman al-Saud, *Discovery 5* astronaut, 'The first day or so we all pointed to our countries. The third or fourth day we were pointing to our continents. By the fifth day we were aware of only one earth.'[9] This 'one earth' the psalmist sees under the blessed control of his ideal King.

'From sea to sea' (v. 8) may imply from the Red Sea in the south to the long shore of the Mediterranean Sea on Israel's western seaboard, and 'the River' is likely to have been the Euphrates to Israel's north-west – specific geographical features which approximate to the promised boundaries of the land of their inheritance (cf. Exod. 23:31). If so, it is only the nucleus of the full, universal scope of the kingdom, which is finally 'the ends of the earth'.

There is an interesting historical incident relating to the specificity of the early part of verse 8, 'from sea to sea and from the River to the ends of the earth'. In 1870, at the time of the confederation of the British North American colonies of Upper and Lower Canada into the united nation of Canada, the name 'Kingdom of Canada' was canvassed but rejected. Finally, the title 'Dominion' was chosen for the new nation because of the apparent relevance of this verse. Canada, then in prospect and later in reality, stretched from 'sea to sea' – from the Atlantic to the Pacific, 'from the River' (the great St Lawrence, which in those days dominated the prospects, trade and

---

[9] Cited H. Snyder, *Earth Currents* (Nashville, 1995), p. 11.

external relations of the country) 'to the ends of the earth' (most applicable to the polar region to Canada's north). Thus it came to be called 'the Dominion of Canada'.[10]

'To the ends of the earth'

For the psalmist, however, the King's 'dominion' stretches far beyond the limits of Israel or Canada, to embrace the far-flung lands of the entire world, its 'distant shores' (v. 10) and, finally, 'all nations' (v. 11). Notably included are all God's enemies (v. 9), who will 'lick the dust' in humiliation and frustration, as 'all kings . . . bow down' in homage (vv. 9–11).

Again in this blessed prospect we touch a thread running through both Old Testament promise and New Testament fulfilment, a prospect which reaches as far back as the Creator's universal reign: 'In the beginning God created the heavens and the earth' (Gen. 1:1). It is refocused around his redemptive purpose in the promise to Abraham in Genesis 12:3: 'All peoples on earth will be blessed through you', a promise which is reaffirmed through the generations. The psalmists herald God's global rule in their summons to the nations to praise (Pss. 67:3; 96:1; 148:11, etc.). It is also expressed, significantly, in the terms of the Servant's ministry: 'I will make you a light for the Gentiles, that you may bring my salvation to the ends of the earth' (Is. 49:6; cf. Is. 42:6).

'The whole wide world for Jesus'

In the New Testament the universal scope of the kingdom of Jesus lies on the surface of the text. He proclaims the kingdom of God as the foundational reality in his mission (Mark 1:14), a kingdom which has necessarily universal dimensions. He prophesies of people coming from 'the east and the west' to take their places in the kingdom alongside Abraham, Isaac and Jacob (Matt. 8:11). In approaching his cross he anticipates the universal effects and global magnetism of his self-offering in sacrifice: 'I, when I am lifted up . . . will draw all . . . to myself' (John 12:32). As the Risen One he claims as inheritance the visionary dominion of the Son of Man: 'All authority in heaven and on earth has been given to me' (Matt. 28:18; cf. Dan. 7:14). On that basis the church is sent on its universal mission, 'Therefore go and make disciples of all nations' (v. 19), in anticipation of the day when 'every knee [will] bow . . . and every

[10] See 'Dominion', in *Canadian Encyclopedia*, editor in chief James H. Marsh (McClelland and Stewart, 2000), p. 280.

tongue confess that Jesus Christ is Lord, to the glory of God the Father' (Phil. 2:10–11).

Appropriately, the New Testament closes with a vision of his glorious reappearance: 'Jesus Christ . . . the ruler of the kings of the earth . . . On his robe and on his thigh he has this name written: KING OF KINGS AND LORD OF LORDS' (Rev. 1:5; 19:16).

The universality of Christ's reign has the most profound implications for every disciple, as we daily serve the one whose name is Lord, and whose destined inheritance is the whole wide world.

4. Humanity (vv. 12–14)

The ideal King is marked by compassion. He is sensitive when the needy and the afflicted cry out in helplessness (v. 12). Specifically he acts to deliver them from oppressive and violent assaults with their threat of death (v. 13–14). In his sight their lives are 'precious', and he is ever ready to take their cause upon himself and to act for them.

Solomon here speaks more in terms of prospect than of performance. In his great prayer at the dedication of the temple he shows a moving sensitivity to the diverse and deep needs of his people; not only the external threats of plundering enemies (cf. 1 Kgs. 8:44f.), but also 'the afflictions of [each one's] heart' (v. 38) and the personal moral struggle: 'Hear . . . their prayer and their plea . . . When they sin against you – for there is no-one who does not sin' (vv. 45–46). His early reign was marked by a judicious application of compassionate judgment (1 Kgs. 3:16–28). In later years, however, the people were to recall the heaviness of his yoke (1 Kgs. 12:4).

David, Solomon's father, is a better embodiment of the deeply felt, royal humanity celebrated here (cf. 2 Sam. 3:31–39; 9:1–13; 16:5–14; 18:33 – 19:4). But both in the end fall short of the true ideal, an ideal prophetically anticipated in the ministry of the Servant, concerning whom it can be testified, 'A bruised reed he will not break, a smouldering wick he will not snuff out' (Is. 42:3); 'I offered my back to those who beat me, my cheeks to those who pulled out my beard; I did not hide my face from mocking and spitting' (Is. 50:6); 'He was despised and rejected by men, a man of sorrows and familiar with suffering . . . Surely he took up our infirmities and carried our sorrows . . . After the suffering of his soul, he will see the light of life and be satisfied; by his knowledge my righteous servant will justify many, for he will bear their iniquities' (Is. 53:3, 4, 11).

Meekness and majesty

The New Testament fulfilment in the ministry of Jesus needs no 'proof text' demonstration. He was 'the Word made flesh', Emmanuel, 'God with us', true man, true God. The writer to the Hebrews makes telling application.

> Since the children have flesh and blood, he too shared in their humanity . . . we do not have a high priest who is unable to sympathise with our weaknesses, but we have one who has been tempted in every way, just as we are . . . Let us then approach the throne of grace with confidence, so that we may receive mercy and find grace to help us in our time of need. (Heb. 2:14; 4:15–16)

Or, as a twentieth-century poem expresses it:

> The other Gods were strong; but thou wast weak;
> They rode, but thou didst stumble to a throne;
> But to our wounds none but God's wounds can speak,
> And not a God has wounds, but Thou alone.[11]

It is precisely this combination of infinite majesty and power with the deepest, most tender humanity which has been the secret of the perennial attraction of Jesus Christ to the human heart across the ages, and which will find its final expression in the 'new heaven and earth' presided over by an enthroned Lamb with the marks of wounds in his hands and side (Rev. 5:6; 21:22; 22:14).

5. Felicity (vv. 6–7, 16–17)

This final characteristic of the ideal King in some ways gathers up all the others. His rule's unimpeachable integrity, its unending perpetuity, its all-embracing universality, its bottomless humanity, combine to produce a dominion under which the highest and deepest felicity abounds. 'Abounds' echoes verse 7 with specific respect to its prosperity, which is no mere materialistic abundance, but one which touches the heart and spirit of its subjects.

---

[11] Edward Shillito, 'Jesus of the Scars', in *A Treasury of Christian Verse* (SCM, 1959), p. 114, v. 4.

'Like dew upon the tender herb'

Thus we have the beautiful image of verse 6, 'He will be like rain falling on a mown field, like showers watering the earth.' The picture is more accessible to an agrarian society, but even the concrete-encompassed city dweller can catch the flavour of this blessed picture. The human heart is forever subject to dryness of spirit. Life drains us. The stresses and strains of daily life, with its multiple relational demands and pressing responsibilities, constantly harass and deprive. We find ourselves frequently in 'a dry and weary land where there is no water' (Ps. 63:1).

To all such Jesus comes; to all such he makes himself available. He is the Servant who knows 'the word that sustains the weary' (Is. 50:4). In words expressing his identification with that promised intercessor, he invites us still, 'Come to me, all you who are weary and burdened, and I will give you rest' (Matt. 11:28). 'There is no need of the human heart which Jesus cannot meet, and that is why he belongs to east as well as to west, and why no greater than Jesus will ever come – no other is required!'[12]

The felicity of the Messiah's reign extends also to its outward splendour. Grain and fruits flourish (v. 16); the very earth is caught into the sense of overflowing abundance. Gold, the great index of wealth, is made available to the King, specifically from Sheba (v. 15), presumably an echo of the lavish gifts supplied to Solomon by the Queen of Sheba (1 Kgs. 10:10), which contributed to the astonishing availability of gold throughout his kingdom (2 Kgs. 10:14–21) such that silver was esteemed of little value, 'as common . . . as stones' (10:27).

Of course, the material opulence of the Solomonic vision needs translating in terms of the one who had 'nowhere to lay his head' (Matt. 8:20) and who identified so utterly with the poor as to leave no material legacy at the last beyond the clothes in which he came to his execution (John 19:23). But the splendour of his reign finds its New Testament expression in the visions of the end and 'the new heaven and earth of righteousness', when he will appear 'coming in clouds with great power and glory' (Mark 13:26). The place of his eventual dwelling among his people is depicted as a temple-city ablaze with glory (Rev. 21:23; cf. Ezek. 43:1–5).

Concerning this, we do well to recall the response of the Queen of Sheba when confronted with Solomon's splendour. 'She was overwhelmed' (1 Kgs. 10:5). 'Not even half was told me . . . you have far exceeded the report I heard' (10:7).

---

[12]Edward Norman, quoted Alan Walker, *Christ is Enough* (Wyvern, 1963), Preface.

Jesus refers to her response as a judgment on those who, whether in his own day or in ours, make no effort to view the splendours of the messianic King. If she expended the effort to examine the material and intellectual acquisitions of an earthly potentate, how much more are we obligated to stir ourselves in the examination, contemplation and wondering admiration of our King of Kings. Such will be the delightful occupation of the heavenly order. On that day we will surely echo in our hearts the queen's verdict, 'Not even half was told me . . . you have far exceeded the report I heard.' We will be utterly, and endlessly, overwhelmed.

We need not be surprised that such images of kingly glory as this psalm holds before us penetrated into the core of New Testament anticipations of the heavenly kingdom and its glorious coming King. No wonder the psalm concludes with a doxology: 'Praise be to his glorious name for ever; may the whole earth be filled with his glory. Amen and Amen.' To which we need only add, 'Your kingdom come.' It will!

Summary

Israel's dream of God's sovereign future vindication of his purposes was shaped by the period of significant earthly power and its trappings during the reigns of David and Solomon. Thus the heavenly life, which was later to be seen as the final form of the kingdom of God, was viewed as being anticipated in these monarchies. Specifically they gave token of the integrity, perpetuity, universality, humanity and felicity of that future messianic reign.

Daniel 7:9–14; 12:1–13
5. Either/or

> But at my back I always hear
> Time's wingèd chariot hurrying near,
> And yonder all before us lie
> Deserts of vast eternity.
>
> (Andrew Marvell, 'Upon Appleton House')

We come to the final Old Testament foreshadowing of human destiny, its explicit anticipation of a radical, future intervention of God in human history, and for this we turn to the book of Daniel.

Even on a cursory reading, the book of Daniel is different. Its opening six chapters appear relatively accessible to the modern reader as we accompany Daniel to the land of Babylon during the exile and witness the dramatic events involving himself and his heroic friends, Shadrach, Meshach and Abednego. Chapters 7–12, however, introduce us to a very different, even bizarre, world. In dream-like visions employing vivid symbols, Daniel unveils a series of dramatic, global happenings which bring history as we know it to an abrupt conclusion.

Extensive debates continue to flourish around the sources, literary forms and historical associations of the book of Daniel, and of these chapters in particular. It is sufficient for our purpose, however, to note simply that Daniel represents a point of Old Testament interface with what has been called 'apocalyptic writing'.[1] Of particular note is the relationship of apocalyptic to prophecy. In general the prophets addressed their own day and its issues, though employing in the process a foretelling of God's future acts with respect to Israel and its neighbours. In apocalyptic writing the focus moves clearly towards the future, and the tie with immediate events becomes more tenuous.

---

[1] Cf. explanation of 'apocalyptic' in footnote 10 in Introduction, p. 31.

External factors which arguably promoted the rise of apocalyptic writing were Israel's diminished global status in the centuries following the Davidic and Solomonic eras, and the relative failure of the restoration from exile to revive its national fortunes. A resolution of this apparent contradiction of God's special relationship with Israel is seen to lie *beyond history* in a new divine intervention.

The book of Daniel, particularly its second part, is not an apocalyptic writing *tout simple*. For one thing, it was written before this literary form had been fully developed, and it has other affinities besides apocalyptic. As one writer helpfully notes, wisdom lies in 'interpreting Daniel from his predecessors rather than his successors'.[2] Daniel stands within the inspired writings of the Old Testament and is to be interpreted in terms of that setting.

For its contribution to the Bible's understanding of heaven and hell, we focus on two crucial passages, 7:9–14 and 12:1–4.

1. The kingdom (7:9–12)

We have already noted the significance of the experience of the monarchy in Israel in shaping its sense of the future. In Daniel 7 the notion of kingly dominion is carried a stage further. Here, in a 'vision at night' (v. 2), we meet a series of 'four great beasts' (v. 3), each with affinities to earthly animals. Particular emphasis is given to the fourth creature, 'terrifying and frightening and very powerful' and 'different from all the former beasts' (v. 7).

The meaning of this succession is given a paragraph later. 'The four great beasts are four kingdoms that will rise from the earth' (v. 17). The pattern here is close to Nebuchadnezzar's statue comprising different materials, which was interpreted by Daniel in similar terms (2:31–43). Critically, in both historical panoramas there appears a fifth kingdom in succession to the other four. 'In the time of those kings, the God of heaven will set up a kingdom that will never be destroyed' (2:44). In chapter 7 the arrival of the fifth kingdom is more directly related to God's intervention.

> As I looked [following the succession of the four beasts with their diverse features], thrones were set in place, and the Ancient of Days took his seat. His clothing was as white as snow; the hair of his head was white like wool. His throne was flaming with fire ... Thousands upon thousands attended him; ten thousand times ten thousand stood before him. The court was seated, and the books were opened. (7:9–10)

[2] Adam C. Welch, *Visions of the End* (London, n.d.), p. 129.

The Son of Man

This expression of divine sovereignty is immediately related to

> one like a son of man, coming with the clouds of heaven. He
> approached the Ancient of Days and was led into his presence.
> He was given authority, glory and sovereign power; all peoples,
> nations and men of every language worshipped him. His domin-
> ion is an everlasting dominion that will not pass away, and his
> kingdom is one that will never be destroyed. (7:13–14)

Later in the chapter, as the interpretation is provided, we are told:

> The court will sit, and his [i.e. the fourth beast, which has terror-
> ized the saints] power will be taken away and completely
> destroyed for ever. Then the sovereignty, power and greatness of
> the kingdoms under the whole heaven will be handed over to the
> saints, the people of the Most High. His kingdom will be an ever-
> lasting kingdom, and all rulers will worship and obey him.
> (7:26–27)

The essence of this vision of human destiny is clear enough. Human
dynasties and powers will finally reach their nadir. At that point God
will sovereignly intervene to pass all previous kingdoms and their
inhabitants under judgment and establish his own divine rule. In
contrast to the earthly kingdoms, this heavenly kingdom will
be eternal.

A judgment to come

Thus the vision of Daniel moves us significantly beyond the processes of judgment and recompense which in earlier Old Testament
writing had been primarily located within earthly experience. It faces
us with the thought of a judgment which operates beyond this
present world order and which is directly exercised by God himself,
in anticipation of the writer to the Hebrews, 'People are destined
once to die, and *after that* to face judgment' (Heb. 9:27 NIVI).

Two other features of Daniel's vision call for comment. The first
is the overwhelming sense of the sovereignty of God. Even when a
great and impressive human kingdom is ranged against him and his
people, he simply asserts himself and the 'doom is writ' as far as his
adversaries are concerned (cf. 7:9, 22; 2:44). His rule is an easy one;
he reigns over all in uninhibited majesty.

Here again we encounter the God of Genesis who creates all

things by his word and upon whom everything utterly depends. Furthermore, that sovereignty is not exercised merely with respect to a specific national adversary, but stretches to all nations. He is the universal Lord; his kingdom will fill 'the whole earth' (2:35).

The second notable feature is that 'the books were opened' when the heavenly court began its session. The language is figurative, but immensely vivid. We will return to this image when we expound the 'great white throne' scene in Revelation 20. There again the books are brought forward (Rev. 20:12) as determinative testimony with regard to the exercise of God's judgment. The thought of God having books for recording the past and exercising his judgment finds echo elsewhere (cf. Exod. 32:32; Ps. 56:8; Mal. 3:16).

Emil Brunner makes the solemn application:

> God is not mocked; 'Whatsoever a man sows that shall he reap'. God does not forget. The constancy, the self-consistency of God, which is primarily one of the comforting and glorious things about Him, is a terrible thing in this connection. God does not forget; the injury to the divine order does not heal; this wound remains open eternally . . . All the expressions that are used in the Bible about 'writing down', 'entering in a book', etc. are meant to express this . . . Just as previously it was comforting to know that we could reckon on God, so now it strikes terror to the heart of man to know that we must reckon with Him.[3]

2. The coming one (7:13–14)

The culminating action of the Ancient of Days is to hand over the 'authority, glory and sovereign power' with respect to 'all peoples, nations and those of every language' to 'one like a son of man, coming with the clouds of heaven' (7:13–14). In reflecting on this figure and his identity we can also note that the later delegation of the 'sovereignty, power and greatness of the kingdoms under the whole heaven' to 'the people of the Most High' (7:27) is followed by the affirmation, 'His kingdom will be an everlasting kingdom, and all rulers will worship and obey him.'

What are we to make of this enigmatic figure?

The context of his ministry is important. The appearance of the 'one like a son of man' is the seventh chapter's equivalent to the fifth kingdom of Nebuchadnezzar's earlier dream (cf. 2:44ff.). The

---

[3] E. Brunner, *The Mediator* (Lutterworth, 1934), p. 463.

context is again the reign of God exercised after the demise of the earthly empires, and in particular the especially threatening fourth kingdom, which has been a source of a special persecution of the saints (7:23–25).

Another significant feature is his 'coming with the clouds of heaven' (v. 13). Noting the regular biblical association of clouds with the appearances of the heavenly King, Leupold comments, 'They are His carpet, His mark of identification' (cf. Exod. 13:12f.; 19:9f.; 1 Kgs. 8:10f.; Is. 19:1; Jer. 4:13; Nah. 1:3; Ezek. 10:4; Ps. 18:1, 12; 97:2–4; 104:3f.).[4] The New Testament reflects the same feature with regard to the coming of Christ at the end of the present age. 'At that time men will see the Son of Man coming in clouds with great power and glory' (Mark 13:26; cf. Matt. 24:30; 26:64; Rev. 1:7; 14:14).

The etymological links with 'man' (humankind) are suggestive of a representative meaning. This is borne out in the context, where the beasts in the earlier part of the vision represent human empires (cf. 'like a lion' [v. 4], 'like a bear' [v. 5], 'like a leopard' [v. 6], and 'like a son of man' [v. 13]). Stress in the phrase falls on the humanity of the figure (cf. Ezek. 2:1; 3:6, 8, etc., where Ezekiel is addressed as son of man, i.e. as creaturely man in contrast to God's creative majesty).

Baldwin suggests a similar contrast in Daniel 7 between the earthly kingdoms with their flawed self-confidence and final inhumanity, and the kingdom of the Son of Man where God is recognized and humanity finds its true expression and dignity as those 'made in the image of God'.[5]

Much discussion has been prompted by attempts to find origins for the concept in other Ancient Near Eastern mythologies, without conspicuous success. Jeremias concludes, 'A thorough examination of the comparative material has shown that these hypotheses stand on very flimsy foundations.'[6] The context of judgment is important (cf. Ps. 9:7–19), and was clearly so for Jesus in carrying this passage into fulfilment in his ministry: 'For the Son of Man is going to come in his Father's glory with his angels, and then he will reward each person according to what he has done' (Matt. 16:27); '[The Father] has given [the Son] authority to judge because he is the Son of Man' (John 5:27).

[4] H. C. Leupold, *Exposition of Daniel* (Baker, 1969) p. 308; see also L. Sabourin, 'In connection with Daniel 7:13 it is observed that the coming with clouds is an exclusively divine attribute', cited Joyce G. Baldwin, *Daniel* (IVP, 1978), p. 142, fn. 1.

[5] Baldwin, ibid., p. 148.

[6] Joachim Jeremias, *New Testament Theology*, vol. 1 (SCM, 1971), p. 268.

We should also note the universal scope of this fifth kingdom (cf. Dan. 2:35): 'all peoples, nations and men of every language' (7:14); 'Then the sovereignty, power and greatness of the kingdoms under the whole heaven will be handed over . . . His kingdom will be an everlasting kingdom, and all rulers will worship and obey him' (7:27).

The representation of the vision in verses 26–27 casts the 'son of man' in a new light. Here the judgment of the fourth, persecuting, empire will, at the time of the court's sitting, be handed over to 'the saints, the people of the Most High'.

The Son and the saints

One possibility is to read the 'son of man' in collective terms; the title is simply another way of referring to the people of God. This seems unlikely, not least because the title is not 'son of Israel' but embraces the whole of humanity. Representation appears a better way of understanding this link between the one and the many. There is an interesting parallel in the 'Servant of the Lord' (cf. Is. 42:1f., etc.), which similarly oscillates between the individual and the community (cf. Is. 44:1; 49:3).

In Jesus' fulfilment of the title the individual meaning is strongly asserted. 'Son of Man', or better, as C. F. D. Moule effectively demonstrated, '*The* Son of Man', is the Son of Man which you know about, the 'son of man' of Daniel's vision.[7] The Messiah is consistently thought of in solidarity with the messianic community, a reality represented in the Gospels by the calling (and commissioning) of the disciples who receive the kingdom from the Son of Man. 'Do not be afraid, little flock, for your Father has been pleased to give you the kingdom' (Luke 12:32; cf. Matt. 16:19; Mark 12:9; Luke 11:13; 20:16; John 6:27; 10:28; 14:16).

The Son of Man is accordingly critical to the culmination of the historical process as the empires of the ages are brought to their end in an act of sovereign, divine intervention and judgment. Subsequently he becomes the central figure of a new order in which he exercises absolute dominion and receives universal acclaim and worship. This new age is in some sense shared with 'the saints, the people of the Most High'. It is an everlasting kingdom.

It is not difficult to identify here the framework within which New Testament eschatology was developed in terms of the messianic figure of Jesus. In fulfilment of Daniel's vision we await the majestic

[7] Cf. C. F. D. Moule, *The Origin of Christology* (Cambridge University Press, 1977), pp. 11–31.

appearing of the Son of Man, the universal judgment, and the new heaven and earth of righteousness in which he will reign in uninhibited glory among his people. This vision of Daniel 7, however, is not this Old Testament book's last word on human destiny.

3. The consequences (vv. 12:1–13)

The biblical chapter division here is fairly unhelpful. Verse 12:1 begins, 'At that time,' but to discover what time is in mind we need to go back to the paragraph beginning at 11:40, 'At the time of the end', and even further back, to 11:35, where the first reference to 'the time of the end' occurs.

Antichrist?

What follows in this section beginning at 11:35 is an account of the ruthless, universal king who will assume power in the final period of history. Many commentators, including ancient ones, have noted historical parallels to the reign of Antiochus IV, 175–164 BC. However, the details are less than fully consistent with what is known of that Seleucid king of Syria. It appears much wiser, as Jerome noted in the fourth century, to see a more general reference to manifestations of evil right across the ages which will find a special expression towards 'the time of the end'.

Whether we should use the term antichrist in any straightforward way is open to some question, as Baldwin rightly points out.[8] However, the polarization of good and evil in the world immediately prior to the return of Christ has clear New Testament grounding (cf. Mark 13:9–11, 19; 2 Thess. 2:3, 4; Dan. 12:2).

The demise of this fearful global ruler is stated succinctly at the end of Daniel 11: 'He will come to his end' (v. 45). This paves the way for the account in chapter 12 of the divine intervention which culminates history.

The instrument is Michael (12:1; cf. 10:13, 21). He is met again in Revelation 12:7 and Jude 9, and in each reference is clearly a champion who wars for God's people against the forces of evil, here in Daniel at 'a time of distress such as has not happened from the beginning of nations until then' (12:1). Deliverance follows for God's people, defined in terms of their names being written in the book of life (cf. Rev. 20:12).

---

[8] Baldwin, *Daniel*, p. 199.

Life and death

This brings us to verse 12:2, 'Multitudes who sleep in the dust of the earth will awake: some to everlasting life, others to shame and everlasting contempt.' This is a crucial saying with respect to the development of the Bible's teaching about heaven and hell. Several things are noteworthy.

First, *the slain during the reign of 'Antiochus'*. Against the view that only a limited company are in view here, Wallace's comment is judicious: 'This is one of the great Old Testament affirmations of the resurrection of the body. It has a universal ring.'[9] In other words, we have a prevision here of Jesus' words in John 5:28–29, 'A time is coming when all who are in their graves will hear his [the Son of Man's] voice and come out – those who have done good will rise to live, and those who have done evil will rise to be condemned.'

Second, *the use of the image of 'sleep'* for death has numerous Old Testament (and New Testament) parallels (cf. Ps. 13:3; Job 3:13; Jer. 51:39, 57; Is. 26:19; Mark 5:39; John 11:11; Acts 7:60; 1 Cor. 15:51; 1 Thess. 4:14). It vividly conveys the sense of the temporariness of the experience of death.

Third, *'the dust of death'* is another vivid touch. It harks back to the second creation account in Genesis 2:7, 'the LORD God formed the man from the dust of the ground', and the curse of Genesis 3:19, 'dust you are and to dust you will return'. This allusion is the more striking in view of the fourth notable feature, *'everlasting life'*. The Genesis 'tree of life' finds possible allusion here (Gen. 3:22; Rev. 2:7; 22:2). This is the first occurrence of the phrase in Scripture.

Fifth, *'everlasting contempt'*. Baldwin offers 'abhorrence' as another possible rendering of this word. It is only otherwise found in Scripture in Isaiah 66:24, which represents the closest parallel to verse 2 in the remainder of the Old Testament: 'They will go out and look upon the dead bodies of those who rebelled against me; their worm will not die, nor will their fire be quenched, and they will be loathsome [abhorrent] to all mankind.'[10]

Henri Blocher, attempting to penetrate the mysteries of the final fate of the condemned, speaks of a 'fixity of remorse' and refers to these verses, Daniel 12:2 and Isaiah 66:24, as 'denoting a right attitude, attuned to God's own judgment, towards their past, sinful lives; all creatures will share in God's abhorrence; the lost will be

---

[9] R. S. Wallace, *The Lord is King: The Message of Daniel* (IVP, 1979), p. 194.
[10] Baldwin, *Daniel*, p. 205.

ashamed, theirs will be the ultimate "confusion of face" as they shall be unable to escape the truth of their past actions'.[11]

It would appear, at least on the surface, that the two destinies are equally extended – 'everlasting life' and 'everlasting contempt'. This equipoise of duration is contested by some at present; we will return to the issue in a later chapter. The words of verse 2 have close resemblance to the saying of Jesus in the parable of the sheep and the goats: 'They [on his left] will go away to eternal punishment, but the righteous [on his right] to eternal life' (Matt. 25:46).

Sixth, the most impressive implication to be drawn is *the clear either/or* which is reflected here. There are no third categories or third options as far as human destiny is concerned. All will pass into the new order after the judgment to a future described as either 'everlasting life' or 'shame and everlasting contempt'.

How do we prepare for such a moment? The following verses offer several answers.

First, we should *be wise*: verse 3 celebrates 'those who are wise'. They appear in the previous chapter as 'those who know their God'. We can prepare in no better way for the coming end of all things and our own exposure to judgment than by setting our hearts to know the living God. But this 'knowing God' is not a selfish concern with our own spiritual health, it is a fundamentally outward-looking activity. The wise 'instruct many' (11:33), and here 'lead many to righteousness' (12:3).

The wisdom which prevails in the face of judgment is the wisdom which reaches consciously towards the well-being of others. It is to be noted that Jesus' echo of verse 2 commends to eternal life those to whom he can say, 'I was hungry and you gave me something to eat; I was thirsty and you gave me something to drink, I was a stranger and you invited me in. I needed clothes and you clothed me, I was sick and you looked after me, I was in prison and you came to visit me' (Matt. 25:35–36). It is concerned additionally ('instruct many') that they come to understand the truth of God amid the falsehood of the prevailing evil powers.

Second, we should *be aware*: verse 10 says that 'none of the wicked will understand'. By contrast, the people of God are comprehending. In particular they understand what is happening in the world around them as the end draws near. Greater detail of this period is given in 11:33, 'Those who are wise . . . for a time . . . will fall by the sword or be burned or captured or plundered . . . Some

---

[11] H. Blocher, 'Everlasting Punishment and the Problem of Evil', in *Universalism and the Doctrine of Hell*, ed. Nigel M. de S. Cameron (Paternoster, 1991), pp. 306–307, 309.

. . . will stumble, so that they may be refined, purified and made spotless.' It will be a testing time.

'Many will be purified, made spotless and refined, but the wicked will continue to be wicked' (12:10). Outwardly there is no sign that their faith in God is vindicated by events and experience. The unbelieving world seems impervious to their witness and to the challenge represented by their lives and values. At such times God's people are called to believe that despite appearances God remains on the throne, and his purposes continue to be worked out. Specifically, faith needs to attune to God's use of persecution to sanctify and purify his people. God is ceaselessly at work, his purposes are ever ripening, and we are to be aware of it.

Third, we should *be content*: in verses 6 and 8 Daniel asks for enlightenment concerning how long it will be before 'the time of the end', and what will be the outcome of it all. His angelic interpreter at this point indicates that he cannot give him a full answer. He is told that it will be 'for a time, times and half a time' when 'the power of the holy people has been finally broken' (v. 7), but this is hardly a clear answer. His second request is met with, 'Go your way . . . because the words are . . . sealed' (v. 9). Daniel has to be content with not having all his questions answered and accepting the fact that mysteries remain.

This continues to be the case, not least in our attempt to grasp the details of human destiny. Some things are given us to understand and hold to. Heaven and hell are real. We will face a final judgment after death and then our eternal destiny will be lived out in either heaven or hell. God is utterly fair and just, utterly righteous and holy, and also utterly loving and compassionate. If we trust our destiny to Jesus Christ, we can be assured of eternal life with God in the glory of heaven. We can also be assured that God's final judgment will be utterly just and compassionate with respect to all his creatures. Far beyond these boundary markers we cannot go.

Reinhold Niebuhr in his day complained about some Christians of his acquaintance who worried him because they knew 'too much about the furniture of heaven and the temperature of hell'. In dealing with the life to come and its respective destinations, we need appropriate reserve. Here and now 'we see but a poor reflection as in a mirror' (1 Cor. 13:12). With that we are to be content.

Fourth, we should *be assured*: verse 13 is God's final word to Daniel. 'As for you go, your way till the end. You will rest, and then at the end of the days you will rise to receive your allotted inheritance.' This is God's word to us all.

No matter what the times are like, and particularly if they are hard and unpromising, we are called to continue 'to go our way'. We are to live out our lives faithfully 'to the end', and then to 'rest' from our labours, trials and struggles in the assurance that the God who knows and loves us, and who has given himself for us on the cross, will not abandon us in death, but will 'raise us up' to share in the 'inheritance' he has prepared for us within his coming glory.

Summary

The prospect of God's kingdom noted earlier is now more fully developed. It will arrive from beyond history, and will supersede and pass under judgment all previous earthly kingdoms.

The instrument of this crisis will be the 'Son of Man', a title of the Messiah adopted by Jesus. His reign will be universal and eternal. History will be brought to a climax at which the dead will rise and a discriminating judgment will be passed, resulting in all people being consigned either to 'everlasting life', or to 'everlasting contempt'.

Part Two
Destiny determined:
heaven and hell in the Gospels

Mark 1:15; Matthew 13:24–30, 36–43; 25:31–45
6. Your kingdom come!

He is not the Great – he is the Only!

(Carnegie Simpson)

With the life and ministry of Jesus Christ we arrive at the centre of everything. In terms of the entire human story, our understanding of Christianity, and not least its teaching about human destiny, the appearance of Jesus brings us to the determinative centre.

The kingdom of God

Where do we begin as far as Jesus and his teaching on human destiny are concerned? There is a central category in his thought, which touches every aspect of it – the kingdom of God. Modern New Testament scholarship has united in affirming the cruciality of the kingdom in Jesus' mind. 'In the thought of the Kingdom of God Jesus lives, and works, and dies.'[1] 'The central theme of the public proclamation of Jesus was the kingly reign of God.'[2] The saying in Mark 1:15, 'The kingdom of God is near. Repent and believe the good news!', represents a summary of his preaching.[3]

Jeremias notes the large number of sayings of Jesus in which the kingdom of God features which have no parallels in the literature of the world within which Jesus moved.[4] For our purposes we note that all Jesus says about human destiny is affected by his convictions about the kingdom. Accordingly, we are required to spend a little time clarifying this concept.

[1] A. M. Hunter, *Introducing New Testament Theology* (SCM, 1995), p. 13.
[2] J. Jeremias, *New Testament Theology*, vol. 1 (SCM, 1971), p. 96.
[3] See parallels in Matt. 4:23; 9:35; Luke 4:43; 8:1; John 3:3; 18:36.
[4] Cf. Jeremias, *New Testament Theology*, pp. 32–34.

As we noted earlier, the root of the biblical notion of God as King lay in his having sovereignly created all things. It was deepened by his having delivered Israel from their Egyptian slavery 'with a mighty hand' and settled them in their 'land of promise'. 'The Lord reigns' (cf. Ps. 97:1; 99:1) accordingly became the heart of their creed. When that conviction seemed to be contradicted by Israel's experience of being dominated by other powers, the dream emerged of a new order in which God's kingship would be unambiguously expressed.

Into that tradition, with its kingdom dream, Jesus came and began to minister. The history of the concept makes it clear that the kingdom is not a localized geographical area. Rather is it a dynamic concept; the kingdom of God is God reigning, God's sovereignty expressed.

The kingdom and the end

One further layer of meaning is to be noted. The kingdom is intimately related to the end of history. God's age-long purposes will have their final expression in the age of the Messiah, 'the age to come'. In Jesus' day the 'age to come' was commonly referred to as 'the kingdom of God' (Mark 10:23–30; Luke 18:29–30; 20:34–36).[5] Thus for the first-century Jew the human story had two parts. The first was the period from the creation up to the coming of the Messiah; the second was the period of the messianic kingdom, or, more popularly, 'the kingdom of God', initiated by the Messiah and moving forward into the endless future.

Against this background we can see how startling was the announcement with which Jesus launched his mission, 'The kingdom of God is near' (Mark 1:15). There is general consensus that the verb contains the sense of a new beginning. Jesus is saying more than 'the kingdom will be along before too long now'. He is claiming nothing less than that with his ministry the kingdom has actually dawned – 'the unsurpassable future of God has begun'.[6]

Jesus' use of 'Son of Man' as a form of self-identification is critical in this connection, and entirely congruent with his conviction about the arrival of the kingdom (cf. more than eighty instances recorded in the Gospels, e.g. Matt. 16:13; Mark 14:62; Luke 18:31; John 3:14). His use of the definite article, 'the Son of Man', is

[5] Or, if the pious wished to avoid using the holy name of God, 'the kingdom of heaven', as used commonly in Matthew's Gospel (cf. 4:17; 5:3,10, 17, etc.).

[6] W. Triling, *Christus Verkündigung in den synoptischen Evangelien*, p. 48, tr. as in G. R. Beasley-Murray, *Jesus and the Kingdom of God* (Eerdmans, 1986), p. 73.

critical for clarifying his meaning: 'the' – the one you know, the 'son of man' of Daniel 7, in relation to whose mission the end will appear.[7]

Here, and still to come

Jesus distinguishes two stages in the kingdom's appearance. First, the Kingdom is *now here*. For example, in Matthew 12:28, Jesus says, 'If I drive out demons by the Spirit of God, then the kingdom of God has come upon you,' or, in the sermon at Nazareth, 'The Spirit of the Lord is on me . . . Today this scripture is fulfilled in your hearing' (Luke 4:18, 21). The kingdom is present because the King, the Son of Man, is present.

Second, the kingdom of God is *still to come*. This future reference, which includes Jesus' teaching on human destiny, will occupy us throughout this second main section of the book.

The kingdom and heaven

It is crucial to relate this notion of the kingdom to our understanding of human destiny, i.e. to heaven. What needs to be grasped is that for the Bible, *'going to heaven' is nothing other than participating in the full realization of the kingdom of God.* Our habit today is to think of 'heaven' merely as 'where Christians go when they die'. But the full achievement of God's purpose for his people and his world cannot be confined to issues around our personal survival of death. We need to be very clear that the last word on salvation is not the 'intermediate state' where, as we may believe, God's children rest between death and the return of Christ.[8] To identify this with all that the Bible holds out for the future is to put the emphasis, as far as human destiny is concerned, in a place which is foreign to the Bible. The central thing for Jesus and the apostles, and for the Bible as a whole, is *the final triumph and eternal reign of God.* Whatever our individual prospects may be, and however confidently we may affirm our personal hope of life after death, *the future is finally the future of God,* envisaged as the return in glory of his Son, the messianic King Jesus, the overthrow of all God's enemies and the arrival of the kingdom of God in its fullness – the 'new heaven and earth of righteousness'. 'Going to', or 'being in' heaven means our participation in *that.*

[7] C. F. D. Moule, *The Origin of Christology* (Cambridge University Press, 1977), pp. 11ff.

[8] See discussion in chapter 9.

The full terms of this hope will become clearer as we proceed. We begin with Jesus' 'parables of the kingdom'. Familiarity with these timeless stories has blunted the edge of their sheer novelty. Joachim Jeremias, after a lifetime wrestling with the words of Jesus, gives this assessment:

> We find nothing to be compared with the parables of Jesus, whether in the entire inter-testamental literature of Judaism, the Essene writings, in Paul, or in Rabbinic literature . . . Their nearness to life, their simplicity and clarity, the masterly brevity with which they are told, the seriousness of their appeal to the conscience, their loving understanding of the outcasts of religion – all this is without analogy.[9]

When we ask what the parables are about, we are perhaps surprised to discover that human destiny occupies so much of the centre stage as far as these didactic gems are concerned. So many of them are designed to jolt the hearers out of their complacency with their lives in the present, particularly in view of the fact of our future judgment and its awesome implications. 'The message of Jesus is not only the proclamation of salvation, but also the announcement of judgment, a cry of warning, and a call to repentance in view of the terrible urgency of the crisis. The number of parables in this category is nothing less than awe-inspiring.'[10] We will consider two of them, in detail.

1. The wheat and the weeds (Matt. 13:24–30, 36–43)

This parable is one of the two for which we have our Lord's interpretation. At this time, Jesus' ministry is in its initial phase, centred in his native Galilee region to the north. The kingdom has been announced and its signs are evident. Jesus is the centre of immense interest and has developed a large and growing following.

The storyline

The storyline of this parable would have resonated in that agrarian culture. Weeds were as great a threat then as today, and every bit as prevalent. The particular weed here is probably what is often known as darnel, a poisonous weed closely related to bearded wheat, and in

[9] Jeremias, *New Testament Theology*, pp. 29–30.
[10] J. Jeremias, *The Parables of Jesus*, rev. ed. (SCM, 1972), p. 160.

112

the early stages of growth hard to distinguish from it. It was a common practice to weed out the darnel as it appeared, but in the parable's case the weeds have made significant headway; the roots of the darnel have become so entangled that an attempt at weeding would threaten the crop itself (v. 29). The surprise of the servants at the extent of the infestation (v. 27) leads the farmer-owner to identify the work of an 'enemy' (v. 28). France notes that to sow darnel among wheat was an act of revenge punishable under Roman law, 'which suggests that the parable depicts a real-life situation'.[11] Rather than weeding out the darnel at this point, the owner counsels restraint until the coming time of harvest (v. 30): 'At that time I will tell the harvesters: First collect the weeds and tie them in bundles to be burned; then gather the wheat and bring it into my barn.' The reference to the bundling up of the darnel for burning reflected another common practice in a society where sources of fuel, especially wood, were often limited.

The interpretation

In his interpretation (vv. 36–43), Jesus confines himself to the primary points of comparison. The sower is none other than the Son of Man, himself. The field, the seed, the weeds and the enemy are respectively the world, the 'sons of the kingdom', 'the sons of the evil one' and the devil himself. The harvest is 'the end of the age', with its angelic harvesters (vv. 37–39). Jesus then elaborates on the coming time of judgment with its distinguishing fates for the 'righteous' (v. 43) and 'all who do evil' (v. 41).

The message

The primary thrust of the parable is probably to be derived from its setting in Jesus' ongoing ministry. The kingdom of God has dawned with all its climactic significance for Israel, and indeed for the world. In the proclamation of Jesus, and in his presence among them as the Son of Man, the last hour has struck for human history. Despite these realities, however, the effect is less apparent than might have been anticipated. There is no cataclysmic disruption of human history. The kingdom, though present, is not obtrusive. The transformation of all things is deferred. Life appears in many respects to continue as before. Evil and the reign of Satan do not to this point appear significantly threatened. The light shines, but the darkness has not been put out.

[11] R. T. France, *Matthew* (IVP, 1985), p. 225.

'The enemy'

Specifically, Jesus had referred a little earlier to 'men of violence' who are 'powerfully attacking' the kingdom of God (Matt. 11:12).[12] There is a possible allusion here to the gathering forces of opposition to Jesus (cf. 12:14, 24), the minions of the same satanic foe identified in the parable. The Qumran community on the shores of the Dead Sea saw as one of the marks of the appearing of the kingdom an immediate and radical separation of the 'sons of light' from the 'sons of darkness', and there may well have been others who shared their belief.

A word to John?

Some also see here a possible response to John the Baptist and his followers. John's anticipation of the Messiah was painted in dramatic colours. 'He will baptise you with . . . fire. His winnowing fork is in his hand, he will clear his threshing-floor, gathering his wheat into the barn and burning up the chaff with unquenchable fire' (Matt. 3:11–12). It is perhaps to the point that there is a clear echo of Matthew 3:12 in the words of 13:30. Jesus does not disavow the coming of judgment, nor the appropriateness of the vivid images of harvest and fiery destruction. His ameliorating word, however, is clearly spoken, 'not yet'! 'Whereas John places the shovel in the Messiah's hand to be used speedily, the parable indicates that the hour for the bundling and the burning has not yet arrived; the harvest belongs to an undisclosed future.'[13]

World unredeemed?

Was the claim of Jesus credible? Did the continuing presence of evil and its proponents not speak against the validity of the kingdom's having appeared? More generally, does the continuing reality of evil not undermine the whole New Testament claim for Jesus, and hence all suggestion that our eternal destiny is in some way tied to our response to him? Jewish scholar Martin Buber writes, 'Redemption occurs for ever, and yet none has yet occurred. Standing bound and shackled in the pillory of mankind we demonstrate with the bloody body of our people the unredeemedness of the world.'[14] In that context the parable speaks a clear and relevant word.

[12] Tr. as in Beasley-Murray, *Jesus and the Kingdom of God*, p. 199.
[13] ibid., p. 199.
[14] M. Buber, *Pointing the Way* (New York, 1957), p. 18.

Not yet

The kingdom *has* arrived, but the old order has not yet been swept away. Truly it will be eliminated; the sovereign Lord will not tolerate its opposing, usurping presence for ever. But that is not yet. Today the sons of darkness continue to oppose the sons of light. Today the devil sows his weeds among the crop of the Lord. Today the field is blighted and the harvest obscured. Today we are called to patient waiting, but it is a waiting in anticipation not anxiety. The kingdom *has* been established, God's new day has dawned. The harvest is being nurtured, secret but sure. The final harvest day is already chosen. The Son of Man will come again. Heaven or hell await us all.

'Overlap living'

Although the two kinds of plant grow together in the field, it is not impossible to discern a difference. Even the servants of the owner are perfectly alert to the presence of the foreign growth among the wheat. The meaning of the parable is not that we are to suspend all discrimination and abandon standards. The seed must continue to be sown and good fruit must be sought after and nourished. But in the 'world' (v. 38) in which all this is undertaken, the results will always appear less than perfect. Other voices will be heard, other solutions will be offered, other values will be asserted, and other lifestyles will flourish. The light shines, but it shines in the darkness.

The true elimination of the enemy is the work of the owner and his angels at the time of harvest. We are not capable of making a perfect, discriminating judgment any more than we are able to do perfectly any other of the works of God. 'The reality in view is the inability of man to execute the judgment of God, which corresponds to the inability of man to bring about the resurrection of the dead and the final kingdom.'[15] The attempt to pre-empt God's final judgments will only have a harmful effect on the community of light. 'Judge nothing before the appointed time; wait till the Lord comes' (1 Cor. 4:5). We need not be anxious in the interval, however, for the judgment is sure and it is coming.

What, then, of that future judgment?

Harvest home

In speaking of human destiny, Jesus employs the image of a gathered harvest. Everyone in Galilee knew about 'harvest home'. Most

[15] Beasley-Murray, *Jesus and the Kingdom of God*, p. 199.

had no doubt shared in one, whether in their own local field, or as hired help in one or other of the many great estates which at that time dotted the countryside. They had vivid memories of the assembling of the harvesters and then their dispatch to the crops, sickle in hand, to work their way side by side down the fields. In their imagination they could almost hear the swish of the blades as, with expert swings back and forth, they brought the proud, high-standing stalks of ripened grain to collapse in severed heaps at their feet.

Then would follow the gleaning, as the bundles of severed stalks were gathered up and borne triumphantly into the granary to be beaten and the rich grains freed for flour, bread and health-bringing nourishment. The darnel was left to be swept up in its turn, and bound together as fuel for cooking or winter heat. Most of the readers of this book will relate to all this only at second hand, but with an effort of imagination we can make the transition. What does this picture of harvest convey?

i. A certain end

First, it asserts that the arrival of our eternal destiny is *certain*. In the parable the passage of time and the progress of the growth of the crop in no way affected the inevitability of the coming harvest. The servants desired to anticipate the harvest by immediate weeding, but the owner's response is clear, 'Let both grow together until the harvest' (v. 30).

'Growing together' in its way summarizes the whole human story from the dawn of human civilization to the present. The good and the bad, the servants of God and the servants of Satan, the men and women of ideals and values and the men and women who have depised these very things, those who have aspired to the skies and those who have sunk to the depths, and all the multitudes who have found themselves somewhere between, moving along on the highways of history, born, surviving, developing, maturing, aging, dying – 'growing together' in the great bundle of human life on planet earth. And so it will go on, through the course of this century, this millennium, and on, for as long as history extends, seemingly endlessly on, 'until the harvest'.

Of course some scoff, as they did long ago. 'Where is this "coming" he promised?' (2 Pet. 3:4). The answer is no different. 'The Lord is not slow in keeping his promise . . . He is patient . . . wanting . . . everyone to come to repentance. But the day of the Lord will come like a thief' (vv. 9, 10). The day is already chosen (cf. Acts 17:31) and every passing hour brings it closer, 'until the harvest'.

ii. A supernatural end

Second, this image speaks of the coming of our destiny as a *supernatural* event. The decision to harvest the grain is taken by the owner. The servants have their suggestions and ideas, but the call is not theirs. They may feel ready, they can ask, 'Do you want us to get started?' (cf. v. 28), but it is not their call. They have to wait until the owner gives the word. 'At that time', he says, 'I will tell the harvesters. . .' (v. 30).

Further, it is an action which does not wait until all the weeds have gone from the field. The whole thrust of this parable is that 'both grow together' until the harvest. So it is clearly not a case of the quality of the field improving with the passage of time until all the weeds have died away and a pure harvest is ready to be gathered in. We are thankful, naturally, for every expression of good grain in the harvest field of the world. For a whole series of reasons, we ought to strive energetically to produce that very crop. But the verdict of this parable is that, despite all the efforts and concerns of the servants, the field will produce a mixed yield to the end.

The coming of the harvest will not be determined by the state of the field. So the coming of the Son of Man at the end of history will not be determined by the condition of the world, whether good or evil. The decision lies with God, and he will come from beyond, sovereignly breaking in, and bringing it all to a climactic conclusion. 'I will tell the harvesters.' The God whose voice brought the world into being at the beginning, 'And God said, "Let there be . . .",', is the same God who will speak at the end, 'I will tell the harvesters.'

iii. A significant end

Third, the harvest image reminds us that the coming of human destiny will be *decisive*. 'First collect the weeds and tie them in bundles to be burned; then gather the wheat and bring it into my barn' (v. 30). The harvest means that the old order of things has ended for ever. The weeds are no more in the field; they are bundled up and carried away to be burned. The wheat is no more in the field; it is cut down and gathered into the barn.

The time of growing is over; the time for producing fine heads of grain for the flour to adorn the owner's table with life-giving bread has passed; the time for frustrating the good stalks of grain with constricting weeds and their entangling roots is at an end. Nothing remains the same. The scene of the action changes. Prior to this moment, all eyes were on the field; it was the centre of everything, here was where it all happened. Now the field is left behind. Everything which was there has been taken away. We have moved beyond the field. We are now either at the fire or at the barn. So the harvest is utterly decisive. It inaugurates a new order, beyond the earthly into the heavenly. This earth, as presently experienced, will be no more.

iv. A segregated end

Finally, the coming of the harvest, as Jesus describes it, entails a *divisive* destiny. The clear emphasis falls on the distinct and very different ends to which the wheat and the darnel proceed. For the weeds the end result is 'the fiery furnace' (v. 42); for the wheat the result is 'my barn' (v. 30), 'the kingdom of [my] Father' (v. 43). The teaching here is entirely congruent with Jesus' exposition of the end of history in Matthew 24:1–41. There it is 'the coming of the Son of Man' (24:27), here it is 'the end of the age. The Son of Man will send . . .' (13:40). There it is, 'He will send his angels with a loud trumpet call, and they will gather his elect from the four winds, from one end of the heavens to the other' (24:31), here it is, 'The Son of Man will send out his angels, and they will weed out of his kingdom everything that causes sin and all who do evil . . . then the righteous will shine like the sun in the kingdom of their Father' (13:41, 43).

On one side of the division will be the 'weeds', the sowing and hence the sons of the enemy, the evil one. Along with them will be 'everything that causes sin and all who do evil' (v. 41). The fate of these is indescribably solemn. True, the image of fire – 'bundles to be burned' (v. 30), 'throw them into the fiery furnace' (v. 42) – belongs no doubt to the local colour of the harvest image. That was how the darnel was used in Palestine, as fuel. But one cannot escape the poignant description of the emotional state of those thus designated, 'there will be weeping and gnashing of teeth' (v. 42). Clearly Jesus is referring to immense, almost unbearable, regret. The persons so consigned will be conscious of their fate and will be overwhelmed by the contemplation of it. Such is the destiny which Jesus and the other New Testament writers call hell.

On the other side is the wheat, the 'sons [and daughters] of the kingdom' (v. 38), 'the righteous' (v. 43), the good planting of the Lord of the harvest. They will be gathered and brought into the owner's barn (v. 30). Jesus' fuller unpacking of that is as follows: 'Then [they] will shine like the sun in the kingdom of their Father' (v. 43). The words here are reminiscent of Daniel 12:3, 'Those who are wise will shine like the brightness of the heavens, and those who lead many to righteousness, like the stars for ever and ever.' The image is a powerful one. The children of the kingdom are not merely preserved from the threat of being consumed in the fire, but are destined to glow with heavenly, supernatural light, to radiate the very light of heaven through their lives, and to do that in the context of the permanence and security of the owner's barn, the eternal kingdom of their Father.

v. A searching end

No wonder Jesus' final words are, 'He who has ears, let him hear' (v. 43). In view of the seriousness and importance of the things he has said, Jesus calls us, his hearers, to listen with utmost attention. These things demand the 'ears' and 'eyes of [our] hearts' (cf. Eph. 1:18). Let each of us, author and reader alike, examine our hearts and place again our whole trust for salvation on Jesus Christ, the only Saviour of sinners, by whose grace alone we can be rescued from being 'sons or daughters of the evil one' under the 'dominion of darkness' and brought securely into the 'kingdom of the Son [God] loves' (Col. 1:13).

2. The sheep and the goats (Matt. 25:31–45)

This is one of the best known and, in our own period, most reflected upon of all Jesus' teachings. A. M. Hunter refers to it as 'one of the supreme glories of the New Testament'.[16] Whether in fact it *is* a parable in the strict sense has been disputed. If we retain the usual designation for the moment, however, this is the final parable in Jesus' recorded teaching as Matthew presents it, being followed immediately by the account of the passion (Matt. 26:1ff.). As such, it represents a fitting postscript with its focus on the judgment to which all history is moving. More specifically, it is the concluding unit of a block of teaching concerned with the 'woes' pronounced on the Jewish religious leaders (23:1–39), the signs of the end (24:1–51), and three parables on the return of the Lord (25:1–46). As to the propriety of the 'parable' designation, many recent interpreters suggest other classifications. Beasley-Murray proposes 'a visionary depiction of the judgment of the world'.[17] France offers 'a straightforward judgment scene'.[18]

The pictorial setting, with its separation of sheep from goats, was an everyday occurrence for Jesus' hearers. Bedouin shepherds to this

---

[16] A. M. Hunter, *Interpreting the Parables* (SCM, 1960), p. 89.

[17] Beasley-Murray, *Jesus and the Kingdom of God*, p. 307.

[18] France, *Matthew*, p. 354. Cf. D. Hill, 'an eschatological vision which answers the question: "How, and on what basis is a man to be judged on the final day of reckoning?"', D. Hill, *Matthew* (Oliphants, 1972), p. 330.

day regularly graze sheep and goats together, making necessary a distinct action of separation at the end of the day. The less hardy but almost indistinguishable sheep (not white European varieties) would be taken aside into the shelter of a fold against the cold Middle Eastern nights.

My 'brothers'

Before we try to isolate what this passage teaches about human destiny, a major interpretive issue presents itself: the identity of 'these brothers of mine' (v. 40). Many recent commentators reject any attempt to restrict the meaning to a specific group within the human community. They argue that the 'brothers' of the Son of Man are needy humanity in general, and see here evidence of Jesus' special identification with the poor and oppressed, in accord with his general solidarity with needy humanity demonstrated in his baptism, his table-fellowship with sinners, and above all in his cross.

However appealing this may be in general ethical terms, it requires a meaning for Jesus' 'brothers' at variance with the meaning carried by the phrase at a number of other points within the Gospels. France can even refer to 'brothers' (Gk. *adelphoi*) as 'a term specifically for his disciples';[19] so, explicitly, in Matthew 12:48–49; 28:10. To receive a disciple was to receive Jesus (10:40). We may also note the references to the 'little ones who believe in me' (cf. 10:42; 18:6, 10, 14), and the way in which Jesus sees himself identified with the mission of his followers (on which more below).

Thus to understand the text need not imply any limitation of the universal concern expected of those who profess to follow Jesus. Witness his concern in the Sermon on the Mount that his followers should reflect the undiscriminating love of the heavenly Father:

> Let your light shine before men, that they may see your good deeds and praise your Father in heaven ... Love your enemies and pray for those who persecute you, that you may be sons of your Father in heaven ... If you love those who love you, what reward will you get? ... And if you greet only your brothers, what are you doing more than others? ... Be perfect, therefore, as your heavenly Father is perfect [i.e. in his all-inclusive love]. (Matt. 5:16, 44–48)

To this James, and also Paul, would sound a loud 'Amen' (cf. Jas. 2:14–26; Rom. 13:8–10).

[19] France, ibid., p. 357.

Hiding?

This particular issue of interpretation must be kept in perspective. Difference of viewpoint here, while no doubt significant for the application of the story, can distract from the urgent issues around future judgment which this 'parable' was surely intended to address. Not for the first time, theological disputation can act as a convenient escape mechanism to avoid having to face God and his searching truth.

What, then, does this 'parable' teach about human destiny?

Future universal judgment

Verses 31–32, which set the scene, are an unambiguous reference to the final judgment anticipated in Daniel 7, at which 'all the nations will be gathered before him'. While it may be true that modern people, in contrast to multitudes of earlier ages, are generally untroubled by thoughts of a future judgment day, that easiness of conscience is finally irrelevant to the question of whether or not it will happen. Here the issue is met with a stark simplicity. Jesus Christ, incarnate God, taught with great frequency and unwavering solemnity the fact of a future divine judgment awaiting every person. If we do not share this belief, we set ourselves up as greater authorities on the spiritual life and post-mortem existence than Jesus, to say nothing of the vast multitudes of his followers through the ages who have embraced this belief with impressive consistency.

However much we need to allow for pictorial elements in Jesus' depiction of the scene (pictures, necessarily, are all we *can* have), the core fact is simple and inescapable. Paul states, 'We must all appear before the judgment seat of Christ' (2 Cor. 5:10). Thus the old slogan, so often the object of the cartoonist's jest, 'Prepare to meet thy God!', is in fact the plain truth for us all. We are all daily moving closer to a final and overwhelming encounter with our Maker.

In that connection the story offers two further salient points. First, the encounter begins here and now. It is in this life that we first meet God, in the needy brothers and sisters of Jesus (v. 40), and perhaps especially in the 'least' of them. This truth bears reflection; the judgment to come will not be an arbitrary, other-worldly event unrelated to the happenings and encounters of our present everyday lives. It is this fact that gives life its moral seriousness, and lends appropriate responsibility to living. What we will hear on the judgment day will be familiar, only too familiar. At the judgment you will meet yourself, and I myself, the people we have been in the lives we have lived. God's will bears upon us here and now in the claims of our conscience. Every moment, as we respond to these claims to one

121

degree or another, whether in affirmation and assent or in rebellion and dissent, we are meeting our Judge. Judgment is the stuff of life. The final judgment will simply bring it all together.

Second, we note the special stress in the story on sins of omission: 'Lord, when did we see you hungry . . . and did not help you?' (v. 44). Sin is not limited to such, nor is good left undone the primary form of sin. On the judgment day 'the books [which] will be opened' will include the record of 'what they [the dead] *had done*' (Rev. 20:12, my italics). However, omitting to do right when we have opportunity to do it is also culpable. It is sobering to note that these sins of omission alone are sufficient to earn for those so failing 'eternal punishment' (v. 46).

Two distinct destinies

The conclusion of the judgment is again unambiguous. In delivering his verdict the King says to those on his right, 'Come, you who are blessed by my Father; take your inheritance, the kingdom prepared for you since the creation of the world' (v. 34). In delivering his verdict he says to those on his left, 'Depart from me, you who are cursed, into the eternal fire prepared for the devil and his angels' (v. 41). The conclusion of the account accordingly reads, 'Then they will go away to eternal punishment, but the righteous to eternal life' (v. 46).

It has to be said, as clearly as words permit it, there is no third option! All humanity are on their way to one destiny or the other. This author and every one of his readers, like every living, breathing person on planet earth at this moment, are either travellers to heaven or travellers to hell.

The finality of the destinies assigned

It is also clear that the judgment arrived at is conclusive. There is no hint in the text of a further probationary period during which the verdict is reviewed, no trace of a 'second chance' subsequent to the verdict with which the proceedings conclude.

The danger certainly exists of overpressing the details here. Much hangs on the literary form we believe we are handling. If this *is* a parabolic passage, then the principle (in general a sound one) that parables were told to make one central point, and hence ought not to be pressed in every detail, is supportive of our exercising reserve in dealing with the details. If, however, as many recent interpreters argue, we are dealing here with a straightforward depiction of the final judgment anticipated by the Son of Man himself, then the details assume larger significance. Certainly the sense of finality appears pronounced. The assize is held in conjunction with the Son of Man coming 'in his glory', and being seated 'on his throne' (v. 31), 'all nations' being gathered in his presence (v. 32). The echoes from Daniel 7 are obvious; we are dealing with the eschatological judgment at the end of time.

Even more impressive in this regard are the references to the two allotted destinations – for those on the right, 'the kingdom prepared ... since the creation of the world' (v. 34); for those on the left, 'the eternal fire prepared for the devil and his angels' (v. 41). The word 'eternal' is significant, and it recurs in the final summarizing statement in verse 46, 'They will go away to eternal punishment, but the righteous to eternal life.' In a later chapter the meaning of 'eternal' as it is used of human destinies will be discussed. Here we focus on the note of finality that clings inseparably to it. The destiny assigned at the judgment seat of Christ is not open to appeal, arguably because it will be recognized as utterly just. It is a final judgment with unalterable consequences.

Jesus as the Judge

This passage reflects a quite astonishing self-consciousness on Jesus' part. The one who will exercise this judgment of the nations at the end of time is 'the Son of Man' (v. 31), the figure of Daniel's prophecy as we would argue, but in the light of Jesus' use of this title, none other than Jesus himself. He is the 'King' (vv. 34, 40) who has brought the kingdom of God, the 'Lord' (v. 44) on whom 'all authority in heaven and on earth' (Matt. 28:18) would shortly be conferred.

The claim being made here is breathtaking. France points out that in some respects Jesus' claim

> goes beyond the vision of Daniel 7, for whereas in that passage the throne was that of God the judge, now it is the Son of Man himself who sits on it as king; moreover 'all the angels with him' probably echoes Zechariah 14:5, where they accompany 'the Lord your God' in his coming to judgment. And in v. 32 the language recalls the gathering of all the nations for judgment in Joel 3:1–12, where again it is God who sits in judgment.[20]

He further notes the congruence of this section with John 5:19–29:

> The Father judges no-one, but has entrusted all judgment to the Son, that all may honour the Son just as they honour the Father

[20] ibid., p. 356.

> . . . he [the Father] has given him [the Son] authority to judge because he is the Son of Man . . . By myself I can do nothing; I judge only as I hear, and my judgment is just, for I seek not to please myself but him who sent me. (vv. 22–23, 27, 30)

We observe additionally that Jesus as Son of Man not only pronounces the judgment but is himself the criterion by which people are evaluated. He is the Christ who is met in 'these brothers [and sisters] of mine' (v. 40). People cannot plead a total ignorance of Jesus, since they have already encountered him in the needy 'brothers'.

This identification of Jesus with his followers (taking 'brothers' in the sense argued for earlier) is also reflected in John 20:23, where Jesus speaks of the disciples actually, in a sense, determining people's destiny by either 'forgiving anyone their sins' or 'not forgiving them their sins'. The meaning here is expressed by John Marsh: 'It is simply the result of the preaching of the gospel, which either brings people to repent as they hear of the ready and costly forgiveness of God, or leaves them unresponsive to the offer of forgiveness which is the gospel, and so they are left in their sins.'[21]

'Christ comes to us', as Calvin was wont to say, 'clothed in his gospel.' Consequently, when we encounter Jesus' message, even though the presentation may be unpolished and the truth crudely stated, we encounter Jesus himself. In such moments we truly stand before the Son of Man, in anticipation of our appearance before him at the end. 'He who receives you receives me' (Matt. 10:42).

The role of 'works'

The criterion of judgment in this story is not the verbal confession of faith but 'righteous' deeds (v. 37). The 'righteous' give title to that description by their acts of caring mercy for the needy brothers and sisters of Jesus. It is a clear statement in the teaching of Jesus of that conviction which James was later memorably to assert: 'Faith without deeds is dead' (Jas. 2:26). Faith is the instrument of our salvation: 'By grace you have been saved, through faith' (Eph. 2:8; cf. Acts 16:31; John 3:16). But genuine faith will affect practice. Believers' behaviour *is* altered, however unaware of it they commonly are themselves, so that actions, particularly towards the disadvantaged and the needy, become a valid criterion of judgment.

Lest this seem to reopen the door to a self-salvation through 'works of love', we dare not miss the notes of grace which run

[21] J. Marsh, *The Gospel of St John* (Penguin, 1968), p. 641.

through the story. First, those on the King's right hand are described as 'blessed by my Father' (v. 34); their blessedness is not self-created by their righteous deeds, but comes from the heart of the Father. Second, their 'reward' is in fact an 'inheritance', which is a benefit received on the basis of another's giving rather than one obtained by personal merit. Third, this inheritance has been 'prepared for you since the creation of the world' (v. 34). Here the note of divine election is sounded, mysterious as that necessarily is. The inheritance is one for which those on the right hand have actually been prepared, prior to any actions on their part. Fourth, the deeds done towards the needy 'brothers' of Jesus are in their essence deeds of grace, actions of overflowing and uncalculating kindness which are the natural fruit of hearts which have themselves received grace. One can note here in parallel Jesus' linkage of forgiveness to the act of forgiving. 'If you forgive men when they sin against you, your heavenly Father will also forgive you' (Matt. 6:14). Jesus' point is not that by our effort to forgive others we earn our forgiveness from God, but that the heart which has been broken in contrition before God and has experienced the wonder of his forgiveness will be capable in a new degree of forgiving wrongs done to it. In that forgiving we give token to the reality of the work of grace within us. Fifth, in further evidence of this grace-based acquittal, we note the surprise expressed by the recipients of the inheritance, 'when? . . . when? . . . when?' (vv. 37–39), making it abundantly clear that there is no sense on their part of acquiring a favourable judgment by their calculating efforts to do good. Good done primarily with a view to personal benefit cannot stand at the judgment as a convincing or authentic expression of love in action.

The meaning of hell

Verse 41 throws some light on the deep enigma of God's punitive judgment in the beyond. A number of features become clear.

Hell consists in *a separation from God*: 'depart from me' (v. 41). In one sense, of course, no-one can escape from God, since all life derives from him. Even hell exists only as sustained by God. There is perhaps an indication of that in the reference to hell as 'prepared for the devil and his angels'. God has to make hell, and God has to sustain hell.

The Bible bears regular witness to the variety of senses in which God is 'present' for us. Adam and Eve, though after the fall still upheld by their Creator, are nonetheless described as 'hiding from God' in the Garden, and though still thus upheld are banished from Eden (Gen. 3). Isaiah can declare in 59:2, 'Your iniquities have separated you from your God; your sins have hidden his face from you.' David in penitence prays, 'Hide your face from my sins and blot out all my iniquity' (Ps. 51:9). The psalmist can also exult, 'As far as the east is from the west, so far has he removed our transgressions from us' (Ps. 103:12). 'You have put all my sins behind your back' is how Isaiah expresses the wonder of forgiveness (Is. 38:17). The writer to the Hebrews goes even further in citing words from Jeremiah centuries before, 'Their sins and lawless acts I will remember no more' (Heb. 10:17; Jer. 31:34). Most profoundly of all, we cannot forget our Lord's cry upon the cross as he 'became sin for us' (2 Cor. 5:17), 'My God, my God, why have you forsaken me?' (Matt. 27:46). These words will be explored later.

Thus the thought of hell as a place 'separated from God', a 'place where God is not', is not so impossible to conceive. In the words of C. S. Lewis,

> The answer to all those who object to the doctrine of hell is itself a question: 'What are you asking God to do?' To wipe out all their past sins and, at all costs, to give them a fresh start, smoothing every difficulty and offering every miraculous help? But He has done so, on Calvary. To forgive them? They will not be forgiven. To leave them alone? Alas, I am afraid that is what He does.[22]

To be forsaken for ever by God; to have our decision to be free of him permanently confirmed: that is hell.

Hell is *for the 'cursed'* (v. 41), those who lie under the ban and condemnation of God. The devil is cursed in the Garden of Eden (Gen. 3:34), a curse which would finally mean the 'seed of the woman' crushing his head. Here the curse attaches to those who, by their refusal to do the works of grace, show that their hearts are closed to grace. In this they identify themselves with 'the devil and his angels'. Thus his curse becomes theirs also. They too will forfeit life.

Hell is *described as a place of fire* (v. 41). The historic links with the valley of Himmon outside Jerusalem are certainly part of the background to this image (cf. Rev. 20:10). The apparently contradictory image of 'darkness' used of hell in Matthew 25:30 (cf. 22:13) is a reminder that we are dealing here with metaphors. The fact that fire commonly destroys what is cast into it has been hailed as support for the eventual annihilation of those banished to hell. We will discuss this position in a later chapter. Whatever the image may imply about the duration of hell, it is on any reckoning a sobering expression of its threat.

[22] C. S. Lewis, *The Problem of Pain* (Macmillan, 1962), p. 128.

Hell was *not 'prepared' for humans, but for devils, and for the arch-devil in particular.* The diabolical rebellion against God's beneficent reign carried out by Satan and his minions bore the seeds of their eventual judgment and banishment. In this sense hell pre-dated the human story; it was never intended for humans. Those who cherish the hope of eventual universal redemption can perhaps find here some modicum of biblical support. The balance of Scripture, however, as we will continue to see, stacks up overwhelmingly against it, to say nothing of the relativization of God's eternal holiness which it involves.

Hell is *'eternal'* (cf. v. 46, 'eternal punishment' and 'eternal fire'). Our fuller discussion of this word will follow in a later chapter, as well as more general reflection on the symbols used about hell and its temporal extension. At this point we note the correspondence established between the duration of heaven and the duration of hell. By the terms of this 'parable', what holds for the one apparently holds also for the other.

The fate which awaits those consigned to hell is 'eternal *punishment*' (v. 46). In other words, hell is *morally deserved.* Hell is the judicial outworking of the wrath of God upon those who have, by their deeds of omission and commission, brought this judgment down upon their own heads. The Judge of all the earth will do justly; how could he who is the origin and standard of all justice do otherwise? There will be no sense of unfairness at his tribunal. No-one will be in hell who does not deserve that fate.

Hell is *a solemn issue.* If these things are valid, and if this gripping drama from the lips of Jesus represents a valid prophecy of the future, then we have the greatest possible need to stop and reflect. Jesus was clearly convinced that he had been appointed by the Father as the universal Judge. He tells us one of the fundamental criteria of that coming judgment, and then he presents us with the awesome consequences – eternal life or eternal punishment. It is time to examine our hearts; it is time to seek the Lord and his mercy. We note the words of Dr Samuel Johnson, as pertinent today as in the eighteenth century: 'I remember that my Maker has said that he will place the sheep on his right hand, and the goats on his left. That is a solemn truth which this frivolous age needs to hear, for it strikes at the very roots of life and destiny.'

The corresponding truths concerning heaven

The dark, oppressive shadow of hell in this passage needs to be balanced with the bright light of heaven which also shines here. Four aspects are highlighted.

We enter heaven at the invitation of the King, the Son of Man, the divine Judge himself: 'Come . . .' (v. 34). This wonderful word echoes through the biblical record. Isaiah eloquently expresses the welcoming heart of God which lies behind it. 'Come, all you who are thirsty, come to the waters; and you who have no money, come, buy and eat! Come, buy wine and milk without money and without cost . . .' (55:1). 'Come unto me,' cries Jesus, 'all you who are weary and burdened, and I will give you rest' (Matt. 11:28). Fittingly, the Bible closes with the same wooing note of invitation. 'The Spirit and the bride say, "Come!" And let him who hears say, "Come!" Whoever is thirsty, let him come; and whoever wishes, let him take the free gift of the water of life' (Rev. 22:17). In that context it is moving to hear the same invitation, 'Come, you who are blessed by my Father; take . . .' (v. 34).

The redeemed are 'blessed by my Father'. The Bible bears continual witness to the love of God and his goodwill towards his creatures. He longs to bless, he waits to show mercy, in unfathomable love he gave his Son to save us from our sins and all their baleful consequences; he yearns for us. Heaven is nothing other than the culmination and the full fruition of the loving heart of God. Here, as heaven is entered, we will understand as never before what it means to be 'blessed'. There is no greater 'blessing' than this, to enter the nearer presence of God, to experience his love anew and, free at last from sin and fallenness, to be able to love, obey, adore and serve him as he deserves. That is heaven: the personal and communal realization of the blessedness of God.

Heaven is an inheritance. In the end heaven is all gift, all grace, all mercy, all undeserved love. But this provision for us was made from the very dawning of God's purposes, 'prepared for you since the creation of the world' (v. 34). Heaven has always been in the heart of God. All his dealings with humankind across the ages have been with a view to this eventual fulfilment, the day when men and women will be 'crowned with glory and honour' (Heb. 2:5–9) and will be what God intended them to be, vice-regents in his renewed creation, the special objects of his boundless and endless love.

Finally, heaven is *an order of existence characterized by life* – 'eternal life' (v. 46). Heaven is the ultimate expression of the life-giving God. It will be life and life abundantly. Negatives will be swallowed up in positives; it will consist in *what we do*, like the righteous in the story. Hence the deeds of the righteous, which secure their eternal salvation because they demonstrate the action of divine grace in and upon them, are seen as the foretaste of heaven. The life of heaven is a life of service, a life of unalloyed, unending, outpoured love.

Summary

Jesus' teaching about human destiny centres on the concept of the kingdom of God, God's reign perfectly fulfilled.

The kingdom came in Jesus; it will come fully when Christ returns. The parables of the kingdom anticipate the events at his coming. It will be like the ingathering of harvest, or the rewards and punishments of a returning king. In both cases a final judgment is central, leading to two contrasting outcomes – one of joyful inheritance, the other of extreme loss and regret.

Mark 12:18–27
7. What about heaven?

and that will be heaven

and that will be heaven
at last the first unclouded
seeing

to stand like the sunflower
turned full face to the sun drenched
with light in the still centre
held while the circling planets
hum with an utter joy

seeing and knowing
at last in every particle
seen and known and not turning
away

never turning away
again

(Evangeline Paterson)

It is Holy Week in Jerusalem, the final week of Jesus' earthly life. He is teaching daily within the great court of the temple, where rabbis met with their disciples to share their insights and to answer questions. The debate which ensues about life after death is one of a series of encounters during that fateful week.

Different groups are identified in Mark's account as Jesus' conversation partners. First into the lists are 'the chief priests, the teachers of the law and the elders' (11:27). An impressive group, of the highest possible authority, no doubt incensed by Jesus disrupting their worship administration by his violent 'cleansing' of the temple area (11:12–17). Their questioning of his authority is peremptorily rebutted as they find themselves facing a disarming question about their view of John the Baptist (11:27–33).

Next up are 'the Pharisees and Herodians' (12:13), normally embittered foes but now united in their opposition to Jesus, as Herod and Pilate would be a few days later (Luke 23:12). Nothing so compounds darkness as the revelation of the light. The Pharisee-Herodian teaser about tax payment to the Romans is brilliantly answered (12:11–15), bringing the Sadducees finally into the ring (12:18). The dialogue which ensues is highly authentic to that first-century temple setting. 'The whole section is thoroughly Jewish in content and manner.'[1]

1. The challenge Jesus faced

The theme of the Sadducees' question is deeply poignant in the light of Jesus' awareness of his own impending death.

> Teacher . . . Moses wrote for us that if a man's brother dies and leaves a wife but no children, the man must marry the widow and have children for his brother. Now there were seven brothers. The first one married and died without leaving any children. The second one married the widow, but he also died, leaving no child. It was the same with the third. In fact, none of the seven left any children. Last of all, the woman died too. At the resurrection whose wife will she be, since the seven were married to her? (12:19–23)

In effect the Sadducees have two questions about life after death: 'What is it like?' and, more fundamentally, 'How is it possible?' They present their questions in terms of a 'now there was' kind of story.

Levirate marriage

Whether an actual case underlay their example is to be doubted. Its biblical base was the Old Testament provision for the continuation of a family line in the case of the death of a male member.[2] In such

---

[1] C. E. B. Cranfield, *The Gospel According to St Mark* (Cambridge University Press, 1959), p. 373.
[2] See Deuteronomy 25:5–10, which is approximately reproduced in the Sadducees' story, and Genesis 38:8.

131

cases the law prescribed levirate marriage, whereby the deceased's brothers were obligated to marry the widow and produce an heir by her, so preserving their late brother's lifeline. 'The law was understood to provide a man with heirs who would preserve his name and inherit his property. The point of the Sadducees' argument is that it is clear from the legislation that Moses did not believe in the resurrection.'[3] How rigorously this law was applied in practice is open to question, but its presence within the written law opened the possibility of this kind of conundrum. The intention of the questioners was to ridicule the whole concept of a resurrection life.

The Sadducees

In examining the challenge to Jesus, a few comments on the Sadducees are in order. They were in effect the high-priestly clique within the Jewish state at the time. In contrast to the Zealots, who constantly stoked the fires of revolution, the Sadducees adopted a pragmatic 'live and let live' policy towards the Roman occupation. They were similarly unadventurous in their theology.

Seeing themselves as the disciples of Moses, they limited the canon of Scripture to his writings, the Pentateuch,[4] and were sceptical about the later and hence, in their view, less authoritative wisdom and prophetic writings. What they did not find clearly taught in the books of Moses they regarded as unnecessary for faith. Notably they rejected angelic intermediaries and an embodied personal existence after death. The clearest assertions of the life to come in the Old Testament occur in passages such as Isaiah 26:19, Daniel 12:2, Job 19:25f. and Psalms 16:9–11 and 73:23f., which of course all occur in the later sections. Hence, 'The doctrine of the Sadducees is this: souls die with bodies.'[5] Their story is predicated on the general assumption among the Jews of the period that any afterlife would be experienced under conditions which were generally continuous with life here and now. Given that assumption, the force of the story is evident. Does the whole idea of an afterlife not involve ridiculous contradictions and fantasies, such as a woman married to seven different husbands? Since Jesus is known to believe in a future life, what answer can he give to this *reductio ad absurdum*?

[3] Morna Hooker, *The Gospel According to St Mark* (Black, 1991), p. 283; also S. R. Driver, *A Critical and Exegetical Commentary on Deuteronomy* (Charles Scribner, 1895), p. 280.
[4] The first five books of the Old Testament, Genesis to Deuteronomy.
[5] Josephus, *Antiquities*, 18:1, 4; cf. Acts 23:8.

2. The response Jesus gave

'Now about the dead rising – have you not read in the book of
Moses, in the account of the bush, how God said to him, "I am the
God of Abraham, the God of Isaac, and the God of Jacob"? He is
not the God of the dead, but of the living. You are badly mistaken!'
(12:26–27). In his response to the Sadducees, what does Jesus teach
about heaven?

a. Heaven is certain

The force of Jesus' argument needs to be felt. 'God' for him, as
for his hearers, referred to the supreme being, the unlimited expression of life, majesty and goodness. This God speaks in the
Scriptures, and hence in the story of the burning bush (Exod. 3:1 –
4:17). God defines himself there as 'the God of Abraham, Isaac
and Jacob'.

The God of the living
That those long-deceased fathers of the nation were no more than
piles of bleached bones when God defined himself with respect to
them was unthinkable; to define himself in terms of heaps of remains
would be so demeaning for God as to represent an impossible
contradiction of his nature. Only if these great figures continued to
live before him, and were the continuing objects of his sovereign
care, sustenance and loving affirmation, could such an identification
have any congruence. 'He is not the God of the dead, but of the
living, for to him all are alive' (Luke 20:38).

What Jesus provides here is a significant and unchallengeable
proof of the survival of death if we affirm the revealed character of
God. In essence Jesus is asserting that, if God is the God of the
Scriptures, a personal, sovereign, caring being who enters into personal relationships with individuals (as the Sadducees would have
conceded), then life beyond death is axiomatic.

'If God be for us . . .'
In his argument Jesus anticipates the exultant strains of Paul in
Romans 8:38, 'I am convinced that . . . death . . . will [not] be able
to separate us from the love of God. . .' Paul is, of course, able to
draw upon the supreme demonstration of that love on the cross.
'He who did not spare his own Son, but gave him up for us all –
how will he not also . . . give us all things', including victory over
death? But the essence of the case is the same – the character
of God.

133

We should not overlook the intellectual brilliance of Jesus reflected in this argument. In Jeremias's judicious words, 'With unsurpassable brevity this sentence says that faith in God includes the certainty of overcoming death.'[6] A heavenly life is assured.

b. Why heaven is certain

Jesus is not merely content with defence. He also moves on to the attack, by exposing the unsupportable grounds upon which the Sadducees' scepticism is based. 'Are you not in error because you do not know the Scriptures or the power of God?' (v. 24). The Sadducees' failure to believe in a life after death is an 'error' of no small proportion, as he asserts at the end of his response. 'You are badly mistaken!' (v. 27).

'He who has the most toys wins'

These words of Jesus are to be taken seriously in our materialistic twenty-first-century culture. Today doubts about life after death are widespread. True, the regular findings of opinion polls, not least in Western societies, indicate a fairly widespread (though decreasing) belief in the survival of death.[7] It is unwise, however, to build too much on these findings. The acid test of any belief, as my philosophy professor taught me years ago, is the difference the belief makes to our values and choices. By that standard, belief in the afterlife is a very rare species. People of our time are patently primarily motivated by the drive to amass wealth and to experience the maximum of pleasure here and now. There is little evidence anywhere of a willingness to forgo present satisfactions in order to achieve larger satisfactions in a life hereafter. The 'treasures on earth' have almost totally eclipsed any concern for the 'treasures in heaven'.

Tragically, though probably not surprisingly, there are even versions of the Christian faith on offer which appeal quite blatantly to the same materialistic instincts. There is simply no credible evidence that for Westerners in particular the prospect of a life to come, with its call for restraint here and now and its prospect of a personal moral inventory after death, is a significant constraint on behaviour. There is even evidence of an unwillingness to deny present satisfactions to

---

[6] J. Jeremias, New Testament Theology, vol. 1 (SCM, 1971), p. 184.
[7] See e.g. R. G. Bibby, Fragmented Gods (Irwin, 1987), p. 67; for Canada, 69% believe in life after death in some sense. The figures for the USA are very similar; a 1996 Gallup poll gave a finding of 71% believing in some form of life after death. In the UK, however, that figure was 54% in 1957 and just 27% in 1991 (Steve Bruce, Religion in Modern Britain [OUP, 1995], p. 51).

secure a sustainable quality of life on this planet for our children and grandchildren. Present consumption to gratify present desires is the virtually universal rule on planet earth as we move forward in the third millennium.

The reply of a Jewish student to a New Testament scholar a few decades ago still stands as a barometer of the world view of both modern and postmodern culture. 'If I could really think, like our fathers, of this life as a mere few seconds' preparation for eternity, it would make a lot of difference. But I can't. Can you?'[8]

Jesus' response to that mind-set is a stark one: 'You are badly mistaken!' Thus one of the primary, and largely unquestioned, assumptions made about life in the third millennium – that it is confined to our earthly span – is, according to Jesus, fatally flawed. Nor is this a secondary issue; being wrong about our destiny is being wrong at the centre. Modern civilization is adrift from truth. But is there a basis for the hope of life after death? Jesus points to two undergirding certainties, the Bible and the power of God.

i. The afterlife is sure because of the witness of the Scriptures (v. 24)
Specifically he points to Exodus 3:6, significant not least because it falls within the books of Moses whose authority the Sadducees were prepared to acknowledge. Other scriptures Jesus might have cited are Psalms 16:10 and 48:15, Job 19:26 and Daniel 12:1–3. Even one clear reference would have sufficed, since for Jesus Scripture is divinely given truth.[9] The Creator Lord of life and death, and hence the supreme authority on matters of human destiny, personally assures us that we will live for ever.

When the divine inspiration which is affirmed by Jesus with respect to the Old Testament writings is extended similarly to the New Testament, the accumulated biblical evidence for immortality is of avalanche-like proportions. It is the universal premise of every contributor to the New Testament, and expresses itself throughout their writings.[10]

To question the fact of conscious, personal existence after death is therefore to fly in the face of the cumulative evidence of the written Word of God, an authority of sufficient veracity for Jesus Christ, the only sinless mind in history, and the supreme authority on spiritual life and destiny, to stake his own life upon its truth. To deny the life

[8] Cf. J. A. T. Robinson, *But That I Can't Believe* (Fontana, 1967), p. 44.
[9] For Jesus' belief in the divinity and hence authority of the written Scriptures, cf. Mark 4:1–11; 8:31; 9:31; 10:33–34; cf. the author's *Know the Truth* (IVP, rev. ed. 1998), pp. 41–43.
[10] See e.g. 1 Cor. 15:51f.; 1 Pet. 1:3f.; Heb. 9:27; 1 John 3:2f.; Jude 7, 21.

to come is to pit ourselves and our woefully limited understanding against the massive twin authorities of the God-inspired Scriptures and the undeviating conviction of Jesus Christ.

ii. The afterlife is sure because of the power of God (v. 24)
Jesus identifies a further ground of the Sadducean scepticism: they had a limited view of God's ability; their God was too small.[11] God's limitless power is revealed supremely at two points. The first is in creation. Isaiah celebrates God's omnipotence in a lyrical outburst.

> Who has held the dust of the earth in a
>   basket,
>   or weighed the mountains on the scales
>   and the hills in a balance? . . .
> 'To whom will you compare me?
>   Or who is my equal?' says the Holy One.
> Lift up your eyes and look to the heavens:
>   Who created all these?
> He who brings out the starry host one
>   by one,
>   and calls them each by name.
> Because of his great power and mighty
>   strength,
>   not one of them is missing.
>
> (Is. 40:12, 25–26)

The second demonstration of God's omnipotence is the resurrection of Jesus from the dead, significantly to take place within a few days of the conversation with the Sadducees. '[He] was declared with power to be the Son of God, by his resurrection from the dead' (Rom. 1:4). The resurrection is in itself a further conclusive demonstration of the life to come, but viewed as another expression of the limitless energies of God it would undergird Jesus' appeal to 'God's power' as a basis for belief in the afterlife. In Romans 4:17 Paul neatly brings these two manifestations of God's sovereign power together: 'God . . . gives life to the dead and calls things that are not as though they were' (cf. 1 Cor. 1:28).

Such a God of omnipotent power is hardly to be conceived as incapable of preserving human life through the ravages of death, and

---

[11] H. B. Swete wrote, 'The Sadducees showed themselves incapable of conceiving a power which could produce an order entirely different from any within their experience. They assumed either that God could not raise the dead, or that he could raise them only to a life which would be a continuation . . . of the present' (*The Gospel According to S. Mark* [Macmillan, 1898], p. 280).

of recreating those who have physically perished in a new order beyond the grave. That he is so able is demonstrated not least by the fact that he has already done it! He has brought the present order, and each individual within it, into being out of nothing. That there is now, as a matter of fact, 'something and not nothing' implies that there can also be 'something and not nothing' on the other side of death.

The ground on which both pieces of evidence rest is implicit – the faithfulness of God.[12] The Exodus reference cited by Jesus (v. 26) points to a God who, in faithfulness to his children, will not abandon them in the grave. 'The God who fondly cares for his people here and now will not go back on his promise and forsake them in death.'[13]

God's faithfulness to his promises and his purposes calls finally for the operation of his power in the formation of a new heaven and earth to be the eternal home of his people. God is faithful, so death will die.

c. What heaven is like

While many of our questions about the nature of the heavenly life must, by the nature of the case, remain unanswered, a few clues can be detected in Jesus' comments.

i. 'The dead rise'
This phrase in verse 25 implies the continuing of self-conscious, personal identity after death. The same 'selves' who passed into death will emerge beyond it. Names may change, as will, on an unimaginable scale, the context in which our 'self' will function. Altered too will be our moral nature, since 'we shall be like him' (1 John 3:2) – for all of us a change of gigantic proportions. But the awareness of 'me' as a discrete, thinking, feeling, experiencing self will continue.

ii. Sex in heaven?
'They will neither marry nor be given in marriage; they will be like the angels' (v. 25). This statement has been commonly understood to imply a non-physical, non-sexual and hence purely 'spiritual' existence in heaven. It has also contributed to a rather disapproving view of sexual passion, even within the marriage covenant. It is to be

---

[12] Cranfield, *The Gospel According to St Mark*, p. 376: 'The kernel of the argument is the faithfulness of God.'

[13] H. Anderson, *Mark* (Oliphants, 1976), p. 279.

questioned whether Jesus' statement holds these implications. Morna Hooker notes,

> In speaking of marriage Jesus would have been concerned, as was normal at that time, with questions of property and legitimacy, and what he is rejecting is the notion that this social contract continues in the resurrection life. The implication is perhaps that the limitations of this bond will be removed in the age to come, allowing a richer and deeper experience of human relationships in an existence very different from that of this age.[14]

Peter Kreeft courageously tackles the question 'Will there be sex in heaven?' in his stimulating book entitled *Everything You Ever Wanted to Know about Heaven . . . but Never Dreamed of Asking.*[15] He correctly comments that in one important sense there *will* be 'sex in heaven' in that gender distinctions will be preserved; the continuity of personal identities implies the continuity of gender identities.

Further, the love for our brothers and sisters within the family of God which will be perfected in heaven surely ought not to be anticipated as a passionless, anaemic business. It will be purged of all sinful, selfish elements and will no longer, as Jesus implies, express itself in genital sexual intimacy. However, the idea that in heaven our love for those of the other gender, as for those of our own gender, will be immeasurably richer, deeper and mutually more satisfying than anything we can know here on earth is surely a biblically grounded anticipation. Jesus' words certainly do not disavow it.

What, then, does 'neither marry nor be given in marriage' imply? Certainly it indicates an end to the exclusiveness of the marriage relationship. Love for others will be marked by that indiscriminate inclusiveness which in the present order the unmarried are uniquely able to reflect.

iii. Will we recognize one another?

Will we then have no special place in our hearts for our earthly beloveds? If the life beyond is in a real degree continuous with the present, it can be fairly assumed that memories of present relationships, purged and cleansed of sinful limitations, will also survive. Certainly, if Jesus' life after his resurrection represents a model,

---

[14] Hooker, *The Gospel According to St Mark*, p. 284.
[15] P. Kreeft, *Everything You Ever Wanted to Know about Heaven . . . but Never Dreamed of Asking* (Ignatius, 1990).

there can be no need for anxiety on this score.[16] Hence we may be confident that the realities implicit in our present 'giving in marriage' will have some perfected equivalence, a surviving awareness of specialness and belonging. As C. S. Lewis suggests, we will not love our earthly beloved less in the eternal order, but in fact will love them more.[17] However, it will be under such conditions, as Jesus makes quite clear in this passage, that the issues raised, for example, by a second marriage will not represent a shadowing embarrassment.

iv. Greater love

None of this must be taken to imply that the heavenly order will offer lesser love gifts. If the expressions of love are less physical, they are surely not less fulfilling, enriching or delightful, shot through as they will be with the presence in the beloved of the Ultimate Beloved.

Loving our human other will become a means as never before of directly experiencing that Love which is the ground and glory of all true love. If the exclusivity of marriage and family recedes in some respects, it is only so that we may discover an expansiveness of embrace of the whole human family, comprising the age-long, multifaceted people of God.

In these ways, as in so many others, what we have gained will infinitely outweigh what we may seem to have given up. In these, as in all things, our reaction to heaven will be, 'You have saved the best till now' (John 2:10).

v. Ministering spirits

'They will be like the angels in heaven.' This further clarifying phrase primarily serves to contrast present genital sexual relationships as the means to human reproduction with the relationships to be enjoyed hereafter. It may not be wholly illegitimate, however, to see it as a pointer to other conditions of life in heaven.

The angels consistently appear in Scripture as 'ministering spirits' (Heb. 1:14) occupied with the service of God. This aspect of the life to come is also indicated in Revelation 22:3.[18] Similar indications appear in the parables of service, such as the parable of the ten minas in Luke 19:11–27, where the reward for faithful service is new

---

[16] Note his continuing relationships with Mary (John 20:10–18), Thomas (20:24–29) and Peter (21:15–22).

[17] C. S. Lewis, *The Four Loves* (Fontana, 1963), pp. 125–128.

[18] The Greek here is *latreia*, which can also be rendered 'worship', but 'serve' appears more probable, though the distinction is never absolute.

responsibilities: 'Take charge of ten cities' (v. 17).[19]

Angels are also consistently associated with worship (cf. Is. 6; Rev. 4), finding life through unbroken adoration of their ever-blessed Creator. To such we too will aspire, and the anticipation of it thrills the heart.

Angelic beings are seen in Scripture to wield impressive power and to possess capacities beyond those available to mortals (cf. Dan. 10:4–9; Rev. 19:14). The heavenly order will open us to new gifts and abilities, which in new, exciting and enriching ways will further contribute to the glory of our God.

d. Who heaven is for

Those who share the heavenly order are referred to in general as 'the living' (v. 27). God is the 'God of the living'. This, of course, resonates with the many references to 'eternal life' in the New Testament. Jesus is 'the life' and gives life to those who believe in him. In the new world death has been 'swallowed up by life' (cf. Is. 25:8; 1 Cor. 15:54). Two characteristics of this 'life' may be noted: its *embrace* – it is communal; and its *essence* – being identified with God.

Life together

The *communal embrace* of the life to come is evident in a series of images throughout Scripture. Heaven is envisaged as a perfect city (Heb. 13:14), a victorious kingdom (Heb. 12:28), a holy temple (Ezek. 40 – 48), and a wedding feast (Rev. 19:7). Some particular features of community are expressed here that are worth drawing out.

It will be a community in which the separation of the generations will be transcended. Thus Abraham will be set in the company of his son Isaac and his grandson Jacob, whom he never met during his earthly life. How the distinctive perspectives of the differing generations will be unified is beyond our present comprehension, but that they can be so will present no difficulty to the one who created and now sustains each one. There is a thrilling glimpse of the entrancing possibilities of this transgenerational interaction in the account of the transfiguration, when 'Moses and Elijah appeared in glorious splendour, talking with Jesus. They spoke about his departure, which he was about to bring to fulfilment at Jerusalem' (Luke 9:31). In this conversation the life of heaven is movingly anticipated. Centuries will fall away, and lives separated by long tracts of time

[19] Swete, *The Gospel According to S. Mark*, p. 251.

will commune and find common cause with those of other ages. Strikingly, Jesus and his mission form the uniting centre of this 'conversation of the generations'.

What riches this anticipates! To be a Christian is first to belong to Christ, but Christ can be known and related to only within his body, which is in the end the whole people of God spread throughout the world and across the ages. That great, swelling company will be our society in the life to come. At the personal level, what possibilities this opens up of conversation and community across the severed generations of our present personal experience!

God is enough

The second aspect of the heavenly life uncovered here is its *essence – identity with God*. It is because God in his infinite condescension is prepared to be called 'the God of Abraham' that Abraham continues to exist before him. The God whose sustaining power alone accounts for our existence in this world will be the only continuing ground of our existence in the world to come. 'You will be my people, and I will be your God' echoes like a chorus to every verse of the Old Testament. In the New Testament that all-encompassing intention of God is grounded in the new covenant sealed in the blood of the Redeemer. It is in being known, called, affirmed and held by God that our life in the heavenly world will consist. To be his, and his eternally – that is heaven.

3. Implications

It remains to note the challenge of this passage for our culture. It directly confronts two of its commonest assumptions, examined below.

a. 'Sex is the ultimate human self-expression'

There are few things that so clearly characterize our time as its pervasive concentration on sex. Much of this is driven by the media, as well as by the vast financial profits which can be made from feeding this insatiable desire. The profits are made because the sex impulse is in general such a strong one, and many people are obviously prepared to be continually stimulated and exploited. The idea that there may be deeper joys and more lasting fulfilments in life than sexual ones is almost shocking to many contemporary ears. Yet such is the witness of this dialogue of Jesus and the Sadducees. As the celibate singleness of Jesus demonstrates, the perfect human life does not necessarily include or demand genital intercourse.

This truth needs to be articulated carefully lest we seem to confirm the common stereotype of Christianity as repressive, killjoy and anti-sex. Our sexuality is given us by God our loving Creator, the same God who will meet and fulfil us in the heavenly life. As his good gift, our sexuality is to be received with thanksgiving. As far as the form of its expression is concerned, Paul helpfully reminds us, 'Each of you has your own gift [Gk. *charisma*] from God; one has this gift [marriage], another has that [singleness]' (1 Cor. 7:7 NIVI).

Sexual intimacy is neither ultimate nor eternal. Accordingly the individual who is unmarried, like Jesus, is certainly not consigned thereby to a second best. Paul is even prepared to claim that, in some circumstances, the unmarried are at an advantage (1 Cor. 7:32–35).

Something better awaits and beckons us all. We shall be 'like the angels', which means not neutered, anaemic spirits, but full, free and liberated persons in whom all the possibilities of our God-given humanity will burst forth in undreamed-of fulfilment.

C. S. Lewis in his allegory of heaven and hell, *The Great Divorce*, appropriately depicts the denizens of heaven as solid, substantial and radiant beings, whereas by contrast the citizens of hell are insubstantial, oily wraiths. Real life lies before us; the present, including our present experience of sexuality, is but a pallid anticipation.

b. 'Death ends life'

Modern people are not anticipating an afterlife. 'This life is all you have, so enjoy it before it's over.' In this assumption our generation is sadly, even tragically, wrong – like the Sadducees, 'badly mistaken'.

In one of his short stories, *The Valley of the Blind*, H. G. Wells depicts a tribe living in a remote valley in the depths of a great mountain range where, during an epidemic, the entire community loses the capacity for sight. As a result, in the course of time, generations arise in that tribal community who have no concept of a visual world. They live out their whole lives without realizing that there is a further, magnificent dimension to existence. In a real sense we live in such a society. Our this-worldliness has become inbred. We no longer live towards eternity. We are in the Valley of the Blind. And so we are 'badly mistaken'. We need to have our eyes opened again to the fact that there truly is a life to come – vast, awesome and endless.

142

Summary

Jesus refutes the Sadducees, contemporary deniers of a life to come. He alleges that they make three mistakes: they fail to reckon with the faithfulness of God, the truth of Scripture, or God's almighty power.

Heaven is real, but it will be different. It will involve a new inclusiveness in relationships, new opportunities for service and worship, and a new identity with God. Jesus' view of life here and hereafter challenges our assumptions – about the primacy of sex in relationships, and about the confining of life to this earthly span.

Mark 9:42–48
8. So what about hell?

'How would ye like to be tied to a tree, and have a slow fire lit up around ye? Wouldn't that be pleasant, eh, Tom?'

'Mas'r, I know ye can do dreadful things, but' – he stretched himself upwards and clasped his hands – 'but after ye've killed the body, there ain't no more ye can do. And oh! there's all eternity to come after that!'

(Harriet Beecher Stowe, *Uncle Tom's Cabin*)

The leading English philosopher Bertrand Russell held the view that, for all that might be said positively about the teaching and character of Jesus Christ, it was overshadowed on the negative side by his belief in hell.[1] Well, did Jesus believe in hell? And what did he teach about it? It is time to confront these questions directly. We choose as the textual basis a paragraph in the central section of Mark. The setting, as always, has to be noted, albeit in this case very briefly.

With Caesarea Philippi and the transfiguration behind him (8:27 – 9:13), Jesus embarks upon his final journey to Jerusalem and his death. The disciples, with only a limited comprehension of the implications, accompany him. They too will face a cross, Jesus tells them (8:34), and he instructs them about what that will mean – for one thing, death to their personal ambitions (9:33–34). Their discipleship model is not a king in his splendour, but a child in his helplessness (9:35–37). Such humility of attitude will show itself in generous judgments of others (9:38–41). But 'dying with Jesus' will express itself in a further way – it will cause the disciples to cherish the 'little ones who believe in me' (9:42). In this they will distinguish themselves from those others who 'cause one of these little ones . . . to sin' (9:42). Such people face the awful prospect of hell.

[1] B. Russell, *Why I am not a Christian* (Simon and Schuster, 1957), p. 17.

Jesus asserts three aspects of hell in these verses, examined in detail below.

1. Why there is a hell: the sin that merits it

Several issues call for comment. Who, for example, are 'these little ones'? In the first instance they are infant children such as the child Jesus has just held in his arms. In Matthew the connection is made explicitly (cf. Matt. 18:5–6). Luke's setting of the saying (cf. Luke 17:1f.) shows that a wider principle is being asserted here, and so the 'little ones'[2] can be referred more generally to weak and vulnerable disciples (cf. Rom. 14; 1 Cor. 8:9) like, perhaps, the exorcist in verse 38. Schweitzer is probably not wrong to stretch the reference to all Jesus' disciples, his 'little flock' (Luke 12:32) who are the 'poor in spirit' (Matt. 5:3).[3] Once again, as we noted in the exposition of the judgment scene in Matthew 25, response to Jesus is response to his followers. The affectionate note should not be missed: Jesus cherishes those who believe in him, and does so individually. Even 'one' so offended is known to him and causes him concern.

Also, what is meant by 'cause to sin'? The verb literally means 'cause to stumble', or 'trip up'. It is used earlier in Mark to refer to those who 'fall away' from discipleship like seeds without roots, and in 6:3 of the effect of Jesus' claims on his native community in Nazareth, 'They took offence at him.' It has the force here of 'destroy spiritually'.

'Let the children come to me . . .'

The context of the persecution of the church in Rome, to which this Gospel was written, would probably have prompted an application to its perpetrators. But all who by their teaching and writing cause simple believers to lose their convictions are here given cause for reflection. Since spiritual convictions and moral values are so closely related, this warning surely also envelops all who consciously pervert the behaviour and moral values of others, especially the young. Paedophiles, abusers of children, internet pornographic predators and drug pushers come readily to mind, but the expressions of this sin are global in their scope. According to a 2001 United Nations Report, 'the trafficking of children for sexual exploitation has reached alarming levels. As many as 30 million children are victimised, largely with impunity.' Mention should also be made of

[2] The word in the Greek text is actually different from that used in v. 36.
[3] E. Schweitzer, *The Good News According to Mark* (SPCK, 1971), p. 197f.

children pressed into intolerable forms of employment, and forcibly recruited as soldiers by corrupt regimes. And where do we all stand in the light of a figure of twenty thousand children dying every day in our world from preventable causes? In the light of verse 47, there is only one word of application required: beware!

Is anything worth it?

The degree of seriousness attached to such 'causing to stumble' is vividly conveyed by Jesus. Even a horrible death such as drowning (particularly abhorred by people of Jesus' day) is preferable to the fate awaiting all such 'stumblers'. This saying echoes the terrible indictment passed upon Judas: 'Woe to that man who betrays the Son of Man! It would be better for him if he had not been born' (Mark 14:21).

Even the most radical of sacrifices – Jesus vividly cites physical mutilation (vv. 43, 45, 47) – is to be chosen rather than the terrible consequences of this form of sin. More generally, Jesus is recognizing that the issues which surround human response to him are so immense that personal sacrifice, even to the point of forfeiting life itself, is not too much to contemplate. There are some things so important, and specific sin on this scale is one of them, that nothing is too great to give up in order to avoid the implications which attach to it. Jesus says that such forms of sin, unless wholeheartedly repented, will necessarily and inevitably lead to hell.

2. What hell is like: the fire that 'never goes out' (vv. 43–48)

Jesus now speaks of the fate awaiting such sinners in the most solemn terms. He speaks of hellfire. This is one of Jesus' fullest accounts of the nature of hell, and it can serve as an appropriate point from which to summarize his teaching on this topic.

We note first the specific terms in which Jesus speaks of hell.

'Fire' (Gk. *pur*) is used in verses 44, 48 (citing Is. 66:24) and 49. It also occurs in verse 46, but that piece of text has limited manuscript support; we may presume that a copyist added this to balance out verses 43 and 45.

'Hell' (Gk. *geenna*) is used in verses 43, 45 and 48. The word *geenna* comes from the Hebrew *ge-hinnōm*, the valley of Hinnom, a ravine south of Jerusalem once linked with the pagan God Moloch and the disgusting rites associated with him (2 Kgs. 23:10; 2 Chr. 28:3; 33:6; Jer. 7:31; Ezek. 16:20; 23:37) which were proscribed by

God (Lev. 18:21; 20:2–5). Josiah, in the course of his reforms, further defiled the valley by making it a place for the dumping of filth and the bodies of criminals (2 Kgs. 23:10). There is some evidence that it was still in use in the first century as a rubbish tip, complete with smouldering fires. In amplification Jesus cites Isaiah's description of the fate of those who have excluded themselves from the 'new heavens and the new earth' which culminate the prophet's vision of the future (v. 48. Is. 66:24; cf. 65:17 – 66:23).

'*Salt*' (Gk. *halas*) appears in verse 49. The final allusion to fire links it to salt. This sentence is a bridge into several sayings about salt gathered in verse 50. The linkage is not crystal clear, and the form of the text is itself somewhat uncertain. The idea of fire's purifying property is probably in mind, along with the reminder that the true disciple cannot contemplate the judgment of the wicked without recognizing that he or she will also face a searching test (cf. 'Everyone will be salted with fire', v. 49), perhaps already anticipated by the fires of persecution currently raging around the Christians to whom this Gospel was addressed.[4] Four further general comments are in order.

a. The context

The danger at this point is to become so engrossed by the issue of the meaning of hell that we forget the context of these sayings. Callous indifference to and ruthless exploitation of the vulnerable, notably children, was a feature of the first-century world as it is of ours. Jesus is warning us that the perpetrators of such behaviour are responsible directly to God, who sees and knows all, and that there will be a terrible accounting at the last day for all such.

While the range of this warning is arguably universal, it is first directed to disciples who have thrown in their lot with the Christ who is on his way to the cross. Accordingly, issues of hell cannot be confined to the non-Christian world beyond the doors of the church. Jesus himself during his ministry had relatively little contact with that wider world. With a few exceptions, such as the Syro-Phoenician woman (Mark 7:24–30), the Gentile centurion (Luke 7:1–10), or Pilate at his trial, Jesus' ministry was wholly with Jews who had universally professed loyalty to God and his covenant with

---

[4] Cf. Lantham, cited H. B. Swete, *The Gospel According to S. Mark* (Macmillan, 1898), p. 213, 'If the preserving principle embodied in the apostles, and which was to emanate from them should itself prove corrupt, then where could help be found? If they the chosen ones became selfish, if they wrangled about who should be the greatest, then the fire which our Lord had come to send upon the earth was clearly not burning in them, and whence could it be kindled afresh?'

Israel, hence all his references to hell were to such an audience. That the teaching on hell is also to be addressed, when appropriate, to Gentiles is clear from references such as Paul's witness in Athens, and the warnings of God's wrath on human wickedness given generally in Romans 1. It is also indicated by Jesus' linkage of hell to the universal judgment he will exercise as the Son of Man at the end of the age (e.g. Matt. 25:32, 41).

Nonetheless, warnings about the dangers of hell, as this passage makes clear, are not out of place within the community of faith. Ralph Martin makes trenchant application:

> Jesus' warnings were meant to shake his hearers out of their complacency. They were thinking 'The Gentiles will burn in hell'. Jesus turned it around, 'you will suffer in an awful place like Gehenna if you live in a way that causes other people to stumble through your bad example' . . . These 'uncomfortable words' of Jesus were spoken whenever leaders of others placed stumbling blocks in the path of simple folk and tried to stop and thwart their entry into the Kingdom of God. Sermons on hell are just as needed today, provided we aim their thrust at the people who most need to hear them . . . as warnings to Christians, especially those who are lax and careless, and above all, judgmental of all and sundry.[5]

b. Sacrifice

The reference to 'cutting off' a member of the body, whether hand, foot or eye, has evoked debate. Some Christians, notably the Early Church theologian Origen, have taken Jesus' words literally and undergone castration. Others think Jesus is arguing in a purely hypothetical way here, using an *ad hominem* argument to show the disciples the futility of trying to change our behaviour by altering outward factors, for instance by removing a hand or an eye (after all, that would still leave the other one, which would be as prone to temptation). By this interpretation Jesus is driving them to realize that what is needed is not a partial alteration but a change of heart and will.[6] This may be rather too subtle, and ignores the facts that much temptation *does* arise from our physical context, and that we *are* capable of bringing change to our lives through self-denial.

Arguably Jesus is recognizing that sacrifices of this nature *can* be helpful, always bearing in mind his larger point that *anything* is

---

[5] R. P. Martin, *Mark* (John Knox, 1981), p. 55.
[6] R. C. H. Lenski, *The Interpretation of St Mark's Gospel* (Augsburg, 1964), pp. 404–406.

worth sacrificing for the sake of preserving our spiritual integrity. John Stott applies this helpfully:

> The command to get rid of troublesome eyes, hands and feet is an example of our Lord's use of dramatic figures of speech. What he was advocating was not a literal self-maiming, but a ruthless moral self-denial. Not mutilation but mortification was the path to holiness he taught ... If your eye causes you to sin because temptation comes to you through the eyes (objects you see), then pluck out your eyes. That is, don't look! Behave as though you had actually plucked out your eyes and flung them away and were now blind and *could* not see the objects which previously caused you to sin.[7]

c. The awesomeness of Jesus' language

We cannot ignore this aspect. Reduced to its core, he is asserting (a) that this life is a time of responsible action; (b) that we are especially accountable for the ways in which we influence others; (c) that God is very concerned about the influence we have on the weak and vulnerable, such as little children; (d) that to be the means of the spiritual destruction of such as these is almost intolerably serious; (e) that the consequences are so grave that no sacrifice in this present life is too great to secure the avoidance of such influence. All kinds of self-limitation here are preferable to the fate that awaits us hereafter.

d. The nature of this fate

Jesus' primary image is 'fire', or 'hell, where the fire never goes out' (v. 46). It is impossible to eliminate the element of conscious suffering from this image. The language is metaphorical; we are dealing with realities to which we can in principle have no direct access this side of the end of the world. Pictures are therefore all we have. The pictures are God-given, and hence are to be received as the normative images for these realities, but they are only a starting point and do not tell us everything. Not surprisingly therefore, there is a multiplicity of pictures given in Scripture of both hell and heaven. The pictures of heaven will occupy us in other chapters; they are by any reckoning multiple and diverse. So also with hell.

Hell is here 'fire [that] never goes out' (v. 44), a place where 'their worm does not die' (v. 48), and 'fire is not quenched' (v. 48). Elsewhere hell is a place of 'darkness' or 'outer darkness' (Matt. 8:12; 22:13; 25:30; 2 Pet. 2:17; Jude 14); 'a lake of fire' (Rev. 19:20; 20:10,

[7] J. R. W. Stott, *The Message of the Sermon on the Mount* (IVP, 1978), p. 89.

14, 15; 21:8); a place where we can be 'beaten with blows' (Luke 12:47); a condition which evokes 'weeping and gnashing of teeth' (Matt. 8:12; 13:42; 22:13; 24:51; 25:30); a fate describable as being 'shut out from the presence of the Lord' (2 Thess. 1:9).

However, even when we affirm that this language is metaphorical, and the suffering concerned is accordingly essentially mental and spiritual rather than physical, the presence of some profound degree of conscious anguish is inescapable. Hell is terrible by any measure and, as Jesus indicates, everything is worth sacrificing in order to avoid it. There is no more terrible prospect conceivable than of being consigned to hell.

3. The duration of hell: how long will hell last?

On the surface, the words of Jesus recorded here appear to answer straightforwardly the question of the duration of hell. In hell 'the fire never goes out' (v. 44), in hell 'their worm does not die' (v. 48), in hell 'the fire is not quenched' (v. 48). Other examples of this seemingly unambiguous statement of the eternity of hell come in Isaiah 66:24, cited by Jesus in this passage; Daniel 12:1, 'others [will wake] to shame and everlasting contempt'; Matthew 3:12; Luke 3:17, 'unquenchable fire'; Matthew 25:41, 'the eternal fire prepared for the devil and his angels'; Matthew 25:46, 'they will go away to eternal punishment'; 2 Thessalonians 1:9, 'they will be punished with everlasting destruction'; Hebrews 6:1–2, 'the elementary teachings about... eternal judgment'; Jude 7, 'the punishment of eternal fire'; Jude 13, 'blackest darkness' reserved 'for ever'; Revelation 14:11, 'the smoke of their torment rises for ever and ever'; Revelation 20:10, 'they [i.e. the devil, the beast and the false prophet] will be tormented... for ever and ever'; and possibly also 2 Peter 2:9, 'continuing their punishment' (though some take the sense here to be 'kept for punishment until the day of judgment').

Not surprisingly, therefore, the vast majority both among general Christian believers and the church's teachers have believed, though seldom without considerable inward struggle, that the Bible teaches the endless duration of hell. Although labels are not always helpful, this can with justice be called the 'traditionalist' view. Set against that is an alternative view, commonly referred to as 'conditionalism'. These two options do not exhaust the possibilities, but for the purposes of this discussion it will be enough to relate to these two 'classic' positions.[8]

[8]See the bibliography for sources representing the different sides of this issue. Titles marked with an asterisk are particularly relevant.

Conditionalism argues that hell is not 'everlasting' as far as the conscious experience of those consigned to it is concerned. Most commonly the conditionalist agrees with the traditionalist in anticipating a final judgment at which all the dead will be raised up to appear. Those who are appointed to hell will suffer a period of conscious pain, understood in whatever terms the biblical symbols such as fire and outer darkness are taken to imply. At some point thereafter, however, for the conditionalist, those in hell are annihilated, ceasing to exist. Support for this version of the negative side of human destiny is sought in several areas.

The language used

'Fire', as in this passage in Mark 9, has the property of consuming what is thrown onto it. Thus the language which alludes to its being 'eternal' (Matt. 25:41; 18:8) or 'never going out' or 'not being quenched' (vv. 43, 48; Is. 66:24) can be fairly thought to refer, not to a condition of unending conscious pain for those exposed to it, but rather to the *eternal effects* of being so consigned. This also explains the cases where the two destinies are set side by side as equally 'eternal', notably in Matthew 25:46.

Note is further made of the term 'destruction', which is often used in relation to hell as pointing to the condition of being 'destroyed', i.e. brought to an end (Matt. 10:28; Phil. 3:19; 1 Thess. 5:3; 2 Thess. 1:9; 2 Pet. 3:7), and hence the equivalent to another commonly used referent of hell, 'perish', which means to come to the end of conscious life (John 3:16; 10:28; 17:12; Rom. 2:12; 1 Cor. 15:18; 2 Pet. 3:9, etc.).

The word commonly rendered 'eternal' in our New Testament translations is in fact literally 'of the age (to come)'. Thus it refers in the first instance to a particular quality of life, rather than to its durational quantity.

The gift of immortality

Conditionalists, who get their 'label' from this tenet ('conditional immortality'), argue that humans are not inherently immortal. Only God is inherently immortal (as 1 Tim. 1:17 affirms). Our immortality (living for ever) is therefore a further gift of God beyond our creaturely life, and totally conditional on his decision to impart it to us. Those who do not commit themselves to the salvation offered them in Jesus Christ are simply denied this further impartation of life in the world to come.

Broader concerns

'Everlasting punishment' is alleged to be impossible to reconcile (a) with God's love, since a literally 'everlasting' torment for anyone, no matter how wicked, is simply unthinkable in a being who is defined as love; (b) with God's justice, since there is no clear equivalency between sins committed during this life and an endless punishment for them, and there is also lacking in the idea the distinction which both biblical teaching (cf. Matt. 11:20–24; Luke 11:47–48) and moral instinct call for, between different degrees of wickedness and hence different degrees of punishment; and (c) with God's victory, since the endless continuation of hell in God's world undercuts the fullness of his triumph in Jesus Christ over all evil.

Predictably, none of these grounds of support for conditionalism have escaped criticism in the discussions around this issue. As to the language employed in the texts referring to hell, it has been observed that 'destroy' (*apollymi*) and its congates have a range of meanings, not all of which involve the ending of existence. It is also said that 'fire' is metaphorical, hence reference to the various properties of fire are not necessarily determinative of its meaning, especially when 'fire' regularly occurs in phrases which appear to stress the endless duration of the experience of those so consigned. Some maintain that 'eternal' is indeed 'of the age (to come)', but everything depends on how that age was understood. First-century sources appear to support the view that the *quantity* (i.e. its lasting for ever) was at least as pronounced in the meaning attached to 'eternal' as its *quality* as life of the new order.

As to immortality, the full force of 1 Timothy 1:17 must be conceded. Inherent immortality, what Jesus referred to as 'having life in himself' (John 5:26), an attribute shared also by 'the Son', is a uniquely divine quality. All immortality referred to humans, whether before or after the fall, or even in the eternal age, is necessarily a gift of the self-existent Creator of all life. That being said, however, it is noted that immortality in this derived sense has commonly been seen as bound up with what is involved for humans in being created 'in the image of God', and as contributing accordingly to that inherent dignity and worth which attaches to every human person, and which was massively underwritten by the extent to which God was prepared to go to reconcile us to himself. Recent understanding of the 'image of God' in terms of our capacity to mirror God's being-in-community is not incompatible with this traditional perspective, indeed arguably enhances it in that our mirroring of God's trinitarian community-in-love is only meaningful if it carries within it the promise of *eternal* human relationships.

Did Christ go to the unfathomable limits of Calvary, it is asked, for those who only carry the *potential* for a God-reflecting, eternal existence? Perhaps he did, but most interpreters over the centuries have assumed that the value placed upon them by his deed, a value traditionally associated not least with their immortality, was already true with respect to them, rather than being potentially attainable by them.

As to the difficulty of reconciling an eternal state of conscious punishment with God's love, justice and victory, the points are well taken. Nonetheless, those who choose to retain the traditional understanding of the texts in question point out that God's love needs to be defined in biblical terms and hence in relation to God's holiness and wrath against sin; that comparative duration of time is not necessarily a helpful way of evaluating the seriousness of sin, since sin is by definition directed against an infinite God. Distinctions in the degree of punishment, which Scripture certainly recognizes, are not irreconcilable with everlasting punishment, nor, traditionalists argue, are these distinctions in any event clearly secured by the conditionalist alternative. They also argue that, while God's full and final victory assuredly must not be called into question, how precisely that works out needs reverently to be left to God to express.

This author has to acknowledge that for him, although the prospect of an endless punishment is an almost unthinkable one, even with respect to the most depraved, and while several of the issues raised by conditionalists give cause for careful (and prayerful) reflection, the case for a revision of the traditional understanding concerning the meaning of the texts in question appears to fall short of compelling demonstration.

John Robinson's great seventeenth-century assertion, 'God has yet more light and truth to break forth from his Word', needs to be given its full hearing. The Holy Spirit is alive in the church, we cannot be forever limited by the interpretations of our forefathers. That being said, however, the sparsity of support over the centuries for the conditionalist view, when it was regularly found in groups which at other points maintained clearly heretical positions, must at the very least give cause for pause. In other words, since interpreters over the centuries have overwhelmingly leaned to the traditional view, both among the church's most revered teachers as well as the mass of its Bible-taught believers, for conditionalism to prevail would need a very clear and persuasive case to be made for it from the relevant biblical material.

Further, and in this general connection, if Jesus himself held a 'conditionalist' view of hell, then it is surprising that there is no report in his teaching of his clearly disavowing the 'traditional' interpretation. While it is likely that no single understanding of the fate of those rejected by God overwhelmingly prevailed in Jesus' day, it is clear that Gehenna, with its 'eternal burnings', had come to be distinguished from *Hades*, the word commonly used to refer to the abode of the godly after death. In this regard the Pharisees, in contrast to the Sadducees, held to a continuing life after death for all, and in the case of those outside the covenant a future of endless divine judgment. Since this view was the one consciously upheld by many of those who peopled his audiences, and bearing in mind the numerous opportunities he had to do so, Jesus' failure to issue any clear disavowal of a 'traditionalist' understanding is significant.

This author's conclusion, therefore, must be that the duration of hell, for Scripture generally and specifically as reflected in Jesus' words recorded in Mark 9:42–49, is everlasting. There are, however, a number of other considerations which bear upon this issue.

i. The common ground
It is important to note, as does the report *The Nature of Hell*,[9] that there are many points of agreement shared by those who may disagree about the duration of hell. We will reflect and amplify the list offered there.

1. God is the creator and upholder of all life. All people are accordingly accountable to him for their lives.
2. In the pursuance of his purposes God has already determined a coming day of judgment.
3. We will all meet God on the day of judgment when our entire lives and deeds will be assessed in his presence.
4. None of us will be able to survive that scrutiny on the basis of our personal moral and spiritual achievements, for 'all have sinned'.
5. Our only hope will be Jesus Christ, his perfect life of righteousness and his death for our sins. Our hope will lie in these having been applied to us, and then and there availing for us.
6. Although the only basis of our acceptance will be Jesus Christ and our embrace of him, the judgment will also take account of how our faith has affected our lives.
7. God himself in the person of his Son will effect the judgment.
8. We recall from the teaching of Jesus that faith may be 'as a grain

[9] *The Nature of Hell*, report by the Evangelical Alliance Commission on Truth and Unity Among Evangelicals (Acute, 2000).

of mustard seed', and also his repeated warning of some degree of surprise on the day of judgment.

9. Those so united to Christ as to be able to claim justification through him will be granted a place within the new, eternal order of the kingdom of God, the 'new heaven and new earth of righteousness'.

10. Those who fail the scrutiny of the day of judgment will be assigned to hell. Not all will be saved.

11. There will be some variety in the degree of punishment, and hence of suffering, in hell.

12. While the images used of hell are necessarily metaphorical, we cannot evade the clear impression that hell is experienced as an existence of conscious and terrible judgment.

13. This assignment to hell is irrevocable. There will be no 'second chance'.

14. The redeemed who enter the 'new heaven and earth' will be completely fulfilled, particularly through a new, all-pervading relationship to God, which no unhappiness will mar.

This list is not exhaustive. The general point to be made here is the need to keep the disagreement over the duration of hell in some proportion.

One of the glories of evangelical faith is its essential assertiveness; by its very definition it lives to make certain specific and definitive pronouncements, to proclaim 'good news'. Not all of these pronouncements are positive, since we need to declare the tragedy of human rebellion and fallenness. But in general we agree with Luther: 'Nothing is more familiar or characteristic among Christians than assertion. Take away assertions, and you take away Christianity.'[10] The gospel at heart is about assertions, concerning who God is and what he has done for the world in Jesus Christ. The list above allows extensive scope for those who hold varying views of the duration of hell to make affirming assertions concerning it, and to make them together.

ii. The Lordship of Jesus

One of the primary considerations for any Christian must be the teaching, and hence the mind of Jesus. As Jesus himself noted in John 13:14, his being our Lord and being our teacher belong inseparably together. We cannot with integrity own him as Lord and then set to one side or leave open-ended what he believed and clearly taught. What did Jesus believe concerning hell? The points made above in

[10] Martin Luther, *The Bondage of the Will* (Jas. Clarke, 1957), p. 67.

expounding his teaching in Mark 9 are representative. In essence: it is real and it is terrible.

True, the kingdom of God is the centre of Jesus' message. It has come in Jesus and will be culminated in the future at his coming again. At that time there will be a universal, final judgment. Those who experience God's rejection will be assigned to hell. While hell is not central, therefore, neither is it peripheral. Hell belonged to the mental furniture of the mind of Jesus as the form of penal condemnation awaiting those who fell under judgment at the time of the final appearing of the kingdom of God.

In response to Bertrand Russell,[11] it *is* patently possible to be a person of the profoundest humanity – as Jesus most surely was by every relevant measure – and also to affirm the fact of the everlasting penal consequences of sin.

Since Jesus believed in hell, it should be part of our mental furniture also, as the form of judgment which will befall those rejected by God on the coming day of judgment. We too need to embrace the awfulness of hell.

Here distinctions between the different ways in which people understand the duration of hell become of lesser significance, unless we are persuaded that the interpretation being offered is a *clear* dismissal of the authority of Scripture. Hell is a terrible prospect and one from which we all need to recoil in horror for ourselves, and also for others who may be consigned there. Being 'correct' or 'enlightened' or 'biblical' on the issue of the duration of hell is secondary to the question of whether or not we reflect an attitude towards it which corresponds to that of Jesus. Jesus cannot be Lord if we do not submit to his teaching, and that includes, among other things, his teaching concerning the reality and the awfulness of hell.

iii. The justice of God

When Abraham was faced with God's impending judgment of Sodom and Gomorrah, and the peril which that posed for his nephew Lot, he resorted to pleading the justice of God: 'Will not the Judge of all the earth do right?' (Gen. 18:26). He did not plead in vain. In the resulting destruction of the cities, the wicked and the righteous were treated with appropriate discrimination. The Judge of all the earth did right.

The same question needs to be posed in relation to the fact and the conditions of hell, not least its duration. Will not the Judge of all the earth do right? God, by all definitions, is the epitome, the ground and the ultimate expression of justice. Can we not trust him

[11] See p. 144.

in this matter of final judgment to act in accordance with his character? When the final judgment is pronounced on us all it will be, and will be seen to be, perfectly right, utterly just, unequivocally proper, and receptive of the fullest approval of every conscience. No single human person will be dealt with in a manner that is even fractionally in diminution or in excess of what, in God's loving and holy presence, will be seen to be just. If one may so put it, not one individual will spend one millisecond longer in hell than is their just desert.

Paul's claim that God is both 'just and the one who justifies those who have faith in Jesus' (Rom. 3:26) is to the point. Our salvation derives from the unimpeachable justice of God as truly as it derives from his eternal love; he will be no less just and loving in his judgments – indeed, he cannot be; to imagine otherwise is to impugn the character of God. Despite divergences of interpretation, we can all anticipate the utter justice of his future judgments and even in anticipation celebrate them. Let God be God! We do exactly that by reposing our restful trust in what he will do. He *will* do right. We can count upon it.

iv. The limits of language

The question of the duration of hell confronts us with the issue of the relationship of language with its words, symbols, images and metaphors on the one hand, and the realities to which they point on the other. The problem is made more acute in the case of heaven and hell by virtue of the fact that, in the strictest sense, we do not have any direct experience of either.

Of course, we add as a caveat that to become a Christian involves the receipt of the Holy Spirit, who is himself the 'down payment' of the life of heaven. In one sense the Christian can, and does, claim that 'in some sense and in some degree' heaven's delights and blessings are 'begun below'. But the fact of fallenness and the continuing presence of the old nature are also realities. Faith is ever far from perfected and our obedience to God's will strictly circumscribed. God may, by his Spirit, come upon us at certain moments with signal effusions of grace and power, and, yes, Paul can bear witness to an experience of being 'caught up into the third heaven . . . into paradise' (2 Cor. 12:2–4). That, however, was Paul, and the revelations given to him cannot be separated from his unique role as an apostle of Christ. It is striking to note that Paul dates this experience very precisely, 'fourteen years ago', which leads us to assume that such heavenly encounters were in no sense normal or regular. The Bible's language concerning the life beyond conveys the clear impression that it will only take a moment spent in heaven or hell to recognize that we are in a very different form of existence from anything which has come our way on planet earth.

So we return to the issue raised above. How can language created and shaped by earthly experience be related to heavenly or infernal realities? The obvious thing to say is that it can only be done with limitation and with difficulty. This does not imply any qualifying of the full inspiration or the truly divine character of the Scriptures. Their words are God's words to us. He has spoken to us of heaven and hell *in so far as we are able to receive impressions of these realities while still on this side of the great divide that separates us from them*. To hold tenaciously to the words of Scripture, and to embrace them in their full trustworthiness, is to receive the truest impression of the realities which await us beyond death that we are capable of receiving as redeemed sinners. But the words, images, metaphors and pictures, while never misleading us, necessarily will not fully inform us.

In his discussion of spiritual gifts and the supremacy of love in 1 Corinthians 13:8–12, Paul contrasts the experience of the two orders, earth and heaven (or what he calls 'the coming perfection', v. 10). He uses four analogies to clarify this distinction. First, *spiritual gifts* are temporary; they belong to the 'not yet' of this life. They do have significant contributions to make (chapters 12–14), but 'they will cease' when 'the perfect' comes (vv. 8, 10). Thus our experience of God now, and his present working through us by the Spirit, will be in principle so different from what awaits us that what we know now will be viewed in hindsight as actually terminated in the light of what we will have come to experience there. Second, in relation to *the process of human maturation*, the experiences of childhood, its speech, thought forms and ways of reasoning, are so different from those employed by us in our adulthood that we inevitably 'put them behind us' (v. 11). They may represent some kind of preparation for adult functioning, but in practice we renounce them. We do not do that any more! Third, *a reflection in a first-century mirror* was very much less sharp and accurate an image than that given by direct sight. No-one would choose the former 'poor reflection' over the latter 'face to face' image. And how much less if the latter is a 'face to face' with the Lord himself in his coming glory (v. 12a). Fourth, *our present knowledge of ourselves* is partial; how little we really understand ourselves! Even after a lifetime of reflection and experience, we often feel we are no nearer understanding the mystery of our personhood than when we began the journey of self-awareness. How fractional is our self-understanding in comparison with God's perfect and exhaustive knowledge of who we are (v. 12b). So will our heavenly knowing be in contrast to our knowing now.

The cumulative impact of these four images is impressive. What we now know of the life to come, whether of heaven or of hell, is a degree of knowledge which is so ephemeral that it will actually pass away like present spiritual gifts, a measure of understanding which will prove as irrelevant as childish burblings, an awareness which will be as forgettable as the image in a tarnished mirror compared with direct sight, and a comprehension which will, when heaven and hell actually dawn, be seen to be as limited and as mistaken as our present self-knowledge.

One particular feature of our present, partial knowledge of the life to come which suffers from these limitations is *our experience and sense of time.* What will 'eternal' look like after the new order breaks in? What will an 'everlasting' existence be experienced as, whether in heaven or hell? The answer is simple – we do not fully know. The only thing we can say with complete confidence is that it will be different. God, as we saw in the opening chapter, is the Creator of all things. Specifically he is the Creator of time (Gen. 1:5, 'and there was evening, and there was morning – the first day'). Time is not a second God which exists for a moment apart from God. Time is a creaturely servant of God, available to him, and hence in principle open to being altered, modified and differently experienced by us *as God may choose.*

It is surely in this light that we need to respond to issues around the duration of hell. What does 'everlasting' mean when referred to either heaven or hell? In the end we do not fully know, and in principle cannot, beyond what Scripture gives us to know from its images and language. We do need to wrestle to bring consistency to its witness, and relate that to our earthly experience as best we may, and hence formulate our doctrines. We may conclude, as does this writer, that by the terms in which Scripture speaks of this order, hell is eternal in its duration. That means hell is strenuously and assiduously to be avoided. On that there can be no question, and the language of Jesus on this point is particularly eloquent and awesomely solemn.

For the rest we must surely leave this issue in the hands of the Lord, trusting him to do what is utterly just and right by each of his creatures, confident that no-one will be treated other than as they deserve, assured that hell will never be other than a fully appropriate destiny for all those consigned to it – in both its experienced nature and its experienced duration.

We bow before him in worship, the Father, the Son and the Spirit, acknowledging him – one God of glorious and infinite Majesty, Love, Light and Sovereign Power. Prostrate in his presence, we put our hands to our mouths and abase ourselves in humility and dependence, acknowledging him as the Lord over all, who is served in time and eternity, who holds every person in his hands, both here and hereafter,

159

who will judge all people at the last and assign to each their appropriate destiny. He is the Lord, he alone, and before him all that we know and experience is as nothing. And in that act of self-obeisance which is our joy, fulfilment and deepest freedom, we leave it thankfully in his hands to determine the destiny of all, which will mean his so acting in perfect love and perfect justice, that with reference to these future judgments we, with all the host of heaven, will fall before him in adoring worship and praise.

> Great and marvellous are your deeds,
> Lord God Almighty [including your deeds of final judgment].
> Just and true are your ways,
> King of the ages [including your assignment of human
> destinies].
> Who will not fear you, O Lord,
> and bring glory to your name?
> For you alone are holy.
> All nations will come and worship before you,
> for your righteous acts have been revealed . . . Hallelujah!
> For our Lord God Almighty reigns.
> Let us rejoice and be glad and give him glory.
>
> (Rev. 15:3–4; 19:6b–7)

4. The unlimited life (vv. 43, 45, 47)

In the swirling debates around the nature and duration of hell which this passage has brought to the surface it is easy to miss the fact that Jesus in this passage refers to *two* destinies, not one. He speaks here of *both* hell and heaven. Admittedly the latter is less prominent, understandably so since Jesus is here primarily warning his hearers about the dangers which a loss of childlike humility can breed. But his inducements towards heaven are as real as his dissuasions concerning hell. He speaks of the happy alternative to 'going into hell' as 'entering life' (vv. 43, 45); and then more substantially in verse 47 of the 'better' alternative, which is 'entering the kingdom of God'. It is an alternative which is only made possible by the amazing love of God expressed in that very journey Jesus is taking to Jerusalem – to death on a cross on behalf of all the sinners of the world (9:31; 10:45; 14:22–24).

This better alternative is a supremely attractive one. So much so, Jesus argues here and elsewhere (cf. Matt. 5:27–30), that no sacrifice is too great in order to secure it. It is not just that hell is so terrible, but that heaven is so wonderful that every effort is to be made and every possession, if necessary, relinquished in order to arrive there.

We recall at this point the setting of Mark's writing – the church of Rome. Peter, the dominating figure in that congregation, whose reminiscences (according to good tradition) Mark has recorded in his Gospel, has paid for his faith with his life. As the Neronian persecution falls more generally upon the church, the cost of following Jesus becomes daily more evident. Baptism with water may very well be the prelude to baptism in blood. To follow Christ in Rome is an extremely costly enterprise, but to give up all is not to lose. Everything here is worth losing if it leads to the incalculable gain of 'life' everlasting.

We can perhaps fittingly conclude this chapter, and our reflection on this solemn passage, with some words of George Adam Smith, commenting on the words of Isaiah 66 cited by Jesus at verse 48 of our passage.

> It is a terrible ending, but upon the same floor Christ set his teaching – the gospel net flung wide, but only to draw in both good and bad upon a beach of judgment; the wedding feast thrown open and guests compelled to come in, but among them a heart whom grace so great could not awe even to decency; Christ's gospel preached, his example evident, and himself owned as Lord, and nevertheless some whom neither the hearing nor the seeing nor the owning with their own lips did lift to unselfishness or stir to pity. Therefore he who had cried, *Come all unto Me*, was compelled to close by saying to many, *Depart from Me*. It is a terrible ending, but one only too conceivable. For though God is love, we are free, – free to turn from that love; free to be as though we had never felt it; free to put away from ourselves the highest, clearest, most urgent grace that God can show. But to do this is the judgment. *Lord, are there few that be saved?* The Lord did not answer the question but by bidding the questioner take heed to himself: *Strive to enter in at the straight Gate.*[12]

Summary

Jesus teaches that sin, such as the abusive destruction of children, leads to hell. Hell is a terrible fate, like being thrown into a fire. It is so terrible that no sacrifice is too great to make in order to avoid it. It is terrible not least in its duration. But it is not inevitable; there is also the possibility of eternal life in the kingdom of God.

[12] G. Adam Smith, *The Book of Isaiah*, vol. 2, The Expositors Bible (Hodder, 1910), p. 467.

Luke 23:32–43
9. When heaven begins

When I die – I do not die anymore, however – and someone finds my skull, let this skull still preach to him and say: I have no eyes, nevertheless I see Him; though I have no lips, I kiss Him; I have no tongue, yet I sing praise to Him with all who call upon His name. I am a hard skull, yet I am wholly softened and melted in His love; I lay here exposed on God's Acre, yet I am there in Paradise! All suffering is forgotten! His great love did this for us when for us he carried His cross and went out to Golgotha.

(Kohlbrugge)

A problem issue which often brings puzzlement to the Christian's prospect of heaven is this: When does it begin? Does it begin at the moment of death, or at the glorious appearing of Christ at the end of the age? Put another way, what do we make of the period between the moment of the individual Christian's death, and the moment of joyful resurrection in a new body when Christ returns in glory? This is the question of the 'intermediate state'.

For our textual anchorage we travel to the very centre of the biblical story – the death of Jesus Christ, and Jesus' words of assurance to the crucified criminal, 'I tell you the truth, today you will be with me in paradise' (Luke 23:43).

In common with the other evangelists, Luke notes that Jesus has company at his crucifixion. 'Two other men, both criminals, were also led out with him to be executed' (23:32). Ellis argues that for Luke this is 'the core of the episode'.[1] As Jesus hangs on the cross, the ironic title of kingship fixed above his head, he is the object of a fourfold assault. The *people* 'hurled insults at him' (Mark 15:29), the Jewish *rulers* 'sneered' at him (Luke 23:35), the *soldiers*

[1] E. E. Ellis, *The Gospel of Luke* (Eerdmans, 1974), p. 267.

'mocked' him (v. 36), and finally *one of the criminals* 'hurled insults' at him (v. 39).

This last takes us to the interaction with the criminals (vv. 39–43). There is an almost surreal quality to this conversation between the three men, hanging as they are by the final thread of their earthly lives, bound so strangely and tragically together in the maelstrom of events sweeping through Jerusalem that Passover two millennia ago. One of the criminals throws Jesus' claim back in his face. 'Aren't you supposed to be the Messiah, God's promised Saviour? Then get on with it and save us all, and you'd better be quick about it!' (cf. v. 39). Underneath the challenge lies the implied insult. 'Messiah, eh? Some Saviour you've proved to be! You couldn't save yourself, never mind us, or anybody else, you misguided, pathetic dreamer!'

His companion rebukes the imprecator. Has he momentarily forgotten his own terrible plight? He too is about to appear in the presence of his Maker, and will arrive there as a justly condemned criminal. This is no moment for adding to the litany of his sins by berating a patently guiltless man (vv. 40–41). 'Then he said, "Jesus, remember me when you come into your kingdom"' (v. 42).

What does this request imply? What did the crucified criminal believe? He certainly knew himself to be guilty of the charges leading to his execution. 'We are punished justly' (v. 41). To this extent, the happening on Calvary that Good Friday retained an element of true justice. He also believed Jesus to be innocent of the charges brought against him. 'This man has done nothing wrong' (v. 41). Further, he believed that for all three there was a continuation of life after they expired on their crosses – for him and his companion an impending accounting before God; for Jesus an appropriate vindication. But what did he believe that vindication of Jesus would amount to? We can never know precisely, but clearly the title over Jesus' head reading 'THIS IS THE KING . . .' resonated for him. As a Jew he would have been familiar with the messianic expectation. In some real sense, despite the utter contradiction expressed in Jesus' helplessness in death, and the shame attaching to its form, Jesus *was* the long-expected King, on his way to claim his throne, and as such was one whose good offices could be entreated.[2] As Plummer pertinently notes, 'Some saw Jesus raise

---

[2] The precise interpretation of the criminal's beliefs about Jesus is muddied by uncertainty about the original form of the phrase 'come into your kingdom'. There is manuscript support both for the sense 'when you enter (now) through your death into your reign', and for 'when you come (again) in the glory of your reign as King'. On the whole, the latter meaning is to be preferred; thus I. H. Marshall, 'The reference is to the *parousia* of Jesus as the Son of Man as a

the dead and did not believe. The robber sees him being put to death, and yet believes.'[3]

It is in response to this plea, with its implicit confession of faith, that Jesus makes the statement which raises directly the issue of the intermediate state. 'I tell you the truth, today you will be with me in paradise' (v. 43). In grasping Jesus' meaning, there are several points to note.

First, the importance of this saying is underlined by the words 'I tell you the truth' (Gk. *amen, amen*). Obviously the setting of the saying would in itself eliminate any casual utterance. All is solemn in such proximity to death. However, Jesus' use of the phrase additionally implies that his comment has behind it the whole weight of his conviction concerning the fate of the dead.

Second, is 'today' to be linked prospectively ('today you will be with me in paradise'), or retrospectively ('I tell you the truth today – you will be with me in paradise')? Apart from the awkwardness of the construction grammatically if the latter was the intended meaning, a linkage to 'I tell you the truth' destroys any significance in Jesus' use of 'today'. The temporal reference is then reduced to the level of the bland. (Obviously Jesus *is* saying the word 'today', but who would descend to such banality at a time like that?) The clear meaning of verses 42–43 is that the criminal believes Jesus can receive him when he returns as messianic King in his future glory, to which Jesus responds that his being with Jesus after death will in fact happen 'today'. The criminal has confessed a faith in Jesus and his mission which so unites him to Jesus' person that the triumph over death which Jesus will realize that very day will be shared with this criminal. In St Ambrose's words, *Ubi Christus, ibi vita, ibi regnum* – 'Wherever Christ is, there is life, and there is the kingdom.' 'In our Lord's answer, the word "today" stands foremost, because Jesus wishes to contrast the nearness of the promised happiness with the remote future to which the prayer of the thief refers. *Today*, before the setting of the sun which is shining on us.'[4]

Third, 'paradise' is a Persian word meaning 'walled garden' or 'park'. It is used in the LXX for the Garden of Eden and became a type

---

future event associated with the raising of the dead. The criminal thus regards Jesus as more than a martyr; he implicitly confesses his faith that Jesus is Messiah or Son of Man' (*The Gospel of Luke* [Paternoster, 1978], p. 872).

[3] A. Plummer, *The Gospel According to S. Luke* (T. and T. Clark, 1922), p. 535.

[4] F. Godet, *A Commentary on the Gospel of St Luke* (T. and T. Clark, 1875) on 23:43. 'It is here clearly taught that the saved, immediately after death associate spiritually with Jesus in heavenly bliss' (N. Geldenhuys, *Commentary on the Gospel of Luke* [Marshall, 1950], p. 615).

of the future bliss of God's people (cf. Is. 51:3). It came to be seen as the intermediate resting place of the souls of the righteous dead.[5] It is used in 2 Corinthians 12:4 and Revelation 2:7 (the only other New Testament occurrences) as a symbol of heaven and its joys. The paths of glory lead not to but from the grave.

Fourth, the phrase 'with me' is immensely important, and links this expression of the future hope of the believer to Jesus' words in John 17:24 and Paul's in Philippians 1:21. We will examine this later.

What, then, are the implications of this deeply impressive exchange?

1. Jesus is king

In his death Jesus continues to reign as Lord and King. He dies in shame and agony, yet with an unshakeable assurance that death is the doorway to life. So confident is he of this that he can carry his ministry of pardoning mercy to its final, triumphant expression as, in his last moments, he utters a prayer for the pardoning of his enemies and offers the kingdom of eternal forgiveness to a penitent criminal. Hence, as Luke portrays it, his death as a victim on behalf of sinners everywhere is simultaneously that of a victor triumphing over sin and death on behalf of sinners everywhere. At the same moment the cross is a place of abject defeat and desolation *and* a place of absolute triumph and exaltation. He reigns from the tree!

2. God is gracious

This incident reflects the amazing scope of the grace of God. The criminal has nothing to offer Jesus. He is justly condemned for capital crime, as he himself acknowledges. The verdict passed upon his life is accordingly, from a judicial point of view, one of proven guilt. Here is a man who, having received the opportunities that life afforded him, has scattered them to the winds in prodigal disregard. Neither direction from parental teaching, nor the restraints and sanctions of his religious upbringing within the Jewish community, nor the discretion dictated by experience, nor all the impressions of conscience, have deflected him from his pathetic flight into self-destruction and shame. This man has nothing to offer to God. He cannot plead for mercy, for he has nothing with which to earn it. In

[5] So Jeremias, TDNT, V, p. 756.

a sense he cannot even plead for clemency, for he has done nothing to warrant it. He is guilty and can do nothing but anticipate the just judgment of the God from whose mouth he has received the breath of life, before whose face he has squandered it away, and into whose hands he now falls helpless in death.

Amazing grace

Yet it is to *this* man that Jesus says, 'Today you will be with me in paradise'! In this promise lies the entire gospel, and the realization of God as 'the God of the gospel', as Barth put it – a God who, to the final depths of his Godhead, is endless, overflowing grace. In Lacordaire's great sentence, 'If you wish to know what God is like, listen to your own heart beating, and add to it infinity.' No logic can explain this. In one sense there is no justification for it. It flies in the face of the instincts of morality understood as the application of the law of desert; ''tis mercy all!'

This deed of mercy does not set aside all moral considerations, however, for Jesus' ability to address the criminal in this way arises from his dying *for* as well as *with* him. The guilt and shame of the criminal's life is not forgotten or ignored. It is accepted and passed under judgment, but the judgment is enacted not on the right or left crosses, but on the central cross of Jesus. In the staggering wonder of God's atoning love the crosses reverse, and the cross of just punishment becomes the cross of Jesus, and the cross of innocence becomes that of the criminal. Thus Jesus dies not for himself but for the others beside him. The guilt which nailed him to the cross is their guilt, and ours.

3. Judgment is real

Set against this glorious exhibition of divine mercy, this gripping story also confronts us with the solemn warning represented by the other criminal who did *not* repent and seek mercy, the man who died with bitter insults for Jesus upon his lips.

For this second criminal, as for us, death will one day stand before us, staring us in the face and holding before our eyes in that moment our utter helplessness and endless need of mercy. To resist the appeals of grace at that time is to put ourselves in a place where grace no longer reaches. It is to put ourselves in the place of judgment. As has been observed, 'One was saved that none might despair, but only one that none might presume.'

4. Life conquers death

One of the unambiguous implications of this story is the fact of life beyond death. 'Today you will be with me in paradise' is the promise of Jesus to every dying disciple. The precise nature of Jesus' presence we will consider below. What is not here in question is that our self-conscious 'I', our sense of personal identity (*'you* will be with me') and our awareness of the Living Christ all go with us into and beyond death.

5. An intermediate state?

At issue here is the condition and experience of believers between their moment of death and their participation in the parousia of the Lord. The word 'today' is obviously the critical one. Murray Harris comments, 'However it be interpreted, it seems incontestable that "today" refers to the day of the crucifixion, and that the man was granted far more than he asked for. He had requested favourable treatment in the distant or undefined future: he was promised personal relationship in the immediate future – "Today, with me."'[6] How are we to think of this 'state'?

Some Christian thinkers question the reality of such an 'intermediate' condition. For them the difficulties surrounding this 'state' are so great that they believe it is wiser to think of the continuing life of the disciple simply in terms of his or her participation with Christ in the glory of the new heaven and earth inaugurated when he returns. Why do they reach this conclusion?

a. Some searching questions

i. Does the prospect held out in the 'intermediate state' not detract from the glory and completeness of the coming victory of Christ?

'Does the doctrine of the intermediate state not suggest that there can be a perfect blessedness that has not shared in the ultimate victory of Christ, and the last and decisive triumph over the last enemy, death, and the revelation of the new heaven and the new earth?'[7] Similarly, in so far as this state is given prominence, does it not introduce an unhelpful, and even unbiblical, duality into the

---

[6]M. J. Harris, *Raised Immortal* (Eerdmans, 1983), p. 136.
[7]G. C. Berkouwer, *The Return of Christ* (Eerdmans, 1972), p. 39, paraphrasing the view of P. Althaus; Berkouwer himself affirms the idea of the intermediate state, cf. chapter 2 passim.

Christian's future prospect, so that the one great expectation of the Scriptures, the glorious appearing of the Son of Man, is replaced by a two-stage process?

This objection, though significant, need not be conclusive provided that we carefully maintain the clear New Testament focus on the parousia of Christ as the true goal and crowning expression of the Christian's victory over death.

To be thus focused need not preclude sounding an anticipatory note of triumph when a Christian dies. A Christian's moment of passing calls for the joyful declaration that the 'time between', awaiting the Lord's return, is also a time of Christ's victory. Further, we can affirm that believers who have passed out of earthly time are secure in the keeping of their Lord until the day they will participate in the renewal of all things. In this connection we recall the martyrs under the altar calling out, 'How long...?' (Rev. 6:10). For them also the focus is on the coming of the Son of Man, but that does not exclude either their present security or their sense of victory.

Among those most challenged by this strand of the Christian's hope are clergy responsible for sharing God's words at funeral and memorial services. A careful balance is called for. On the one hand, the hope of personal survival through Christ's death and rising must be sounded very clearly, and with a pastoral sensitivity which conveys the hope of a real, ongoing life in God for those we may have loved and lost awhile. On the other hand, that word of comfort and assurance must be set within the context of the future ultimate victory of Christ over the last enemy, when 'with all the saints' the loved one will enter into the fully emergent kingdom of the Lord.

ii. Does the idea of an 'intermediate state' not reflect a 'spiritualizing' instinct which denigrates the human body by suggesting that we can have a meaningful, indeed a full and satisfying, relationship with the Lord apart from the body?

While the question is again a salutary one, the 'intermediate state' need imply no such denigration. That soul and body can be distinguished is a biblical idea, as Christian tradition has consistently affirmed (cf. Matt. 10:28; Rev. 6:9; 20:4). Blocher asserts, 'The duality of soul/spirit and of body which is peculiar to human nature belongs to the propositions of Biblical anthropology . . . Duality stands out unambiguously in the New Testament, just as it does in the Judaism of that era.'[8] Provided that we continue to affirm the essential provisionality of the intermediate state, and make clear that the goal of

---

[8] H. Blocher, *In the Beginning* (IVP, 1984), pp. 87–88; cf. L. Boettner, *Immortality* (Presbyterian and Reformed, 1956), pp. 115ff.

Christ's saving work as far as the believer is concerned is always an embodied existence within 'a new heaven and a new earth', no denigration of the body appears implied.

iii. Is there not here a significant loss of the corporate, kingdom dimension of Christ's victory in favour of a narrow, self-focused, preoccupation? Should we really as Christians be focused on this 'private blessedness, without communion with the people of God, without considering the victory of Christ and the Kingdom'?[9]

This question has considerable force. It is another way of noting that the focus of the Bible lies in the parousia and the fullness of the kingdom of God. In Scripture this prospect is consistently anticipated in corporate terms. The image of the post-mortem experience as a lonely journey to a personal beatific vision of God finds little support. For the Bible we are to expect a *social glory*, a life with others as well as with God. The intermediate state, however, need not exclude some sense of community, although the true reality of the Christian's future is of life within the community of the Holy City which will appear when Jesus comes again.

iv. Does belief in an intermediate state not betray a failure to face the judgment represented by human death?

By assuring ourselves of the passage into Christ's immediate and joyful presence, do we not evade rather than face what it means to be a sinner before God? Should we not courageously submit to the inevitable implications of our sin and fallenness in the darkness and silence of death?

Again, while this point is well taken, the intermediate state need not imply any evasion of 'the wages of sin'. Death's sting is truly felt, no matter the circumstances or the degree of conviction with which Christians experience the passing of a loved one. The pain often goes very, very deep, and commonly the wound never fully heals. A conviction that the beloved is now 'with the Lord', while clearly a source of comfort, may do little even after the passage of time to counteract the numbing blow of the loss. That, at least, is the experience of this pastor.

b. The elimination of time

One way of resolving the difficulties attendant upon an 'intermediate state' is to note that, since time was created by God, it is in principle totally relative. Hence, it is argued, dying can be thought

[9] P. Althaus, *Die leitzen Dinge*, tr. as in Berkouwer, *The Return of Christ*, p. 39.

169

of as passing into the eternal state where time is no longer meaningful as a measure of experience. Thus, when the believer dies, he
or she passes out of the time sequence as we know it into the eternal
order. *From their personal perspective*, the next conscious moment
for the dead will therefore be the parousia and the receipt of their
heavenly bodies, when presumably time in some sense is restored
to them.[10]

We argued in chapters 1 and 8 that, since time was created, our
experience of time may be genuinely, even radically, different in the
new order. However, entirely to eliminate all sense of temporal succession in the beyond appears to raise questions about the value of
temporal existence. Berkouwer notes, 'It is precisely within time that
man's life can obtain profound meaning in the service of the living
God. To see time as the essential structure of the fallen cosmos . . .
and so to conclude that this structure must be abolished, can only
threaten the meaning of our earthly existence.'[11] While this caution
is principally addressed to those who dream of a non-temporal or
supra-temporal eternity, it is not without force whenever time seems
in danger of elimination. More significantly, however, this non-
temporal interpretation does not appear able to take seriously
enough the temporal dimension of the relevant biblical texts which
we address below in 'Biblical boundaries'.

c. The notion of purgatory

In Roman Catholic theology as formulated at the Councils of
Florence (1438–45) and Trent (1545–63), the intermediate state is
viewed as a condition of moral development in which the dead are
purged (hence 'purgatory') from the residual elements of their fallenness to prepare them for entry into heaven. 'The Roman Catholic
view adds to the concept of an intermediate state the possibility of
real purgation after death while in that interim state, and the possibility of being aided by those who are still on earth.'[12]

This idea has no defensible biblical support. Texts which have been
adduced, such as 1 Corinthians 3:11–15 with its reference to

---

[10] Cf. T. F. Torrance, *Space, Time and Resurrection* (Handsel, 1976), p. 102; S. H.
Travis, *Christian Hope and the Future of Man* (IVP, 1980), pp. 111–112. In his discussion of 2 Corinthians 5:1–10 Murray Harris 'inclines' to a not entirely different
perspective in presenting the view that believers do receive their new bodies on
death, but that this condition remains hidden until its open manifestation at the
parousia (Harris, *Raised Immortal*, pp. 98–101).

[11] Berkouwer, *The Return of Christ*, p. 43.

[12] Z. A. Hayes, 'The Purgatorial View', in *Four Views on Hell*, ed. W. Crockett
(Zondervan, 1992), p. 99.

'escaping through the flames', or Matthew 12:31–32 with its alleged implication of sins which will require forgiveness during the heavenly life, fall far short of the requirement. In 1 Corinthians Paul is talking about the assessment of Christian ministries, not people's essential standing with God. The reference in Matthew 12 to not being 'forgiven in the ... world to come' appears to be simply a vivid way of expressing the eternal effects of unforgiven sin.

The notion of purgatory is incompatible with the freedom and fullness of God's grace, and the exercise of his sovereign power which is able, immediately upon death, to transform us into his likeness. Purgatory cannot stand in the face of the clear meaning of Jesus' words to the criminal, '*Today* you will be with me in paradise.' If ever there was a candidate for purgatory, it is this man. His life, to its final moments, has been lived away from God. He has literally nothing to offer to God in terms of a process of sanctification in his life. If anyone needs to be taken away and cleaned up before being ready for communion with the holy Son of God beyond the grave, it is surely he. Yet to him Jesus gives the assurance of immediate access to paradise, in the company of Jesus himself.

Further, the idea of our intercessions availing for the dead is similarly devoid of a scriptural basis, and seriously compromises the sufficiency of the sole mediation of the Lord Jesus Christ. More generally, it conflicts with the Bible's unwearying insistence that 'salvation is of the Lord'. He, and only he, can effect our salvation and transformation. Purgatory is, in the end, irreconcilable with grace.

d. Biblical boundaries

All these questions and the diversities of interpretation require us at the very least to ensure that our thinking about the intermediate state is kept within clear biblical boundaries. Does the notion have adequate biblical justification?

While the focus in Scripture is clearly on the glory of Christ's coming, the Bible does also witness to believers being 'with him' beyond death prior to the ultimate triumph. Apart from anything else, the 'today' of Jesus in Luke 23:43 cannot be eliminated. We can set alongside it the occasions of reappearance after earthly death of Samuel (1 Sam. 28:11–19), Moses and Elijah (Luke 9:28–33). Other references to be considered are Acts 7:55–56; 2 Corinthians 5:4; Philippians 1:23; Luke 16:19–31; Revelation 5:13; 6:9–11; 15:2ff. and 19:1ff. We can also note Jesus' mention of the patriarchs 'living unto God' in Luke 20:38. Thus a two-stage process in some sense does not appear entirely foreign to the witness of Scripture.

This biblical strand is admittedly not particularly thick, but it is real nonetheless. Berkouwer speaks perceptively of a 'clear whispering'.[13] This may be to understate, but it sounds an appropriately cautionary note. We recall that the Bible often uses 'sleep' to refer to this condition (Mark 5:39; John 11:11; Acts 7:60; 1 Cor. 15:51; 1 Thess. 4:14). This is a telling metaphor for some of the things which death implies – rest from labour, easing of responsibility, abstraction from immediate involvement in events, a different kind of awareness and, perhaps most important of all, the certainty of reawakening at a future point. While not saying everything, it draws attention to the relative passivity of the intermediate state.

e. With Christ

The best and simplest expression of this dimension of the Christian hope is to understand it in terms of Jesus' words to the criminal, as a life 'with me'. It is also how Jesus expresses it in his prayer in John 17:24: 'I want those you have given me to be with me where I am, and to see my glory' (cf. Luke 16:22; Rev. 6:9). It is in these terms, too, that Paul describes the intermediate state in Philippians 1:23: 'to depart and be with Christ'.

To refer to this condition as 'going to the Lord' is fitting, not just because no higher benefit can be conceived, but also because this 'beginning' of our victory over death is only possible because of Christ's triumph over all death's dimensions in his cross and resurrection. As the Christian burial rite variously expresses it, it is because he has passed through death and 'by his rest in the tomb has sanctified the graves of the saints' that the tomb offers this authentic hope.

We will live beyond death and experience what might be referred to as a first, provisional instalment of Christ's cosmic conquest over all death's power, only because of his facing it for us and drawing its sting. All the victory, and hence all the glory here, is his alone. One day, like the penitent criminal at Calvary, we will, by grace, be 'with him in paradise'.

f. The distant triumph song

What more can we say of this state? Perhaps we may look forward also to some sense of community, since to be 'in Christ' is necessarily to be at one to a new degree with all who are his.

[13] Cited A. A. Hoekema, *The Bible and the Future* (Paternoster, 1978), p. 94, fn. 20.

The 'communion of saints' which is given biblical underpinning in Hebrews 12:22–28 affords a fundamentally corporate and supramundane picture of the people of God. The worship setting of the Hebrews passage is salutary (12:18–21). We are never 'nearer', if one may so express it, to those who have gone before us, 'the spirits of the righteous made perfect' (v. 23), than when we gather with the family of God in worship. There are times in that kingdom context when, as many would testify, the gulf separating the church militant on earth from the church triumphant in heaven seems significantly reduced.

In all of this, however, the question put by 'the souls of those who had been slain because of the word of God' depicted in Revelation 6:10 remains an impressive one: 'How long, Sovereign Lord, holy and true, until you judge . . .?' In other words, whatever the experience of the intermediate state may amount to, it is not the end of the journey in any sense. It has within it a deep and ineradicable limitation. It will not do in itself; it is not enough; it will not truly satisfy either ourselves, or our blessed Lord. Its effect will be to kindle anew within us the cry of the church across the ages: 'Come, O Lord! . . . Amen. Come, Lord Jesus' (1 Cor. 16:22; Rev. 22:20).

Summary

Jesus assures the dying criminal of life with him in paradise 'today'. The Bible appears to uphold the idea of an 'intermediate state', despite the searching questions to which it is exposed. This continuing, personal consciousness after death awaits the fullness of the Christian hope at the parousia of Christ.

Matthew 27:45-50
10. Hell on earth: the death of Jesus

> In the strange mercy of God the cup of his righteous wrath against
> the sin of the world is given into the hands, not of his enemies, but
> of his beloved Son. And he will drink it down to the dregs until
> the moment comes when 'I thirst' gives place to 'It is finished'.
>
> (Lesslie Newbigin, *The Light Has Come*)

Hell is 'in' today. 'My years in Auschwitz – hell on earth!' 'My heart
attack was hell on earth!' 'My five years of hell with an abusive
husband!' '"It was hell today on the Centre Court" says tennis star.'
By a strange irony, at a time when the word 'hell' has almost entirely
dropped from the language of the church, and from its preaching in
particular, hell is one of the staples of everyday discourse.

Some of the experiences mentioned above were undoubtedly terrible, but literally speaking, they were not 'hell on earth'. Only once
in all history has there truly been 'hell on earth' – when Jesus Christ
took our place on the cross and bore the wrath due to us for our sins.

We will explore that overwhelming truth in this chapter, and in
the process will discover what we can learn about hell from this
event. In doing so we will be able in some degree to rebut the criticism to which those who write or speak on this theme are exposed
– that since hell is a state which will only be experienced after earthly
existence is relinquished, any attempt to describe it is doomed to
failure from the start. Up to this point we have defended our exploration of hell (and heaven) by noting that, while *we* have no personal
access to the experience of hell, the all-knowing God does, and he
has informed us of it in Scripture. We now offer a second line of
defence: we may validly speak of hell (and heaven) because at one
point in space and time, one unique moment in Jerusalem two thousand years ago, both hell and heaven made their appearance
on earth.

174

For our encounter with 'hell on earth' we will use Matthew as our source.[1] Jesus having been duly arrested, tried and condemned (26:47 – 27:31), Matthew sets the scene of the crucifixion by noting first Jesus' refusal of the narcotic offered to dull the pain of the impalement (27:34), and then the dividing of his garments among the soldiers (v. 35). Mark interjects the exact time at which he was bound to the cross – 'the third hour', 9.00 a.m. by our reckoning (15:25). Matthew notes the title above Jesus' head (27:37), the presence of the criminals crucified on either side (v. 38), and the mocking of both the passers-by (vv. 39–40) and the Jewish leaders (vv. 41–43).

Matthew then moves to the conclusion at the ninth hour (v. 45f.). During the three-hour interval there has been 'darkness . . . over all the land'.[2] Its appropriateness needs no comment. Scripture provides fitting commentary: 'The light shines in the darkness' (John 1:5); 'this is your hour – when darkness reigns' (Luke 22:53b).

Matthew then tells us that at 'the ninth hour', at the end of the three-hour period of darkness, 'Jesus cried out in a loud voice, "*Eloi, Eloi, lama sabachthani?*" – which means, "My God, my God, why have you forsaken me?"' (v. 46). These words are possibly the most challenging in the entire Bible as far as the interpreter is concerned. We will attempt an approach to them below.

Jesus' words lead some bystanders to imagine a plea for Elijah's intervention (v. 47f.). There is some evidence that Jews of the period had a belief in the efficacy of Elijah and his prayers.[3] A further drink is offered to Jesus (v. 48). He gives a final loud cry, and dies (v. 50). Matthew concludes with the information that the veil in the temple was at that very time torn in two (v. 51), that the Roman centurion supervising the execution testified, 'Surely he was the Son of God!' (v. 54), and that a group of women stood by at some distance (vv. 55–56).

What light does this death scene throw on the enigma of hell? We can best answer that by viewing the death of Jesus through the lens of three interpretive phrases. Each will in turn take us a step closer to the revelation of hell in this event.

---

[1] Mark could as easily have been chosen; the two accounts are very close, which has led many scholars to postulate a common source document used by both, often referred to as 'Q'.

[2] There is probable interesting corroboration of this remarkable phenomenon in pagan sources. Both Thallus, the first-century Samaritan historian, and the second-century Greek historian Phlegon make apparent reference to it; cf. Paul Barnett, *The Truth about Jesus* (Aquila, 1994), pp. 18–19.

[3] Cf. Jas. 5:17–18; Jeremias in TDNT, II, p. 935f.

1. The principle of substitution

Considered simply as a story of heroic yet tragic death, the crucifixion of Jesus grips the heart and imagination as few other deaths in history. Here is the tragic hero at the end of a life of consummate service and self-giving, pursued and finally overtaken by his jealous enemies. Despite his capture and inevitable execution, he faces his final, agonizing moments with deeply moving dignity and courage, even to the point of expressing forgiveness for those who have maliciously plotted his downfall. It is unforgettably impressive.

God was in Christ

For the biblical writers, however, there is something else at work in all this, another whole dimension. The death of Jesus is not merely a personal event, the final chapter in the fascinating story of Jesus. The claim of the Scriptures is that this is also a global event. Jesus is more than a private individual, he is a corporate person. Like Adam before him, he represents the entire race. 'Just as the result of one trespass was condemnation for all people, so also the result of one act of righteousness was justification that brings life for all people . . . just as through the disobedience of the one man the many were made sinners, so through the obedience of the one man the many will be made righteous' (Rom. 5:18–19 NIVI).

Thus the death of Jesus Christ is to be understood as *God's deed for all humanity*. Adam acted for all people when he sinned, thereby making sin and death realities in every human life. Jesus acted for all when he died, thereby making righteousness and eternal life possibilities for every human being.

How did the death of Jesus achieve this?

In our place

The key which unlocks this mystery is the word *substitution.* Christ in his death stood in our place and bore on our behalf the just judgment of God against our sin. 'Christ died for our sins' (1 Cor. 15:3); 'Christ died for sins once for all, the righteous for the unrighteous, to bring you to God' (1 Pet. 3:18). C. E. B. Cranfield expresses it memorably: 'God, because in his mercy he willed to forgive sinful men and women, and being truly merciful, willed to forgive them, righteously, that is without in any way condoning their sin, purposed to direct against his own very self in the person of his Son the full weight of that righteous wrath which they deserved.'[4]

---

[4] C. E. B. Cranfield, *The Epistle to the Romans,* vol. 1 (T. and T. Clark, 1975), p. 217.

The notion of substitution is rooted deeply in the soil of the Old Testament. It appears in the sacrificial rituals whereby slain victims were presented on behalf of worshippers, the forfeited life of the animal substituting for the forfeited life of the sinner (e.g. Lev. 1 – 7). It is expressed at the heart of Israel's faith in the Passover ritual, based on Israel's remarkable liberation from Egyptian oppression when the lamb 'without blemish or spot' died in substitution for the life of the firstborn son of every Jewish household (Exod. 12–13). Substitution surfaces again in the Day of Atonement ritual (Lev. 16) which called for the giving on the worshipper's behalf of two sin-bearing goats, the one to be slain, the other driven to a solitary place (Lev. 16:21–22).

Substitution finds its climax in the self-giving ministry of 'the Servant of the Lord', who was to be 'pierced for our transgressions', upon whom was 'the punishment that brought us peace', and upon whom 'the LORD has laid . . . the iniquity of us all' (Is. 53:5–6). The New Testament is clear that all of this was fulfilled in Jesus (John 12:38; Matt. 8:17; 1 Pet. 2:22f.; Acts 8:30–35).

Jesus himself claimed it in two crucial sayings: 'The Son of Man . . . [came] . . . to give his life as a ransom for many' (Mark 10:45); and, at the Last Supper, 'This is my blood of the covenant, which is poured out for many' (Mark 14:24). Paul gathers up this witness: 'God demonstrates his own love for us in this: While we were still sinners, Christ died for us' (Rom. 5:8). The sense of bearing a penalty on behalf of another is so clearly present in these references that this interpretive key is often referred to as 'penal substitution'. James Packer states,

> Christ Jesus, moved by a love that was determined to do everything necessary to save us, endured and exhausted the destructive divine judgment for which we were otherwise inescapably destined, and so won for us forgiveness, adoption and glory. To affirm penal substitution is to say that believers are in debt to Christ specifically for this, and that this is the mainspring of all their joy, peace and praise both now and for eternity.[5]

In the death of Jesus God acts *for us*. Jesus takes our place and bears himself what is due to us – the just penal retribution which God is bound to exact for the sin which is an ineradicable part of our lives.

Hell for us

Crucially, since the final content of that penal retribution is banishment to hell, his substituting himself for us to bear the full effects of

[5] J. I. Packer, TB 25, 1974, p. 25.

God's wrath implies that his substitionary suffering *must have included this hell-experiencing element.* To bear all the other implications of our sins but to leave unborne the experience of hell would empty his claim to be an all-sufficient Saviour of sinners. Only if Jesus' death includes the equivalence of hell can it properly and effectually be the means of our salvation. Christ's saving us *through* the cross must mean that he endured hell *on* the cross. The cross was 'hell on earth'.

2. The significance of Christ's death

The second step in the exploration of 'hell on earth' is to identify what it is about the cross which gives it this hellish meaning. For the Bible writers the equivalence of hell appears to lie in Jesus' *death*. We have assumed that in the previous section. It is time to justify it.

To understand the location of 'hell on earth' requires being clear about two things: the Bible's estimate of the significance of death generally, and of the death of Jesus specifically.

Sin and death

In Scripture death is never a neutral, amoral phenomenon, a purely natural fate. Such a view is not only conspicuous by its absence, it is basically alien. What stands before us is the consistent association of death with guilt and sin. Death is 'the wages of sin' (Rom. 3:23); 'sin . . . leads to death' (Rom. 6:16); sin 'results in death' (Rom. 6:21); it is the inevitable result of living 'according to the sinful nature' (Rom. 8:13); sin is 'the sting of death' (1 Cor. 15:56); death is the fruit produced by sin (Rom. 7:5); sin is, in James's vivid picture, the womb in which death is conceived and from which it emerges to hunt and finally slay humankind (Jas. 1:15).

This line of teaching carries forward the prophetic witness of Ezekiel and Jeremiah 'that everyone will die for his own sin', and reaches back to the Garden of Eden, in Genesis 2 and 3, where God's prohibition of Adam (Gen. 2:17) carried the fatal warning, 'when you eat of it you will surely die.'

Thus 'sin entered the world . . . and death through sin', and in this way death spread to all, because 'all sinned' (Rom. 5:12). 'Death came through a man' (1 Cor. 15:21), and 'sin reigned in death' (Rom. 5:21; cf. Heb. 2:14; Luke 1:79; Rom. 7:29; 8:24; 1 John 2:9).

This is all in essential harmony with the teaching of Jesus recorded in John, where to believe in him is to pass 'from death to life' (5:24; 8:51; 11:25), and with Jesus' observation, recorded in

Matthew 8:22, 'Let the dead bury their own dead.' It is not acciden-tal that the father of the prodigal can affirm, 'This son of mine was dead' (Luke 15:24).

For the Bible, then, death is a profoundly moral reality. It is the witness to God's claim upon humanity, and to humanity's resistance of the claim. In death our sin becomes open and naked as the truth of our life. Death is therefore, to use James Denney's words, 'the sac-rament of sin',[6] or in Karl Rahner's vivid phrase, 'guilt made visible'.[7] The terror of death is disclosed here, for in death we see ourselves as we are before God – as those who have lived throughout our allot-ted time in rebellion against him and in guilt before him, in rejection of his claim upon us and in repeated disobedience to his good will. In our death all the illusions are stripped away; all the pathetic rags and tatters with which we seek to cover ourselves from exposure to that awful gaze, all are here torn aside and blown away. Whether it be the sham religion, the so-called 'Christian' service, the frantic philanthropic activity, the prayers and cheery smiles, the devotions and sacrifices, the public displays and the private gestures – all fall away, swept aside and scattered to the winds by the tempest of the divine judgment that falls upon us in death. 'The soul who sins . . . will die' (Ezek. 18:20).

This, for the Bible, is the meaning of death, of our death – *the judg-ment of God* – and any other description is the merest tinkering with externals. Death is not a natural phenomenon which allows us to shrug our shoulders and mutter, 'Ah well, we can't live for ever!' For in truth we were created to do just that. We were destined for immor-tality and, as immortals made for everlasting fellowship with God, we shall and must last for ever. In this light we see death for what it is, as the enemy, the intruder, the tumbril of the evil one bearing us away.

The judgment which is death

Even in this, however, the deepest and darkest thing has not been said, for the true terror of death is not that in it we escape from God, but precisely that in it we meet him. In Karl Barth's sombre words,

> Death as it meets us can only be understood as a sign of God's judgment. For when it meets us, as it undoubtedly does, it meets us as sinful and guilty people with whom God cannot finally do

---

[6] James Denney, *The Death of Christ* (Hodder and Stoughton, 1903), p. 285.
[7] K. Rahner, *On the Theology of Death* (Burns and Oates, 1961), p. 57.

anything but whom he can only regret having made. For man has failed as his creature. He has not used the freedom in which he was privileged to exist before God. He has squandered it away in the most incredible manner. He can hope for nothing better than to be hewn down and cast into the fire.[8]

That is the meaning of death, our death. It is God's act of judgment which we have brought down upon our own heads by our identification in the whole tenor of our lives, as well as in myriads of specific acts, with that foul, malignant dimension of resistance and antipathy to God which Scripture refers to as the demonic, the anti-kingdom of bottomless iniquity.

Death, however, is not the exhausting of judgment – it is rather its foretaste and prelude. 'People are destined once to die, and after that to face judgment' (Heb. 9:27 NIVI). Our present death is therefore the prelude of the terrors of the second death (Rev. 2:11; 20:6, 14), for everyone must appear before the judgment seat where books are to be opened and secrets uncovered, and the thoughts of every heart revealed (2 Cor. 5:10; Rev. 20:12; Rom. 14:12).

Such is death for the Bible, and it is this view of it which lies behind and is expressed in the truth at the heart of the cross. 'Christ died for us.' Here is the hell in the cross, for Christ bore our hell in his dying for us. He died our death, the death of the sinner who, as the object of God's wrath, receives in death the first fruits of the eternal dying which is hell.

But can the 'first fruits' be the equivalent of the full harvest? Can a temporary, momentary experience of death be the equivalent of an 'everlasting' death? To engage that question means opening up our third principle.

3. The experience of separation

This is the final step towards the uncovering of hell at the cross. The principle of substitution established the basis of this disclosure. The significance of death clarified the location of this revelation of hell. We come now, as close as we may penetrate it, to the unveiling of hell at the cross – the experience of separation.

Probably the most striking feature in Matthew's account is the terrible cry wrung from the heart of Jesus at the conclusion of his hours of agony, 'My God, my God, why have you forsaken me?' (27:46). What meaning are we to give to these words?

[8] K. Barth, *The Doctrine of Creation*, CD III, 2 (T. and T. Clark, 1958), p. 597.

Abandoned

The first observation is that they accord with Matthew's general presentation of Jesus' death as an experience of abandonment. It begins in the Garden of Gethsemane as the 'inner circle' of his disciple companions are unable to support Jesus in his agony and repeatedly fall asleep (26:36–45). It continues as the disciples 'deserted him and fled' (26:56). His loneliness before his accusers is underlined: '"He is worthy of death," they [all] answered' (26:66). And all the while Peter, one of his closest friends, is betraying him: 'I don't know the man!' (26:72). Soon the crowd is shouting, 'Crucify him! . . . Crucify him!' (27:22, 23). He is a helpless pawn in the hands of the Roman soldiery (27:27–31). Finally, at the cross, the passers-by, the chief priests and the teachers, and then one of the criminals crucified with him, all combine to hurl abuse at him (27:38–44).

So Jesus moves step by terrible step into the place of utter isolation and forsakenness. Even the comforting embrace of the daylight is withdrawn, the sun is shut out as the darkness engulfs him. But the most terrible step is still to be taken. At last it comes upon him. At the end of three hours in utter, appalling aloneness, the terrifying cry is torn from the heart of one entering the final, unspeakable abandonment – by his Father. 'My God, my God, why have you forsaken me?'

A hard saying

Some have sought to evade, on a number of grounds, the difficulties attendant on attributing this saying to Jesus. The difficulties centre on considerations such as its appearing to undermine conviction about his divine person or the integrity of the Trinity, or its incompatibility with the victory he won at the cross, reflected for instance in the cry, 'It is finished', with which John concludes the account of Jesus' life (John 19:30).

That the Early Church struggled with the saying is not in doubt. Possibly its appearance in only two of the Gospels suggests that struggle, as may the presence of variations in the textual tradition of Mark's record of the cry (Mark 15:34). For them, as for us, this is 'a hard saying'.

Others urge that we do not simply take the words at their face value. 'Never was there an utterance that reveals more amazingly the distance between feeling and fact.'[9] In other words, Jesus was mistaken. He no doubt *felt* abandoned by the Father, but he was not so

[9]T. R. Glover, *The Jesus of History* (London, 1917), p. 192.

in fact. This, however, encounters the huge difficulty of imputing a basic misunderstanding to Jesus, and that in the area of his relationship to the Father, where by any standard his perception was matchless.

Another tack is to note that the words are a quotation from Psalm 22:1. The claim then is that Jesus was in the process of reciting the whole psalm, which of course ends with the triumphant assurance of God's purpose, 'Dominion belongs to the LORD and he rules over the nations . . .' (v. 28). Either he was interrupted in his recitation by his expiring in death, or the quoting of the opening words carry the implicit affirmation of the rest of the psalm. Either way, the difficulty of verse 1 of Psalm 22 quoted in isolation is overcome. As one writer aptly notes, however, 'The awful cry which startled the onlookers cannot be reconciled with a devotional exercise.'[10]

The full import of the words must be retained. In his dying Jesus experienced in real and authentic measure that terrible, indescribable separation from God which sin brings. In these final moments on the cross, as he entered the valley of the shadow of death and tasted in fullest anticipation that abandonment which his death must mean, Jesus cried out in words which accurately expressed the experienced reality of these moments, 'My God, my God, why have you forsaken me?' 'The burden of the world's sin, his complete self-identification with sinners, involved not merely a felt, but a real abandonment by his Father.'[11]

The cup of wrath

We need to exercise care in how we express this horror. It is not enough to think here only of an abandonment, terrible as that must have been, set against the history of Jesus' unique, lifelong oneness with the Father. Abandonment alone does not plumb the depths of this; there is something else at work here. Help in interpretation can perhaps be derived from 2 Corinthians 5:17, 'God made him who had no sin to be sin for us'; from Galatians 3:13, 'Christ [became] a curse for us'; and perhaps most of all from the experience of the agony in the Garden of Gethsemane, where the language – 'he began to be greatly amazed and sore troubled' (Mark 14:33) – is referred to by Morris as 'almost shocking'.[12]

[10] H. Maynard Smith, *Atonement* (London, 1925), p. 155.
[11] C. E. B. Cranfield, *The Gospel According to St Mark* (Cambridge University Press, 1959) , p. 458.
[12] L. Morris, *The Cross in the New Testament* (Paternoster, n.d.), p. 46, where also is found this rendering of Mark 14:33.

What was it, we dare to ask, that in prospect so unhinged him? What did he discern in the shadows of the garden that caused him to start back in such terror? The key to that agony is surely caught in the words of his prayer, 'Let this cup pass from me . . .' (Matt. 26:39 RSV). The 'cup', to one raised in the Old Testament Scriptures as Jesus was, has only one possible meaning – the cup of the wrath on human sin (cf. Is. 51:17–22; Jer: 25:15–28; Zech. 12:2). What overwhelmed Jesus in the garden and produced in him a consternation that bordered on derangement was, if we may so put it, the looming figure of the Father in the holy fire of his wrath.

Hence we dare not fall short of asserting that on the cross, in his death, Jesus faced and experienced the wrath of God; or, to put it more theologically, in the cross God turned the reality of the eternal, divine displeasure against the sin of our race *in upon himself in the person of his well-beloved Son*. Hell is not merely the absence of God; it is the absence of God which is the inevitable concomitant of the holy, divine antipathy to sin and evil. 'Christ as reprobate bears damnation on his shoulders to defend and shelter those who are in Him from it, however deserved.'[13] He bore damnation; he entered hell. That is the meaning of the cry of dereliction.

'He descended into hell'

There is a significant historical perspective on this. In the Apostles' Creed the clause 'crucified under Pontius Pilate' is followed by 'he descended into hell'. It can be argued that, back in the fourth century when the creed was composed, 'hell' commonly implied only the nether regions, i.e. the Old Testament *Sheol* (*Hades* in Greek), the abode of the dead, without the punitive implications which attach to hell in the New Testament. Accordingly, Christ was thought of as going, after the experience of death, to announce his victory to those who had died in preceding generations, and to bring deliverance to the Old Testament saints. Scriptures, notably 1 Peter 3:19, 'he went and preached to the spirits in prison', and 4:6, 'the gospel was preached even to those who are now dead', were seen as support for this 'post-mortem' ministry of Jesus.

The issues here are complex, however, as a reference to any responsible commentary on 1 Peter will reveal. Wayne Grudem argues persuasively that the reference in 3:19–20 is to Christ's preaching *through Noah* during the time the ark was being constructed.[14] But

---

[13] J. S. K. Reid, SJT, 1, p. 181; J. H. Newman speaks in similar vein, seeing in the cry 'the agony of hell itself', cited Morris, ibid., p. 49, fn. 95.
[14] W. Grudem, *1 Peter* (IVP, 1988), pp. 157–161, 203–239.

Cranfield's observation is not without force: 'The best thing is to rec-
ognise that we encounter here a mystery, which is still a secret from
us, and reverently accept the hint – for a hint is all that is given us –
and thank God that the reach of Christ's saving activity is not limited
by our desire to get things neat and tidy in pigeon-holes of our
choosing.'[15]

Calvin, following Luther before him, sees the phrase 'he descended
into hell' as of great significance, noting 'how important it is to the
sum of our redemption, if it is left out much of the benefit of Christ's
death will be lost'.[16] This is because the phrase, Calvin believed, refers
not to some post-mortem ministry of Jesus.[17] His 'descent into hell'
is a statement of what was entailed in his bearing our sin on the cross.

> The Creed [in this phrase] sets forth what Christ suffered in the
> sight of men, and then appositely speaks of that invisible and
> incomprehensible judgment which he underwent in the sight of
> God in order that we might know not only that Christ's body was
> given as the price of our redemption, but that he paid a greater and
> more excellent price in suffering in his soul the terrible torments
> of a condemned and forsaken man.[18]

In other words, his 'descent into hell' is a comment on *what was happening on the cross,* and specifically in his death thereon, rather than
a speculative hint as to what might have been happening in the period
immediately following.[19]

Our wrath-bearer

Underlying this interpretation is a powerful theological consideration which we noted earlier. If we understand the cross in substitu-
tionary terms, i.e. as an action 'for us', and if we are to understand 'for
us' to mean that Christ takes our very place and, in that place of ours,
accepts on our behalf entire responsibility for the whole burden of
our sins, then we are driven to understand the death of Jesus on the
cross in these terms. One of the primary implications of being sinners
is that we are the objects of God's just judgment; we are 'by nature

[15] C. E. B. Cranfield, *The First Epistle of Peter* (SCM, 1950), p. 86.
[16] J. Calvin, *Institutes*, II, XVI, 8, p. 513.
[17] On 1 Pet. 3:19 Calvin is prepared to allow some kind of proclamation to the
deceased saints of the victory of the cross. Cf. *The Epistle of Paul the Apostle to
the Hebrews, and the First and Second Epistles of St Peter* (St Andrew, 1963),
pp. 514–515.
[18] Calvin, *Institutes*, II, XVI, 8, p. 516.
[19] Cf. K. Barth similarly, *Dogmatics in Outline* (SCM, 1949), p. 118f.

objects of wrath' (Eph. 2:3). For Christ to take our place therefore necessitates his taking that divine wrath upon himself in our stead. To carry every other implication of our sinnerhood but to leave this particular implication uncarried would be fundamentally to flaw his saving work. To be a complete and sufficient Saviour he must save us from every effect of our sins. If he achieves this by taking our place and bearing these implications in himself, then he must, of necessity, in some way and at some point, bear in himself the pains and terrors of hell. Only thus are we delivered from them. The claim of the Scriptures is that, in unfathomable love and mercy, he truly bore them – by dying our death (cf. Rom. 3:25; 1 John 2:2; Gal. 3:13, etc.). Thus the cross was precisely, as Calvin argues, 'hell on earth'.

4. Hell in the light of the cross

We ask finally what all this means for our overall theme. What of the meaning of hell in the light of the cross, and of the cry of dereliction in particular?

Infinite suffering, infinite atonement

Two things call for comment in the light of this. The first refers to *the duration of hell.* Those who have argued in recent times for the limited duration of hell[20] see in this disproportion a justification of their viewpoint. If what Christ suffered was 'hell on earth', then clearly hell cannot be of everlasting duration, otherwise there is no real equivalence between his sufferings and those of the condemned. This objection, however, tends to isolate one factor in God's judgment, its temporal duration, from all its other dimensions. If time is the fundamental issue, then certainly Christ could not be thought of as literally bearing 'hell' on the cross. But the primary reality in the death of Christ is surely the nature of the one who endured it. '*Christ died for our sins.*'

The measure of the seriousness and extent of the judgment borne on the cross is the person of the crucified. The witness of the New Testament is that none other than the God-man, Jesus Christ, the everlasting Son of God become human, died on the cross. His infinite person endured the sufferings of the crucifixion. In that sense the sufferings were infinite by every possible measure. The agony of God is by the nature of the case an infinite and eternal agony. Precisely the anguish and pain of hell in all its dimensions, as it will

[20] See chapter 8, pp. 150–161.

be experienced eventually by the impenitent, was experienced by Jesus in his dying. He endured hell for us on the cross.

The nature of hell

What then *is* hell in the light of the cross? Here is the second area for concluding comment, the *nature of hell*. Three words come to mind.

First, hell is *darkness*. The three hours of darkness while Jesus hung on the cross are eloquent in this regard (Matt. 27:45). Darkness recurs in a number of the texts where hell is mentioned. There is notable Old Testament anticipation of this metaphor for judgment, including the 'darkness that can be felt' of the plague in Egypt (Exod. 10:21). Darkness is variously seen as the destiny of the wicked (cf. 1 Sam. 2:9; Job 18:18; Prov. 4:19). It is the fate of those who go down to the grave (Ps. 88:12; Eccles. 6:4). The coming Day of the Lord will be a day of darkness (Joel 2:2, 31; Amos 5:18, 20; Zeph. 1:15). Isaiah pictures those who turn from the Lord to spiritualist mediums and occult diviners as being 'thrust into utter darkness' (Is. 8:22).

The New Testament texts come most commonly from the lips of Jesus. 'The subjects of the kingdom [those assigned it but who have proved unworthy] will be thrown outside, into the darkness' (Matt. 8:12). The attendants of the king in the parable of the wedding banquet are instructed to deal with the guest who despised the king's invitation by appearing at the banquet without proper clothing: 'Throw him outside, into the darkness' (Matt. 22:13). The servant in the parable of the talents who hid his talent is to be punished with the judgment, 'Throw that worthless servant outside, into the darkness' (Matt. 25:30). Jesus issues his appeal as the one who will be 'lifted up' and warns his hearers of the solemn consequences of rejecting him. 'Walk while you have the light, before darkness overtakes you' (John 12:35). In his Acts 2 sermon Peter refers to the association of darkness with the final judgments of God (Acts 2:20). And there is reference to darkness in association with the future of the ungodly: 'Blackest darkness is reserved for them' (2 Pet. 2:17; Jude 1:13). In Revelation the anti-kingdom of the beast 'was plunged into darkness' (Rev. 16:10). This metaphor exposes the woeful superficiality of notions of hell which presume on its offering cheerful camaraderie and pleasurable diversions.

Second, hell is *terror*. There is a dimension of fearfulness and dismay associated with the cross which permeates the record of Jesus' death, all the more impressive in that the accounts are given in such an unadorned, almost unemotional manner. The reference in Matthew to an earthquake with its resultant rending of tombs, causing the centurion and all those who were with him, hardened soldiers to a man, to be terrified; Luke's reference to the 'mourning and wailing' of the women (Luke 23:27) and the concluding reaction, 'When all the people who had gathered to witness this sight saw what took place, they beat their breasts' (23:48); and John's detail of the piercing of Jesus' body with a spear (John 19:34), when added to the references to darkness and the terrible cry of dereliction, all add up to a sense of pervasive fear and deranging terror. Hell is not a place where anyone will find pleasure or comfort.

Third, hell is *exclusion*. The way Matthew draws attention to the increasing abandonment of Jesus was noted earlier. The final element, the abandonment reflected in the cry of dereliction, focuses this most profoundly.

This way of understanding hell has support from several comments of Jesus. 'Away from me, you evildoers!' (Matt. 7:23) comes in the context of final judgment. 'I don't know you or where you come from. Away from me, all you evildoers!' is his final word in the parable of the householder (Luke 13:25, 27). The foolish virgins in the parable of the virgins hear a similar awful word, 'I tell you the truth, I don't know you' (Matt. 25:12). In the same chapter, those on the left hand in the vision of the end hear the King say, 'Depart from me, you who are cursed . . .' (Matt. 25:41). Paul speaks similarly of those who 'do not know God . . . They shall suffer the punishment of eternal destruction and exclusion from the presence of the Lord' (2 Thess. 1:9 RSV). Romans 9:3 has also been noted in this connection: 'I could wish . . . myself . . . accursed and cut off from Christ for the sake of my brethren.' Cranfield comments on these words, 'Nothing less than the eschatological sentence of exclusion from Christ's presence is involved.'[21]

For many interpreters this is the nearest we can come to a definitive description of hell. C. S. Lewis identifies three basic images which give some sense of meaning to hell – punishment, destruction, and exclusion.[22] The third of these, exclusion, is focused in Jesus' terrible cry – although, as we saw earlier, the exclusion motif cannot be finally separated from the punishment aspect. The horror of the separation lies in its being the experienced form of the divine antipathy which is God's holy wrath. K. S. Harmon, in noting this emphasis, cites Donne: 'When all is done, the hell of hells, the torment of torments is the everlasting absence of God, and the everlasting impossibility of returning to his presence . . . to fall out of the hands

---

[21] Cranfield, *The Epistle to the Romans*, vol. 2, p. 458; cited K. S. Harmon, 'The Case Against Conditionalism', in *Universalism and the Doctrine of Hell*, ed. M. de S. Cameron (Paternoster, 1991), p. 219.
[22] C. S. Lewis, *The Problem of Pain* (Macmillan, 1962), pp. 120–126.

of the living God is a horror beyond our expression, beyond our imagination.'[23]

Alone, for ever

The cry of Jesus reverberates for us still. Even if the experience of being eternally excluded from God's presence is what the lost have themselves chosen as the outworking of a self-centred life, the prospect remains a terrible one. To be utterly left alone, to have that ultimate freedom for which we have struggled through life conferred upon us for ever, to know that the God who made us in love and for love, and who in incredible mercy has given himself on our behalf, has now finally withdrawn from us, to know that we are the God-forsaken for ever more – that is surely, as Donne claimed, 'the hell of hells'.

Yet it is only too true and only too real, and the cross more than any other alleged 'hell' of human experience presents it to our consciousness. *That* was 'hell on earth', when Jesus died. It is the supreme argument for escaping it, but in the wonderful, unending mercy of God it is also the only, and yet eternally sufficient, means to that escape. He bore hell for us all.

Summary

In the death of Jesus we have a direct space-time encounter with hell. His self-substitution for us on the cross meant his taking on our behalf all the consequences of our sins. That necessarily implies that the cross included the experience of hell. Since death is the final 'wages of sin', it was in his dying that he experienced hell. The essence of that experience is disclosed in his cry of dereliction, 'My God, my God, why have you forsaken me?' Hell is revealed as abandonment by God.

---

[23] *Sermons IV*, 86, cited K. S. Harmon, 'The Case Against Conditionalism', in *Universalism and the Doctrine of Hell*, p. 220.

John 20:1–31; 21:1–25
11. Encountering heaven: the risen Jesus

> When Christ left the grave, it was not merely an announcement that there is a hereafter and a life beyond – which in any case the apostles knew already; it was the shattering of history by a creative act of God . . . When Paul met the risen Christ on the Damascus road, the blinding thing about the encounter – it literally blinded him for three days – was that in that moment he looked face to face, without any veil between, upon the eternal purpose of God.
>
> (James S. Stewart, *A Faith to Proclaim*)

In the last chapter we considered the implications of the fact that hell was once 'on earth'. In this chapter we will conduct a similar investigation as far as heaven is concerned. It too has appeared among us! In the resurrection of Jesus and his ministry among the disciples during the forty days between the resurrection and ascension, we are in touch with 'heaven on earth' in a very real sense (Acts 1:3). As with all our anticipations of heaven, not every question we have can be answered even from our chosen source. Many of them can, however, and we will see how far the evidence takes us.

The resurrection of Jesus and the life of heaven can be linked in two general ways. First, the reality of Jesus' conquest of death secures the prospect of life after death. It establishes the veracity of our heavenly hope. Second, the ministry of the risen Jesus during the forty days prior to his ascension throws important light on the nature of the heavenly life.

1. The fact of heaven

The resurrection did not take place in a vacuum. It happened within a specific nation at a particular stage of their national and religious development. We need to start, therefore, by setting the resurrection of Jesus against the background of first-century Jewish beliefs about such a happening. When we consider this context we discover that the link to the life of heaven is actually *fundamental to the very notion of resurrection*. In other words, for the first-century Jew, resurrection meant nothing less than that heaven had already arrived.

Your kingdom come

Jewish expectation in the time of Jesus was centred on the hope of the coming of the kingdom of God, as we observed in chapter 6. This hope had roots reaching back into the Old Testament. 'The faith of the Old Testament rests upon two certainties, equally profound and indissolubly bound together. The first is that God has come in the past and . . . intervened in favour of his people. The other . . . is the hope that God will come anew in the future.'[1] This hope of God's future action, whether in the canonical writings or in the literature of the apocalyptists, was in essence the expectation that he would break decisively into history and inaugurate a new order, the kingdom of God. The instrument of this intervention was the Anointed One, the promised Messiah. For Judaism, conviction about the resurrection of the dead thus lay within this larger prospect of national and, indeed, cosmic resurrection whereby all things would experience the renewing touch of the appearing God.

Easter surprise

Against that background, Jesus' resurrection was in a real sense an anomaly. We could in effect apply to Jesus the words used by Paul of his personal, post-resurrection encounter with Jesus, 'as to one abnormally born' (1 Cor. 15:8). 'Resurrection' for Jews meant two things necessarily – a physical grave-emptying event, and the dawn *in its fullness* of the endless era of the kingdom. Resurrection would therefore only happen at the end of all things and the beginning of a newly constituted heaven and earth. What they were not prepared for – and the emergence of this conviction among the disciples, Jews

[1] G. Pidoux, cited G. R. Beasley-Murray, *Jesus and the Kingdom of God* (Eerdmans, 1986), p. 3.

to a man, is all the more impressive on this account – was an authentic grave-emptying resurrection *before the coming of the end.*

Historically speaking this context needs to be retained, and hence the resurrection needs to be understood from this perspective – as the space-time appearance of that which will finally consummate and renew history. It is the future in the present, the end in the here and now.

> The resurrection of Jesus . . . has to be understood as *the* eschatological event pure and simple. The reality of the resurrection is already the eschaton, and does not merely have a relation to it. All the Last Things have their ground in the Risen Christ and are bound up with him. That is why the resurrection is the ground of the Christian hope of eternal life and of our knowledge of the consummation of the world.[2]

Putting it at its simplest, the resurrection of Jesus *is* heaven on earth!

So much for the resurrection within its first-century setting. The link between the resurrection and heaven can also be made at a more general, universal level. Considered as a space-time happening, it answers definitively for all peoples and for all times the elemental human question of whether there is life after death.

Someone has come back

In the course of discussions of this question over the years, I have not infrequently been faced with the observation that, since no-one has ever come back from the other side of death to tell us, we can never really know what lies there. But the Easter happening demonstrates that this is precisely the truth of it – someone *has* come back! Jesus, who beyond any reasonable doubt died on the cross on Good Friday, was radiantly alive on Easter Sunday.

The resurrection of Jesus is much more than a conclusive argument for life after death, but it is also that. If Jesus rose from the dead, then there is no room for doubt that death is not the end of our journey. If Jesus truly rose, then there is for every person a heaven to embrace and a hell to shun.[3]

---

[2] W. Kunneth, *The Theology of the Resurrection* (SCM, 1965), p. 242.

[3] We can identify with the observation of C. E. M. Joad, when noting that if he were allowed to interview any personage from the past he would wish to speak to Jesus of Nazareth, and put to him 'the most important question in the world, "Did you or did you not rise from the dead?"'; cited M. Green, *The Day Death Died* (IVP, 1982), p. 15.

This is Christianity!

In drawing this conclusion, it is to be noted that the resurrection of Jesus is not a peripheral truth as far as the Christian faith is concerned. In a real sense, the faith which meets us in the pages of the New Testament is resurrection faith. James Denney asserts with justice that the resurrection and subsequent exaltation of Jesus is 'the first, and last, and dominating element in the Christian conscious of the New Testament'.[4] In similar vein James Stewart asks, 'What is the most characteristic word of the Christian religion?' He answers himself, 'resurrection'.[5] Historically speaking, when every account is taken of the impact of the personality of Jesus, every allowance made for the depth, insight and novelty of his teaching, and every possible force attributed to the power and pathos of his love, had his crucifixion been the ending of Jesus, there simply would have been no Christian church rising phoenix-like out of the ashes of his death to carry his message to the ends of the earth, and to such effect that two thousand years afterwards a third of the world is prepared to acknowledge his truth and profess some degree of allegiance to him. In a real sense, the resurrection is what created Christianity.

John's account

John, representing all four evangelists, shares his account of it in the final two chapters of his Gospel. It begins with the discovery of the empty tomb (20:1–9). Mary Magdalene is the first to stumble on it as she goes with the other women (cf. the 'we' in v. 2) to visit the tomb. Peter and John are then alerted and confirm her report (vv. 3–8). In the case of John, the tomb itself and the orderliness of its contents are sufficient to lead him to the conclusion that Jesus had risen. 'He saw and believed' (v. 8), a realization which is soon shared by Mary as she is afforded the incredible privilege of a personal meeting with the one she first mistakes for the gardener – 'Rabboni!' (vv. 10–16).

Soon all the apostles are engulfed in it as Jesus appears among them that Easter evening (vv. 19–23), experiencing the 'overjoy' of it all (v. 20), and receiving Jesus' solemn commission and a promise of the means for its fulfilment (vv. 21–23). Thomas has missed out on this meeting, but for him too Jesus appears (vv. 24–29). 'Put your finger here; see my hands. Reach out your hand and put it into my side. Stop doubting and believe.' His words evoke Thomas's timeless response, 'My Lord and my God!' (v. 28).

[4] James Denney, *Studies in Theology* (Hodder and Stoughton, 1904), p. 49.
[5] J. S. Stewart, *Heralds of God* (Hodder and Stoughton, 1946), p. 87.

192

Then in Galilee a further encounter follows, as a repeated miracle of an astonishing catch of fish reveals his presence (21:1–14) and leads to a public reinstatement of Peter and his recommissioning for ministry (vv. 15–17). The account ends with a prophecy concerning Peter's and John's future service, and a reference finally to Jesus' return in glory (vv. 18–23).

So, for John, as for the others, the story of Jesus goes on after Calvary. He has risen from the dead. He belongs to all time and all ages.

'Beyond the sunset'

For us, as for John, that means life after death. Paul uses a vivid metaphor in 1 Corinthians 15:20, 'Christ has indeed been raised from the dead, the firstfruits of those who have fallen asleep.' The dead of the ages are like seeds fallen into the earth, hidden from view and silent beneath the soil of human mortality and corruptibility. In rising from that same levelled soil, Christ is the first seed to burst through the surface into new life and visibility. In that emergence is the promise and proof of the coming harvest, when 'all who are in their graves will hear his voice and come out' (John 5:28). Someone has come back! To use Victor Hugo's image, 'The grave is not a one way street; it is a thoroughfare.'

For centuries in Europe, people debated the question as to whether there was a land beyond the western horizon, beyond the sunset. Some said there was, others expressed their doubts. Then one day Columbus and his men sailed out from Europe across the vast Atlantic Ocean and into the sunset. They discovered the land of the Americas. When they returned, they could say, 'There *is* a land out there beyond the sunset – we've been there, and we know!'

In the same way, for generations people have debated the question of life after death. Some have said, 'Yes, there is a life beyond the grave.' Others have denied it, 'No, there isn't.' Then one day Jesus sailed out into that 'undiscovered country', and he came back, and in coming back still says to us, in Isaac Watts' verse:

> There is a land of pure delight
> Where saints immortal reign;
> Infinite day excludes the night,
> And pleasures banish pain!

'There *is* a heaven after death. I've been there, and I know!'

2. The form of heaven

The resurrection of Jesus differs in important respects from the full glory to be inaugurated at his return. Hence it represents 'heaven on earth' in an attenuated form. Nonetheless, there are significant points of identity which enable us to use the New Testament accounts of his post-Easter ministry as significant pointers to life in the heavenly era.

What, then, may be deduced from it as far as the heavenly life is concerned?

a. Heavenly life is personal life

The Jesus we meet after the resurrection is clearly the same person as the figure met in the Gospel records prior to his resurrection. The Jesus whose words and deeds are recorded in John 1 – 19 is the same one met in John 20 – 21. John conveys that by referring to Jesus showing the disciples 'his hands and his side' (20:20). The man who had hung upon the cross at the conclusion of his years of association with them is the one who now stands before them. Luke makes the same point more directly by citing Jesus' words, 'It is I myself!' (Luke 24:39).

This continuity of Jesus' personhood is also expressed in the moving encounters with individuals after the resurrection, which John sensitively records – Mary (20:10–18), Thomas (20:24–29) and Peter (21:15–22). In each case Jesus draws upon his previous knowledge of them, in Mary's case with the deeply moving recitation of her name, 'Mary!' (20:16), reflecting a relationship of profoundest mutual understanding and awareness. In Thomas's case Jesus recites back to him his very conditions for belief, 'Put your finger here . . .' (20:27), evoking Thomas's 'My Lord and my God!', the personal 'my' surely reflecting an assured confidence that the one before him is no other than the Jesus he knew and followed during his years as a disciple. With Peter the exchange is based upon the validity of John's exclamation in 21:7, 'It is the Lord!' – this is the Jesus we have followed through the years. The interaction in 21:15–17 draws directly on Peter's earlier pledge of loyalty, and hence is only coherent in terms of the continuity in Jesus' person, as is the call to Peter to love Jesus and Peter's heartfelt comment, 'You know all things; you know that I love you' (21:17).

We can therefore conclude with conviction that life in the heavenly world will preserve personal identity. There will be continuity of our personhood. We can banish all fear of being absorbed into the 'All' which Buddhism holds before us, or reincarnated in some other life form as in the post-mortem prospect of Hinduism. Both of these visions are mistaken, and promise so much less than what awaits us in the biblical vision. The self with which we were endowed by the Creator in his gift of life to us, the self whose worth was secured for ever in the self-substitution of God for us on the cross, *that self* will endure into eternity. We ourselves, and not another, are destined to behold the face of God and share the life of heaven. Death cannot destroy us. Our personhood is immortal. By God's faithful grace we shall endure eternally.

b. Heavenly life is Christ-centred life

This second feature is arguably the most significant. The dominating theme in these final two chapters of John is the significance of the resurrection for *Jesus himself.*

Thus in 20:17 the discovery of the resurrected Jesus by Mary Magdalene is not the stopping point for the narrative. In a sense, Mary wants to make it so by 'holding on' to Jesus (v. 17). He gently but firmly resists her attempt to detain him, and directs her to his further progression as he 'returns to the Father'. Similarly, in the upper room appearance in 20:19–23, while the joy of the disciples at meeting him is not overlooked (v. 20), the focus is again on Jesus himself as he directs them towards the mission they are to pursue at his command, a mission patterned on the sending of the Son by the Father, and hence a mission in which the sender (Jesus) is the central reality. It is the mission of Jesus through them. For its pursuance they are assured of the gift of the Spirit with its authoritative and redemptive implications. The appearance to the disciples when Thomas is present follows (vv. 24–29), climaxing in the great Christological confession, 'My Lord and my God!' (v. 28). The final section in 21:1–22 centres on the mission of Jesus and unfolds its further features – the basic reliance on Jesus which fruitful work requires (vv. 1–14); the repentance and personal love-commitment to Jesus which alone qualifies for leadership in his mission (vv. 15–17); the care and nurture which his mission will necessitate (vv. 15–17); the price which service for Jesus may demand (vv. 16–19); and the partnership which mission for Christ will involve (vv. 20–22). Appropriately the section, and the Gospel, concludes with a clear reference to Jesus' return (vv. 22–24) and a summarizing reference to the inexhaustible riches of his person and work (v. 25).

The other Gospels are no differently centred in their record of the post-resurrection ministry of Jesus. In Matthew we have the great Christological declaration of 28:18, 'All authority in heaven and on earth has been given to me', followed by the 'great commission',

'Therefore go . . .', culminating in the declaration, 'I am with you always, to the very end of the age' (28:20), implying his presidency over the mission and its culmination in his glorious reappearing at 'the end'.

Mark's account involves some difficult textual issues, but at the very least there is the great Christ-centred Easter announcement, 'You are looking for Jesus the Nazarene, who was crucified. He has risen!' (16:6). Verses 9–20 may reflect later first-century witness, but significantly the focus is consistently on Jesus and his mission, 'Go into all the world and preach the good news to all creation' (16:15), followed by a reference to Jesus being 'taken up into heaven' and enthroned in the place of supreme authority 'at the right hand of God', while the mission proceeds and 'the Lord worked with them', confirming his word by the 'signs that accompanied it' (16:19–20).

Luke describes Jesus' post-resurrection ministry in 24:13–53, giving special prominence to the way he 'explained to them what was said in all the Scriptures concerning himself' (24:27; cf. 24:44), with again the proclamation of the mission of Jesus, its divine resourcing (vv. 47–49) and Jesus' ascension to glory (vv. 50–52). Nor should we overlook Luke's further account of the ministry of the risen Lord in Acts 1:1–11, a ministry focused on his bringing the disciples absolute proof of his resurrection triumph and completing his teaching 'about the kingdom of God', which would certainly have contained references to his glorious return when the kingdom would have been consummated. The confirmation of that occurs in the subsequent, consistently Christ-centred preaching of the apostles (Acts 2:22–36; 3:13–36; 4:9–12). The Acts description concludes, in accord with the Gospel accounts, with the mission of Jesus pursued in the divine enablement of the Holy Spirit (v. 8), and his ascension (vv. 9–11).

The point is almost too obvious to need stating. *The revelation of the life of heaven given in the risen life of Jesus is of a life centred on the service and glory of the Risen One.*

Not surprisingly, the glimpses of the heavenly order afforded in the book of Revelation have the exultant hosts contemplating the 'Lamb, looking as if it had been slain', 'the Lion of the tribe of Judah, the Root of David', and bursting into praise: 'Worthy is the Lamb' and, more fully, 'To him who sits on the throne and to the Lamb be praise and honour and glory and power, for ever and ever!' (Rev. 5:5–6, 12, 13)

Nor need we eliminate the dimension of mission. The hints of a further world of service are not to be overlooked (cf. Matt. 25:21, 23; Rev. 22:3). Who may guess what further experiences of mission await in the new order? The glories of Jesus' person, the celebration of his work and, as he sends us, the further exploits in his service – these, we may confidently anticipate, will be the centre and all-absorbing concerns of the heavenly life.

c. The heavenly life is a liberated life

The Jesus who meets us in the Gospel records of his earthly life is pre-eminently the liberated human. His is freedom from the bondage of sin, from the promptings of the inner fallen nature, from the memory of past failures and present guilts. He is liberated also from the limits of fallen understanding, and from the errors and confusions which flow from it. His is freedom from the intransigence of physical forces such as disease and death, or waves and winds. His is freedom from an ignorance of God and his purposes. His is freedom from the incapacity or unwillingness to love without limit, from the desire to cling to life rather than surrender it at love's demand. No wonder that at the heart of his preaching was the offer of freedom to those who came to him.

In the glimpses afforded of his life beyond resurrection we find those freedoms even further enhanced. At the physical level he can appear, disappear and then reappear at will;[6] at the moral and spiritual level there is a freedom from the awful burden of responsibility for the completion of his mission; at the relational level there is a new freedom to indwell and personally identify with all who belong to him. Such is the promise of the heavenly life – an existence of boundless freedoms.

Some of the heavenly freedoms will be ones that Jesus never required – the freedom from a fallen nature, and freedom from the guilt of sin. But we too can anticipate, on the model of Jesus' post-resurrection ministry, a new openness to the 'material' world with new possibilities of its energies and forces being open to our direction. Implicit in that lies a new harmony and partnership, such as Paul referred to in Romans 8:21, with a natual order liberated from 'its bondage to decay'. On the basis of the Gospels' evidence we can also anticipate wonderful new possibilities in mutual relationships, as we are set free to love as never before. Freedom awaits, and beckons. Like Martin Luther King Junior, in the words etched on his gravestone, we will be 'Free at Last!'

d. The heavenly life will be an embodied life

We confront here the fact which all the evangelists are careful to stress, that the tomb of Jesus was emptied by his resurrection. As we

---

[6] Cf. John 20:19, 26; Luke 24:15, 31, 36, 51.

noted above, no Jew would have embraced a claim to authentic resurrection which did not involve that. Since the Creator God had placed his stamp upon the material world as surely as upon the transcendent spiritual order ('In the beginning God created the heavens and the earth' [Gen. 1:1]), the only kind of resurrection which would represent a true victory over fallenness would be one in which physical as well as spiritual processes of dissolution were overcome.

The physicality of the resurrection is emphasized by Jesus himself in his drawing attention to the wounds still visible in his body and even, in Luke's account, in his sharing a meal with the disciples. They must grasp that this is not a matter of a 'spirit appearance', but the utterly unprecedented, unique, world-transforming, heaven-anticipating, sovereign action of the Creator in the first instalment of remaking the world. That was what happened at Easter, and the embodied nature of the Risen One is critical to its reality.

Accordingly, we need to banish from our minds anticipations of heaven in terms of a 'spiritual' order 'away beyond the blue'. The Bible's final promise in both Testaments is of a 'new heaven *and earth*' (Is. 65:17; 66:22; 2 Pet. 3:1f.; Rev. 21:1, 5). The essential movement at the end is accordingly not so much a 'taking up' into the heavens above but a 'coming down' of the glorified Son of Man, who will be viewed as 'coming', i.e. 'coming to us'. In Revelation 21:2 the New Jerusalem, the eternal home of the saints, is seen as 'coming down out of heaven from God'. Thus the prospect is of new bodies (not no-bodies!). The Jesus who says, 'Touch me and see; a ghost does not have flesh and bones, as you see I have' (Luke 24:39); who 'showed them his hands and his side' (John 20:20); who said, 'Put your finger here; see my hands. Reach out your hand and put it into my side' (John 20:27) – this is the Jesus who draws back the curtain on the heavenly life and shows us what it will be like: embodied!

True, there will be difference as well as sameness, discontinuity as well as continuity – thankfully and necessarily so. For sin is no more, and hence all the destructive and limiting powers of sin and its attendant physical corruption are also 'no more'. But we will rise to a new life *in the body*.

e. The heavenly life is a communal life

One of the clearest features of Jesus' activity in the records of his ministry after Easter is his solicitous care for his disciples. Gathering them in a group, he spends such time with them as they need to become utterly persuaded of the truth of his resurrection (Acts 1:2), to arrive at a fuller understanding of the kingdom of God (1:3), and to become conscious of the massive task he has for them to perform (1:4–8).

It is perhaps his ministry to the individual, however, which is so indicative of the 'heavenly communality'. His interactions with Mary Magdalene (John 20:10–18), Thomas (20:24–29) and Peter (21:15–22) are replete with such profound understanding, sensitivity and loving concern that one is almost drawn to argue that the experience of the cross brought Jesus even closer to those whom he had drawn to himself over the years of his public ministry. If that is to overstate it, then at least we may note the astonishing degree and depth of his mutual care and commitment. What foretastes of heaven this holds out! There, as this modelling of Jesus indicates so enticingly, we shall love one another as never before, and shall enjoy in that heavenly world the righteousness of true, pure, committed relationships of absolute love for every one. What a prospect! How desirable heaven is.

f. The heavenly life is a fulfilled life

'Peace', Jesus' first word of greeting in the upper room on Easter evening (John 20:19), gathers up so much that is significant. Behind that word lies the great Hebrew term *Shalom,* which means wholeness, or completeness, and embraces the blessings of righteousness, justice, joy, peace – indeed, everything good at the hand of God. *Shalom* implies spiritual perfection, and the complete fulfilment of our lives as the creatures and children of the triune God. It is a promise that all the potential of our lives here will at last be released, and we will become through God's renewing grace all that we were eternally intended to be. That is heaven.

Through these forty unique days the life of heaven was experienced in our world, teaching us to anticipate the eruption within the terms of this world of the life given by the Creator at the beginning, reborn and renewed, and finding glorious release in a new heaven and earth.

The presence of the Risen One is the proof that this is no wishful thinking on our part, no idle dream or escapist projection. God reigns. All things are from him. He has come in Jesus; he will come again in Jesus. At his coming the glory of heaven will break in upon us. Heaven is coming, and it is as certain as the empty tomb of the Lord.

Summary

The life of Jesus during the forty days after his resurrection, as he came and went among the disciples, is a real expression of the life of heaven within earthly parameters. Accordingly, we can derive from it authentic impressions of heaven. Among other things, heaven is shown to be:

- a personal life in which our individual identity will be preserved;
- a Christ-centred life focused on the blessed person of the Lord himself;
- a life of new and glorious freedoms;
- an embodied life with a continued, albeit renewed, tangibility;
- a communal life lived in perfect love with 'all the saints';
- a fulfilled life in which all our potential will find complete and satisfying expression.

Part Three
Destiny declared: heaven and hell in the rest of the New Testament

Acts 17:22–34
12. An unpopular perspective

> Go on dear friends, but an inch of time remains, and then the
> eternal ages roll on forever; but an inch in which we may stand and
> proclaim the way of salvation to a perishing world.
>
> (Robert Murray McCheyne)

This third and final part will focus principally on heaven and hell in
the apostolic writings. We precede that, however, with a fascinating
glimpse of the first Christian generation bearing its witness to these
very realities. This historical interlude is entirely appropriate, since
the issue of human destiny can never be merely abstract or theoretical. These are deeply personal issues which are raised for specific
people in specific historical contexts.

Two worlds in collision

The setting is the apostle Paul's visit to Athens. The date can be
accurately plotted – AD 50. Paul is in the course of his second mis-
sionary journey. What had begun as a follow-up to his first journey
– 'Let us go back and visit the brothers in all the towns where we
preached the word of the Lord and see how they are doing' (15:36)
– had, perhaps inevitably, developed a life of its own, as Paul was
directed by the Spirit into the unexplored field of Europe (cf. 16:9,
'Come over to Macedonia and help us'). Following the excitement,
and costliness, of the ministry in Philippi (16:11–40; cf. 1 Thess.
2:2), Paul, Silas and Timothy moved southwards into the adjoining
province of Achaia. Churches were planted at Thessalonica and
Berea (17:1–15). When things became too hot in Berea due to agi-
tators from Thessalonica (17:13), Paul was escorted on to Athens,
there to await his companions, who were presumably to follow

after making sure the seed sown in Berea had safely 'taken' (17:14–15).

From the perspective of the history of human culture, Paul's arrival in the city was both dramatic and portentous. Here was the encounter of two worlds. The Athens of the first century AD was in some senses a far cry from the glory of its prime in the fifth century BC, when the full flowering of its cultural life was to represent one of the building blocks of subsequent Western and, indeed, global civilization. While much of that former grandeur had dissipated, Athens remained in many senses the intellectual capital of the ancient world, and Paul, as a student and graduate of the not insignificant city of Tarsus, would no doubt have been well aware of Athens' history and stature.

However much Paul must have stirred with interest as he approached the city, he entered it not as a tourist but as an apostle of Jesus Christ. And so the ancient order of classical paganism and the new order of nascent Christianity came face to face. Although nothing of this significance would have been observed by the casual onlooker, Paul was bringing in his person ideas and convictions that within a few centuries would usurp the place of the pagan dynasties and usher in a new world of human experience, reflection and imagination. Here was a new order which would take its inspiration not from Athens but from Jerusalem, and from a crucified Judean carpenter rather than a Greek philosopher, poet or politician. In its meeting with Paul, however little it guessed the significance at that moment, ancient Athens was for the first time face to face with the world of tomorrow.

Zeal for your house

If Paul was impressed by the Athenian cultural legacy, that is not indicated in the text of Acts 17. What concerned him was the ubiquitous, 'in your face' idolatry of the city (v. 16). This 'greatly distressed' him. The Greek verb used here, *paroxynō*, has associations with deep feelings including anger. So he was 'outraged' (REB), 'revolted' (NJB), 'provoked' (RSV). The sight of these multiple expressions of paganism, with their patent ignorance of the true God and the dishonour done by them to God's name, drove Paul to bear witness. The text records three distinct places where his witness was expressed, the Jewish synagogue, the forum or marketplace where debate was the staple diet (v. 17), and finally, at their invitation, before the elite intellectual club known as the Areopagus (vv. 18–19).

The content of the apostle's witness needs note, though it hardly surprises us. 'Paul was preaching the good news about Jesus and the resurrection' (v. 18). In other words, he was sharing the one message guaranteed to overthrow the pagan idolatry with its God-dishonouring pretensions and to enthrone the living God in the hearts and lives of the Athenians. In his presentation of this 'good news' in the Areopagus, Paul announced that God 'has set a day when he will judge the world with justice' (v. 31).

Before we take that proclamation of judgment any further, it is worth making note of Paul's audience. Luke's account notes the two primary schools represented, the Epicureans and the Stoics (v. 18).

The Epicureans, followers of Epicurus who had died in 270 BC, taught that the gods were remote from human affairs. The world and life within it were a matter of pure chance; there was no immortality and no judgment to come. The aim was therefore to enjoy life as far as possible without the shadows of pain, passion or fear. Paul may be reflecting a popular summation of the Epicurean view in 1 Corinthians 15:32 (citing Is. 22:13), 'Let us eat and drink [and enjoy ourselves as best we may], for tomorrow we die [and that will be the end of us].'

By contrast the Stoics, disciples of Zeno who had died in 265 BC, taught that there was a supreme god, the 'world's soul', who determined everything and acted in everything. Fate therefore reigned and life was best pursued by accepting it as it is, living according to nature, and developing indifference to both pleasure and pain.

With this background in mind, we move on to look more closely at Paul's words to the Athenians. His teaching on judgment has several aspects worthy of note.

1. The source of judgment: the nature of God

Paul is in no degree awed by the Athenians' philosophical traditions. Taking his point of contact from a local shrine, he accuses them of a fundamental and pervasive ignorance of God (v. 23). He then proceeds to educate them by expounding in their hearing the character and deeds of 'the true and living God'. Like the author of Genesis, the apostle recognizes that the issue of judgment can only be raised properly in the light of a clear and comprehensive understanding of God. Paul asserts no less than seventeen truths about God.

1. God is the Creator of all things: 'God . . . made the world and everything in it' (v. 24); 'We are his offspring' (v. 28), citing the pagan author Aratus.
2. God is the sustainer of all things: 'God . . . gives all men life and breath and everything else' (v. 25).

205

3. God is ruler over all things: 'God . . . is the Lord of heaven and earth' (v. 24).
4. God is a transcendent spirit: 'God . . . does not live in temples built by hands' (v. 24); 'we should not think that the divine being is like gold or silver or stone' (v. 29).
5. God is perfectly complete in himself: 'God . . . is not served by human hands, as if he needed anything' (v. 25).
6. God is a purposive and active God: 'from one man he made every nation . . . that they should inhabit the whole earth; and he determined the times set for them and the exact places where they should live' (v. 26).
7. God is a personal, relational being who seeks relationship with his creatures: 'God did this so that men would seek him and perhaps reach out for him' (v. 27).
8. God is immanent within the world: 'God . . . is not far from each one of us' (v. 27); 'in him we live and move and have our being' (v. 28), citing the pagan poet Epimenides.
9. God is our Father, in the sense that our life comes to us ultimately from him: 'We are his offspring' (v. 28).
10. God is a merciful being: 'In the past God overlooked such [idolatrous] ignorance' (v. 30).
11. God is a morally righteous being who calls all people to repent of wrong: 'God . . . commands all people everywhere to repent' (v. 30).
12. God is a God of justice: 'God . . . will judge the world with justice' (v. 31).
13. God's purpose in human history has reached its critical goal in the mission of Jesus Christ: 'God . . . now . . . commands all people everywhere to repent. For he has set a day when he will judge the world with justice by the man he has appointed' (v. 31).[1] The fact that Paul asserts this without providing the Old Testament justification (assuming that Luke's account is an accurate transcription of Paul's address) would be explicable on the grounds that his audience had no direct acquaintance with the Scriptures.
14. God has raised Jesus to life after his death: 'God . . . [raised] him from the dead' (v. 31).
15. God has already set a time when all people will be passed under judgment: 'God . . . has set a day when he will judge the world' (v. 31).

---

[1] 'Man' here is probably an allusion to the 'son of man' = 'man' = humanity, of Daniel 7:13, the one appointed as judge of all. Cf. W. Neill, *The Acts of the Apostles*, NCB (Oliphants, 1973), p. 192.

16. God will judge all people at that set time by Jesus Christ: 'God
    . . . will judge the world . . . by the man he has appointed' (v. 31).
17. God has provided a universal sign of his correspondingly univer-
    sal judgment by raising Jesus from the dead: 'God . . . has given
    proof of this to all men by raising him from the dead' (v. 31).

A crash course in theology

One cannot read this list without astonishment. What Paul gave the
Areopagus that day was nothing less than a crash course in basic
theology. In particular he taught them a comprehensive doctrine of
God. It is remarkably inclusive and expansive. It is, moreover, both
effectively related to the philosophical positions of his hearers and
yet utterly faithful to the revelation of God in the Old Testament
Scriptures. Virtually every basic attribute of God disclosed there is
either asserted or implied.[2] In a day when theology is routinely dismissed as an irrelevant preoccupation for Christian eggheads, it is
time to learn again from Paul. Paul's gospel is rooted in Paul's God.
And Paul's God is not an innocuous, virtually absent being, who
vaguely loves the world and is pleased about Jesus. Paul's God is the
overwhelmingly real and ever-present embodiment of every one of
the above list of attributes, and more besides.

Supremely, Paul's God is the presupposition of every single act
and attribute of Paul's Christ, and to ignore the former is in effect to
empty the latter of all true meaning. We need to be alert to the mistaken and mischievous notion, which is sometimes passed off as the
last word in orthodoxy, that to think long and hard about God in his
triune majesty and mystery is somehow detrimental to a rounded
and happy Christian experience.

The relevance of all this for Christian evangelism is powerfully
spelled out by John Stott:

> . . . all this [truth about God] is part of the gospel. Or at least it is
> the indispensable background to the gospel, without which the
> gospel cannot effectively be preached. Many people are rejecting
> our gospel today not because they perceive it to be false, but
> because they perceive it to be trivial. People are looking for an
> integrated world-view which makes sense of all their experience.
> We learn from Paul that we cannot preach the gospel of Jesus
> without the doctrine of God, or the cross without the creation, or
> salvation without judgment. Today's world needs a bigger gospel,

[2] Cf. C. S. C. Williams, *A Commentary on the Acts of the Apostles* (Black, 1964),
pp. 201–205.

the full gospel of Scripture, what Paul later in Ephesus was to call 'the whole purpose of God' (20:27).[3]

2. The sanctioning of judgment: the presence of God

'God . . . commands all people everywhere to repent' (v. 30). Paul does not hesitate to preach 'Jesus and the resurrection' to the philosophers of Athens, nor to call them to repentance, despite the fact that his sermon may in many cases have been the first time they had heard of the name and the saving work of Christ. This is because, as his sermon makes clear, Paul does not see the obligation laid upon the pagans of Athens to repent of their sins as in any degree mitigated by their ignorance of the coming of Jesus. Indeed, Paul clearly sees this same obligation laid upon the consciences of all people everywhere – 'he commands all people everywhere to repent'. That 'all people' means what it so clearly says, and hence specifically includes all the followers of every other religious tradition on the face of the earth. It is notable that Paul is not alone in this insistence. When addressing a Gentile audience in the home of the Roman Cornelius, Peter spoke of Jesus as 'the one whom God appointed as judge of the living and the dead' (Acts 10:42), words closely paralleling those of Paul here.

'Not without a testimony'

However unfashionable this truth may have become in our time, for Paul, as we will see more fully in the next chapter, people are not out of touch with God prior to hearing about his coming in Jesus. God is present for every human being; God addresses every human life. 'God . . . has not left himself without testimony', as Paul declared to another pagan congregation in Lystra (Acts 14:17). The Creator, who has made every person (17:24–25, 29), who sustains them every moment in life (vv. 25, 28), who sovereignly determines the context and conditions of their life (vv. 24, 26), who prompts them to seek after him (v. 27), and who in mercy stands ever ready to withhold judgment and overlook the lamentable response they make to his provisions, gifts and initiatives (v. 30), that same God holds all humanity accountable to him. Specifically, he calls all people to renounce their attempt to ignore and live without reference to him. Instead he invites them humbly to seek his mercy.

God's judgment at the last will be just, as Paul makes clear: 'he will judge the world with justice' (v. 31). Indeed, we may go further and

[3] J. R. W. Stott, *The Message of Acts* (IVP, 1990), p. 290.

assert that God's judgment at the end will be the one utterly fair and just judgment in all history, since it will be the judgment of the God who is the personification and eternal ground of all justice. That gives no grounds for complacency, however, especially when we recall that he has access to 'the thoughts and attitudes of the heart. Nothing in all creation is hidden from God's sight. Everything is uncovered and laid bare before the eyes of him to whom we must give account' (Heb. 4:12b–13). Among the 'thoughts and attitudes of the heart' are surely those intimations which come to every person of their creaturely dependence and moral obligation – which, if heeded, as we may surmise on the basis of Jesus' remark 'whoever has will be given more' (Matt. 13:12; 25:29, etc.), will grow to a greater clarity of understanding. Accordingly, as Paul argues here, it is this which represents a sufficient basis for God's universal summons to repentance.

Paul's call for repentance, which simply echoes the earlier preaching appeals of John the Baptist (Matt. 3:1–12), Jesus (Mark 1:14; Luke 13:1–5; Matt. 11:20–24) and Peter (Acts 2:37–39; 3:19), carries a further significant implication: that the response to the gospel which God seeks is always at root a moral response. It requires a new estimate of our past – a realization that it has been lived in contradiction to God's will for us, a decision to renounce that lifestyle, and a commitment to live henceforth in obedience to God.

3. The specificity of judgment: the day of God

'God . . . has set a day when he will judge the world' (v. 31). Not only is the coming judgment certain because of the demand for accountability inherent in all moral experience, but Paul goes so far as to assert that the time and circumstance are already determined. We not only know it will happen, we know when it will happen: on 'the God-set day'. We also know who will act as the Judge: 'the man he has appointed', the God-man Jesus Christ.

This truth is predicated on the truths about God which Paul has expounded previously – that God made everything and is Lord of heaven and earth (v. 24), that God determined the times set for the lives of men and women in his world (v. 26), and that 'he now commands all people everywhere to repent' (v. 30).

In the calendar of God

Thus God, as Lord of human life in all its aspects, is Lord over all lifespans, whether of individuals or civilizations. For him the end is as real as the beginning, and every moment between. We, by contrast, cannot alter the past nor determine the future. All we have any mastery of is the elusive present, which forever slips through our fingers and escapes our grasp. For us, therefore, the question of the end is one we can speculate about, dismiss, dread, or ignore. We can reflect on the delay in its arrival and conclude that it will never come. We can suppress God's witness to us and persuade ourselves that it is only a myth, or an empty threat conjured out of the Christian imagination to try to secure conformity to its standards. Such is our strange freedom, for the present. But God cannot do that; to do so would be to deny his own truth. The day is coming, every hour brings it closer. He has already chosen it. It stands before him now, as it has from the dawn of time. It is entered into every calendar in heaven. It is inevitable, unavoidable and sure.

Further, the Judge is already appointed. Jesus Christ will judge all people. How serious, therefore, to have resisted and rejected him in this life, or to have used his name only as an expletive, or to have persecuted his followers, or to have cared nothing for his teaching, or to have trodden his holy laws underfoot, or to have made no contribution to his work in the world, or never truly to have prayed in his name, or to have neglected our many opportunities for helping 'the least of these brothers of mine' (Matt. 25:40). For whether we relish the thought or not, he is already appointed. We will appear before him. He will be our judge. On that we have not been consulted.

4. The scope of judgment: the world of God

'He has set a day when he will judge the world.' There is no evasion of this summons. To every person there will come the call to appear. No excuses will prevail and no reasons for absence will be relevant. All will be there, every man, every woman, every child, every person without exception. 'People are destined once to die, and after that to face judgment' (Heb. 9:27 NIVI).

The resurrection of Jesus is the proof of all this, Paul argues (v. 31), on several grounds.

1. The resurrection proves the judgment because it demonstrates the fact of life after death. When we fall helplessly into the hands of God at the end of our lives, the God who has given us life will meet us and in that future order will hold us accountable for the use we have made of life here.
2. The resurrection proves the judgment because, by setting Jesus on the other side of death, it makes him a presence and a reality

when we pass into the eternal order. It therefore underscores the fact that 'we must all appear before the judgment seat of Christ' (2 Cor. 5:10). All of us, irrespective of our attitudes to him here, are going to encounter him there.

3. The resurrection proves the judgment because it authenticates Jesus' claim to be the Son of Man prophesied in Daniel 7:13 whose function it is to open the books and to render judgment at the end.

4. The resurrection proves the judgment because the universally public nature of the resurrection – 'he has given proof of this to all' (v. 31) – implies the universally public nature of the judgment to come.

5. The seriousness of judgment: our personal response to God

The nature of God has been stated; he is all of the things asserted by Paul, and more. The fact of his coming to us in Jesus Christ has been proclaimed, along with the triumphant significance of his resurrection. The solemn implications have been spelled out. Through Christ's coming, his death for us on the cross, and his resurrection from the dead, God invites us, no less than the bemused philosophers of Athens, to 'repent' (v. 30) and to 'reach out ... and find him' (v. 27). What response are we making? The text spells out the possibilities. There are three.

The first is to *dismiss* this message. 'Some of them sneered' (v. 32).[4] Some of them still do. In the end, of course, the laughter of those who sneeringly dismiss the gospel will be drowned out by the laughter of God himself as he comes in victory over all his enemies at the last. 'The One enthroned in heaven laughs; the Lord scoffs at them' (Ps. 2:4). God's amazing respect for the personal dignity of his creatures extends to the point of permitting their rejection of him. No greater mistake is imaginable, but we can make it, and then spend eternity with our regrets.

The second possible reaction to his gospel is to *defer*. 'We want to hear you again on this subject' (v. 32). This response is, of course, better than the first. Indeed, since only a tiny minority of people accept the gospel the first time they hear it, most people who become Christians spend some time in this second category. Jesus himself spoke about the need to count the cost of commitment before embarking upon it (Luke 14:25–33). So far as it goes, this is an acceptable response. It is critical, however, that this should represent

---

[4] Cf. 'burst out laughing' (NJB).

only a temporary stopping place. If we remain in this mind-set, then we will not escape the fate of those who took the first course. Good intentions alone will not save us if they do not lead on to good further action. Sooner or later, the third form of response must be embraced.

The third possibility is represented by those who *decide to believe*. They are described in the text as those who 'became followers . . . and believed' (v. 34). They are named in several cases, Dionysius, and Damaris (v. 34). That in itself is significant, for our response needs to become personal – *my own* personal 'believing' in 'the man God appointed', Jesus Christ as Lord and Saviour of *my life and destiny.*

The 'believing' has two preliminary steps which Paul specifies. The first step is to 'repent' (v. 30), to acknowledge our sin before God and renounce it. This is exactly what Paul's Master had called for in response to his own preaching (Mark 1:15; Luke 13:1–5). The second step is to 'reach out for him' (v. 27), to seek him and entrust ourselves to him as he has drawn near to us. That means finally committing ourselves to his Son Jesus Christ, by 'believing in the man appointed'.

The naming of those who responded has two other possibilities in application. One is the indication it gives that it is only at the moment of crowning Christ as Lord of our lives that we truly begin to be ourselves. Only as a man or woman 'in Christ' do we truly have a name and an identity. The other is that our response to the call of Christ in the gospel while here on earth has its counterpart in heaven – where our names are from that moment inscribed in the Lamb's 'book of life' (Rev. 3:5; 20:12; 21:27) and written on the heart of God (cf. Is. 49:16).

If we do 'decide to believe', we are given the wonderful assurance by the Judge himself that on that appointed day he will 'acknowledge [your] name before my Father' (Rev. 3:5).

Summary

Paul's preaching at Athens is a fascinating cameo of early Christian witness. Notably, in the sophisticated setting of the Athenian Areopagus, he proclaimed God's future judgment. He rooted the fact of judgment in the character of God. He argued for its propriety on the grounds of God's presence in every human life. He announced that the time of God's future judgment is already determined, as is the identity of the Judge – Jesus Christ. He claimed the judgment to be universal in its scope. He called for the only proper response to this prospect – repentance and faith.

Romans 1:18 – 2:11
13. The revealing of wrath

Abandon Every Hope, Who Enter Here.
(Dante Alighieri, *The Divine Comedy*)[1]

In turning to the New Testament letters for their contribution to understanding human destiny we begin, appropriately, with the letter which more than any other has shaped Christian thought over the centuries, Paul's letter to the Romans. Calvin's often quoted comment, 'When anyone understands this epistle he has a passage opened for him to the understanding of the whole Scriptures', is as valid for our understanding of heaven and hell as for any other branch of Christian truth.

We will examine two sections, the first relating to hell (1:18 – 2:11), and the second (in the next chapter) to heaven (8:16–39).

Reasons for Romans

Although the 'reasons for Romans'[2] have stirred considerable discussion in recent years, the circumstances behind this letter are widely agreed upon, and are indeed indicated in the text.

First, Paul was about to launch a new phase of his apostolic ministry. As a result of ten years of strenuous, indefatigable labour, he was able to make the astonishing claim, 'From Jerusalem all the way

---

[1] 'Inferno', canto III, inscription above the gateway to hell, tr. H. Allen Mandelbaum.

[2] The phrase is the title of a monograph by A. J. M. Wedderburn (T. and T. Clark), 1988. For other contributions see J. A. T. Robinson, *Wrestling with Romans* (SCM, 1979); Wm. S. Campbell, *Paul's Gospel in an Intercultural Context. Jew and Gentile in the Letter to the Romans* (Peter Lang, 1991); E. P. Saunders, *Paul and Palestinian Judaism* (SCM, 1977); J. R. W. Stott, *Romans: Good News for God's World* (IVP, 1994), pp. 26–36.

around to Illyricum [the Roman province on the eastern shore of the Adriatic Sea] I have fully proclaimed the gospel of Christ' (15:19). Paul is not finished, however, since his commission was to the entire Gentile world (Acts 9:15; 22:21; 26:1). Accordingly, once he has made a further journey to Jerusalem to deliver the fruits of the 'contribution for the poor among the saints in Jerusalem' (15:26), his ambitions lie westwards to the unevangelized field of Spain (15:24).

It is likely that Paul saw the Roman church, which he had long hoped to visit (1:13), as affording a base for his new western Mediterranean ministry, rather as Antioch had done for his ministry in the eastern Mediterranean (cf. 15:24, 'I hope . . . to have you assist me on my journey'). The letter, which he commits to Phoebe who is journeying to Rome (16:1), spells out the full terms of his message so that the church in Rome can be fully acquainted with it, and by implication be made comfortable in the task of supporting him in his future labours to the west.

A second reason for the letter, which some recent interpreters suggest may have been the primary one, was to address the polarization which had arisen in the Roman congregation (or house congregations) between Christian-former-Gentiles and Christian-former-Jews, a concern reflected in the assertion which pervades the letter of the fundamental equality of Jews and Gentiles in Jesus Christ.

After his preliminary greetings and comments about his plans, Paul comes immediately to a great summarizing statement of the gospel, as the divinely originated means of the operation of 'the power of God for the salvation of everyone who believes: first for the Jew, then for the Gentile' (1:16). The gospel is the revelation of 'a righteousness from God . . . that is by faith from first to last' (1:17). In a series of majestic steps, he then proceeds to unpack the terms of this gospel.

The first step is to clarify the need of humanity in its sin; this is the 'bad news' to which the 'good news' (the gospel) comes. The goodness of the gospel message arises from its being a glorious solution to the problem posed by human sin. Only in terms of this antithesis can we truly appreciate the wonder of God's grace and the fullness, sufficiency and power of his salvation.

The peril of pluralism

Today's pluralistic instincts are inimical to antitheses. Since no single viewpoint is a final perspective, truth lies in the amalgam of diverse positions. Absolute contradictions are anathema. Thus the claim that good and evil, God and Satan, heaven and hell, God's righteousness and human godlessness, represent irreconcilable antitheses is seen as basic misunderstanding at best, and intolerant prejudice at worst. One of the widely followed gurus of our time, Deepak Chopra, captures the essence of the present mood with his slogan 'everything is good' – there are no ultimate contradictions; all roads, specifically the good and the evil, will finally arrive at the same destination. Paul begs to differ.

His primary conviction is contained in verse 18, 'The wrath of God is being revealed from heaven.' Four questions arise: What is meant by 'the wrath of God'? Against whom is this wrath directed? What is the cause of God's wrath? What has the wrath of God to do with hell?

1. What is meant by 'the wrath of God'?

God's wrath may be defined as 'the holy revulsion of God's being against all which is the contradiction of his holiness'.[3] God resists, as of necessity he must, all that stands opposed to his Godhead. He reacts to all such in that holy antipathy which expresses his eternal Lordship. In his faithfulness he is unalterably consistent with his revealed character. He embraces good and resists evil. To put this another way, he takes being God seriously. Indeed, as Brunner points out, it is this fact that gives life its seriousness: 'If God did not take himself seriously what else could be taken seriously?'[4] This perfect, settled, holy antipathy to all sin and evil is his wrath.

God's wrath is not, as is sometimes alleged, a crude piece of anthropomorphism. Nor is his wrath arbitrary, fitful, or subject to emotion, as our own is. It is eternally consistent and unchangeable. God's wrath is 'his holy hostility to evil, his refusal to condone it or come to terms with it, his just judgment upon it'.[5]

2. Against whom is this wrath directed?

God's wrath is directed against 'all the godlessness and wickedness of men [and women] who suppress the truth' (v. 18). At first sight God's wrath might be considered impersonal, directed not in the first instance against people but against their godless and wicked

[3] J. Murray, NBD, p. 1109.
[4] E. Brunner, *The Christian Doctrine of God* (Lutterworth, 1949), p. 161; cf. also L. Morris, *The Apostolic Preaching of the Cross* (Tyndale, 1955), pp. 174ff., 208ff.
[5] Stott, *Romans*, p. 72.

deeds. This distinction, however, is in the end somewhat formal, since the godless and wicked deeds are performed by moral agents, i.e. the men and women who commit them, and the judgment which these deeds evoke is necessarily directed against those who perpetrate them.

3. What is the cause of God's wrath?

In essence we have already answered this question. God is wrathful against human godlessness and wickedness. 'Godlessness' (*asebeia*) is the effective denial of God. Stott helpfully explains it as 'the attempt to get rid of God and, since that is impossible, the determination to live as though one had succeeded in doing so'.[6] Since the primary commandment is to love God (Matt. 22:37–38), or to acknowledge him alone as our God (Exod. 20:30), the greatest sin lies in denying him in the sense of dismissing him by living in conscious disregard of him. This brings God's wrath upon us.

'Wickedness' (*adikia*) relates to sin's assault upon God's will, upon his just ordering of the world and of human life. It is the disregard for God's law by the breaching of it. And since God's law is the expression of his nature, it is finally another form of human denial of, and resistance to, God. This also brings God's wrath upon us.

The argument throughout this section is predicated on the assumption of a particular series of relationships and the moral realities arising from them. In the following verses Paul stakes out that relational and moral 'grid' on the basis of which his initial assertion about God's wrath is both made sense of and justified.

Before expounding these truths with some thoroughness, we can posit and answer our fourth question.

4. What has the wrath of God to do with hell?

The answer is 'just about everything', for hell is simply the locational expression of God's wrath in post-mortem experience. Hell is the eternal form of God's wrath. The implication of this equation is a significant one, however, for the relating of hell to the divine wrath is a reminder that hell is not merely a negative reality, like the absence of God. It is true that the sense of separation from God is a terrible dimension of hell, as we saw earlier, and one with clear biblical warrant. But this separation is also a punitive and judicial separation.

[6] ibid., p. 72.

It is the express, personal judgment of God directed towards, and centred upon, the individual concerned. Hell is his just and personal judgment on those who in 'godlessness and wickedness' set themselves against him.

Brunner's definition of the divine wrath is therefore applicable directly to the experience of hell: 'the working out of the Divine Glory upon those who refuse to give Him glory; the working out of the Holiness of God against him who irreverently, godlessly, does not acknowledge Him'.[7]

All these truths about God's wrath are based upon certain theological and moral convictions which represent the framework of ideas within which the notion of the divine wrath has currency. It has five interlocking aspects – deity, responsibility, iniquity, antipathy and mercy.

a. Deity

God is the great central thread which runs through the letter to Romans, as through the entire Bible. Thus in the opening section of the letter Paul defines himself as 'set apart for the gospel of God' (1:1). His ministry is directed 'by God's will' (1:10). This gospel concerns 'the Son of God' (1:4), 'the power of God' (1:16) and 'the righteousness of God' (1:17), and reveals 'the wrath of God' (1:18). In later chapters, to give the merest indication, God is 'the God who gives life to the dead' (4:17), the God who 'in all things . . . works for the good of those who love him' (8:28), the God 'from [whom] and through [whom] and to [whom] are all things' (11:36), 'the only wise God [to whom] be glory for ever' (16:27). As begins the Bible, 'In the beginning God . . .' (Gen. 1:1), so begins the thought world of the apostle Paul: everything, literally everything everywhere and in all times, is predicated on the reality of God. He is the great elemental reality which underlies all other reality.

To God be the glory

One of the clearest and most impressive indicators of this God-centredness is Paul's habit of breaking into doxological outbursts in the course of his writing. In Romans he writes of 'the Creator – who is for ever praised. Amen' (1:25); and later he comments, 'Thanks be to God – through Jesus Christ our Lord!' (7:25); or again, 'Oh, the depth of the riches of the wisdom and knowledge of God! How unsearchable his judgments, and his paths beyond

---

[7] Brunner, *The Christian Doctrine of God*, p. 162.

tracing out . . . For from him and through him and to him are all things. To him be the glory for ever! Amen' (11:33, 36); or finally, 'Now to him who is able to establish you by my gospel and the proclamation of Jesus Christ . . . to the only wise God be glory for ever through Jesus Christ! Amen' (16:25, 27). Paul inhabits a world in which God is the ever-present, all-embracing and supremely praiseworthy reality.

For Paul this God is active rather than passive. He does things. Specifically, he creates: 'For since the creation of the world . . .' (1:20); 'the Creator – who is for ever praised' (1:25). There is a good case to be made that the Genesis account of creation and the fall is the unidentified 'text' underlying these verses.[8] God creates, and we exist as his creatures. He willed our being and called into existence the relational and physical framework within which we live. This implies that we are utterly dependent upon God and irreducibly responsible to him. Hence our reaction to God *can* be passed under judgment (1:20, 25; 2:15).

b. Responsibility

This represents for Paul the inevitable consequence of our creation. Since God has given us life, we are radically dependent upon him and accountable to him. So we are 'without excuse' (1:20), our 'consciences also bearing witness, [our] thoughts now accusing, now even defending' (2:15).

Not without witness

God has acted to make himself known. Paul writes, 'What may be known about God is plain to them, because God has made it plain to them' (1:19).

God's revealing of himself has reached humanity along several avenues. First, the creation itself points to God, specifically 'his eternal power and divine nature', which are 'clearly seen' (1:20). Second, there is the 'inward law' in the human conscience: 'The requirements of the law are written on their hearts, their consciences also bearing witness' (2:15). Paul is referring here to the distinction between right and wrong which is basic to human experience, along with the sense of responsibility towards doing right and refusing wrong. This activity of conscience is known both negatively, 'their thoughts now accusing', and on occasion positively, 'now even defending them' (2:15). Third, for the privileged people of Israel (2:17 – 3:8), there is the written law of God: 'They have been

---

[8] So Morna Hooker, 'Adam in Romans 1', in NTS 6, 1959–60.

entrusted with the very words of God' (3:2); 'you [Jews] are instructed by the law' (2:18) and even 'brag about the law' (2:23). For the apostle there is no such thing, strictly speaking, as a godless man or woman.

No godless people
However unpopular this perspective may be at the present time, it was clearly the view of Paul that God 'did not leave himself without witness' (Acts 14:17 RSV) and that he accordingly speaks to all people, irrespective of race, age, religious tradition or educational opportunity. The fact of the created world around us, the pressures and conflicts of conscience within us, and the written Scriptures when they are available to us, are all witnesses to God's being and nature.

Atheism is not viewed by Paul as a defensible stance. That people do deny God's existence would have been known to him, as it is to us. But the teaching of Romans 1:18–32 is that 'atheism' is finally only possible by consciously refusing God's self-revelation. Obviously the level of clarity in this witness varies with individuals and social contexts. Paul admits as much in his reference to the 'advantages' possessed by the Jews. This distinction echoes Jesus' recognition of different levels of opportunity and hence responsibility (Matt. 12:39–42; John 19:11). This passage in Romans does not require us to argue that God is equally clearly disclosed to all people, but simply that in some genuine degree he has not left himself 'without witness', and hence all people are accountable to God for their lives with reference to him.

Much still needs to be done by the church through its global witness to clarify and deepen this awareness of God. It is encouraging nonetheless to be able to record that, while of course allowance has to be made for factors such as geographical location and affordability, eight out of every ten people in the world today have access to the entire Bible in their own language, and nine out of ten have access to a New Testament.

Hence all the three forms of God's self-revelation noted by Paul in Romans 1:18 – 3:8 are relevant to a significant portion of the world's peoples. And of course, since 'the very words of God' now mean the New Testament as well as the Old, the revelation of God today commonly includes its supreme expression – Jesus Christ, 'God with us'.

God has spoken. God constantly speaks. In creation, conscience and Scripture God draws near to his creatures and summons them to acknowledge him by worshipping, obeying and serving him.

c. Iniquity

God has spoken – but humanity has refused to listen. God's witness has been 'plain' (1:19), 'clearly seen' (1:20), 'understood' (1:20), and 'known' (1:21). That truth about God is possessed by us is evidenced by our being described as having subsequently 'exchanged' it (1:25), i.e. given away what was, by implication, previously ours. In similar vein, it was a 'knowledge of God' that we did not 'retain' (1:28). It included the moral perception that 'those who do [wicked] things deserve death' (1:32), i.e. wrongdoing deserves and earns appropriate punishment.

Holding down the truth

This widespread human rejection of the revelation of God is described as 'suppression' (v. 18). The verb used here can also be rendered 'hold down', 'stifle',[9] or 'bury out of sight, obliterate from the memory'.[10] Paul's point is that, far from delighting in this revelation and hence in the God to whom it points with a view to loving, adoring and serving him, humanity consciously tries to eradicate it. Like the citizens in Jesus' parable, we hurl our defiance against the claim of God: 'We do not want this man to reign over us' (Luke 19:14 RSV).

Thus human ignorance of God is finally a wilful, deliberately chosen ignorance. We have become people with 'foolish, darkened hearts' (1:21) as far as knowing God is concerned. We have chosen the 'lie' (that there is no God, or at least no God who has any claim upon us) in place of the 'truth' that God is (1:25). We have dismissed the truth of God as 'not . . . worthwhile' (1:28), or 'not fitting' for us, in other words, not to our liking, not perceived as serving our interests. We have therefore forfeited such knowledge as we had received, particularly in the sphere of moral conduct (cf. 1:28, 'he gave them over to a depraved mind'). Paul's general conclusion on this basis is therefore irresistible: as sinners we are 'without excuse' (1:20).

d. Antipathy

'God cannot be mocked', Paul had written to the Galatians (Gal. 6:7). Here he spells out the terms of that divine reaction to human 'godlessness and wickedness' – his just wrath (1:18).

---

[9] Stott, *Romans*, p. 72.
[10] C. E. B. Cranfield, *The Epistle to the Romans*, vol. 1 (T. and T. Clark, 1975), p. 112.

God's wrath has several forms. It can be seen at work in the moral depravity of human nature. What began in the sphere of worship as a turning aside from the true God to the worship of idols became a debasement of their behaviour. 'Although they claimed to be wise, they became fools and exchanged the glory of the immortal God for images made to look like mortal man and birds and animals and reptiles' (1:22–23). Humanity must have a god, if not the true God then an idolatrous replacement. Thus the link between idolatry and immorality is clearly established. The truly fearful dimension of this, however, is that God is at work in this deterioration. Three times Paul sounds the terrible indictment, 'God gave them over in the sinful desires of their hearts to sexual impurity' (v. 24); 'God gave them over to shameful lusts' (v. 26); 'God . . . gave them over to a depraved mind, to do what ought not to be done' (v. 28).

'He gave them up'
This immorality, which is the result of God's 'giving up', finds expression in idolatrous acts in which unconditional service is rendered to the creaturely (v. 25). It is expressed in all homosexual and lesbian acts (vv. 26–27).[11] It is expressed in 'every kind of wickedness, evil, greed and depravity' (v. 29). God's wrath in this sense is not so much his active confrontation with evil as his non-confrontation. It is God withdrawing his restraining hand as far as the manifestations of evil in the human heart, and in human society, are concerned. In fearful judgment he allows evil its head, so that men and women may be brought face to face with their moral impotence and moved to repent and cry to God for his mercy.

It may be that we are given here some sense of one of the horrors of hell. 'Hell is a condition in which life is lived away from God

[11]The traditional understanding of vv. 26–27 as a condemnation of non-heteroexual genital liaisons has been challenged in recent times on two grounds: (1) that what Paul is actually condemning here is the use of boys in pederasty; and (2) that the group he is targeting are heterosexual people who are indulging in homosexuality and hence acting in a way that is 'unnatural' for them. People of homosexual instincts are claimed not to be in Paul's sights here since their homosexuality is, for them, 'natural'. The evidence for so reading these texts is lacking. R. B. Hayes has provided ample evidence that 'natural' and 'unnatural' were 'very frequently used . . . as a way of distinguishing between heterosexual and homosexual behaviour'; and further that the modern distinction between orientation and behaviour is 'to introduce a distinction entirely foreign to Paul's thought-world'. Cf. Richard B. Hayes, 'Relations Natural and Unnatural . . .' in JRE, Spring 1986, p. 192, cited Stott, *Romans*, pp. 77–78. We can also observe Dunn's comment. 'The condemnation of homosexuality here is a characteristic expression of Jewish antipathy towards the practice of homosexuality so prevalent in the Graeco-Roman world. Paul's attitude is unambiguous' (J. G. Dunn, *Romans* [Word, 1988], vol. 1, p. 72).

and all the restraints of God's holiness.'[12] In hell the 'giving up' is complete and evil is allowed unrestrained influence. This is not, of course, to eliminate the directly punitive aspect of hell (see below), however it is a salutary corrective to the much trumpeted 'delights' of escaping from God and the stultifying shackles of conscience. This secular utopia is no mere dream. It does exist; its name is hell.

Some have argued that Paul, in referring to 'God's wrath being revealed from heaven', also has in view the manifestation of his wrath in the cross. We have asserted earlier[13] that the death of Jesus was in very truth 'hell on earth'. Hence the claim that God's wrath was poured out in Jesus' death is a valid insight. It is in fact borne out by the whole 'propitiatory' (Gk. *hilasmos*) atonement category (cf. Rom. 3:25; 5:8–11; 2 Cor. 5:19; Heb. 9:5; 1 John 2:2; 4:9f., etc.). Whether Paul has the cross primarily in view in 1:18 is less certain, however. The phrase 'God's wrath being revealed' has appeared to most interpreters to refer to the revealing of his wrath in the moral decay of civil society which is spelled out in the following verses. If the cross *is* indeed in Paul's mind here, in anticipation of his clear reference to it in 3:25, 'God presented [Jesus Christ] as the one who would turn aside his wrath' (NIV, mg.; cf. also 5:9), then it affords on the one hand a further witness to the reality of the divine displeasure (sin can be pardoned only by being passed under judgment), and on the other the clearest possible witness to the unending love of God in the midst of his wrath ('God so loved the world that he gave his one and only Son').

The wrath to come
There is, however, another form of the divine wrath which is certainly in view in this section of Romans – God's *future* wrath. In Romans 2 Paul turns to those 'moralists' who do not identify with the behavioural corruption of Graeco-Roman society vividly portrayed in 1:18–32, but instead pass judgment on it from their higher moral vantage point.[14] 'You fail to see', says the apostle, 'that your "moral" lifestyle is entirely God's gift, intended to lead you to repent of those personal sins which you yourselves in different ways also

---

[12] D. M. Lloyd-Jones, *Romans, 'The Gospel of God'* (Banner of Truth, 1985), p. 392.

[13] See above, chapter 10.

[14] The precise identity of this group in Romans 2 has been much debated. The traditional view, that the Jews are in Paul's mind, has recently been upheld by Cranfield, *The Epistle to the Romans*, vol. 1, p. 137ff., and Dunn, *Romans*, p. 76f. Alternatively, they may be Gentile moralists, so Stott, *Romans*, p. 50f.; F. F. Bruce, *The Epistle of Paul to the Romans* (Tyndale, 1973), p. 82.

commit. If, as truly as the Gentile sinners, you fail to repent of these and seek God's mercy for yourselves, "you are storing up wrath against yourself for the day of God's wrath, when his righteous judgment will be revealed"' (2:5). On that day, for those who are self-seeking and who reject the truth and follow evil, 'there will be wrath and anger. There will be trouble and distress for every human being who does evil: first for the Jew, then for the Gentile' (2:8–9).

Paul has four further things to say concerning this divine antipathy against human sin expressed in the judgment to come.

First, *the basis of judgment* will be human behaviour. 'To those who by persistence in doing good seek glory, honour and immortality, he will give eternal life' (2:7). But 'for those who are self-seeking and who reject the truth and follow evil, there will be wrath and anger' (2:8). Or again, 'There will be trouble and distress for every human being who does evil' (2:9), and there will be 'glory, honour and peace for everyone who does good' (2:10).

Does this imply self-salvation? Hardly so, for to argue this would be to contradict Paul's whole presentation of the gospel in this letter: '[We] are justified freely by his grace through the redemption that came by Christ Jesus' (3:24); 'Therefore, since we have been justified through faith, we have peace with God through our Lord Jesus Christ, through whom we have gained access by faith into this grace in which we now stand' (5:1; cf. Rom. 10:8; 11:6).

What Paul is drawing upon in these references to the basis of judgment in 2:6–10 is the public nature of the coming judgment. 'God will judge men's secrets through Jesus Christ' (2:16). Our judgment will not be on the basis of what we may claim to be, but on the basis of what we *actually are*. Are we true Christians, those who have repented of our sins and trusted in what Christ did for us in his wrath-bearing sacrifice on the cross? If so, there will be evidence of that when our lives are scrutinized on the judgment day, evidence in terms of our goals ('glory, honour and immortality'), what Paul referred to in Colossians as 'the things above' (3:1).[15] There will also be evidence in terms of our behaviour: what we have done will be seen to include what is 'good' (2:10).

In interpreting this we should note that the alternative, in the case of those for whom there will be 'wrath and anger' at the judgment day, is 'self-seeking' (2:8). The 'good' which by contrast is proof of salvation will necessarily include unselfishness, the 'works of love' as Luther liked to call them, which, however we may bewail their

---

[15] Stott interprets these goals as '*glory* (the manifestation of God himself), *honour* (God's approval), *and immortality* (the unfading joy of his presence)' (Stott, ibid., p. 84).

limitations, are nonetheless a supreme evidence of the work of grace in our hearts. The flowers and fruits of grace grow only from the soil of grace. In the end we will find ourselves affirming in another phrase of Paul (taken somewhat out of context), 'All this is of God!'

The exposure in the case of those who will receive wrath on 'the day of God's wrath' (2:5) will reveal 'self-seeking' as their goal (2:18), and 'rejection of the truth [of God]' (cf. 1:25) and 'evil-doing' as their actions (2:9). Behaviour will be the basis of judgment.

Second, *the range of the judgment* will involve 'each person' (2:6), 'every human being' (2:9). It will involve the entirety of a person's life, including his or her 'secrets' (2:16).

Third, *the agent of the judgment* will be Jesus Christ. He will pass the judgment in person. How critical, then, that we should know him and entrust our destiny to his work of sin-bearing on our behalf.

Fourth, *the outcome of the judgment* offers only two possibilities. One is 'eternal life' (2:7), also described as 'glory, honour and peace' (2:10). The other is 'wrath' (2:8), also described as 'trouble and distress' (2:9).

A final truth, however, needs to be drawn from these opening paragraphs of the letter to the Romans, one more aspect of the relational and moral 'grid' within which God's wrath is expounded.

e. Mercy

God's wrath is not inevitable in any specific case. God's wrath is not the gospel; rather it is the dark background against which the gospel blazes with glory. For Paul is coming to Rome with *good news* – the 'good news' for which his life has been set apart (1:2); the 'good news' which God 'promised beforehand through . . . the Holy Scriptures' (1:3); the 'good news' concerning 'the Son of God . . . Jesus Christ our Lord' (1:3, 4); the 'good news' which is 'the power of God for the salvation of everyone who believes' (1:16); the 'good news' in which 'a righteousness from God is revealed . . . this righteousness from God [which] comes through faith in Jesus Christ to all who believe' (1:17; 3:22); the 'good news' that we are 'justified freely by his grace through the redemption that came by Christ Jesus' (3:24); the 'good news' that God is 'just and the one who justifies those who have faith in Jesus' (3:26); the 'good news' that Jesus was 'delivered over to death for our sins and was raised to life for our justification' (4:25); the 'good news' that 'since we have been justified through faith, we have peace with God through our Lord Jesus Christ' (5:1); the 'good news' that 'God demonstrates his own love for us in this: While we were still sinners, Christ died for us' (5:8); the 'good news' that 'since we have now been justified by his blood, how much more shall we be saved from God's wrath through him!' (5:9).

No matter the fact or degree of our sinning ('for all have sinned' [3:23]), we need not fear hell and wrath. In his love, God has come in person in Jesus Christ and has taken his just wrath upon himself on the cross: 'Christ died for us'; 'God presented him as a sacrifice of atonement, through faith in his blood' (3:25). Even as his antipathy to human sinning was awakened by our wilful disobedience, God was reaching into his heart to give expression to his almighty compassion and mercy. That reaching brought forth his dear Son. In the sacrifice of Jesus, God gave his very self for us all – as Johann Rothe wrote, 'O love, Thou bottomless abyss!' If we turn from our sin to him we will pass from the dark, terrible prospect of eternal death to the glorious, liberating prospect of eternal life. This is our God – what better news can there be?

Summary

The definitive statement of the Christian gospel in the letter to the Romans begins by confronting the 'bad news' of human sin: it evokes 'the wrath of God'. God's wrath may be defined as God's implacable antipathy to all evil. God's wrath is directed against all 'godlessness and wickedness'. God's wrath is expressed in hell, which is the final and eternal form of his wrath. God's mercy is the 'good news'. In the giving up of Jesus Christ, God's mercy 'triumphs over' his wrath. His mercy is extended unconditionally to all who have faith in Jesus Christ.

Romans 8:12–39
14. The privilege of children

The work which His goodness began
The arm of his strength will complete;
His promise is Yea and Amen,
And never was forfeited yet;
Things future, nor things that are now,
Nor all things below or above
Can make Him His purpose forgo
Or sever my soul from His love.

(Augustus Toplady)

In the previous chapter we considered the 'bad news' of our sin and its inevitable judgment, the dark background against which Paul's real purpose – the exposition of the 'good news' – can be seen in its shining brilliance. That glorious, positive message, 'the power of God for the salvation of everyone who believes' (1:16), is unfolded through chapters 3 – 8. We join the argument in chapter 8 as Paul thinks through the meaning of salvation in the light of the coming triumph of God's purpose. Here is our heavenly hope in its fullest and most thrilling terms.

Romans 8 begins with a sentence which gathers up the achievement of Christ's work for us as expounded in the previous chapters (3:21 – 7:25), 'Therefore, there is now no condemnation for those who are in Christ Jesus' (8:1). Because of Christ's 'sacrifice of atonement' (3:25), his dying 'for us' (5:8), we are free from the guilt that otherwise attaches to us as sinners. Because we are 'in Christ Jesus', his righteousness is credited to us; God the Righteous no longer condemns us. We no longer anticipate 'wrath and anger . . . trouble and distress' (2:8–9), but rather 'eternal life . . . glory, honour and peace' (2:7, 10). The dread of hell is gone; we are on the path to heaven.

As for being sure of our heavenly destiny, Paul offers two major arguments in support, *the ministry of God's indwelling Spirit* (8:12–17), and *the reality of God's triumphant purpose* (8:18–39).

1. The ministry of God's indwelling Spirit (vv. 12–17)

We can distinguish two aspects of the Holy Spirit's ministry in affirming our Christian hope – his work (vv. 14a, 2–13), and his witness (vv. 14b–17). The outcome is the assurance of a heavenly inheritance.

a. The work of the Spirit (v. 14)

'Those who are led by the Spirit of God are the children of God' (NIVI). What does being 'led by the Spirit of God' mean?

At the very least it implies that God the Holy Spirit is a present, perceptible reality in the Christian's life. Since the Spirit is the Spirit of the God of resurrection, his presence means new moral possibilities for every Christian. 'If the Spirit of him who raised Jesus from the dead is living in you, he who raised Christ from the dead will also give life to your mortal bodies through his Spirit, who lives in you' (8:11). This 'giving life' to our 'mortal bodies', which gives evidence of our heavenly destiny, is what Paul refers to in verse 14 as being 'led by the Spirit of God'. Cranfield unpacks the text in this way: 'The daily, hourly putting to death of the schemings and enterprises of the sinful flesh by means of the Spirit is a matter of being led, directed, impelled, controlled by the Spirit.'[1] It is this experience of moral renewal which is the first great assurance of our glorious destiny.

Daring to be holy
This argument may come as a surprise. H. C. G. Moule's observation penned a century ago is still relevant:

> Too often in the Christian Church the great word Holiness has been practically banished to a supposed almost inaccessible background . . . to a region where a few might with difficulty climb in the quest, men and women who had 'leisure to be good', or had exceptional instincts for piety.[2]

[1] C. E. B. Cranfield, *The Epistle to the Romans*, vol. 1 (T. and T. Clark, 1975), p. 395.
[2] H. C. G. Moule, *The Epistle of Paul the Apostle to the Romans* (Cambridge University Press, 1903) , p. 219.

But the standards and achievements of Christian living dare not be measured by our human perceptions or levels of attainment. The standard must be God's Word, and, however uncomfortable this may make us, it is indisputable that Paul speaks here of the life of the Christian *as a life of moral achievement*. We are assured of our title to a place in God's coming holy world by virtue of the fact that we are already experiencing in measure that holy life here and now: 'if by the Spirit you put to death the misdeeds of the body, you will live [eternally]' (8:13). This is what is meant by being 'led by the Spirit' (v. 14). The Puritan William Gurnall put it memorably: 'Say not thou hast royal blood in thy veins, and art born of God, except thou canst prove thy pedigree by daring to be holy.'[3] In applying this truth several comments are in order.

First, we should note that the standard attained is a *personal* one. What the Spirit of God achieves will necessarily vary from individual to individual. For example, the degree of sin's domination prior to the Spirit's 'arrival' will vary. What the Spirit is faced with, if one may so speak, is as diverse as the individual personalities and natures concerned. Thus what for one might be a glorious evidence of the Spirit's presence and hence the token of a heavenly inheritance, for another might be, at least as externally perceived, something which they might be thought to have been capable of attaining by the agency of their natural grace and personality apart from the Spirit's indwelling.

What *is* promised is that, if Mr White becomes a Christian, he will be a better Mr White. But that says nothing about whether the Christian Mr White is in all respects better than non-Christian Mr Brown, who in turn, if converted, will be a better Mr Brown, but not necessarily better in all respects than non-Christian Mr Green, and so on. Putting this another way, comparisons between Christians as far as their moral and spiritual attainment is concerned are usually poorly informed, and commonly unhelpful.

Taking this a step further, we can say that the judgment of the Spirit's ministry is a *hidden* one. Only the God who alone 'knows us' (1 Cor. 13:12) can assess what our degree of holiness is at any time, which is why, appropriately, he alone will be the judge on the last day. At that time he will 'bring to light what is hidden in darkness' so that 'each [Christian] will receive his [or her] praise from God' (1 Cor. 4:5) – and, as a basic ingredient of that affirmation, the gift of a heavenly inheritance.

Second, the standard is *not perfection*. Perfection is what heaven is about, and we are certainly not there yet. Romans 8 was written to

[3] Cited J. C. Ryle, *Holiness* (Jas. Clarke, 1952), p. 32.

real people who retained their 'body of death' (7:24) and who, like Paul, regularly found themselves crying, 'What a wretched person I am!' (7:25). Cranfield's observation is apt.

> [Those indwelt by the Spirit] fulfill the law (8:4) in the sense that they do have real faith in God [which is the law's basic demand], in the sense that their lives are definitely turned in the direction of obedience, they do sincerely desire to obey, and are ever striving to advance ever nearer to perfection. But as long as they remain in this present life their faith is always in some measure mixed with unbelief, their obedience is always imperfect and incomplete.[4]

This 'striving' is Spirit-induced, however, and hence gives evidence of a heavenly destiny. In the words of Calvin, it is not that Christians are 'wholly free from vice', but that they 'heartily strive to form their lives in obedience to God'. We may similarly note the observation of David Smith, 'The believer may fall into sin, but he will not walk in it.'[5]

It is worth noting several of the ways in which Paul refers to this *inner working of the Spirit*. In verse 5 the Spirit's presence issues in 'a mind set on what the Spirit desires', which Cranfield helpfully understands as 'allowing the Spirit to determine the direction of their lives'.[6] God's call and will become the ultimate determination of the believer's goals and values. Even though at times this direction may become indistinct, we can never finally lose a concern for God and his will for us. Every Christian can surely find some echo of this.

According to verse 7, what the Spirit promotes is the opposite to a mind 'hostile to God'. Again, every Christian can recognize themselves even though at times we are aware of disobeying God in specific ways. A consistently hostile attitude to God is what we have left behind in becoming Christians. The evidence of the Spirit in our lives is that we approach God with freedom and pleasure rather than hostility or revulsion. So, 'By him [the Spirit] we cry *"Abba, Father"'* (8:15), in anticipation of the day when we will run into our Father's arms in eternity.

Third, *backsliding* is a sad possibility in every Christian's life – but there is always a way back. So Peter can fail Jesus in a spectacularly

---

[4] Cranfield, *The Epistle to the Romans*, vol. 1, p. 384.
[5] Cited J. R. W. Stott, *The Epistles of John* (Tyndale, 1964), p. 135.
[6] Cranfield, *The Epistle to the Romans*, p. 386.

public manner, and yet be restored (Mark 14:66–72; John 21:15–18). So Demas can be 'in love with this present world' and forsake a servant of God in his time of need (2 Tim. 4:10). So Mark can quit his assignment, and yet prove 'useful' to Paul's ministry at a later time (Acts 13:13; 15:36–39; 2 Tim. 4:11). So there can be a loss of a 'first love' which can still be repented (Rev. 2:4–5). Failure need never be final for any of us. The Spirit's evident presence will always be a fluctuating reality at best, but heaven is not forfeited by failure.

Fourth, it is worth noting here something that is commonly overlooked: that this teaching on the attainment of holiness is addressed to *a corporate body*, a *church* composed of a number of individuals bound together by the Holy Spirit. Paul is writing 'to the Romans'. The point is so obvious, yet it is consistently missed. The victory that is held out here is accordingly, to a real degree, *a communal reality*.

When one reflects that the great bulk of New Testament teaching on the Christian life is contained in letters addressed to congregations rather than to private individuals, the implication is surely clear: the life of spiritual victory, which is a witness to our share in the coming glory, is envisaged only in the context of a community where our personal limitations and weaknesses are compensated for and complemented by the strengths and responses of our brothers and sisters.

It is significant in this connection that the Spirit is immediately affirmed as a 'Spirit of adoption', of family belonging. The point here is *not* about belittling the searching summons to holiness which every Christian faces. Rather it is about asserting that our responding to that summons in a way which shows the Spirit's presence in our lives is rendered significantly more possible when we are involved in real Christian community. Readers who feel that the call to holiness is a losing struggle at this point may need to make the discovery that the step closer to God which they need to take is, in practice, a step closer to God's people.

Gathering it up

Being a Christian, then, means being indwelt by God the Holy Spirit in such a manner that his indwelling presence makes a difference in our lives, not least in terms of our concerns, interests and desires; and further that this difference is one of the grounds of our assurance that we will one day share the life of heaven.

b. The witness of the Spirit (vv. 14b–17)

Paul now picks up the family image of verse 14 to identify a second, closely related, way in which the indwelling Holy Spirit assures the Christian of his or her share in the heavenly glory.

The essence of his case is conveyed in verse 16, 'The Spirit himself testifies with our spirit that we are God's children.' What is this 'testimony'? It is the persuasion the Spirit brings that we *are* God's children. The familial reference is critical to the apostle's point here. The Spirit is 'the Spirit of sonship' (v. 15). 'Sonship' is the word for 'adoption', *hyiothesia*. F. F. Bruce explores the implications:

> The term 'adoption' may have a somewhat artificial sound in our ears; but in the Roman world of the first century AD an adopted son was a son deliberately chosen by his adoptive father to perpetuate his name and to inherit his estate; he was in no way inferior in status to a natural son and might well enjoy the father's affection more fully and reproduce the father's character more worthily.[7]

'Our Father'

The Spirit's witness is his giving to Christians a persuasion that God has chosen and received them into his family, and that they are henceforth his true sons or daughters. The experience by which this familial relationship is demonstrated is our approach to God in prayer. We are delivered from fear (8:14) and instead 'cry, "Abba, Father!"' (8:15).

This phrase is a striking, even exciting one. *Abba* is an Aramaic word, the language spoken by Jesus in the everyday context. The reference to Jesus is key because *Abba* was consistently used by our Lord in his prayers. Of the twenty-one prayers of Jesus that have come down to us, with the single significant exception of the cry of dereliction, he uses the '*Abba*, Father' form.[8]

Thus the Spirit witnesses to our intimacy with God by emboldening us in prayer to draw near to the Father with the very word of address used by Jesus the eternal Son (cf. Gal. 4:6). Not surprisingly, Paul immediately goes on to speak of us as 'co-heirs with Christ'

---

[7] F. F. Bruce, *The Epistle of Paul to the Romans* (Tyndale, 1973), p. 166.

[8] This was revolutionary. We have considerable liturgical and devotional material from the inter-testamental period, rabbinic sources, and Qumran, and nowhere in all of this outpouring of prayer is *Abba* used in addressing the deity; in its way a remarkable testimony to the unique sense of intimacy which Jesus knew in relation to the Father.

(v. 17). We are God's co-heirs because, as the indwelling Spirit in prayer testifies, we are previously his co-children!

c. The outcome – assurance of heaven (v. 17)

The two aspects of the Spirit's ministry – work and witness – have the same result. By inclining us towards obeying God (his work), and by freeing us to approach God (his witness), he gives us the basis for assurance concerning our standing with God. We are his beloved children. This assurance also has a future reference point: 'Now if we are [God's] children, then we are heirs . . . that we may also share in his glory' (v. 17).

The key is again 'adoption'. As we saw above, the adoptee might with complete propriety enjoy the fullest rights and privileges within the family, including specifically the right of inheritance. This is precisely our case, Paul asserts. 'If we are children [as our crying *Abba* proves], then we are heirs – heirs of God and co-heirs with Christ, if indeed we share in his sufferings in order that we may also share in his glory' (v. 17). Five aspects of our heavenly inheritance can be seen here.

i. Its basis

We are heirs 'with Christ'. None of this is our natural right. Only because Jesus is the Son of God and 'bought [us] at a price' (1 Cor. 6:20) do we have peaceful access to the Father, whether now on earth or then in heaven.

ii. Its certainty

Our being heirs 'with Jesus' means that our inheritance is a shared one – astonishingly, we share it with Christ. But in his case the heavenly inheritance is already enjoyed by him *beyond death*, 'at the Father's right hand' (e.g. Heb. 1:3; Acts 7:56). So, if our inheritance is identical to his, then it follows that part of that inheritance must lie *beyond death, 'with him in glory'* (Col. 3:2).

To see him enthroned, as Stephen did in Acts 7:56, is not only to be given a vision of our Lord's triumph and eternal kingship, it is also to be given a vision of our own coming triumph and elevation. In Cranfield's words, 'He has already entered upon the inheritance for which we have still to wait, and this fact is the guarantee that we too, who are his joint-heirs, will enjoy the fulfilment of our expectations.'[9]

[9]Cranfield, *The Epistle to the Romans*, vol. 1, p. 407.

iii. Its extent

Adoption as practised in the Roman world carries the astonishing implication that the adoptee could have equality of status with the natural child. In the case of Jesus and ourselves, the degree of parallel is necessarily circumscribed. As we noted above, Jesus, as the Saviour Son of God, is the only reason why we have been adopted into God's family in the first place.

Perhaps, however, we may retain Paul's remarkable image in one regard. May we not affirm that the love the Father has for his unique, eternal Son Jesus is echoed in his love for us, his adopted children? Jesus affirms exactly this in his prayer in John 17:23: 'May they be brought to complete unity to let the world know that you . . . have loved them even as you have loved me.' Thus Jesus becomes a paradigm of the Father-love of God for all his children. 'The sentence that mankind craves from stories – The Maker of all things loves and wants me'[10] is here given its grounding. He does!

iv. Its condition

This identity with Jesus has a further dimension – 'if indeed we share in his sufferings' (v. 17). It is likely that Paul has in mind here the call to identify with Jesus in our daily lives in the world. 'The reference is . . . to that element of suffering which is inseparable from faithfulness to Christ in a world that does not know him as Lord.'[11]

The application is clear. To stand for the truth of Christ today, and to implement the values of his kingdom, will necessarily, sooner or later, lead us into suffering. This is becoming a more dangerous world in which to be identified with Jesus (Phil. 1:29). It has been reliably computed that on present trends one in two hundred Christians alive today will be martyred. The claims we are called to make as Christians for the uniqueness of Jesus and for his being the only way to the Father are anathema to a world where inclusiveness, relativism and the easy tolerance of options is the prevailing style, and where the fanatical pursuit of other global dominions is on the increase.

The point of verse 17, however, is that, far from our rejection and humiliation in the eyes of the world implying that we are less than God's own children and contradicting the idea that we are on our way to receiving our heavenly inheritance, this very suffering is proof of our title to it. 'The essence of discipleship is union with

---

[10] Reynolds Price, cited P. Yancey, *The Jesus I Never Knew* (Zondervan, 1995), p. 269.
[11] Cranfield, *The Epistle to the Romans*, vol. 1, p. 408.

Christ, and this means identification with him in both his sufferings and his glory.'[12]

v. Its form
Two phrases are used to denote the inheritance. We are 'heirs of God', and 'sharers in his glory' (v. 17). God's glory is the outpouring of his majesty, God's 'God-ness' becoming visible. There is biblical witness to it in many places (cf. Exod. 24:16; 2 Chr. 7:1; Ezek. 1:28; 2 Cor. 4:6; 2 Pet. 1:16–17). The promise of heaven is nothing less than that we shall share this divine glory: 'We rejoice in the hope of the glory of God' (Rom. 5:2). 'By the glory of God is meant that illumination of man's whole being by the radiance of the divine glory which is man's true destiny, but which was lost through sin.'[13]

The other descriptive phrase, 'heirs of God', possibly means not just that God in grace has made us his heirs, but that the inheritance to which he has thus appointed us consists of God himself. 'It is difficult to suppress the richer and deeper thought that God himself is the inheritance of his children.'[14] Nothing higher or greater is possible to contemplate. 'He who has God and everything else has no more than he who only has God.' To possess and be possessed by him, the ever-blessed Trinity, is all that we can ever wish for. Heaven, in the end, is simply the eternal enjoyment of God. And it is sure.

Richard Baxter, in his classic on the life of heaven, *The Saints' Everlasting Rest*, speaks of this as the 'fruition of God', which he describes as 'the heaven of heavens . . . in these mutual embracements of love does it consist. To love and be beloved: "These are the everlasting arms that are underneath. His left hand is under their heads and with his right hand he embraces them."'[15]

2. The reality of God's triumphant purpose (vv. 18–39)

The ministry of God's indwelling Spirit, examined above, is Paul's first ground for our assurance of heaven. Now we move on to consider his second major argument, which concerns God's purpose. Paul develops this second ground for our 'certain hope' along two lines. First, everything is actually moving towards the final

[12] J. R. W. Stott, *Romans* (IVP, 1994), p. 235.
[13] Cranfield, *The Epistle to the Romans*, vol. 1, p. 260.
[14] J. Murray, *The Epistle to the Romans* (Eerdmans, 1986), vol. I, p. 298.
[15] R. Baxter, *The Saints' Everlasting Rest* (Wesleyan-Methodist Book Room, n.d.), p. 18.

fulfiment of God's purpose (vv. 18–30). Second, nothing conceivable can stand in its way (vv. 31–39). We will look at both these lines of thought below.

a. Everything is moving towards it (vv. 18–30)

Paul produces two witnesses for his argument. We can see this working out in *creation* (vv. 18–22), and we can see it working out in *Christians* (vv. 23–30).

God's triumphant purpose is already being realized in creation. What does 'creation' mean here? Since the opening chapters of Genesis play such a significant role in Paul's whole exposition in Romans, we can helpfully think of 'creation' as everything covered by God's creative acts in Genesis 1:1–25. Cranfield's proposal, 'the sum-total of sub-human nature, both animate and inanimate', seems about right.[16] Since God made and hence upholds it all (as we saw in chapter 1), it needs to be encompassed within any fully biblical vision of his divine purpose. Paul asserts three things concerning it: the creation is expectant, frustrated and, finally, liberated.

i. The creation is expectant (v. 19)
'The creation waits in eager expectation for the sons of God to be revealed' (v. 19). It is not unhelpful to recall that 'expectant' is the word commonly used of mothers-to-be. That precisely captures Paul's point. The creation is pregnant, longing to arrive at the moment of birth, or perhaps 'rebirth', the word used by Jesus in Matthew 19:28, 'when everything is made new again' (NJB). It comes as no surprise, therefore, when Paul uses this precise image in verse 22: 'We know that the whole creation has been groaning as in the pains of childbirth right up to the present time.' The birth image is also reflected in the notion of the messianic 'birthpangs' (or 'woes'). This widespread first-century notion held that the messianic age would be preceded by a period of upheaval in the physical world and marked distress in human affairs.

Thus we are part of a created order in which there are unfulfilled possibilities, and inarticulate longings for a fulfilment which can only be realized 'when the sons [and daughters] of God are revealed' (v. 19) – i.e. when at the coming of the Son of Man in glory his children will experience their true liberation, their 'sharing in his glory' (v. 17; cf. Mark 13:8).

---

[16] Cranfield, *The Epistle to the Romans*, vol. 1, pp. 411–412.

ii. The creation is frustrated (v. 20)

'The creation was subjected to frustration, not by its own choice, but by the will of the one who subjected it, in hope . . .' (v. 20). Paul draws upon the Genesis 3 account in which the fall draws into its shadow the creaturely order within which Adam and Eve had formerly exercised their regency. 'Cursed is the ground because of you . . . It will produce thorns and thistles for you, and you will eat the plants of the field' (Gen. 3:17–18). 'The one who subjected it' in verse 20 is God, in his judgment following Adam and Eve's disobedience. 'Not by its own choice' implies that this curse (cf. the 'bondage to decay', v. 21) refers probably to the endless cycle of nature, memorably noted by the Preacher in Ecclesiastes:

> The sun rises and the sun sets,
> and hurries back to where it rises.
> The wind blows to the south
> and turns to the north;
> round and round it goes,
> ever returning on its course.
> All streams flow into the sea,
> yet the sea is never full.
> To the place the streams come from,
> there they return again.
> All things are wearisome . . .
> Is there anything of which one can say,
> 'Look! This is something new'?
>
> (Eccles. 1:5–8a, 10)

iii. The creation is liberated (v. 21)

'. . . in hope that the creation itself will be liberated from its bondage to decay and brought into the glorious freedom of the children of God' (v. 21). The goal towards which the presently frustrated creation reaches longingly is the 'new life' which is waiting to emerge from the womb of the fallen creation. This life is nothing less than the emergent 'new heaven and new earth of righteousness' (cf. 2 Pet. 3:1; Is. 65:17ff.; 66:22), when the 'children of God' are revealed at the parousia of the Lord (v. 19).

There is a salutary pointer here to the full terms of God's salvation. It embraces not merely humans, or even additionally supernatural moral agents such as angels; it will involve nothing less than all forms of his creation. The heavenly order is also earthly. We are destined for a transformed world.

From his patient body pierced
Blood and water streaming fall;
Earth and sea and stars and mankind
By that stream are cleansèd all.[17]

The larger point is that the apostle, looking at creation through the eyes of faith, is able to identify in the terrestrial order salient pointers towards the coming glory. But he has an even more pertinent piece of evidence:

God's triumphant purpose is already being realized in Christians (vv. 23–30). He notes four expressions of this: the Spirit's presence and prayers, and God's providence and perspective.

i. The Spirit's presence (vv. 22–25)
Paul has identified a 'groan' of longing in creation (v. 22); he now speaks of another longing 'groan' – in the hearts of Christian disciples. 'Not only so, but we ourselves, who have the firstfruits of the Spirit, groan inwardly as we wait eagerly for our adoption . . . the redemption of our bodies' (v. 23). Paul's 'plotting' of this experience in terms of the Holy Spirit accords with what we observed in verses 4–13. The Spirit indwells our lives, and it is his presence which gives rise to our 'groaning'. How can that be?

We note that the Spirit is within us as 'firstfruits' (Gk. *aparchē*). One of the great annual feasts of the Jews, in which Paul as a Pharisee would regularly have participated, was the 'Feast of Weeks' (Lev. 23:15; Exod. 23:18). The Feast of Weeks, which preceded the 'Feast of Ingathering', was not so much a celebration of the full, ingathered harvest as a celebration of the *promise* of it, expressed in the appearance of the first stalks of grain.

Accordingly, it was a time of joyful *anticipation* of the harvest which had yet to blossom and be gathered. If we recall that the other name for this feast was Pentecost (literally 'fifty', because it was to be celebrated fifty days after the great Passover celebration), we can see the wonderful overruling of God. It was at this feast of anticipated harvest that the Holy Spirit came in power at the birthing of the New Testament church as described in Acts 2. No wonder Paul uses this image here. The Holy Spirit is God's first sheaf – his foretaste, literally, of the future heavenly harvest home. His presence in our lives creates the longing for his fullness when, as C. S. Lewis said, 'in the land of the Trinity', God the Father, Son and Spirit will be 'all in all', or 'everything to everybody' (1 Cor. 15:28). To taste it is to acquire an insatiable appetite for more. That

[17] Cited J. Philip, *Christian Maturity* (IVP, 1964), p. 12.

is our groaning as Christians, and it signals the coming triumph of God's purpose.

This tension is clearly evident in our physical bodies. Salvation here and now does not deliver us from weakness, disease, ageing or death. But one day the full harvest will be brought in, which means the 'redemption of our bodies' (v. 23) and the conferring of new bodies, 'like his glorious body' (Phil. 3:21) and hence without weakness, without susceptibility to disease, ageing, weariness, pain, corruption or death.

The range of this 'firstfruits' principle is broader than the physical, however. Paul has eloquently expounded earlier in this letter the realities of the 'old self' (6:6) and 'another law at work in the members of my body, waging war against the law of my mind and making me a prisoner of the law of sin at work within my members' (7:23), evoking the agonized cry, 'What a wretched man I am!' (v. 24). Our 'groan' is also a longing for the day when sin's inner base of operations within us will be wiped out for ever, to say nothing of the elimination of the devil and his beguiling snares. Thus we 'groan inwardly as we wait eagerly for our [full, future] adoption'. It is not yet ours, and so we are called to patient, hopeful waiting (vv. 24–25).

We can identify one further dimension of our 'groaning': the longing within, not just for our own personal redemption, but for the redemption of the world, the ending of the long night of evil, sin, pain and death. No-one who identifies with the agonies of the world, to say nothing of the agonies which are personalized in a regular way among family and friends, can do anything but long fervently for the coming resurrection of all things. This 'groaning' underlies the petition of the Lord's Prayer, 'Your kingdom come', and the cry of Paul in 1 Corinthians 15, 'Even so, come Lord Jesus!'

The reference to the indwelling Holy Spirit as 'firstfruits' calls for one further comment. Several Old Testament passages associate the ministry of the Holy Spirit with the new age of the kingdom (Ezek. 39:29; Joel 2:28f.). Jesus makes this linkage when talking to Nicodemus of the need to be 'born again' for entry into the kingdom (John 3:3), an experience which he explains as being 'born of water and the Spirit' (3:5). So the life of the new heavenly order is identified with that divine life who is the Holy Spirit. In technical theological language, the Spirit is an eschatological Person: in indwelling our lives he imparts to us the very life of the inaugurated and coming kingdom of God.

Another closely related Greek New Testament word is *arrabōn*, also used of the Spirit's presence in the Christian's life (2 Cor. 1:22; 5:5; Eph. 1:14). This word comes from first-century business. When a contract was entered into one paid an *arrabōn*, a 'deposit' which guaranteed the full payment to follow.

This has relevance to the issue noted earlier, that the subject of this book is entirely speculative since heaven and hell are both, by the nature of the case, entirely unknown by us during this lifetime. We responded by arguing that they are not unknown to God and he can, and has, informed us of them in his revelation in Scripture, and also by noting that Jesus' death and his ministry between the resurrection and ascension represent genuine projections of hell and heaven within our space and time. At this point we can enter a further rejoinder. Heaven is not totally unknown by us in this lifetime if we have experienced the Holy Spirit's rebirth and indwelling presence. For he is the 'firstfruits' of the life of heaven. The Holy Spirit is truly 'glory begun below'.

ii. The Spirit's prayers (vv. 26–28)

The Holy Spirit not only creates this longing for our full redemption, he also helps us cope with its deferment. We are at present ignorant about many, many things, not least concerning God and his will for us. Our prayers are regularly uninformed, even misdirected. But the Holy Spirit helps us by the fact that '[he] himself intercedes for us with groans that words cannot express' (v. 26). He works in and through our broken, misdirected prayers to present them on our behalf to the Father in a form appropriate to the fulfilling of God's purpose, and in relation to which the Father can grant an affirming answer. As John Stott helpfully expresses it, 'The inspiration of the Spirit is just as necessary for our prayers as the mediation of the Son. We can approach the Father only through the Son and only by the Spirit.'[18]

Paul refers here to a ministry of the Spirit which is seldom recognized and yet which continues to be fundamental to the blessing and direction of every Christian's life. It must also inspire us with hope to know that in this sense 'we are not alone' as we pray.

One other point of note is the reference to the 'third groan'. There is the groan of creation (v. 22), the groan of the Christian (v. 23), and now the groan of the Spirit (v. 26). Some interpreters have hesitated to assign this activity to the Spirit on the grounds that involvement in a groaning, struggling activity is incompatible with the Spirit's deity. But if God is truly involved in our lives, and if he has truly identified with us in the man Jesus and his 'loud cries and tears' (Heb. 5:7), it is difficult to see a problem with the Spirit's 'groans'. What marvellous encouragement this represents in portraying a God who

[18] ibid., p. 244.

identifies deeply with our human struggles and helps us in the midst of them.

The larger point must not be missed, however: the Spirit heals and redirects our prayers precisely in order that our prayers should become a genuine medium for the fulfilment of God's purposes in the present and the future. No less than his enabling us to cry '*Abba, Father*', the Spirit's enabling of our intercessions is a pointer to the coming day of glory when we 'shall know fully even as [we are] fully known' (1 Cor. 13:12).

iii. God's providence (v. 28)
'We know that in all things God works for the good of those who love him, who have been called according to his purpose' (8:28). This is a remarkable claim and it has, not surprisingly, occasioned much debate.

We note what Paul does *not* say here. He is not promulgating his version of the idea taught by the Enlightenment philosopher Leibnitz, that 'this is the best of all possible worlds'; nor is he proclaiming, like Deepak Chopra in our own time, that 'everything is good', nor is he commending the Buddhist road to happiness through a courageous acceptance of life in all its aspects, both pleasant and painful. For the apostle, life is a meaningful process in which the loving, sovereign Creator is at work fulfilling his *eternal purpose* of conforming all who will come to him to the 'likeness of his Son' (v. 29). In achieving this goal in the lives of 'those who have been called', he is able at his pleasure to cause 'all things' to contribute to the realization of that 'good' purpose of Christlikeness.

iv. God's perspective (v. 30)
This purpose of conforming us to the image of Jesus Christ has four distinguishable phases: 'Those he *predestined*, he also *called*; those he called, he also *justified*; those he justified, he also *glorified*' (v. 30, my italics).

'Predestined' means that God intended this for us from the beginning of time. It is rooted finally in what he has chosen and willed for us.

'Called' means that the eternal purpose became actual in our experience when, hearing of his love in Christ, we committed ourselves in faith to be his. 'He called you . . . through [the] gospel, that you might share in the glory of our Lord Jesus Christ' (2 Thess. 2:14).

'Justified' means that in believing in Christ we were so united to him in his death that our sin and all its attendant guilt was borne by Christ for us, and all his perfect obedience and righteousness was eternally credited to us.

'Glorified' refers to the completion of God's purpose of grace, such that we are changed in nature to become Christlike, 'conformed to the likeness of his Son' (v. 29), and hence radiating his divine glory.

Especially striking is the tense of this fourth verb, 'glorified'. It is in the same tense (aorist) as the preceding three, used of actions regarded as already completed. James Denney appropriately comments, 'The tense in the last word is amazing. It is the most daring anticipation of faith that even the New Testament contains.'[19] It is accordingly a fitting final word for this remarkable paragraph, in which the certainty of the Christian's participation in the coming glory is so profoundly and repeatedly asserted.

b. Nothing can stand in the face of it (vv. 31–39)

Paul rounds out this *tour de force* of the triumphant purpose of God with a final, lyrical section in which he surveys all its conceivable threats. There are three possible directions from which our future full salvation can be threatened. First, and most fundamentally, it can be threatened by *God himself*. Should he change his mind and heart towards us, then clearly our hopes are destroyed. Second, it can be threatened *by ourselves*, by the fact that we have been and continue to be, even as Christians, sinful men and women. Third, it can be threatened by *other alien forces*, whether physical threats in this life or alien spiritual forces here or hereafter. Paul faces each of these in turn by means of a series of questions which he hurls at a supposed interlocutor.

i. The threat from God

'If God is for us, who can be against us?' (v. 31). This is the supreme consideration, and he will return to it in conclusion (v. 39). The force of the assertion is unchallengeable. God being 'for us' is, in one sense, all we need to know. But can we be sure that he is, and will continue to be, 'for us'? Paul answers in radiant confidence, 'Yes, he is, and will be for ever!' How can he be so sure? He can be sure because of Jesus Christ. 'He who did not spare his own Son, but gave him up for us all – how will he not also, along with him, graciously give us all things?' (v. 32).

We know we have God for ever 'for us' because of what he did in giving up his Son for us on the cross. The love that drew salvation's

---

[19] J. Denney, *St Paul's Epistle to the Romans*, The Expositor's Greek Testament, vol. II (Hodder and Stoughton, 1901), p. 652.

plan, the love that bled and died for us at Golgotha, cannot fail to give us every other thing that we need, whether in time or eternity. And among these 'other things' is our eternal life to his honour and glory.

ii. The threat from ourselves

'Who will bring any charge against those whom God has chosen?' (v. 33). Paul now considers the objects of this infinite divine act of mercy. What about the fact that charges *can* be brought against us? What about the sins that litter our lives? What about the countless ways in which we have declared as vehemently as Peter, 'I don't know this man' (Mark 14:71)? What about the many sins committed, not only before we made our Christian profession, but subsequent to it?

Paul's reply is again clear and defiant. 'It is God who justifies. Who is he that condemns?' (vv. 33–34). God has justified us through the cross. The guilt accruing from all our sins, whenever committed, however frequently committed, whatever their form, whatever their consequences, was accepted by Jesus Christ and his perfect righteousness was credited to us. All our sins have been pardoned, even those not yet committed. God our Maker has committed himself to our pardon; he himself is the one who has justified us in Christ.

But what of Christ the Judge? Will that judgment day not bring our sins once more to light and thereby destroy our hope of acceptance? No. He, the Judge, himself died for our sins. He, the Judge, was raised again in witness that his pardoning sacrifice was accepted on our behalf. He, the Judge, is our advocate, even now pleading our case in the presence of God. We need not fear: what we *are* will not threaten what we *will become*.

iii. The threat from other forces

Paul addresses first those *tangible threats in this life* which might seem to separate us from Christ and his love. 'Shall trouble or hardship or persecution or famine or nakedness or danger or sword [separate us from him]?' (v. 35). These very things are already rehearsed in Scripture as the lot of the children of God (v. 36, 'as it is written'). In the midst of even the most fearful physical danger, says Paul, we can be 'more than conquerors' through his loving presence, which will continue to surround us. Even if life is forfeited, we pass into his nearer presence.

What of more sinister enemies, the *spiritual forces* that might assault us in this life or in the dark, unknown world beyond the grave? Again Paul has his answer ready, and in essence it is the answer he gave to the first challenge. If God is for us in his love, then he is more than a match for all such spiritual powers, whether they be met in 'death or life'. If God be for us in his love, then 'neither angels nor demons . . . nor any [other spiritual] powers' can ultimately threaten us, whether they meet us in 'the present', in this life, or in 'the future', in the world beyond the grave. If God be for us in his love, then 'neither height nor depth' can ultimately threaten us (vv. 38–39). This last possibly refers to the astrological spirit forces which in the first century were widely believed to control human life and destiny, or perhaps, as Cranfield suggests, noting Psalm 139:8, 'neither the highest height nor the deepest depth (or should we say "neither heaven nor hell"?)'.[20]

Having reeled off the specifics, Paul can conclude with an all-inclusive final cry of victory, '. . . nor anything else in all creation, will be able to separate us from the love of God that is in Christ Jesus our Lord' (v. 39).

Nothing needs to be added, or can be. The case is made. Every possible counter-argument has been honestly considered and conclusively answered. The threatening tyrants have all been met and mastered. The Christian, the object of the endless, all-vanquishing, personal love of God in Jesus Christ, is a person of certain hope. Heaven is assured.

Summary

Paul argues that, as the children of God, Christians possess a heavenly inheritance which awaits them. They can know with fullest conviction that this is so. The grounds of that assurance are twofold. First, the work of the Holy Spirit, as he morally renews them and frees them to approach God. Second, God's triumphant purpose, as it can be seen working out in creation, and in Christians, the children of God who are the personal objects of his invincible love.

[20] Cranfield, *The Epistle to the Romans*, vol. 1, p. 443.

1 Corinthians 15:1–58
15. An embodied hope

Make no mistake: if he rose at all
it was as His body;
if the cells' dissolution did not reverse, the molecules
   reknit, the animo acids rekindle,
the Church will fail.

Let us not mock God with metaphor,
analogy, sidestepping transcendence;
making of the event a parable, a sign painted in the
   faded credulity of earlier ages;
let us walk through the door.

(John Updike)

Leon Morris refers to 1 Corinthians 15 as 'The classical Christian discussion of resurrection.'[1] It certainly comprises the fullest exposition in the Bible of the form of the Christian's future.[2]

Paul had been the instrument God used to found the church in Corinth during AD 50 (cf. Acts 18). After his departure various difficulties had arisen, and '1 Corinthians' gives a clear picture of several of these.[3] The church was being shaken by polarized loyalties to different Christian teachers, divisions which were at root a love affair with

---

[1] L. Morris, *The First Epistle of Paul to the Corinthians* (Tyndale, 1958), p. 203; cf. Gordon Fee, '[This chapter is] one of the greatest theological treasures of the Christian Church' (*The First Epistle to the Corinthians* [NIC, 1988], p. 717).

[2] Cf. J. Hering, *The First Epistle of St Paul to the Corinthians* (Epworth, 1962), p. 156: 'The doctrine of the resurrection is like the keystone of the structure of the apostle's religious thought. In it his Christology, soteriology, and anthropology are culminated.'

[3] The letter in our New Testament with this heading was not the first letter Paul wrote to the church (see 5:9).

Hellenistic 'wisdom' (1:10 – 3:23); a group of influential members questioned Paul's apostolic status (4:1–21), an issue which would become the dominant concern addressed in 2 Corinthians; the congregation had become morally lax (5:1 – 6:20); it was in danger of dividing along economic lines (11:17–34); it was plagued by a group of 'hyperspirituals' who greatly overvalued and overindulged glossolalia (12:1 – 14:40); and it wobbled in its understanding of the Christian hope (15:1–58). Not your perfect church!

It is the latter problem concerning Christian hope which immediately concerns us (15:1–58). What did the errant members in Corinth believe about the Christian's future? Their view appears in Paul's question in verse 12, 'If it is preached that Christ has been raised from the dead, how can some of you say that there is no resurrection of the dead?' In other words, granted that you believe in the resurrection of Christ, how can you then deny the future, *bodily* resurrection of believers? It is fairly clear from Paul's extended exposition in verses 35–58 of the physicality of the coming resurrection of Christians that their objections centred around the corporeal aspects of the future life.[4] What was the root of this rejection of the body? The most likely source, as Fee argues, is that:

[it] reflects the conflict between them and Paul over what it means to be *pneumatikos* ('spiritual'). In their view, by the reception of the Spirit, and especially the gift of tongues, they had already entered the true 'spirituality' that is to be (4:8); already they had begun a form of angelic existence (13:1; cf. 4:9; 7:1–7) in which the body was unnecessary and unwanted, and would finally be destroyed. Thus for them life in the Spirit meant finally ridding oneself of the body, not because it was evil, but because it was inferior and beneath them; the idea that the body would be raised would have been anathema.[5]

So we move on to Paul's great defence of the *bodily* form of our heavenly hope. We can distinguish three stages in his presentation: its sure basis, its special form, and its glorious character.

1. Our embodied hope – its sure basis (vv. 1–34)

The assured basis of our hope is the resurrection of Jesus from the dead. The empty tomb of Jesus and his risen life after death

[4] So Fee, *The First Epistle to the Corinthians*, pp. 713–716; also M. L. Soards, 1 Corinthians, NIBC (Hendrickson, 1999), pp. 314–316; R. B. Hayes, *1 Corinthians* (Knox, 1997).
[5] Fee, ibid., p. 715.

(vv. 1–11) demonstrate beyond any question both the reality of a life beyond the grave and the embodied nature of that life. Thus, '*Christ died* [his body was subjected to the destructive forces of death] . . . *he was buried* [as a continuing embodied person he was laid in the tomb] . . . *he was raised on the third day*', as an embodied person at a datable moment in time (vv. 3–4, my italics). His body participated in that supernatural act of renewal. Accordingly, 'he appeared to Peter' (v. 5). As this reanimated, embodied person he was encountered in a form which was registered by human eyes, at specific occasions in space and time. In other words, the resurrection of Jesus, the epicentre of the Christian faith (vv. 3a, 11), was *a bodily event*.

Physical resurrection

It is only in these terms that the idea of resurrection would have had any force for the first Christian witnesses or their followers in Palestine. For the Hebrew consciousness, with their strong doctrine of the Creatorhood of God (Gen. 1:1), resurrection *could only mean a physical event*. Earl Ellis notes, 'It is very unlikely that the earliest Palestinian Christians could conceive of any distinction between resurrection, and physical grave-emptying resurrection. To them an *anastasis* (resurrection) without an empty grave would have been about as meaningful as a square circle.'[6] Hence the 'new thing' which the apostles preached was not so much the miracle of bodily resurrection; they and the great majority of their Jewish contemporaries already believed in that as part of the apocalyptic conclusion of history. The 'new thing' was the occurrence of a specific event of resurrection *in the midst of history* – the end without the other accompaniments of the end.

The Corinthians, by contrast, owed their mental origins not to Jerusalem but to Athens (which interestingly, and surely not insignificantly, was visible from the 'Acrocorinth', the tall hill at the foot of which Corinth lay). It is therefore in this Hellenistic context, where the dualistic instincts fostered by classical Greek philosophy had elevated the 'soul' at the expense of the body, that Paul has to reassert the 'holiness' of the body, and hence the embodied nature of the Christian hope.

---

[6]E. E. Ellis, *The Gospel of Luke* (Eerdmans, 1974), p. 273; cf. E. L. Bode, *The First Easter Morning* (Biblical Institute Press, 1970), pp. 162–163, who argues similarly that the Jewish mentality would never have accepted a division between two bodies, one in the grave and one in the new life.

He was seen

That these post-resurrection encounters with Jesus took place is for Paul irrefutable, and he sees his own meeting with the risen Jesus as part of the evidence. 'He appeared to me also' (v. 8). 'You can check all this out for yourselves,' he is saying when he notes that 'most' of the five hundred who had met the risen Jesus on one celebrated occasion were still around (v. 6). As C. H. Dodd puts it, 'There can hardly be any purpose in mentioning the fact that most of the five hundred are still alive, unless Paul is saying, in effect, "the witnesses are there to be questioned".'[7]

It is difficult even two millennia later to resist the overwhelming historical probability attaching to these visible, datable, bodily appearances of Jesus. 'That the disciples had experiences in which they believed they met Jesus risen from the dead is as incontrovertible as the fact that they saw him hanging on the cross on Good Friday.'[8] Nor is their explanation of these experiences – that in them they had actually met with the bodily raised Jesus of Nazareth – easily interpreted in a way which does better justice to the facts. The radical transformation which overtook them after the crucifixion is left without adequate explanation on any other supposition than the one they themselves consistently gave for it – that the resurrection had actually happened as a space-time event.

As Paul argues, however, we cannot stop there. Not simply a freakish oddity, a meteor fallen from some alien sky, *the resurrection cannot be isolated*. Specifically, it sets in motion two irresistible forces. The first is the future resurrection of the whole people of Christ, and the second is the eventual defeat of death. Paul supports this argument by appeal to both logic and life experience.

The appeal to logic

If the Corinthians believed in the resurrection of Jesus, and they did (vv. 1–2, 11), then to fail to believe in the consequent resurrection of Christian believers was logically nonsense, on six grounds.

1. It would mean that Jesus himself had not been raised (vv. 13, 16).
2. It would mean that the preaching of the gospel in Corinth by Paul and others had been a waste of time and that their faith, which had been based on that preaching, was in fact empty (v. 14).

[7] C. H. Dodd, 'The Appearances of the risen Christ', in *More New Testament Studies* (University of Manchester Press, 1968), p. 128; cited W. L. Craig, *The Son Rises* (Moody, 1981), p. 94.

[8] G. R. Beasley-Murray, *The Resurrection of Jesus Christ* (Oliphants, 1964), p. 16.

3. It would mean that he and the other apostles (such as Peter) and teachers (such as Apollos) had been guilty of propagating falsehood (v. 15).
4. It would mean that the atoning value of Christ's death was emptied, and hence their sins remained unpardoned (vv. 15–17).
5. It would mean that the 'dead in Christ' are in fact finally and eternally 'lost', perished for ever (v. 18).
6. It would mean that their condition, as those who have forsaken this world in the interests of a heavenly hope, is in fact 'pitiable' (v. 19).

After delivering this nightmarish catalogue of negatives, Paul reaches eagerly for the gospel trumpet and scatters them with a mighty blast. 'But Christ has indeed been raised from the dead, the firstfruits of those who have fallen asleep' (v. 20). Christ has been raised, and therefore his people will be also. Hallelujah! He uses three arguments to drive his point home.

Horticulturally speaking, like the first sheaf of grain that God called his people to bring to the temple in thankful anticipation of the harvest, so Christ, God's great 'first sheaf' (cf. vv. 20, 23), is presented as the harbinger of the coming harvest of the dead.

Theologically speaking, the solidarity of all people with Adam by which his act of disobedience has implications for the whole race (v. 21, 'since death came through a man'; v. 22, 'in Adam all die'; cf. Rom. 5:12–21), anticipates the solidarity of all Christ's people with him so that 'in Christ all will be made alive' (v. 22).

Christologically speaking, in terms of Christ's person and ministry, his resurrection proves that he has triumphed. He is the victorious Lord, who now, as it were, 'holds the reins of the reign of God'; 'he hands over the kingdom' (v. 24). Christ's Easter triumph must therefore be completed by his glorious return, and that 'return' is the future point at which death, 'the last enemy', will be destroyed (vv. 24, 26).

The significance of this for the Corinthian superspirituals was twofold. First, the supreme transformation was *future*. 'Then' the resurrection life would begin for believers. Second, the resurrection was a reversal of death with its physical destructiveness, and hence was an event ushering in a new, deathless form of *physical* life – the eternal life of heaven.

The appeal to life experience

This brings Paul to his further argument in support of the fact of the embodied future life of Christians, the appeal to life experience

(vv. 29–34). Just as the logic of their beliefs drove them to affirm the bodily hope, Paul's and the Corinthians' Christian lifestyles only made sense on the basis of a bodily hope. Paul notes three things.

The first point he makes deals with their concerns about the dead (v. 29). Not surprisingly, this text has evoked endless debate. Some forty different interpretations have been proposed. The notion of 'baptism for the dead' appears to run directly contrary to (a) Paul's consistent teaching that salvation is by grace alone, rather than a humanly generated salvation; (b) his consistent teaching on the need for personal faith for salvation, and hence the disavowal of a faith exercised vicariously by others; (c) his consistent teaching that ceremonies cannot save, whether circumcision under the old covenant or baptism, by implication, under the new; (d) his consistent view that death is a judgment brought by sin and ends the opportunity for salvation.

It is probably best to see this as a practice in which some, perhaps only one or two, of the Corinthians have engaged without Paul's blessing. This is already a very long letter, not short on admonition, and arguably Paul has no stomach for firing yet another salvo at the congregation, particularly if only a small number of the Corinthians are involved in this error.

In an *ad hominem* argument, therefore, he simply notes that the practice of a 'baptism for the dead' is entirely inconsistent with a purely spiritual hope (to say nothing of its theological heterodoxy). It is inconsistent because any baptism which has even the most tangential link to Christianity is linked to the death and resurrection of Christ, and hence, if these 'odd' baptisms had any degree of theological propriety attached to them, it could be so only if Christ was truly raised, which (to recap the argument of verses 1–28) determines the form of the Christian's future as an *embodied* one. Further, it is inconsistent because these baptisms show on the part of those performing them a concern for those who had died, viewing them as persons who are still 'alive' in some sense so as to be susceptible to influence by the actions of those being baptized for them. But the resurrection of Jesus is the ground of the conviction that these deceased believers *are* alive, and since the resurrection of Jesus was a bodily one, then (again recapping verses 1–28) the implication of performing these baptisms, whether or not the people concerned had realized it, is that those who do this believe in *a bodily hope*.

The second point Paul makes concerns his privations for the gospel (vv. 30–32a). Pursuing his mission continued to be a matter of immense, daily sacrifice for Paul. The words of the risen Lord outside Damascus had proved only too accurate, 'I will show him how much he must suffer for my name' (Acts 9:16).

If there is no bodily resurrection leading to an embodied heavenly life, all this sacrifice is quite meaningless. Then, 'Let us eat and drink, for tomorrow we die' (v. 32). Only a gospel which includes the future judgments on sin and the future rewards for faithful service in an embodied heavenly life can sufficiently justify the depth of suffering which its service may presently demand of those embracing it.

Paul's third point concerns the character of God (vv. 32–34). His quotation from Isaiah 22:13 directs him along an apparent tangent in which he remonstrates again with the moral libertines in the Corinthian congregation. '. . . stop sinning; for there are some who are ignorant of God' (cf. 5:1–13; 6:12–20). There is a linkage with his larger argument, however. The plea for repentance is predicated on the assumption that knowing God carries with it the instinct to renounce sin. The God with whom we have to do is the ground and source of all moral distinctions, and hence he is the one to whom we must give account at the last.

2. Our embodied hope – its special form (vv. 35–50)

In verses 1–28 Paul has argued that Christ is risen in an embodied form, which is the proof that his people will rise in similarly embodied terms. He now imagines a questioner who poses the question, 'How are the dead raised? With what kind of body will they come?' (v. 35)

How is it possible?

Part of the hesitation about bodily resurrection arises from the sheer difficulty of imagining it at the physical level. Dreams of the heavenly life are much easier to sustain against our recurrent doubts if they are set in some 'spiritual' order in the mysterious yonder. The moment we begin to anchor our hope in meaningful continuity with present physical existence, we are immediately forced to come to terms with the sheer, hard facts of human corruption and destruction in death. To this challenge Paul now turns.

He bids us contemplate the natural world. He returns once more to the *horticultural* sphere (vv. 20, 23), noting first that the production of the new form in the case of plant reproduction requires the 'death' of the earlier form (echoing Jesus' words in John 12:24, 'unless a grain of wheat falls to the ground and dies, it remains only a single seed. But if it dies, it produces many seeds'). Death is the means whereby the new life is produced. Second, what is sown in the ground is in no degree identical to what will grow out of the ground

(v. 37). Thus the small, indistinguished seed bears no apparent relation to the laden ear of corn. The distinction, however, is as God has
determined it (v. 38).

Paul then moves to the *biological* sphere (v. 39), noting the diversity of life forms represented by humans, animals, birds and fish. The
point is that God, the sovereign Creator, can give life, not least physical life, in as many diverse forms as he may please.

Turning then to the *terrestrial* order, he notes again the difference
of form and the splendour attaching to each (vv. 40–41). Thus the
earthly is to be distinguished from the celestial (v. 40), and within the
celestial order the sun is to be distinguished from the moon, and
within the constellations a distinction is to be made between their
particular stars (v. 41).

Paul's primary point in all these illustrations is *the diversity of life
forms which yet retain a common physicality.*

The same, yet different

Turning now to the case of 'the resurrection of the dead' (v. 42), he
identifies a similar diversity, which he teases out in the form of four
contrasts, between the form and condition of life here in this present
world, and the changed yet continuing life of the resurrection order.

Cleverly returning to the image of sowing and producing after
death which he employed in verses 36–37, he distinguishes in turn
(a) between the 'sowing', which is the 'perishable body' (*phthora*),
and the subsequently produced, 'raised from the dead' form, which
is the 'spiritual body' (*aphtharsia*) (v. 42); (b) between the 'sowing'
in 'dishonour' (*atimia*), and the produced, 'raised from the dead'
form in 'glory' (*doxa*) (v. 43); (c) between the 'sowing', which is in
'weakness' (*asthenia*), and the produced, 'raised from the dead' form,
which is in 'power' (*dynamei*) (v. 43); and (d) between the 'sowing',
which is 'a natural body' (*sōma psychikon*), and the produced, 'raised
from the dead' form, which is 'a spiritual body' (*sōma pneumatikon*)
(v. 44). This last is particularly significant for Paul's case against the
Corinthian 'spirituals'.

The spiritual elite

Gordon Fee argues that the Greek term *pneumatikos* ('spiritual') had
in all probability become something of a slogan with this group of
Corinthians. They were the 'spiritual elite', as distinct from the
common herd of the rest of the congregation, and as distinct from
Paul, who, despite his credentials and previously effective ministry
(he had been the church's founder!), was also now beneath them.

They had 'arrived', as their profuse tongue-speaking demonstrated. They were already 'heavenly ones' using the language of angels (13:1), the 'spirituals' who had left the body and earthly considerations behind them.

For some this even implied leaving behind the moral restraints around indulging in sex with a prostitute (6:12–20), since that was on the lower level of merely physical appetite and did not enter the higher 'spiritual' sphere where they essentially moved. Paul's probably deliberate linkage of 'body' with 'spiritual' would therefore have hit them between the eyes. It was no doubt meant to. But this identification is simply the conclusion of his entire argument throughout the previous paragraphs.

Made like him

The apostle has one more stage to cover in this exposition of the condition of the Christian after 'the end' has arrived (15:24). This final step is a critical one, because it brings the argument full circle. He began with the resurrection of Christ as the *basis* of our hope, and he returns there finally in exploring the *form* of our hope. In the end, our end is Jesus. It is from him we have come and to him we are going. He is 'the Alpha and the Omega' for his people (Rev. 1:8), the 'author' and 'perfecter' of our faith (Heb. 12:2). Jesus shapes our destiny, and does it specifically by his ministry as the last Adam (15:45).

Characteristically, Paul turns to Scripture for his clinching evidence. He has already referred to the Adam–Christ analogy in verse 22 (cf. Rom. 5:12–21, where Paul develops more extensively the similarities and dissimilarities of the two 'archetypal' Adams). Here Paul takes up Genesis 2:7, referring to the creation of the first Adam as a 'living being' (v. 45), made 'of the dust of the earth' (v. 47), an 'earthly man' (vv. 48, 49). We share this 'earthiness', and by implication will continue to do so, until the coming (again) of the 'last Adam' (v. 45), the 'life-giving spirit' (v. 45), 'the man from heaven' (vv. 47, 48, 49). At this point (by implication, not until then) we who 'have borne the likeness of the earthly man' will 'bear the likeness of the man from heaven' (v. 49).

Paul thus clarifies, first, that we have not yet arrived, we will arrive when Christ appears and we are transformed into his likeness; second, that the one to whom we will be conformed, and hence the goal to which we aspire and which will express our final destiny, is the risen Jesus, the 'heavenly *man*'. We need to recognize a genuine degree of continuity between our existence here and our existence hereafter. Thus the message of the great cry 'I am making everything new!' that will echo across the coming day of nuptial glory when Christ and his church at last embrace at the marriage supper of the Lamb (Rev. 21:5), does not mean a totally *de novo* recreation. 'A new earth' means what it says. Personally we will have, not 'no bodies' but 'new bodies', not a purely 'spiritual' existence, but a gloriously 'supernatural' existence, an existence that can be expressed no better than by the apostle here: we shall be like him who was raised from the dead, 'we [shall] bear the likeness of the man from heaven' (v. 49).

If it be asked 'how?', we can only remind ourselves of the activity of the Creator to whose work Paul has just alluded by his reference to Genesis 2:7. He who 'made all things out of nothing by his Word' is not going to find the challenge of this universal resurrection an insuperable problem. As Jesus said to the Sadducees when their doubts about the physicality of the new order robbed them of their hope, 'You are in error because you do not know the Scriptures or the power of God' (Matt. 22:29).

With complete confidence concerning the process, we, like Paul, 'eagerly await a Saviour . . . the Lord Jesus Christ, who, by the power that enables him to bring everything under his control, will transform our lowly bodies so that they will be like his glorious body' (Phil. 3:20–21).

3. Our embodied hope – its glorious character (vv. 51–57)

Paul stays with that great future event, and for a moment allows the Corinthians with their problems and heartaches to recede into the background. His heart and mind quicken with expectation as he contemplates the finale of history, and the coming coronation of his Lord.

Although he has trenchantly defended the importance of present bodily existence, Paul is not in danger of overvaluing it. This present existence lies under the curse of sin, fomented by the law (cf. v. 56; Rom. 7:11, etc.), and is moving inexorably to the judgment represented by death (v. 21; Rom. 6:23). Hence perishable 'flesh and blood' (v. 50) cannot represent the final form of God's glorious salvation, nor can it in its present form be the instrument through which we fully experience it. The kingdom of God, the summation of God's redemption, needs a new form of humanity (v. 50; and as he has just argued in vv. 44–49). So we look forward to a moment of divine intervention when that necessary transformation will be effected. Paul notes several features of this great coming metamorphosis.

The way it will be

First, it is *known only by God's gracious revelation*, which is what 'mystery' means here (v. 51) – something previously hidden but now made known. That allusion to our dependence on God's initiative for our knowledge of these things is pertinent. In these 'last things', as in all other things, we see 'but a poor reflection' (13:12). We know 'in part', but only 'in part'. Dogmatism is unwise in this area of Christian truth. 'Mystery' in its technical sense, as here, includes 'mystery' in its more regular sense. 'He who has ears to hear, let him hear.'

Second, it will be *a moment of all-encompassing change*, affecting equally those alive at the time and those who 'sleep' in death (v. 51).

Third, it will be *instantaneous*. Paul's way of expressing that is 'in the twinkling [or the blink] of an eye' (v. 52).[9]

Fourth, it will be *an act of divine sovereignty*. The allusion to the trumpet conveys that powerfully. The Lord God Almighty will act. 'When the author walks on to the stage the play is over.'[10] It will be, literally, 'curtains' for human history and for human life as it has been experienced since the creation. In this connection we should note the title given to Jesus in Paul's concluding cry in verse 57, '. . . the victory through our Lord Jesus Christ'. 'Lord' needs particular note. It will be the act of him who both 'died and returned to life that he might be Lord of both the dead and the living' (Rom. 14:9). To him be all the glory! The hope is not the invasive unleashing of transcendent power, a 'fireworks display' of the sovereign majesty of God. It is a *personal* event, the coming in glory of the Lord Jesus Christ. Overwhelming divine majesty will accompany it, but its heart and centre is personal. It is *his* coming, *his* appearing, *his* triumph. Our response to that prospect is therefore not merely an unnerving awe at the manifestation of God's power, but also a heart-leap of love at the appearing and crowning of God's dear and ever-blessed Son, our very Saviour, Jesus Christ our Lord.

Fifth, *it will bring change* – particularly, in keeping with the theme of this chapter, to death's ability to terminate life. Perishability and mortality will be no more (v. 53). The apostle presses this home with a defiant challenge based on Hosea 13:14, 'Where, O death, is your victory? Where, O death, is your sting?' (v. 55).

---

[9] Cf. Eugene H. Peterson, *The Message* (Navpress, 1993), p. 434, 'You hear a blast to end all blasts from a trumpet, and in the time you look up and blink your eyes – it's all over.'

[10] C. S. Lewis, *Mere Christianity* (Macmillan, 1943), p. 66.

Death, you've had it!

The underlying reality, of course, is the resurrection of Jesus (vv. 1–28), an event to which Paul has had indubitable, first-hand access. 'He appeared to me' (v. 8). In these verses he exposes the implication of that fact – that death is mortally wounded. Its days are numbered; its reign is broken; its own demise is certain. Colloquially we could perhaps render verse 55, 'Death, you've had it! Your number's up! You're history!' In that blinding moment of revelation on the Damascus highway, Paul had not only seen the Lord Jesus in his triumphant majesty, but he had also glimpsed the age-old tyrant, death, lying broken beneath the feet of Jesus, Christ's sword of righteousness transfixing its evil heart.

Not only is death due for termination, but also its two henchmen – sin, which gives death its shadowing, destructive right to us, and the law, with its impossible demand for perfect righteousness and its power to entice our fallen hearts into sin's poisonous embrace (v. 56; cf. Rom. 7:7–25). These too have died in the death and rising of Jesus our Lord. Victory, total, final victory, over these deadliest of enemies is ours in promise, and will be ours in practice, when our Victor appears. 'Thanks be to God!' (v. 57).

The last words

The last word has surely been spoken. We are caught up with the apostle in the raptured anticipation of the coming victory; faith rises over our habitual doubts. In our mind's eye we see death falling to defeat and the door swinging open to a beckoning, heavenly eternity. For a shimmering moment we gaze through the portal into the adoring, dancing eyes of our Risen Lord.

Paul is not finished, however, and his further sentences of application speak volumes for the integrity of his mind and heart. It is not merely that as always his theology is applied, though there are far-reaching lessons there. More specifically, Paul is saying something which powerfully illustrates the character of the Christian hope. It is not in essence a comforting pillow which enables us to escape in imagination to an existence of bliss beyond the earthly horizon. Heaven is, in fact, of the greatest earthly use. Indeed, without its prospect earthly life can never fulfil its God-intended purpose. So, after the extended exposition of the coming, cosmic resurrection and the heavenly life into which it will usher us, Paul has a 'therefore . . .' (v. 58). The fact of Christ's resurrection, and the prospect of our own, properly has three effects.

First, *it strengthens love*. 'My dear brothers . . .' writes Paul. No, we are not mistranslating that. Yes, this is written to the Corinthians. Here is a glorious fruit of contemplating the coming triumph: it awakens, as almost nothing else will do, our sense of mutual belonging, a belonging to *all* God's people, who, whatever their present limitations, are destined to 'bear the likeness of the man from heaven' (v. 49). As Paul contemplates the glory that he will share with these sinning, hurtful, immature, but ultimately Christlike miscreants in the church at Corinth, the sense of common belonging and the anticipation of the eternal fellowship surges through him. The Holy Spirit's gift of a love which 'is patient [and] kind . . . is not easily angered . . . keeps no record of wrongs . . . [and] always perseveres' (13:4, 5, 6, 7) is quickened within him. And so he bursts out, 'my dear brothers and sisters' (v. 58 NIVI).

Second, *it stabilizes faith*. 'Stand firm. Let nothing move you' (v. 58, lit. 'be steadfast and immovable'; cf. 'be strong and steady' NLT). The basic meaning is clear enough. Paul is calling for steadfastness on the part of the Corinthians, certainly apt in view of their turbulent congregational life. But he is probably also consciously building on his exposition of the Christian hope. Few things more readily promote steadfastness than the assurance of an eventual, assured victory. It anchors the soul in times of trial and uncertainty, when familiar landmarks become indistinct and long-standing securities are swept away. We can stand firm if we know that a Risen Lord is by our side, and that we are destined, no matter the depth or duration of our present challenges, to prevail to the end and, at the last, to take our place in the New Jerusalem when death has lost its sting for ever.

Third, *it stimulates service*. 'Always give yourselves fully to the work of the Lord, because you know that your labour in the Lord is not in vain' (v. 58). This final application is a fitting conclusion to a section which was begun (in 15:1–2) with a concern as to whether Paul's labour might have been in vain at Corinth. Here he answers his own anxiety. Between the expressed concern and its reassured answer lies Paul's exposition of the resurrection of Jesus and the final resurrection of his people.

There is no greater encouragement for misunderstood, failing, discouraged servants of Christ than the truths of verses 3–57. For one thing, they remind us that the ultimate evaluation of Christian ministry has not yet taken place. No matter how our work may be judged here, the one ultimately valid judgment still awaits. We may yet make the happy discovery that Christ's judgment is more understanding and generous than that of his followers.

Indestructible

More substantially, the fact of the resurrection of Jesus and the coming resurrection of his people means that a dimension of eternity is imparted to all service for Christ. J. B. Phillips draws out this implication memorably. 'Let nothing move you as you busy yourselves in the Lord's work. Be sure that nothing you do for him is ever lost or ever wasted.'[11]

Every kingdom work, whether publicly performed or privately endeavoured, partakes of the kingdom's imperishable character. Every honest intention, every stumbling word of witness, every resistance of temptation, every motion of repentance, every gesture of concern, every routine engagement, every motion of worship, every struggle towards obedience, every mumbled prayer, everything, literally, which flows out of our faith-relationship with the Ever-Living One, will find its place in the ever-living heavenly order which will dawn at his coming. It is, and will be, so utterly worthwhile – because he rose.

Summary

The hope of a heavenly life is securely rooted in the historically validated resurrection of Jesus. Our resurrection will be patterned on his. Jesus rose 'in the body', and so will we. There are helpful analogies of this in the created order. Our heavenly, embodied life will begin when Christ returns, but it has significant implications for our lives in the present.

---

[11] J. B. Phillips, *Letters to Young Churches* (Bles, 1947), p. 66.

2 Corinthians 4:16 – 5:6
16. Ministering in hope

> If you read history you will find that the Christians who did most
> for the present world were precisely those who thought most
> about the next. It is since Christians have largely ceased to think
> of the other world that they have become so ineffective in this.
>
> (C. S. Lewis)

The Corinthian congregation posed probably the biggest pastoral
challenge Paul encountered in all of his extensive ministry. By the
time the apostle came to write what we know as 2 Corinthians, the
divisive issues between Paul and the Corinthians had to some extent
receded. There were, however, residual issues for at least some of the
congregation.

1. Paul's personal authority as an apostle was questioned; some
   rated Peter higher. Peter was one of the original apostles, Paul was
   not (Acts 19:1; 1 Cor. 1:12; 9:5).
2. Paul's speaking ability was limited – a big issue for Greeks (2 Cor.
   10:10). Apollos was clearly his superior (Acts 18:24–28; 1 Cor.
   1:12).
3. Paul had refused financial support from them – though he had not
   hesitated to take it from the rustic northerners in Macedonia
   (2 Cor. 11:7–9).
4. Paul had been overzealous in rebuking fornication and temple-
   worship (2 Cor. 7:8ff.).
5. Paul had shown inappropriate vacillation with reference to his
   travel plans (2 Cor. 1:12–17).
6. Paul in general compared unfavourably with the 'superapostles',
   a shadowy, forceful and highly articulate group who had come
   to Corinth following Paul's initial ministry there. They criticized
   his views of the covenant, his lack of superior mystical-spiritual

gifts, his use of money and possibly also his physical weakness (2 Cor. 11:1 – 12:13).

While 2 Corinthians reflects a less sanguine response to all this, the depth of feeling engendered for the apostle has only very recently subsided with Titus's arrival and good report (7:5–16).

The general context of this letter is one of faithfulness in the face of discouragement and difficulty. With great authenticity it takes us right to the heart of the experience of Christian ministry in every generation. No reader who has become involved in the ongoing, demanding business of sharing the gospel and building the church of Jesus Christ in any part of the world will fail to resonate with the passage before us.

1. The rigours of ministry

In 4:8–9, in a sentence of searing realism, Paul characterizes ministry in four vivid Greek words.

First, 'We are *hard pressed on every side*' (Gk. *thlibomenoi*). Ministry means 'living under pressure', which arises from multiple sources, congregation, colleagues, community, pastoral dilemmas, home and family, financial demand, the unremitting duties of ministry, and so on.

In using the term 'ministry' here, and throughout this chapter, we are not simply referring to the 'ordained ministry'. That is not excluded, of course, but we use 'ministry' in its full New Testament sense of the service of the whole body. In Christ all are called to minister (lit. 'serve'), and 1 Corinthians 12, with its image of the church as the body of Christ where each member is equipped to contribute, is clear biblical anchorage for the idea (1 Cor. 12:5–6).

One of the secrets of successful ministry, especially for leaders, is not so much an ability to handle difficult situations, but an ability to cope with many difficult situations at the same time, an ability to 'live under pressure'.

Second, 'We are . . . *perplexed*' (Gk. *aporoumenoi*). This speaks of uncertainty, of being 'doubtful as to which way to take'.[1] The idealistic dream of a walk with God in which every decision is automatically and unerringly directed was clearly not what Paul experienced; nor is it likely to be true for those who step into the hard places on the front lines of ministry today. 'Lord, which way . . .?'

---

[1] C. Hodge, *An Exposition of the First Epistle to the Corinthians* (Banner of Truth, 1958), p. 93.

Third, 'We are *persecuted*' (Gk. *diōkomenoi*). Not all ministry leads to persecution in the sense of a physical threat to life and limb, although there have always been places in the world (and today is no exception) where that degree of opposition is part of the job description. Jesus warned of this (John 15:18 – 16:4). The more general sense of being personally targeted, of being hunted by those who are 'out to get us', is one with which many in ministry at all levels can readily identify.

Fourth, 'We are *struck down*' (Gk. *kataballomenoi*). We could render this as 'punched to the ground'. Paul had experienced that literally at Lystra (Acts 14:19f.). In the service of God there are moments when we too find ourselves lying on our backs, with the referee counting out the seconds somewhere near our heads. That is ministry!

Plastic bags

Whatever its compensations (and Paul will come to them), whatever its rewards (and they are real, as we will note below), whatever its surpassing dignity (and it has never lacked such), ministry is a deeply human activity which again and again faces us with our limitations and the realities of our humanity. 'We have this treasure in jars of clay' (4:7).

The word used here would have resonated for every citizen of Corinth, where a 'jar of clay' could be bought in the market for a copper or two. These were not the beautifully shaped vases created for the mantelshelf, nor even the strong, sturdy pots for cooking or storage. The 'clay jar' (Gk. *ostrakon*) was a cheap, everyday, disposable container. Its nearest modern equivalent is the plastic bag. That, says Paul, is ministry – 'treasure in plastic bags'!

He makes the same point even more graphically in verses 10–12. 'We always carry around in our body the death of Jesus . . . we . . . are always being given over to death for Jesus' sake . . . death is at work in us.'

'If anyone would come after me'

In the final analysis, ministry is not a matter of human frailty; it is a matter of human finality. It is not weakness; it is death. Ministry is the ever-repeated experience of being literally at an end of ourselves. To say that ministry is difficult is to fail to understand it. It is not difficult; it is impossible! Only when we have grasped that, and have begun to live in the light of its implications, can ministry in its apostolic sense begin to operate in our lives.

Christian ministry means being in partnership with Jesus Christ, even to the point where at times we will testify to a 'fellowship of sharing in his sufferings', to a 'becoming like him in his death' (Phil. 3:10). And yet, like Paul, in the face of this impossibility and this dying, life somehow goes on. The rigours are real, terribly real at times, but they do not finish us. We are 'hard pressed' *but* 'not crushed', 'perplexed' *but* 'not in despair', 'persecuted' *but* 'not abandoned', 'struck down' *but* 'not destroyed' (vv. 8–9). The plastic bag flaps and stretches, but it does not relinquish the treasure within.

2. The resources for ministry

Despite these searching rigours, Paul continues in ministry. How can he do it? On the surface there is nothing to explain it. This accounts for the appeal to Psalm 116:10, 'It is written: "I believed; therefore I have spoken," ' and continues, 'with that same spirit of faith we also believe and therefore speak' (v. 13). Paul continues to preach, the ministry moves forward, God's work gets done. On what basis? The answer can only be located from the perspective of faith. From the perspective of mere sight there is nothing to explain how ministry happens. What happens to enable ministry is the operation of the supernatural; it is the work of God, discerned only in faith. Paul identifies three of these faith resources, the third of which will be our primary concern.

a. The presence of Jesus

This was the truth which came wonderfully alive for Paul during his ministry in Corinth at a time of deep discouragement. 'One night the Lord spoke to Paul in a vision: "Do not be afraid; keep on speaking, do not be silent. For I am with you . . ."' (Acts 18:9–10). Christian ministry is not in the end our ministry for Christ, but Christ's ministry through us. 'The ministry of Jesus is the standard and pattern of the Church's task; but, more than that, the Church's task is the continuation of the ministry of Jesus . . . All our endeavours are to be understood as ways in which the Risen Lord continues his work in the world.'[2] While humanly impossible, ministry *is* effective because we are not alone in the pursuit of it. Paul refers to this as the 'treasure' we carry in our 'plastic bag' humanity (v. 7), 'the light of the knowledge of the glory of God in the face of Christ' (v. 6).

[2] T. W. Manson, *The Church's Ministry* (Hodder and Stoughton, 1948), pp. 32–33.

b. The work of the Spirit

The second resource is the work of God the Holy Spirit. In 5:5 Paul asserts, 'God . . . has given us the Spirit.' 'Given' here has the force of 'imparted to'. Here is a further, massive encouragement for the Christian servant who is crushed beneath the cares and demands of his or her calling. No Christian can be described in adequate terms if account is not taken of the divine indweller, of him who 'lives with you and will be in you' (John 14:17).

We recall the image in Bunyan's *Pilgrim's Progress* when Christian is shown a man lighting a fire in the Interpreter's House, and then another pouring on water to douse it, but always unsuccessfully, as the flames stubbornly refuse to be extinguished and ever and again flare up with new energy. Pilgrim, at a loss to understand the phenomenon, is taken behind the fire into the adjoining room and there sees a third figure who is constantly pouring oil on the fire from behind. So God the indwelling Spirit, the heavenly Paraclete, again and again, in the face of the devil's repeated assaults, rekindles and invigorates the faith of God's servants.

c. The hope of glory

Of the three resources Paul discerns, this third appears to carry the greatest influence for the apostle at this point. We will examine it in some detail, considering its certainty, its contours, and its consequences.

i. The certainty of the hope

The return of the Lord and the heavenly resurrection are central for the apostle. We noted earlier Paul's image of ministry as a kind of living death (vv. 10–12). Only in terms of a faith which 'sees the invisible' is ministry possible (v. 13; cf. Heb. 11:27). But where is faith grounded? 'We know [for sure] that [God] raised the Lord Jesus from the dead' (v. 14). Paul's bedrock remains immovably located at the tomb in Jerusalem and on the road to Damascus. He has met the Risen One; the resurrection is an unquestionable fact.

It is also a massively potent fact. Christ's rising means that God 'will also raise us with Jesus and present us with you in his presence' (v. 14). Here is the final horizon of ministry: the return of the Risen One in glory and the gathering of all his people to him. So, a little later, 'we must all appear before the judgment seat of Christ, that each one may receive what is due to [them] for the things done while in the body' (5:10). All our endeavours are moving inexorably towards that coming encounter with the Lord. Paul refers to the future hope a third time in 4:17 as 'an eternal glory' which awaits us after our present, earthly troubles are over. He is in no doubt that the eternal order will one day overwhelm earth's little day.

ii. The contours of the hope

What will it be like? Since we have no direct experience of the 'eternal glory', we can only project it in imagination in contrast to present earthly conditions. Paul does that concisely in 4:17–18. The future state is contrasted to our present one in four respects:

1. The present is 'light', the future is 'weighty'.
2. The present is 'troublesome', the future is 'glorious'.
3. The present is 'momentary', the future is 'eternal'.
4. The present is 'seen', the future is 'unseen'.

The contrast continues in 5:1–5. The images flow into one another and disentangling them is not easy.

Life here is a *'tent' existence*, as contrasted with the heavenly life in a 'building'. Being a tent-maker by trade (cf. Acts 18:3), this image would have been an obvious one for the apostle. Two points are made by this metaphor. First, tents are exposed to storms and other external forces. They provide no great security, as every camper has learned. By the same measure, life here is vulnerable, subject to chance and change. By contrast, our heavenly life is secure, like a solid building, impervious to storm or other threatening external forces. Life in a tent is transient. Its appeal lies precisely in its ability to be moved around easily. It is the form of residence of the traveller and the pilgrim.

So it is with our earthly life: we are 'strangers and pilgrims' (1 Pet. 2:11), with no permanent residence. The last call will come, the final tent site will be abandoned, and our pilgrimage will be over. By contrast, the heavenly life is rooted and permanent. We are 'settled' in the 'building not built by human hands', in that home which Jesus went through death and resurrection to prepare for us (John 14:1–2). There time no longer 'bears all its sons and daughters away'. We will always 'have time' for whatever is given us to do, for we will have eternity.

In another image used by Paul in these verses, life here is like a regular *suit of clothes*, so that death will mean being for a time 'unclothed'. By contrast, life after the coming of the Lord will be like being given an 'over-clothing' (the verb in verses 2 and 4, *ependuō*, means 'to put on over').[3] Heaven means being 'over-clothed', or perhaps 'fully clothed', since there we are entirely provided for.[4]

The 'naked' condition is arguably that of the intermediate state,[5] which, while offering a new sense of the presence of the Lord, is in another sense 'less' than life here because of the loss of embodied existence. This lack will be more than corrected when the provisionality of the intermediate state gives place to the full life of glory, and we reach the true goal of existence, being 'invested' in the 'spiritual body' which is the 'likeness of the man from heaven' (cf. 1 Cor. 15:44b–49).

This view of the passage is the more likely, bearing in mind the 'superspirituals' at Corinth. Although their influence may have declined, the apostle does not miss an opportunity to make again the point of 1 Corinthians 15:35–49, that the Christian hope is not some disembodied 'spiritual' state. As with the tent/building contrast, we are reminded by this clothed/unclothed/superclothed image of the abundance and all-sufficiency of the heavenly life. The desirability of this condition is reflected in another Pauline use of the 'groan' image (cf. Rom. 8:22, 23, 26); 'we groan and are burdened; because we . . . wish . . . to be [over]clothed' (v. 4). To know the limitations of embodied life here is to long, not for death with its unclothing, but for life in all its fullness, including our new heavenly bodies, which will 'swallow up' God's children on that day.

Closely allied to the first image is probably a third, the distinction between being *'at home'* and being *'away from home'* (vv. 6–8). In this life, for all our knowledge of God and our belonging within his family, we are never entirely 'at home'. To a degree our local church can become a further dimension of 'home' for us, and in so doing can be an earthly pointer to the unseen home that awaits us. We cannot enter or possess it while 'in the body' (v. 6), by which Paul means, surely, in this present earthly body. It is beautifully defined as 'at home with the Lord' (v. 8).

Since that future residence is defined in terms of a closeness of relationship to the Lord, this present one is accordingly distinguished from it by being 'absent from the Lord'. True, he is ever 'with us' here (Matt. 28:20, etc.), and we are 'with him', but by comparison it is as though this present is an 'absence' in contrast with the coming 'presence'.

[3] G. Abbot-Smith, *A Manual Greek Lexicon of the New Testament* (T. and T. Clark, 1937), p. 166.
[4] This passage is a well-known crux of interpretation and various positions are taken on what Paul can mean by being possibly 'found naked' (5:3). The matter is helpfully discussed in M. Harris, *Raised Immortal* (Eerdmans, 1983), pp. 219–226.
[5] See chapter 9.

What, then, is this embodied hope like? It is in a solid, secure environment; it is a state of being invested with life in all its fullness; it will afford a sense of being 'at home' as never before, in the presence of the Lord.

iii. The consequences of the hope

How does this heavenly hope make a difference to Christian ministry? For Paul, as we saw earlier, it can *transform suffering* (4:8–12). The suffering focused on here arises in the course of ministry. Service for Christ costs. Some of the cost arises from the contradictions of the fallen world in which we are called to serve, but the Christian servant is also called to suffer with and for the church. Paul's suffering at the hands of the Corinthians was of that variety. He refers to it more generally in 11:28, 'the daily pressure of my concern for all the churches'.

Paul's conviction is that such suffering is fruitful; it 'achieves' (4:17) in several ways. First, it makes clear that *the effectiveness of our ministry does not derive from ourselves, but from the Lord who indwells us.* This is the force of verse 7, 'We have this treasure in jars of clay to show that this all-surpassing power is from God and not from us.' The battered, inwardly or outwardly bleeding figure of the Christian servant is an eloquent statement of our utter weakness and is, accordingly, the clearest possible indication that the glory for anything achieved must be directed to its proper source. It causes 'thanksgiving to overflow to the glory of God' (v. 15).

The same reality surfaced through Paul's wrestling with 'the thorn in the flesh' in 12:7–10. For all its repulsiveness, the 'thorn' had a ministry, to humble him, and to keep him utterly weak, and hence utterly dependent upon the grace and strength of his risen, ever-present Lord. 'Therefore I will boast all the more gladly about my weaknesses, so that Christ's power may rest on me. That is why, for Christ's sake, I delight in weaknesses, in insults, in hardships, in persecutions, in difficulties. For when I am weak, then I am strong' (12:9–10; cf. 13:4).

James Denney makes a trenchant application of this principle in sentences that have lost none of their relevance.

> One would sometimes think, from the tone of current literature, that no person with gifts beyond contempt, is any longer identified with the gospel. Clever men, we are told, do not become preachers now – still less do they go to church . . . Perhaps this is not so alarming as the clever people think. There have always been men in the world so clever that God could make no use of them; they could never do His work, because they are so lost in admiration of

their own. But God's work never depended on them, and it does not depend on them now. It depends on those who, when they see Jesus Christ, become unconscious, once and for all, of all that they have been used to call their wisdom and their strength – of those who are but an earthen vessel in which another's jewel is kept . . . God will always have his work done by instruments who are willing to have it clear that the exceeding greatness of the power is His, and not theirs.[6]

Second, suffering in Christ's service is 'productive' in the light of his heavenly appearing in that it *gives clear title to our belonging to him*. In 5:10–11 Paul refers to the astonishing identity which those sufferings establish between Christians and their Lord. The effect of the suffering is that 'the life of Jesus [is] revealed in our body'. It is in this sense that the 'troubles' of our service 'achieve for us an eternal glory' (v. 17).

Luther spoke of the inevitability of trials for all who would be conformed to Christ: 'The more Christian a person is the more sufferings and deaths they must endure.' William Law writes in similar vein, 'It would be strange to suppose that humankind were redeemed by the sufferings of the Saviour to live henceforth in ease and softness – suffering cannot be necessary for atonement and then Christians be excused from suffering.'

Third, our trials in the ministry of Christ are fruitful in that they have *life-giving potency as far as others are concerned*. They actually help those to whom we minister in their progress along the pathway to glory. This is the force of verse 12, 'So then, death is at work in us, but life is at work in you.' God will make our struggles fruitful, both in ourselves and in others. Indeed, there often appears to be a law at work in relation to the service of Christ that the greater our pain the greater our power, or better, the greater the power of God through us.[7] One recalls the comment attributed to Elgar concerning a singer of great natural talent: 'She is good, but she will be great – once she has suffered.'

Fourth, the future 'eternal glory' brought transformation to Paul's sufferings in that it *gave them their proper proportion*. In the light of the coming glory, the sufferings of our service are in the end 'light and temporary', in no way to be compared with the weight of everlasting glory for which they are preparing us.

[6] J. Denney, *The Second Epistle to the Corinthians* (Hodder and Stoughton, 1916), p. 160.
[7] 'We are weak in him . . . to serve you' (13:4); and 'We are glad whenever we are weak . . . for your perfection' (13:9).

Such was Paul's perspective, and in the strength of it he soldiered on for Christ, knowing that to all his exhausting labours and daily trials there would come an end. How frequently he must have anticipated that longed-for moment when he who had taken Paul's place on a bloodstained cross outside Jerusalem, he who had laid his pierced hand on the apostle outside Damascus, would call him hence, the fight fought to the finish, the race run to the end and the faith preserved, there to present his weary, careworn servant with the imperishable crown of righteousness. To win that approval and the eternal glories which it anticipated made it all utterly worthwhile.

As well as transforming suffering, Paul discovered that his hope of heaven also *energized his ministry* and his service. The glorious, coming climax of the ages is, for Paul, a major stimulus to his ministry. For one thing, *it establishes accountability.* 'We make it our goal to please him . . . For we must all appear before the judgment seat of Christ, that each one may receive what is due to [them] for the things done while in the body' (5:9–10). 'Since, then, we know what it is to fear the Lord, we try to persuade men' (5:11). Fear is not the only motive for ministry, nor is it the highest. But it is a motive, and it arises directly from the apostle's conviction concerning the coming glory. We too must stand to give account and, like Paul, it is surely of the greatest prudence to prepare ourselves for this personal accounting.

There is another motivation for ministry which also springs from our future hope. The coming glory also establishes ministry's *overwhelming worthwhileness.* 'The one who raised Jesus from the dead will also raise us with Jesus and present us with you in his presence' (4:14). All Paul's struggles for the Corinthians were vindicated from this perspective. In a striking image, Paul shares his anticipation: these often trying disciples at Corinth were a gift he would personally present to his returning Lord, and thereby enhance his glory on that day of coronation. 'I am jealous for you with a godly jealousy. I promised you to one husband, to Christ, so that I might present you as a pure virgin to him' (11:2). The coming meeting with the Lord would be a love encounter in which Paul would pay back at least something of the infinite debt he owed to Christ, by laying at his feet the fruit of all his struggles – the body of Christ in Corinth, a bride made ready for the embrace of her bridegroom. Nor does he stop short of the full terms of that great purpose. 'Our prayer is for your perfection . . . aim for perfection' (13:9, 11).

Here is the motivation for Christian ministry that is without rival or peer, and it flows directly from our Christian hope. In some way of which we have no direct understanding, *what has been achieved in the Lord's name here on earth will contribute to, even enrich, that day of days.* The praise which will surround the Saviour's head from the serried ranks of the redeemed of all the ages will be enhanced in the measure to which the bride of Christ has been conformed through the passage of the years to the likeness of her Lord. For this reason also, for this reason especially, 'we make it our aim to please him'.

Summary

The hope of heaven is a major resource in God's service. In general, it puts our trials in context. In its light they are seen to be temporary and insubstantial. More specifically, it uncovers the values which can be produced by trials experienced in ministry:

- Making clear that God is the one at work through us.
- Showing our identity with our suffering Lord.
- Promoting the growth of those to whom we minister.
- Reminding us that the true fulfilments in God's service lie beyond this life.

Further, the heavenly hope energizes our service.

- It faces us with our future accounting to the Lord.
- It holds out the wonderful prospect that our service here can enhance Christ's glory there.

1 Peter 1:3–9
17. Suffering in perspective

> It is not a smooth and easy way, neither will your weather be fair
> and pleasant; but whosoever saw the invisible God and the fair
> city, makes no reckoning of losses or crosses.
>
> (Samuel Rutherford, Letters)

In turning to Peter's first letter, we continue to explore the link
between the heavenly hope and the fact of suffering.

1. Here

Peter's readership is made up of both Jewish and Gentile Christians
in the churches of the Asia Minor area, which approximately corre-
sponded to present-day Turkey. His purpose in writing is primarily
to bring hope and encouragement to believers facing the threat of
persecution. Barclay characterizes the context.

> The persecution when it came was confined originally to Rome,
> but the gateway to persecution had been opened and in every place
> the Christians were ready victims for the mob . . . For ever after the
> Christians were to live under threat. There were times when the
> mob loved blood and there were many governors ready to pander
> to their blood-lust. It was not Roman law, but lynch-law which
> threatened the Christians. From now on the Christian was in peril
> of his life. For years nothing might happen; then some spark might
> set off the explosion and the terror would break out. That is the
> situation at the back of First Peter.[1]

[1] W. Barclay, *The Letters of James and Peter* (St Andrews, 1976) p. 150.

'You shall stretch out your hands'

Whatever the situation at the precise time of writing, it is clear that Peter had a sense that things were soon to get worse, and events proved him right. Peter's own position was indicative of how the wind was blowing, for within a relatively short period he would be arrested and executed on the Appian Way outside the city. Peter is writing also for himself.

He begins with praise, 'Praise be to the God and Father of our Lord Jesus Christ! In his great mercy he has given us new birth into a living hope through the resurrection of Jesus Christ' (v. 3). The blessing of God ('Praise be . . .') was a characteristic feature of Jewish prayers, not least in the liturgy used daily in the synagogue. This was Peter's background, so parallels from that setting are not surprising. In particular we can compare Peter's benediction here with the synagogue form known as the Second Benediction, 'Blessed are/Praise be to you, O Lord, who gives life to the dead. . .'

'God was in Christ'

In two critical respects, however, Peter's benediction moves on a different plane. First, God has been redefined. This is a crucial point. He is not just 'Lord' in the sense of being ruler of the world and protector of Israel. He is now defined in terms of his coming in Jesus Christ, the God to whom he had submitted himself and served as his God and Father. 'For Jesus according to his human nature God is his God, and for Jesus in his deity God is his Father; his God since the incarnation, his Father from all eternity.'[2] Christianity brought to the world nothing less than a new way of understanding God, and it is there, finally expressed in the doctrine of the Trinity, that its irreducible uniqueness lies.

Second, there is a change in the terms of God's Lordship over the forces of corruption and death. Whereas the Jewish Benediction can only refer to God as the one who in general 'gives life to the dead', that divine mastery has found specific, world-transforming expression in his raising of Jesus from the tomb.

On the morning of 27 August 1883 the major part of the island of Krakatoa, between Java and Sumatra, was blown up in a mind-numbing volcanic explosion, the largest, most awesome explosion ever recorded. It was heard as far as 3,000 miles away. Stones, ash and dust shot up seventeen miles above the earth's surface. Entire forests were buried under the debris. One hundred and fifty miles away the

---

[2]R. C. H. Lenski, *The First Letter of Peter* (Augsburg, 1966), p. 31.

sky was darkened and people had to use lamps at midday. The tidal waves reached as far as Cape Horn, about 8,000 miles distant. Weather and sunsets were dramatically affected around the world for many months after.

On Easter Sunday morning, at a tomb in the city of Jerusalem, an explosive event occurred which had some similarities in the spiritual realm. Jesus Christ rose from the dead, and the effects continue to reverberate around the globe. It is this fact, the resurrection of Jesus, which is the dominating reality underlying Peter's hopefulness in the face of the trials which he and his readers are undergoing, or are about to undergo.

The resurrection has three discernible effects – celebration, regeneration, and the promise of heaven.

i. A reason for celebration
Into the lives of these converted slaves, scattered among the great pagan cities of antiquity, there had broken a glorious hope. Christ himself had loved them and given himself for them. Christ had risen, and was now and always with them. They would spend eternity in his presence. Formerly nobodies, they were now 'a chosen people, a royal priesthood, a holy nation, a people belonging to God' (2:9). They were part of the family of God. Small wonder that they would have resonated to Peter's call for worship. Christ was risen, the world was reborn: praise be to God indeed, and for ever!

ii. The source of regeneration
Through the resurrection 'he has given us new birth' (1:3). As Jesus had anticipated in his dialogue with Nicodemus (John 3:3ff.), and as Ezekiel and Jeremiah had promised centuries before (Ezek. 35 – 37; Jer. 31; cf. Joel 2:28–32), God the Holy Spirit had come to them (John 14:15f.; 16:7f.; cf. 20:22). The new life which had brought Jesus from the dead had reached out to touch them also. Slaves they might be still in the eyes of their often pitiless owners, but in Christ they were free for ever. The basis of this new life lay not in themselves, but outside them: 'In his great mercy he has given us new birth.' They were accordingly endlessly in debt for a gift which they could never repay. James Stewart commented, 'None who is too proud to be infinitely in debt can ever be a Christian.'[3]

iii. The promise of our heavenly destination
Through the resurrection we have come 'into an inheritance that can

---

[3] Cited in John N. Gladstone, *A Magnificent Faith* (Lancelot, 1979), p. 39.

never perish, spoil or fade' (v. 4). Cranfield powerfully sets this Christian hope against its pagan background.

> The most striking characteristic that distinguished the early Christians from their pagan neighbours was their *hope*. When Saint Paul described the pagan as 'having no hope', it was no mere rhetorical flourish, but plain truth. The world of ancient Greek and Roman civilisation was a world of fascinating beauty. It could boast of splendid courage, high intellectual power, and superb loveliness of poetry and art; but in spite of all the grandeur and charm it was a world without hope . . . Old age was dreaded as the threshold leading out into the dark and cold . . . Over that classical civilisation death reigned as king of terrors . . . Now by the resurrection of Christ the king of terrors had been dethroned. Unlike their pagan neighbours the early Christians were men and women of hope . . . A new dimension had been given to their lives – the dimension of the future, of eternal life.[4]

2. Hereafter

The word upon which Peter seizes to describe the hope is *inheritance* (v. 4; Gk. *klēronomia*). In the classical world of the first century this referred to property which changed hands when a death occurred. If we think of the death in this case as the death of Jesus, the acquired estate is the full salvation which accrues to his people because of his self-sacrifice.

In using this word, however, Peter almost certainly has in mind its rich Old Testament background. When the confederacy of Israel settled in the land of Canaan following the conquest, that land was, in general, seen as their 'inheritance'. 'I will make your descendants as numerous as the stars in the sky and I will give your descendants all this land I promised them, and it will be their inheritance for ever' (Exod. 32:13).[5] There is also the thought of conferring a right of ownership. Thus the prodigal son in the parable asks for the portion of his father's estate which is his right: 'Give me my share of the estate' (Luke 15:12). Stibbs can observe that *klēronomia* 'includes the idea of full, realised possession, rather than just the title

---

[4] C. E. B. Cranfield, *The First Epistle of Peter* (SCM, 1950), pp. 222–223.
[5] Cf. Lev. 20:24; Deut. 4:21; 19:10; and Heb. 11:8, 'By faith Abraham, when called to go to a place he would later receive as his inheritance, obeyed and went, even though he did not know where he was going.'

to it'.[6] The perfect participle carries that sense of completion – 'it has been carefully already laid aside for you'. Jesus' imagery in John 14 is similar: 'I go to prepare a place for you' (v. 3).

The Christian is a person with two homes, two addresses, two pieces of 'real estate' to which he or she has title of ownership. One is our earthly domicile, that space where we live and which we can in some degree and in some sense claim as 'ours'. The other is beyond the curtain of our mortality, finally revealed in the glory of the parousia, our 'eternal inheritance' which is our 'eternal home' (2 Cor. 5:1).

So Peter reminds the suffering, or soon to be suffering, saints in the churches of Asia Minor that they are the possessors of the title to a glorious new life in the heavenly order, one which is guaranteed on the basis of the historical fact of Jesus' resurrection. He expands this general prospect in three defining negative adjectives, and then one positive one.

a. The inheritance 'can never perish' (aphtharton)

This word expresses the utter security of the heavenly inheritance – in stark contrast to Israel's inheritance in the land, which was endlessly under threat from raiders and marching armies. These threats were not mere formalities. 'In the ninth year of Zedekiah king of Judah . . . Nebuchadnezzar king of Babylon marched against Jerusalem with his whole army . . . and the city wall was broken through' (Jer. 39:1–2; cf. Judg. 3:7–8, 12–14; 1 Sam. 4:1–22; Dan. 9:26). The very geography of the Promised Land, standing astride one of the great trade routes of the ancient world and without clear and secure natural boundaries, made it constantly vulnerable to enemy attack. It was an inherently insecure inheritance, as any history of the last thirty years in the Middle East will confirm.

At the domestic level, insecurity is no less a fact of life, as Jesus noted when contrasting the heavenly inheritance with the earthly. 'Do not store up for yourselves treasures on earth, where moth and rust destroy, and where thieves break in and steal. But store up for yourselves treasures in heaven, where moth and rust do not destroy, and where thieves do not break in and steal' (Matt. 6:19–20). Our heavenly inheritance is finally invulnerable: 'For I am convinced that neither death nor life, neither angels nor demons, neither the present nor the future, nor any powers, neither height nor depth, nor anything else in all creation, will be able to separate us [in time or eternity] from the love of God that is in Christ Jesus our Lord' (Rom. 8:38–39).

[6] A. Stibbs, *The First Epistle General of Peter* (Tyndale, 1959), p. 75.

b. The inheritance 'can never spoil' (amianton)

Again the failures of Israel's historic experience may lie in the background. Isaiah complains, 'The earth is defiled by its people; they have disobeyed the laws, violated the statutes and broken the everlasting covenant. Therefore a curse consumes the earth; its people must bear their guilt' (Is. 24:5–6). Jeremiah notes that God had given Israel a fertile land, 'But you came and defiled my land and made my inheritance detestable' (Jer. 2:7). The sin which primarily produced this defilement is idolatry (cf. Jer 3:2; Ezek. 20:43; Hag. 2:14).

By contrast, the heavenly inheritance is safe from every sinful taint. It is a sinless inheritance. The 'sexually immoral [and] the idolaters' are for ever 'in the fiery lake', 'outside' (Rev. 21:8; 22:15). 'No longer will there be any curse' (Rev. 22:3). The bride will be 'beautifully dressed for her husband'; 'without stain or wrinkle or any other blemish, but holy and blameless' (Rev. 21:2; Eph. 5:27). What a prospect is held before us – at last to leave sin and all its defilements behind us for ever. It is nothing less than the prospect of being part of a world which perfectly obeys, worships and serves its God.

c. The inheritance 'can never fade' (amaranton)

The word translated 'fade' is used of flowers which are inherently perishable, an eloquent image in a land subject to withering temperatures. 'The grass withers and the flowers fall' (Is. 40:8). Jesus noted this also: 'See how the lilies of the field grow. They do not labour or spin. Yet I tell you that not even Solomon in all his splendour was dressed like one of these. If that is how God clothes the grass of the field, which is here today and tomorrow is thrown into the fire . . .' (Matt. 6:28–30). James makes a similar point with respect to earthly riches: '[The rich man] will pass away like a wild flower. For the sun rises with scorching heat and withers the plant; its blossom falls and its beauty is destroyed' (Jas. 1:10–11). By contrast, the heavenly inheritance is imperishable. Ours is an eternal home.

Paul's three negative adjectives thus build up a picture of our inheritance as one which is 'sure, pure and will endure', or which 'is untouched by death, unstained by evil, unimpaired by time'.[7] This brings us to Paul's positive assertion.

[7] F. W. Beare, *The First Epistle of Peter* (Oxford, 1958); cited E. Best, *1 Peter*, NCB (Eerdmans, 1971), p. 76.

d. The inheritance is 'kept in heaven for you' (tetērēmenēn)

We could translate this as 'reserved'. A reservation has been made for us personally, as well as for the people of God collectively. This sense of the inheritance being already in place is brought out also by the verbal form. 'Kept' is a perfect participle, used of an action which has already been completed. It has been done; even though 'what we will be has not yet been made known' (1 John 3:2) and the inheritance is invisible at present. 'People are destined once to die' (Heb. 9:27 NIV) is as valid for Christians as for any others. For believers, as for the rest of humankind, 'the paths of glory lead but to the grave'. Invisible though it may be, however, the path goes on beyond the grave, and leads the Christian unerringly to 'the place I have prepared for you' (John 14:2). The same assurance is conveyed by Peter in verse 5, where he speaks of the coming salvation, our inheritance, as 'ready to be revealed'. It is presently veiled, true, but it is already in place, like an object hidden behind a curtain. When the Saviour appears, the curtain will be drawn back to reveal him who has been standing there patiently awaiting the 'curtain call' of the last trumpet.[8] Then he and his eternal salvation, including the inheritance of his people, will be revealed.

Expected
One of the most disconcerting experiences which can come our way is to make a long journey, perhaps even to the other side of the world, and to discover on arrival that we have not been expected. The hotel reservation has not been made, or, even more devastating, the friendly home is all locked up and the warm welcome we have anticipated over the miles is not awaiting us, due to a mix-up of dates or the loss of a letter or e-mail. Heaven, however, is guaranteed not to disappoint. At the end of this journey, above all others, a welcome awaits us, and our place is already prepared. It is being 'kept' for us. Not only is that inheritance 'kept' for us, but we are also 'kept' for it. It is 'kept in heaven for you, who through faith are shielded by God's power until the coming of the salvation that is ready to be revealed in the last time' (v. 6). Here Peter, like Paul in writing to the Romans (cf. Rom. 8:31–34), confronts possibly the deepest anxiety which assaults our hope of heavenly glory. We can affirm that God has prepared it and that, unlike our earthly inheritances, it will never 'perish, spoil, or fade', but rather is kept in anticipation of our arrival to claim it. We are expected.

---

[8] This image actually unpacks one of the primary New Testament words for Christ's second coming, *epiphaneia*, 'unveiling', e.g. 2 Thess. 2:8.

Kept
But what if we fail ourselves? This is our fear. What confidence can we have that *we* will ever arrive in the heavenly order? The prize which is heavenly glory dangles enticingly before us; the key to our inheritance is in our hands, and we see the door of our heavenly home in the distance – but what if we are beguiled by our fallen hearts and lose the way, and so never arrive? What if, in our sinful folly, we throw away the key?

Such fears are answered in this great assertion, '[We are] kept . . . by God's power until the coming of the salvation' (v. 5). The verb 'kept' here is used in the sense of 'putting under guard'. In a similar sense we read in Galatians 3:23, 'Before this faith came, we were held prisoners by the law, locked up until faith should be revealed.'[9]

This 'keeping' is 'through faith', which may indicate the human means by which the keeping is effected. Bearing in mind the whole thrust of this passage, however, it is possibly also directing attention away from our visible efforts to secure ourselves, to the miracle of the constant, unseen, keeping power of God. As Cranfield rightly notes, using a different metaphor, 'It would be but a poor providence, if it shielded us from the troubles of this life and then were to fail to bring us to our inheritance in the end. It would be like bringing a ship safely through the perils of the high seas and then failing to navigate the river mouth.'[10]

Peter's use of 'salvation' in this verse has future rather than past or present reference. While we thank God for all that our salvation may bring us in this life, 'to identify our present experience as Christians with what the New Testament terms salvation is a disastrous illusion'.[11] Thank God there is more to come – much, much more. The contemplation of this glorious, assured prospect brings joy (v. 6).

3. Hallelujah!

'In this you greatly rejoice.' Thus Peter brings us again to the note of praise with which he began the paragraph, 'Praise be . . .' (v. 3). But it is not a joy unrelated to present, more sobering realities: 'though now for a little while you may have had to suffer grief in all kinds of

---

[9] Paul uses the same verb in 2 Corinthians 11:32 with reference to the gates of Damascus being 'guarded'. 'God has put us under arrest, as it were, to keep us safe for his day' (E. P. Clowney, *The Message of 1 Peter* [IVP, 1988], p. 49).
[10] Cranfield, *The First Epistle of Peter*, p. 25.
[11] ibid., p. 26.

trials' (v. 6). The heavenly hope is not a mental illusion or an emotional crutch. It makes a real difference in the present, not least in the 'grievous' present.

Peter now unfolds the ways in which the hope of the heavenly inheritance impacts on our painful experiences, and in particular those which arise from our being faithful Christian disciples. Jesus had promised, we recall, that following him would not be a comfortable journey. 'Those who love their lives will lose them, while those who hate their lives in this world will keep them for eternal life. Whoever serves me must follow me' (John 12:25–26 NIVI). Peter had lived out his post-resurrection, apostolic life with the prediction of his future martyrdom hanging over his head (cf. John 21:18, 'when you are old you will stretch out your hands', a first-century euphemism for death by crucifixion). To follow Jesus in life would be best understood at times as following him into death (cf. Luke 14:25–33).

Billy Graham, in his book *Till Armageddon*, gives a list of 'all kinds of trials' which the Bible predicts for God's children, as drawn up by Dr Finis Drake. It is a remarkable list covering twenty distinguishable forms of trial.[12] Peter's message is clear: on the day when you are called to bear any one of these trials, recall the heavenly prospect which lies before you. In the light of that coming inheritance we can take heart: our trials have a purpose; they will be productive; and they will pass.

a. Purposeful

'You may have had to suffer.' There is a conditional sense here, 'you *may* have had to suffer', but the construction used 'assumes the reality of the condition, "if necessary, [as it is]"'.[13] Calvin comments,

---

[12] Billy Graham, *Till Armageddon* (Word, 1981), pp. 94–96. Dr Drake's 'Twenty trials': (1) Persecutions for righteousness (Matt. 5:10; 13:21; Mark 10:30; John 15:20). (2) Revilings and slander (Matt. 5:11–12; 10:25; Acts 13:45; 1 Pet. 4:4). (3) False accusations (Matt. 10:17–29). (4) Scourgings for Christ (Matt. 10:17). (5) Rejection (Matt. 10:14). (6) Hatred by the world (Matt. 10:22; John 15:18–21). (7) Hatred by relatives (Matt. 10:21–36). (8) Martyrdom (Matt. 10:28; Acts 7:58). (9) Temptations (Luke 8:13; Jas. 1:2–16). (10) Shame for his name (Acts 5:41). (11) Imprisonments (Acts 4:3; 5:18; 12:4). (12) Tribulations (Acts 14:22; 2 Thess. 1:4). (13) Stonings (Acts 14:19; 2 Cor. 11:25). (14) Beatings (Acts 16:23; 2 Cor. 11:24–25). (15) Being a spectacle to the world (1 Cor. 4:9). (16) Misunderstandings, necessities, defamation and despisings (1 Cor. 4:10–13). (17) Troubles, afflictions, distresses, tumults, labours, watchings, fastings and evil reports (2 Cor. 6:8–10; 11:26–28). (18) Reproaches (Heb. 13:13; 1 Pet. 4:14). (19) Trials (1 Pet. 1:7; 4:12). (20) Satanic opposition (Eph. 4:27; 6:12).

[13] E. D. Hiebert, *First Peter* (Moody, 1984), p. 80.

His purpose was to show that God does not thus try his people without reason, for if God afflicted us without a cause it would be grievous to bear. Hence Peter has taken an argument for consolation from the design of God, not because the purpose always appears to us, but because we ought to be fully persuaded that it ought to be so, because it is God's will.[14]

Peter's exhortation later in the letter underlines the lesson. 'Dear friends, do not be surprised at the painful trial you are suffering, as though something strange were happening to you' (4:12). God works in our trials. They are not accidental.

b. Productive

Peter uses a vivid image to convey this next profound truth. Just as precious metals (he instances gold) are put into the furnace in order to be purified, and hence increase their value, so the faith of the Christian is purified through the experience of trial. Indeed, Peter asserts that the parallel is imperfect, since in practice gold is an ultimately perishable substance, whereas faith is imperishable like its inheritance (cf. v. 4, 'can never perish'). Among other things, faith becomes more precious through the experience of trial in that it is thereby 'proved genuine'.

The Old Testament contains several echoes of this teaching. 'I have tested you in the furnace of affliction' (Is. 48:10). 'He knows the way that I take; when he has tested me, I shall come forth as gold' (Job 16:10). One particular aspect of this productivity from trials is specified by Peter: 'that your faith . . . may be proved genuine and may result in praise, glory and honour when Jesus Christ is revealed' (v. 7). Peter is assuring his readers that God is not unaware of the pains they endure for him, and that he who is no-one's debtor will appropriately reward and honour those who have suffered for him (cf. Rom. 2:29; 1 Cor. 4:5; 1 Pet. 5:4). Thus, as Stibbs notes, 'The praise and honour and glory which genuine faith will secure in the day of full disclosure will, from one standpoint, be given to the true believers by the approving Lord.' But he continues, 'From another standpoint they will be given to the Lord himself, who is thus openly shown to have been worthy of trust by both the devotion and the experience of those who trusted him.'[15]

In terms of our trials bringing honour to the Lord himself, we can compare also the testimony of Joni Eareckson-Tada. 'I don't really

---

[14] J. Calvin, *The Epistle of Paul the Apostle to the Hebrews and the First and Second Epistles of St Peter* (Saint Andrew, 1963), p. 235.

[15] Stibbs, *The First Epistle General of Peter*, p. 78.

mind the inconvenience of being paralysed if my faithfulness to God while in this wheel-chair can bring glory to Him.' She then applies this truth. 'Have you considered the potential glory your faith can give to God if in your "wheel-chair" you remain faithful?'[16] Hudson Taylor notes one particular aspect of this 'resulting in praise and glory and honour': 'Difficulties afford a platform upon which God can show himself. Without them we could never know how tender, faithful and almighty God is.'

c. Passing

The trials are, Peter notes, 'for a little while' (v. 6). Concerning them we can always echo the recurrent phrase of the Authorized Version, 'it came to pass'. Even if this life does not bring relief, from the perspective of the coming of the Lord and the ages of eternity, these trials are 'momentary', as Paul argued in 2 Corinthians 4:17. Thus we look beyond the present to the future, past present brokenness and pain to the coming wholeness and the triumph of the Lord. The trials will pass, but the triumph is for ever.

Desmond Tutu reflects this perspective in a sermon preached at one of the lowest points in the struggle for human rights in South Africa.

Humanly speaking it seems quite hopeless. But we are not alone. Man, this is God's world. He is in charge. The kingdoms of this world are becoming the Kingdom of our God and of his Christ, and he shall reign forever and ever! . . . The resurrection of Jesus is our guarantee, that right has triumphed, and will triumph over wrong, that good has triumphed and will triumph over evil; it is our guarantee that love has triumphed and will triumph over hate. You and I know that Jesus has broken down all kinds of walls of separation. You and I know despite all the evidence to the contrary that we, black and white together, are one in the Lord, we, black and white together, are one in the Spirit. You and I know that we will hold hands, black and white together, with our heads held high as we stride into the glorious future God holds out to us . . . for the fulfilment of the vision of St John the Divine: 'After this I looked, and there was an enormous crowd – no-one could count all the people! They were from every race, tribe, nation and language, and they stood in front of the throne and of the Lamb, dressed in white robes and holding palm branches in their hands. They called out in a loud voice, 'Salvation comes from our God, who sits on the throne, and from the Lamb.'[17]

[16] Joni Eareckson and Steve Estes, *A Step Further* (Zondervan, 1979), p. 41.
[17] D. Tutu, *The Rainbow People of God* (Doubleday, 1984), p. 40.

We cannot stop here, however. We cannot stop with Peter's recognition that through Christ and his coming triumph all our earthly trials are sanctified, given perspective, invested with meaning, and made productive of glory and praise. Wonderful as that no doubt is, there is something beyond that. Rather, there is someone.

d. The person of the Lord

The prospect of Christ 'being revealed' (v. 7) brings Peter back to the present, to the risen, living Lord in whom both he and his readers believed (v. 8, 'you believe in him', or perhaps 'you trust' or 'rely upon'). Peter had the great privilege of countless memories of his years with Jesus to draw upon when he thought of Christ. His readers, however, had not, and still did not see him ('you do not see him now'). That is no final inhibition as far as faith is concerned. Knowing him now is knowing him as the one we love ('though you have not seen him, you love him'). There is no more glorious fruit of faith than this – to love Jesus.

The apostle Peter could never forget that this was what the Lord had searched for in Peter's heart after the tragedy of his betrayal. 'Do you love me? . . . Do you love me? . . . Do you love me?' (John 21:16–17). Nothing was of greater importance as Jesus recommissioned his penitent apostle. Nothing is above that, nothing beyond it. It is the supreme gift of faith, and arguably the best reason of all for being a Christian – to know him as our beloved Lord. Duncan Campbell speaks for every Christian heart when he writes, 'I want to say reverently and humbly that for me the greatest reality, the greatest fact in life is just the presence of the Lord Jesus. And I love Him; that to me is greater than preaching, it is greater than seeing revival . . . the greatest thing of all is just to have fellowship with Jesus.'[18]

To know that is to be immediately in worship. It is to sing 'hallelujah' in our deepest hearts. Peter speaks of it as the door to being 'filled with an inexpressible and glorious joy' (v. 9). The word 'inexpressible', or 'unutterable', occurs only here in the New Testament, and speaks for itself – in fact, it says nothing because no words are adequate! Words fail, worship becomes speechless adoration, and joy engulfs the heart, a 'glorious joy'. Wayne Grudem suggests that it is 'joy that has been infused with heavenly glory and that still possesses the radiance of that glory'.[19] It is a joy which is in essence 'the salvation of our souls'.[20]

---

[18] D. Campbell, *The Price and Power of Revival* (Parry Jackman, 1956), p. 36.
[19] W. Grudem, *1 Peter* (IVP, 1988), p. 66.
[20] The NIV 'for' (v. 9) is probably mistaken; cf. ibid., p. 67.

Salvation in the end is Jesus himself – his anticipation in the Old Testament, his realization in the New. Salvation is Jesus Christ the Lord – his incarnation, his holy, obedient life and ministry, his unspeakable death for our sins, his glorious resurrection on the third day, his ascension to the Father's right hand, his present reign, his glorious return and everlasting kingdom. To know him is to know all that, and it is salvation – past, present and future, salvation for time and salvation for eternity. Its final word is again and again, 'Hallelujah!' 'To him who sits on the throne and to the Lamb be praise and honour and glory and power, for ever and ever!' Amen.

Summary

Peter is addressing Christians facing big trouble. Persecution is imminent. He tells them that the resurrection of Jesus has redefined God, brought new spiritual life, and guaranteed a heavenly inheritance. This inheritance is already in place. In its light the trials are seen as purposeful, productive and passing, and preparatory to meeting their beloved Lord.

2 Peter 3:1–14
18. Why live differently?

Christian: 'We are going to Mount Zion.'
Then Atheist fell into very great laughter.
Christian: 'What's the meaning of your laughter?'
Atheist: 'I laugh to see what ignorant persons you are, to take upon you so tedious a journey, and yet are like to have nothing but your travel for your pains . . . There is not such a place as you dream of in all this world.'
Hopeful: 'What! no Mount Zion! Did we not see from the Delectable Mountains the Gate of the City? . . . Now do I rejoice in the hope of the Glory of God.'
So they turned away from the man; and he, laughing at them, went his way.

(John Bunyan, *The Pilgrim's Progress*)

As he writes his second letter, Peter is aware that his ministry is nearly at an end. 'I know that I will soon put [the tent of this body] aside, as our Lord Jesus Christ has made clear to me' (1:13–14). His overriding concern is understandably for the health of the churches he is soon to leave behind.

Specifically, the letter addresses the harmful influence of false teachers. Their teaching is usually seen as a precursor of Gnosticism, a pseudo-Christian heresy which became a major challenge to the faith during the second century.[1] Rooted in Hellenistic thought, Gnosticism taught the radical disjunction between the material and spiritual worlds. God resided in the spiritual order and had no

---

[1] J. N. D. Kelly, A *Commentary on the Epistles of Peter and Jude* (Black, 1977), p. 237; R. H. Strachan, *The Second Epistle General of Peter*, Exp. Gk. Text (1897–1910), pp. 5, 116. For another view of the heresy see R. J. Baukham, *Jude, 2 Peter* (WBC, 1983), p. 156f.

dealings with the evil, material order. Salvation lay in escape from the prison of the material world into the upper spiritual realm. This liberation was possible only for those with a special 'inner spark' (*pneuma*), provided that they received the necessary special knowledge (*gnōsis*, hence 'gnosticism'). One of the tenets of the heretics was their denial of eschatology: since God is not ultimately concerned with this earthly order, and hence is indifferent to the present process of history and to the future of the space-time world, there is no future climax. Theirs was a theology without a heavenly hope.

Peter's main riposte comes in the third chapter, and clearly demonstrates not only the inadequacy of these pre-Gnostics' doctrinal understanding, but also the significant ethical and moral implications of the true doctrine of the end.

1. Denials of destiny

The false prophets are described as 'scoffers' (3:3), an allusion to their arrogance (cf. 2:10, 'bold and arrogant'). Like heretics in every age, they are serenely assured of their superiority to the 'simple, uninformed believers' whom they have come to liberate by their 'new insights'. They are the people, truth will die with them. They *know*! Peter notes that their breed will be typical of 'the last days' (v. 3). This phrase refers not simply to the final phase of earthly history immediately before Christ's return, but to the entire period of time between the first and second comings of Christ (cf. Gal. 4:4; Heb. 1:2; 1 Cor. 10:11; Acts 2:17). Accordingly, we should not be surprised to meet their kind today.

They have at least two criticisms of the Christian doctrine of the coming parousia of Christ and its accompanying end. First, 'Where is this "coming" he promised?' (v. 4) – there is no sign of this anticipated event. Second, 'Ever since our fathers died, everything goes on as it has since the beginning of creation' (v. 4) – history does not contain any clear precursors to the glorious return of Christ; the world is regulated by processes which do not admit of cataclysmic interventions.

The real motive

There is a further dimension to this criticism which Peter identifies: its motivation. In voicing their criticisms, they are 'following their own evil desires' (v. 3). In other words, the false teachings are the rationalization of false motives; their misdirected desires are the real roots of their misinformed doctrines. Peter has earlier exposed

283

these desires: 'With eyes full of adultery, they never stop sinning; they seduce the unstable . . . appealing to the lustful desires of sinful human nature . . . they promise . . . freedom, while they themselves are slaves of depravity' (2:14, 18, 19). It is not a pretty picture. Accordingly, it comes as no surprise that they deny the coming of the Lord, since one of the primary functions he will perform is to render judgment. There is no 'coming of the Lord' – there daren't be!

2. The defence of destiny

Peter offers a fivefold defence of the coming climax of history.

a. God has spoken

First, he appeals to *the Word of God*. 'I want you to recall the words spoken in the past by the holy prophets and the command given by our Lord and Saviour through your apostles' (v. 2). In this plea Peter neatly summarizes the contents of the Bible, the Old Testament conveniently referred to as 'the words spoken by the holy prophets', and the New Testament categorized as 'the command given by our Lord and Saviour through your apostles'.

Here is the ultimate court of appeal. The Lord God Almighty has spoken! Both Testaments leave no doubt concerning the apocalyptic conclusion to human history.

Old Testament prophecies consistently refer to the coming 'day of the Lord', and to its accompanying universal accounting, the last judgment. They speak too, in many places, of the fact and the forms of the eternal kingdom of the Messiah.

The New Testament speaks with even clearer witness. Again and again Jesus prophesied his coming, both in his parables and in his direct didactic instruction. The combined apostolic writings of the New Testament contain more than 250 clear references. While we dare not assess theological significance in terms of numerical frequency of reference, it is certainly noteworthy that comparatively fewer promises underlie the glory and power of the incarnation with all its epochal import.

Here we encounter one of the great bedrocks of our beliefs about human destiny. God has broken the silence, the Creator and Lord of all has taken initiative to inform us. This 'word of the prophets' is the most 'certain' (1:19) ground of appeal. The prophetic testimony does not reside in the prophet's own will or fancy, but 'men spoke from God as they were carried along by the Holy Spirit' (1:21). God the

Holy Spirit, he who 'searches all things, even the deep things of God, [he who] knows the thoughts of God' (1 Cor. 2:10–11), has spoken. What has he said? The Lord is coming, history will conclude, and heaven and hell will carry the human story into its eternal phase. Thus says the Lord!

b. God has come

Second, Peter appeals to *the coming of God*. This argument occurs in the first chapter. There Peter reminded his readers of 'the power and coming of our Lord Jesus Christ . . . of his majesty', as confirmed by his receiving 'honour and glory from God the Father when the voice came to him from the Majestic Glory, saying, "This is my Son, whom I love; with him I am well pleased"' (1:16–17). Peter is recalling in vivid language the overwhelming impact of the transfiguration. Years later its detail still lingers in his memory, with its mind-blowing impression of the glory of the Lord and the direct, heavenly attestation of his divine status by the voice of 'God the Father'.

Thus the claim of the false teachers that history has never before been cleaved by the intervention of God is mistaken. They ignore the fact of the incarnation. The God of glory has manifested himself in human history in Jesus Christ. Hence the thought of a further 'coming' of Jesus at the climax of history is both entirely credible, in view of the clear historic precedent in his first 'coming', and religiously inevitable, in view of the nature of God (1:3) and the fact of 'the eternal kingdom of our Lord and Saviour Jesus Christ' (1:11).

This point is capable of expansion in terms of the further manifestation of the 'majesty' of our Lord Jesus Christ in his resurrection from the dead. That event may be implicit in the language Peter uses here. However, he does have a further, earlier, instance of God's intervention to which he can appeal. We recall that the criticism he is rebutting is the claim that 'everything goes on as it has since the beginning of creation'. 'Not so,' says Peter. 'You are forgetting the flood!' In the time of Noah, 'the world . . . was deluged and destroyed' (3:6). So again there is historical precedent for the intervention of God. Since Peter's opponents appear to have made some appeal to the Old Testament,[2] their overlooking of this event is mischievous – 'they deliberately forget' (3:5).

This allusion to the flood throws up a further ground of appeal.

---

[2] Cf. 3:16, Peter's reference to a tendency to 'distort . . . the other Scriptures', and similarly his defence of the divine inspiration of Scripture in 1:21, aimed at those claiming 'private' interpretations.

c. God is great

Third, Peter appeals to *the greatness of God*. God's greatness is disclosed in the act of creation. His opponents have foolishly introduced this piece of evidence themselves by their charge that nothing has changed 'since the beginning of creation'. Creation at 'the beginning' is excellent grist for Peter's mill. As he notes, 'the heavens existed' – i.e. came into existence – 'by God's word . . . and the earth was formed out of water' (3:5). Peter has Genesis 1 in mind here, and the reference to water will allow him to anticipate the case of Noah's flood, which, as we noted above, demonstrates the non-uniform nature of history.

God having created the world 'out of nothing' by his word alone is a gift to Peter in his demolition of the heretics, since it establishes an open universe, one which is entirely under the rule of God, and hence in principle constantly open to the special intervention of God. God is accordingly utterly free to terminate the universe and the affairs of our tiny planet howsoever and whensoever he pleases.

A second aspect of Peter's appeal to God's greatness is his lordship over the temporal process. Time is God's servant, hence it is entirely relative as far as God is concerned. For God time has both a brevity, 'with the Lord . . . a thousand years are like a day' (3:8), and an intensity, 'with the Lord a day is like a thousand years' (3:8), which are unknown by us. Accusations of God's 'slowness' in keeping the promises concerning the return of Christ are therefore entirely beside the point. God is in complete control of time and its discerned passage. To accuse him of delay is effectively to ignore, even to blaspheme, his sovereignty, and to question his purpose of love.

d. God is just

Fourth, Peter appeals to *the justice of God*. The story of Noah operates for Peter rather as it did for his Master (Luke 17:26f.; Matt. 14:37f.), as a foreshadow of God's sudden and destructive judgment. Peter alluded to this earlier: 'He did not spare the ancient world when he brought the flood on its ungodly people' (2:5). Now he returns to it: 'By the same word [of God] the present heavens and earth are reserved for fire, being kept for the day of judgment and destruction of ungodly men' (3:7). Thus the return of Christ is demanded by the just character of God. Evil cannot go unpunished for ever. Ungodliness must be brought to book. The story of the flood is a solemn warning to all perpetrators of evil. Beware, 'God cannot be mocked. People reap what they sow' (Gal. 6:7 NIVI).

There is a sobering facet of that future judgment indicated in Peter's following allusion to the relativity of time, 'With the Lord a day is like a thousand years' (3:8). Obviously he is only using this as a loose illustration of time's relativity, but it is worth pursuing the equation. That rate of comparison yields the approximate ratio of one second of our time equalling four days to God. In other words, the intensity of time for God means that what passes us by as a mere moment has the potential to be teased out in the presence of God so that all its features and ingredients are minutely exposed. Jesus made a similar point when referring to the fact that 'men will have to give account on the day of judgment for every careless word they have spoken' (Matt. 12:36), and that 'there is nothing concealed that will not be disclosed, or hidden that will not be made known. What you have said in the dark will be heard in the daylight, and what you have whispered in the ear in the inner rooms will be proclaimed from the roofs' (Luke 12:2–3).

How often we excuse ourselves by alluding to the brevity of the action in question, 'it happened in an instant', or 'the word was out before I could stop it', as if the very intensity of the experience represented some sort of excuse, and since it happened so quickly we are really hardly responsible for it at all. But 'with the Lord a second is as four days'. How little will such appeal stand up on the judgment day, when we appear before the one by whom 'motives are weighed' (Prov. 16:2), and at whose coming 'the motives of people's hearts' will be exposed (1 Cor. 4:5 NIVI).

God's judgments will have a depth and inclusiveness such as have never before obtained nor ever will again. No wonder the book of Revelation affords this awesome picture of the time of judgment:

> The kings of the earth, the princes, the generals, the rich, the mighty, and every slave and every free man hid in caves and among the rocks of the mountains. They called to the mountains and the rocks, 'Fall on us and hide us from the face of him who sits on the throne and from the wrath of the Lamb! For the great day of their wrath has come, and who can stand?' (Rev. 6:15–17).

e. God is gracious

Fifth, Peter appeals to the *grace of God*. The ultimate explanation of the apparent delay in the end is God's heart of mercy. He is a God who 'takes no pleasure in the death of anyone' (Ezek. 18:32). He is a God who 'wants all people to be saved and come to a knowledge of the truth' (1 Tim. 2:4 NIVI). Accordingly, God is pictured by Peter as holding back the coming of judgment so that sinners may have further opportunity to repent and turn to him to find salvation. 'He is patient . . . not wanting anyone to perish, but everyone to come to repentance' (v. 9).

The critics therefore stand to be warned as well as corrected. That they continue to experience the deferment of final judgment is not because they have it right and there is no judgment to come. It is because they have it wrong; there *is* a judgment coming, but the judge is a God who, in his amazing, patient grace, waits for these first-century heretics to come to their senses and submit to the truth of the gospel.

3. The description of destiny

Peter comes finally to the issue which immediately follows: granted the fact of the coming climax of history, what will it be like? Wisely, the apostle confines himself to broad brush-strokes in his depiction of the dawn of the eternal order. In thinking about the end, there is always the danger of saying too much as well as of saying too little. Here, as in other things, the limits of revelation need to be observed. 'What we will be has not yet been made known' (1 John 3:2; cf. Deut. 29:29).

Peter alludes to the end in three texts. 'The present heavens and earth are reserved for fire, being kept for the day of judgment' (v. 7). 'The day of the Lord will come like a thief. The heavens will disappear with a roar; the elements will be destroyed by fire, and the earth and everything in it will be laid bare' (v. 10). 'That day will bring about the destruction of the heavens by fire, and the elements will melt in the heat' (v. 12). To which we can add, 'But in keeping with his promise we are looking forward to a new heaven and a new earth' (v. 13). What can we understand from Peter's descriptions?

a. Climax

The arrival of destiny will be *climactic in its repercussion.* Quite simply, it will bring life on this planet to an end. The long course of human history, from its earliest beginnings to its final preoccupations, will abruptly conclude. That conclusion will be cosmic as well as anthropic. The world which has been our physical context over the centuries and millennia will be no more.

In verse 10 Peter uses an Old Testament phrase, 'the day of the Lord' (cf. v. 12, 'the day of God'). The prophets frequently refer to this coming 'day' as the time of God's judgment both on the nations (Is. 13:6, 9; Jer. 46:10; Obad. 15; Joel 2:13; 3:14), and on Israel (Amos 5:18–20; Is. 2:12f.; Ezek. 13:5; Joel 1:15; 2:1, 11; Zeph. 1:7; Zech. 14:1). Paul also uses the phrase in 2 Thessalonians 2:2, though more commonly links it explicitly to Jesus Christ (1 Cor. 1:8; 5:5; Phil. 1:6,

10; 2:16). The climactic nature of this 'day' is expressed by Peter's repeated use of the word 'destruction' (vv. 7, 10, 12). Fire is the primary physical element mentioned (vv. 7, 10, 12), of such intensity that 'elements will melt in the heat' (v. 12). It is accompanied by a 'roar', signalling an event of hyperdestructiveness which will cause the disappearance of the physical universe as presently perceived (v. 10).

Commentators note the parallels, on the surface, to Stoic visions of the end. The differences are even more marked, however, as the Fathers pointed out.[3] In this imagery Peter is repeating the words of Jesus (Luke 21:25; Matt. 24:29, 35).

When we recall the link between God and fire in Scripture – 'the LORD your God is a consuming fire' (Deut. 4:24), with its echo in Hebrews 12:29, 'God is a consuming fire' – we can express Peter's teaching by the assertion that there is a moment coming in which the world will meet face to face with its God.

b. Surprise

This meeting will be *surprising in its occasion.* 'The day of the Lord will come like a thief' (v. 10). Peter here restates the teaching of his Master (cf. Luke 12:39f.; Matt. 24:43f.) and of Paul (1 Thess. 5:2; cf. Rev. 3:3; 16:15). The inbreaking of destiny will be both sudden and unexpected. The householder does not know that the thief is coming to raid his house, nor when he will choose to strike, which is why he often succeeds in his ploy. So it is with the end. It will happen without apparent warning.

True, Jesus had spoken of 'signs', and of the need for watchfulness (cf. Mark 13:5–37; Matt, 24:3–44), and Paul was prepared to identify certain preconditions (2 Thess. 2:1–12), but only the believing will be alerted. The mass of humanity will be completely caught out, and even for the believer it is questionable how far the 'signs' will escape the ambiguities of all historical perception. In the end, 'the Son of Man will come at an hour when you do not expect him' (Matt. 24:44).

c. Purpose

Finally, Peter says, the end will be *purposed in its function.* The coming of the end, and with it the dawning of human destiny,

---

[3] Cf. Justin Martyr, 'Whereas they [the Stoics] think God himself shall be resolved into fire ... we understand that God, the Creator of all things, is superior to the things which are to be changed' (*Apology,* i. 20; cited E. M. B. Green, *The Second Epistle General of Peter and the General Epistle of Jude* [Tyndale, 1958], p. 133).

whether in heaven or hell, will not be an arbitrary event, uncon-
nected to the historical process which has preceded it. Peter conveys
this connectedness by noting that the 'present heavens and earth' are
'reserved for fire, being kept for the day of judgment' (v. 7), that 'the
earth and everything in in it will be laid bare' (v. 10), and that 'we are
looking forward to a new heaven and a new earth, the home of
righteousness' (v. 13).

From the moment that humanity sinned in the Garden of Eden
(Gen. 3:6), the day of judgment, involving the radical reformation of
the entire fallen order, was implicit. Thus in the present order,
whether we think of human life under the tyranny of sin, death,
wrath and Satan (Rom. 5:12–20; 6:1 – 8:17; 11:32; John 8:28; Luke
11:17–22; Eph. 6:10–20), or of the created, physical order 'groaning'
in anticipation of its coming liberation from the 'bondage to decay'
(Rom. 8:21–22), all things await this coming day of the Lord. It is the
day to which all things are moving on their appointed course as the
triumphant purpose of God emerges beyond the shadows of sin
and destruction.

In the process there needs to be a 'laying bare' of all things (v. 10).
The verb here is much discussed, but a meaning of 'judicial enquiry
culminating in a penal pronouncement' is certainly possible.[4] Such a
meaning would be entirely congruent with the many other biblical
references to this coming 'day of the Lord'.

4. The demonstration of destiny

For Peter, as for all the New Testament writers, belief affects behaviour. The false teachers' denial of the end of history and the coming
day of the Lord with its determination of destiny has serious negative effects on their conduct. Correspondingly, the believer's
embrace of future destiny has significant positive effects. Peter identifies several in concluding his teaching on the end.

a. An inducement to seek salvation

As Peter notes, the end, when it arrives, will bring 'judgment and
destruction' on ungodly people (v. 7). Since we will face an examination which will, as verse 8 implies, be utterly disclosive of our slightest passing thoughts as well as our most visible behaviours, a
judgment in which everything will be 'laid bare' (v. 10), the inducement to seek salvation is overwhelming. It is time to seek the Lord.

---

[4] So F. W. Danker, in ZNW, 1962, pp. 82–86; cited Green, ibid., p. 138.

Peter gives special emphasis to the fact that God holds back his judgment in the hope that 'everyone will come to repentance'. Hence 'our Lord's patience means salvation' (v. 15), in the sense that the deferring of judgment underscores the graciousness of God, and his great willingness to receive and grant salvation to penitent sinners.

In this conclusion Peter sees Paul fully concurring, 'just as our dear brother Paul also wrote to you' (v. 15). It is therefore good to quote Paul saying exactly the same thing, in Romans 2:4, 'The riches of his kindness, tolerance and patience . . . leads you towards repentance.' The coming of the end is a call to salvation.

b. A motivator to pursue holiness

Verse 11 states it unerringly: 'Since everything will be destroyed in this way, what kind of people ought you to be? You ought to live holy and godly lives as you look forward to the day of God.' Similarly in verse 14, 'Since you are looking forward to this, make every effort to be found spotless, blameless and at peace with him.' How does the anticipation of the end promote our holiness?

First, *everything will be 'laid bare' on that day.* The New Testament is eloquent on the fact that, as Paul puts it, 'we must all appear before the judgment seat of Christ, that each one may receive what is due to [them] for the things done while in the body, whether good or bad' (2 Cor. 5:10). Earlier Paul had spoken to the Corinthians of the fact that everyone's 'work will be shown for what it is, because the Day will bring it to light. It will be revealed with fire' (1 Cor. 3:13). Behind these apostolic notes lies the witness of Jesus in his parables of the pounds (Luke 19:11–27) and the talents (Matt. 25:14–30). There is an accounting for every Christian. It will not imperil our status as children of God, and hence our title to a heavenly destiny, but equally it is not a prospect to dismiss lightly. Paul says that the careless Christian will 'suffer loss' on that day (1 Cor. 3:15). While the details of that 'loss' are not supplied, its force is clear. Here is a weighty inducement to holy living.

Second, *the tangible order within which our lives are lived will be destroyed.* The end relativizes all our loyalties within the present order, since 'this world is passing away' (1 Cor. 7:31; 2 Pet. 3:11). We dare not allow this to encourage social quietism or carelessness, not least because, as Paul notes in Colossians 3:22–25, our earthly work, including every expression of love for our neighbours, is part of that by which we glorify our heavenly Lord. But to covet for their own sakes the prizes, rewards and accolades of this present age is, in the light of the coming conflagration, a classic case of mistaken priorities. Jesus' word for all who succumb to such leaves nothing further to be said: 'God said to him, "You fool!"' (Luke 12:20).

By contrast we are to set our sights and our hearts on living 'holy and godly lives . . . spotless and blameless, and at peace with him'. John has the same perspective. 'Everyone who has this hope purifies himself, just as he is pure' (1 John 3:3). We should note Peter's 'make every effort' (v. 14). Holiness of life is finally the fruit of the indwelling Holy Spirit (Gal. 5:22f.; Rom. 8:3–11), but we are called to rouse ourselves to 'work out our salvation in fear and trembling' (Phil. 2:12).

Third, we should note *the condition of the new order which the end will inaugurate.* Peter refers to that new order as 'a new heaven and a new earth, the home of righteousness' (v. 13). We are on our way to a holy eternity, symbolized by a holy city, where 'nothing impure will ever enter' (Rev. 21:27). We are therefore wise to prepare ourselves for that holy world by embracing holiness as our lifestyle here and now. Part of that is listening to our conscience so that we are regularly 'at peace' with God (v. 14).

c. A promoter of energetic service

'You look forward to the day of God and speed its coming' (v. 12). Peter's language has provoked discussion. How can we 'speed', i.e. bring nearer, the 'day of God'? Does this not seriously dilute God's sovereignty? Besides, God himself has already set the day, as Paul informed the Athenians (Acts 17:31), a date so critical that even his blessed Son Incarnate was not informed of it (Matt. 24:36). It would be an astonishing conclusion if uncertainty as to the timing were bound up with God's dependence upon the church's achievement through the ages.

On account of this kind of consideration, the AV translated the phrase 'hasting unto'. Grammatically speaking, however, 'hasten' is closer to what Peter wrote. But need God's sovereignty be impugned by this? The God who foreknows all things, and in that foreknowing set the day, was able to take into account the Spirit-inspired actions of his people through the centuries (cf. Mark 13:10; Matt. 24:14; Acts 1:6–8). Further, Peter in his sermon recorded in Acts 3:19–21 similarly appears to see a linkage between response to the gospel and the return of Christ.

Lest we take too much upon ourselves, however, we should note that when Peter gives the reasons for the delay in the coming of the end (v. 9), he does not list the church's failure to fulfil the Great Commission among them.

Perhaps a surer and less controversial linkage between our service now and the future coming of the Lord is that made by Paul in 2 Corinthians 11:2, where he sees his labours in Corinth (and elsewhere) as 'getting the bride ready' for presentation to the heavenly bridegroom at his coming. This 'getting ready' will obviously include all means used to induce people to become a part of the bride, such as personal witness to Christ, prayer ('Your kingdom come'), and the support of world evangelization. It will also embrace all the means employed towards the church's growth into the likeness of the Lord. The linkage between our service and Christ's coming is here made in a way that truly honours him, and yet takes into account all our present opportunities for service. And the Lord, foreknowing all this, has taken it into account in his setting of the time he has inscribed on the heavenly wedding invitations, a time which, in this sense, we have 'hastened'. Since the coming of the end, and thus the dawning of human destiny, is supremely honouring to the Lord, we need have no hesitation in echoing the cry of 'the Spirit and the bride' as it has echoed through the ages: 'Come Lord Jesus!' (Rev. 22:17, 20; 1 Cor. 16:22).

d. A trumpet call to hope

We have noted this implication in the previous paragraph. It only remains to note the textual base for it. 'As you look forward to this' (v. 12), and 'You are looking forward to this' (v. 14), Peter asserts. He is surely right. Throughout our lives we have been 'looking forward'. As children it was the anticipation of a birthday or the exciting surprises of a Christmas Day. Later it was a party, or a vacation, or a first date, or a graduation. Later still a wedding day, or a promotion, the birth of a baby, or a new home. And later again, the day of retirement, a special anniversary, the arrival of a grandchild. We live our lives 'looking forward'. But none of these 'hopes' is a sure thing. Some miss out on many of them, others would identify other 'dreams' not listed here. For the Christian, however, there is one 'sure and certain hope'. It is the arrival of 'the day of God'. So, 'in keeping with his promise we are looking forward to a new heaven and a new earth, the home of righteousness' (v. 13) – what a great preacher called 'the most glorious promise which is to be found anywhere in the entire Bible'.[5]

This promise delineates the end of sin, the end of Satan, the end of shame and evil, the end of disease, death and despair. This promise

[5] D. M. Lloyd-Jones, *Expository Sermons on 2 Peter* (Banner of Truth, 1983), p. 197.

anticipates the arrival of righteousness, the coming of peace, joy and love, the appearing of God, Father, Son and Spirit, in all his glory, majesty, beauty and grace. This promise embraces entry into the glory of God's unveiled presence, along with all the people of God from this and every age, and the exaltation of the Lord Jesus Christ at the centre of that glory, all in a new world to which there will be no end for ever. When we consider this promise, then hope wells up irrepressibly within us. Amen! Come, Lord Jesus! We are looking forward!

Summary

The whole idea of a climactic end to history has always had its detractors. Peter's defence appeals to five certainties:

- God's promise;
- God's past interventions, supremely in Jesus Christ;
- God's omnipotence;
- God's justice;
- God's grace.

The end will be climactic, unexpected, and purposeful. It is a basis for seeking salvation, pursuing holiness, being active in service, and living in hope.

Revelation 20:1–15
19. Final judgment

> What humanity needs is not the promise of a scientific immortality, but compassionate pity in this life and infinite mercy on the Day of Judgment.
>
> (Joseph Conrad)

In the visions of the book of Revelation we are afforded a last, tantalizing glimpse into the world that opens beyond the final door of history. The glimpse is virtually a blinding one, because the pictures which arise before us are ablaze with colours and images which alternately amaze and appal us. These passages in the book of Revelation are literally the Bible's 'last words on the last things'. In this chapter we focus on 'the last words on hell' in 20:4–15, and in the next chapter we consider 'the last words on heaven' in 21:1 – 22:6. For possibly the first time in this entire survey, heaven and hell are indubitably the primary concern of the passages in question.

The book of Revelation has notoriously fascinated, perplexed and divided its interpreters from the first century onwards. Accordingly, as with almost no other book of the Bible, some contextual notes are essential before we approach the specific passages.

The book's opening sentences allow us to answer some of the more obvious questions.

i. What is it?
It is a 'revelation' (1:1), a disclosure of what was previously hidden. It is also a 'prophecy', since it concerns 'what must soon take place' (1:1).

ii. Who wrote it?
The book was written by 'his [i.e. Jesus Christ's] servant John' (1:1), which we take to be John the apostle, the human author of the fourth

295

Gospel and the 'letters of John'. We note additionally, however, the explicit attribution to Christ himself, 'the revelation of Jesus Christ' (1:1).

iii. Who was it written for?
It was written 'to the seven churches in the province of Asia' (1:4). It is accordingly a message to real people in real human situations, sent by their pastor, John.

iv. What is it about?
In essence it is 'the testimony of Jesus Christ' (1:2), which is filled out as the book develops. Revelation begins with a pastoral address to each of the churches from their exalted Lord (1:9 – 3:22), and then expands to encompass the remainder of the book (4:1 – 22:21) which we can helpfully view as an ellipse with two foci. The foci are 4:1 – 5:14, the vision of the throne of God; and 19:11 – 22:21, the vision of the end.

Our immediate concern is with the second vision, where human destiny is a central interest, but we approach it by way of the first. The essential message of 4:1 – 5:14 is that the God of creation (4:1–11) is the God of redemption (5:1–14), and that all his purposes are accomplished through the crucified and risen Christ (5:6–11).

The critical event is the Easter victory of Jesus, which is pivotal for the whole sweep of human history (6:1 – 19:10), surveyed as the period of time between the two comings of Jesus. We can, not unfairly, characterize these chapters as 'history in the light of Easter', and the final chapters (19:11 – 22:21) as 'the closing events of the Easter drama'.[1]

Two themes predominate, judgment and victory, and both are the work of the Christ, represented in the image of a wounded Lamb, who grasps the scroll representing the mysteries of human life and destiny (5:7). He proceeds to open the scroll (6:1ff.). The sweeping overview of human history which follows (6:1 – 19:10) is unfolded in terms of the imagery of seven seals (6:1 – 8:5), seven trumpets (8:6 – 11:19), and seven bowls (15:1 – 19:10). The prevailing theme is judgment.

These historical judgments culminate in the final judgment scene of 20:4–15, for it is in his 'coming to judge' that the final victory of Jesus is expressed. As his judgments are poured out in final, unsparing wrath upon sin, evil and the devil, the justice of his cause is made ineffaceably manifest. His Easter victory reaches its fullest degree of accomplishment, evoking the celebratory songs of his people: 'Hallelujah! Salvation and glory and power belong to our God, for

---

[1] So G. R. Beasley-Murray, *The Book of Revelation* (Eerdmans, 1974), pp. 108–111.

true and just are his judgments' (19:1–2), and therefore, 'Hallelujah! For our Lord God the Almighty reigns. Let us rejoice and be glad and give him glory! For the wedding of the Lamb has come' (19:6–7).[2]

1. The seat of judgment (20:11–15)

Since history has been concluded, judgment follows. Fittingly, the throne of God dominates the scene (v. 11). The throne was the first object of attention at the beginning of John's exposition, as he passed through the 'door standing open in heaven' (4:1). In Daniel's vision there was reference to a plurality of thrones (Dan. 7:9), and similarly here in 20:4. As the vision develops, however, there is in the end only one, expressing the 'sole and supreme sovereignty of the judge'.[3]

The great white throne

The features of the throne are especially impressed upon the seer. It is 'great', expressing the greatness of the one whose throne it is, and hence his unqualified majesty as the Lord of all. It is 'white', reflecting the unimpeachable and all-consuming holiness of the Lord, the judge of all (v. 11). The throne, however, is finally secondary to him who occupies it. 'Earth and sky fled from his presence, and there was no place for them' (v. 11). In the august, overwhelming presence of the Living God in his majesty, all else collapses into nothingness. The old order, the universe as we now know it, the world and all its life forms, from the teeming galaxies to the infinitesimal particles, all 'flee away' before 'him who sits upon the throne' (cf. 21:5).

2. The scope of judgment

Attention now moves from the Judge to the judged. 'I saw the dead, great and small, standing before the throne' (20:12). The judgment, because it is the final act of history and the gathering up of the human story, is necessarily universal. The Lord of all life now passes all life under his all-determining review. By the very nature of this judgment, no-one can be absented from it. 'The sea', 'death' and 'Hades'

[2] It is to be noted that the judgments unpacked through the Lamb's 'breaking of the seals' in 6:1ff. are closely paralleled by the 'signs' of coming judgment in the discourse of Jesus in Mark 13. Cf. R. H. Charles, *A Critical and Exegetical Commentary on the Revelation of St John* (T. and T. Clark, 1920), vol. 1, p. 158; Beasley-Murray, *The Book of Revelation*, pp. 129–131.
[3] P. E. Hughes, *The Book of the Revelation* (IVP, 1990) p. 218.

are specifically noted as sources from which the dead are assembled (v. 13). Cumulatively, these three represent locations where no human trace is left behind, where it might be thought that people have simply 'gone' into oblivion and hence face no ultimate accounting for their lives and deeds. They represent those whose identity was seemingly partial and almost unrealized, those who left life before ever seeming to have arrived in it, those who lived and died leaving behind no slightest trace on the surface of history, the long-forgotten, the ancient and remote, the inaccessible, the unnoticed and the ignored: all these, without exception, will be there, 'before the throne'.

Further, in this review all human distinctions are irrelevant. 'Great and small' stand together (v. 12). What was claimed, or asserted, or believed concerning any individual during or following his or her earthly life, specifically those comparative assessments whereby one is 'great' or 'greater' and another 'small' or 'smaller', these and all other distinguishing considerations have no meaning 'before the throne'. Like all things earthly, these 'human' judgments have 'fled away'. They have actually never had any final validity; now they are seen to have had none. In the presence of the Lord who is the Judge of all, other judgments are simply irrelevant.

One other specific should be noted: the judgment applies to all. The church is not excluded. Some distinction between the redeemed and the unredeemed is certainly in order with respect to the final judgment of God, and John will come to that as the vision develops. However, we need to note at this point the clear assertion of the *universality* of the judgment. What John sees in his vision is entirely in accord with Paul's assertion when writing to the Christians in Corinth: 'We must *all* appear before the judgment seat of Christ' (2 Cor. 5:10, my italics).

The scope of the judgment is not confined to humans. 'The devil . . . the beast and the false prophet' are consigned to 'the lake of burning sulphur' where 'they will be tormented day and night for ever and ever' (20:10). This infernal anti-trinity was envisaged as forming the final opposition to God in the period leading up to the end (19:17 – 20:3). The lake accordingly represents the final and unalterable victory of the triune God. His original and most formidable foes are overcome and subjected to his just wrath, and their threat to God's endless glory and reign is finally and eternally brought to an end.

We may therefore assert, in the light of this statement in verse 10, that hell was made for the devil and hence in the first instance *not* for humankind. Jesus has a similar implication recorded in Matthew 25:41 concerning 'the external fire prepared for the devil and his angels'. God's loving, eternal purpose did not include hell as far as humans were concerned. It was not God's primary thought in his plan for human destiny. To the hints in Scripture of a pre-mundane fall and rebellion among his angelic creatures we may tentatively trace the 'origin of hell' (2 Pet. 2:4; Jude 6; Matt. 25:41). That hell should exist also for humankind is the supreme tragedy of existence.

One other extension of the judgment is noteworthy: 'Then death and Hades were thrown into the lake of fire' (v. 14). This means that death and the place of the dead have no more power over humanity. In Paul's words, 'The last enemy to be destroyed is death' (1 Cor. 15:26). Here is the pictorial representation of its destruction. It is to be presumed that its residence in the lake is, like that of the anti-trinity, of equally endless duration. On any other interpretation the metaphor of its destruction loses its force, and the song of victory is muted. Death's threat is ended for ever. The life of those who pass into the holy city is therefore endless. 'There will be no more death . . . they will reign for ever and ever' (21:4; 22:5).

3. The standard of judgment

We are now introduced to the criterion which is applied: 'books were opened' (20:12). The background to the idea of divine 'book-keeping' recalls the habits of certain oriental monarchs (notably the Persian kings) of inscribing the doings of their subjects. But there is biblical precedent also: 'All the days ordained for me were written in your book before one of them came to be' (Ps. 139:16; cf. Ps. 69:28; 56:8; Exod. 32:23).

The Judge of all

The meaning is clear: at the final judgment all history stands revealed. This includes, of necessity, all personal histories. The Judge will have in review before him a uniquely comprehensive accumulation of evidence. Nothing will be omitted since, by the nature of the case, everything will be there, from the slightest stirring of thought and feeling, the deep recesses of motivation, the barely ventured word and reaction, all the way through to the most wholehearted and determinative action. Never before nor ever again will there transpire a judgment where the relevant evidence is even remotely as comprehensive.

This point is worth underlining when accusations of unfairness are raised concerning God's judgment. The final judgment will be the only judgment in all of time and history which is *truly* fair. It is perhaps in this context that we should understand Paul's observation that 'every mouth may be silenced and the whole world held accountable to God' (Rom. 3:19). Right of appeal will be available to all on every point, but because the Judge is the God of utter justice and limitless knowledge, the judgment passed will be beyond challenge. We will all have our day in court – indeed, as many days as we might wish for, and access to whatever legal counsel we may wish to engage; but the outcome will be the same and our own consciences will be the primary witnesses. 'Will not the Judge of all the earth do right?' (Gen. 18:25). Indeed he will; indeed he will.

'By their deeds . . .'

Particular note will be made of *deeds* – 'what they had done' (v. 12); 'everyone was judged according to what they had done' (v. 13 NIVI). This might seem a limited basis for judgment, but every deed has a history. What we do is the visible emergence of processes that reach back into our inner beings. Like the iceberg floating on the surface of the ocean, the visible is only a part, commonly only a small part of the whole. In the last analysis, who we are is what we do and what we do is who we are. So it will be *deeds* in their fullest context that will come up for judgment, including inevitably the deeds left undone by the deeds done. Everything attaching to every person covering the entirety of his or her life will be there, 'before the throne'.

Believers in Christ should not despair at this prospect. We recall that Jesus 'went about doing good' (Acts 10:38), and those who claim to be his are surely likely to express their saving relationship with him by a similarly positive and outgoing lifestyle. Living as we do in a world where need abounds on every hand, God the Judge is surely right to anticipate finding in the lives of those who claim to belong to him the instincts and expressions of a concern to help others. Nor need the shut-in, or the physically or mentally handicapped, despair. Cups of cold water given in his name are noted and treasured by this Judge, who understands and knows all. Nor will he overlook that care for others which finds its deepest expression in the ministry of prayer.

4. The survival of judgment

The books which are opened, however, are not identical. One particular volume stands apart. 'Another book was opened, which is the book of life' (v. 12). John referred to this book earlier, in the message to the church in Sardis: 'Those who overcome will . . . be dressed in white. I will never blot out their names from the book of life, but will acknowledge their names before my Father and his angels' (3:5 NIVI; cf. 21:27). The attribution of ownership of the book to the Lamb in this reference is critical for interpreting the nature of this volume. It is the register of all those whom the Lamb acknowledges as his own 'before my Father and his angels' – those, that is, who belong to him.

Here is the distinction alluded to earlier between the redeemed and the unredeemed, the saved and the lost, the children of God and the children of the evil one. That we should be among those so listed could not be more critical, for, 'all whose names were not found written in the book of life were thrown into the lake of fire' (v. 15 NIVI).

By grace you are saved

We should also note that no other means of escape from the 'lake of fire' is identified. In particular, there is no reference to any individuals who escape the lake of fire on the basis of 'what they had done as recorded in the [other] books' (v. 12). Here is echoed the verdict of Paul, 'No-one will be declared righteous in [God's] sight by observing the law' (Rom. 3:20). There is simply no way into the holy eternities of God if appeal is made to what we have achieved by our own moral endeavours, or conceivably will ever achieve in any number of future lives, whether repeated or reincarnated. We are shut up to one way of salvation and one alone – being 'written in the Lamb's book of life'. It is Christ or eternal condemnation. There is no third possibility.

Grounds for acquittal

The means by which this verdict of acquittal is attained is implicit. Since the redeemed no less than the unredeemed are found upon examination 'before the throne' to lack God's perfect righteousness, their acquittal needs a just basis. This lies in their having the Lamb 'acknowledge their names' before the Father (3:5). In probing the significance of that statement, we recall that the Lamb in Revelation is 'a Lamb, looking as if it had been slain' (5:5), and Jesus Christ himself is earlier introduced as 'him who loves us and has freed us from our sins by his blood' (1:5). We may fairly conclude that the acquittal of the redeemed, those 'written in the Lamb's book of life', derives from their having so identified with the Lamb in his dying that his wrath-bearing, sacrificial death becomes theirs. The just judgment of God on their sins *is* executed, at the cross, upon Christ their substitute. He dies in their place, for them. His 'acknowledg-ing' them before the Father is his personal affirmation that their sins have already been passed under judgment when he, the Lamb of God, died for them. The pronouncement of their acquittal is there-fore grounded on their having rested their whole hope of pardon upon Christ's self-substitution for them on the cross. Belonging inseparably to him, his perfect righteousness is also their righteous-ness, and with that comes their title to a place in the righteous eter-nity of God.

5. The solemnity of judgment

Those whose names were 'not found written in the book of life' were 'thrown into the lake of fire' (v. 15). When due regard is paid to the fact that we are in the realm of metaphor here, the prospect for those who do not find acquittal beggars description, and at two points.

First, the experience of anguish which a 'lake of fire' necessarily engenders is overwhelming. Were it not that Jesus uses similar imagery to depict hell, we would be tempted to expunge it from our minds. Whether the experience be physical, mental or spiritual, or any combination of these, is in some sense quite secondary. A con-dition of agonizing personal self-consciousness is at the core of this picture.

Second, this hellish condition is reported to be continuous. The endless duration which attaches to existence in the lake of fire, which is unambiguously referred to in the case of the demonic powers (v. 10), and necessarily implicit in the case of death (v. 14), cannot easily be eliminated for the unredeemed in verse 15. That the unre-deemed continue in their judged state is also the clear impression of the following account of the New Jerusalem, where the condition of the redeemed is contrasted with that of 'the cowardly, the unbeliev-ing, the vile . . . their place will be in the fiery lake' (21:8). Of similar import is the contrast in 22:14–15 between 'those who wash their robes' and hence live within the city, and those who live 'outside'. 'The lake of fire signifies not extinction in opposition to existence, but tortuous existence in the society of evil in opposition to life in the society of God.'[4] (The reader is referred to the discussion of this

[4]Beasley-Murray, *The Book of Revelation*, p. 304. Cf. T. F. Torrance, *The Apocalypse Today* (Jas. Clarke, 1960), p. 171, 'However much there may be that we cannot understand about the mystery of iniquity and its judgment, it is quite clear from the Word of God that those who die in their sins do not pass into nothing-ness and forgetfulness. There is time beyond death, time for the damned as well. And it is because there is such a thing as time beyond that hell is so terrible.'

issue in chapter 8, not least its concluding considerations concerning the creatureliness of time, the necessary limitations placed upon language, and above all the perfect justice and endless love of the one with whom we will have, in the end, to do.)

The Beasley-Murray quotation above helpfully points us beyond the fearful contemplation of hell to the joyful anticipation of heaven, and hence from Revelation 20 and the last judgment to Revelation 21 – 22 and the Holy City. To this, with conscious relief, we will soon turn. Before doing so, however, there are two final points to make from this last judgment scene.

a. The last judgment is a solemn prospect

Despite the humorous dismissal of the last judgment in our culture, its comparative neglect in much theological reflection, and the virtual silence on the subject in the modern pulpit, it is going to happen. The Bible bears witness to it from beginning to end, and no-one spoke more solemnly or more frequently about it than Jesus. Quite apart from these conclusive attestations, the future judgment is actually implicit in every moral instinct and every moral choice. We are accountable for our lives, for our choices, for our decisions, for our relationships, for our attitudes, for our thoughts, words and deeds. Deep within, we know that to be true.

'God has set a day when he will judge the world' (Acts 17:31). When all allowance is made for the accretions of metaphor and vividness of imagery, the portrayal of that event and its outcomes is literally overwhelming. We must each appear in the presence of uncreated holiness. We must stand naked and alone before the Judge of all, who has given us our lives and called us to use them in all their parts and possibilities in his service. To fail that judgment, as in ourselves we invariably must, is to face a destiny of awesome gravity. Hell is for real and is portrayed in language which removes all doubt concerning its fearfulness. Quite simply, it is all that we do not want to experience.

The only way to avoid it, to be able to stand unbowed at the judgment and to pass the all-seeing eye of our Lord and Judge, is to be righteous in the sight of God. None of us have even the remotest hope of achieving that. But, thanks be to God, there is a way of escape, a way of being found righteous before even that all-penetrating eye. In incredible love, the Judge has taken our condemnation and all its last consequences upon himself. The Judge has been judged for us. His sacrificial death on the cross can become our death, his condemnation our condemnation, his acceptance our acceptance, and his righteousness our righteousness. To embrace him by faith as he offers himself in Jesus Christ is to discover what Martin Luther stumbled upon in November 1515, and in that stumble transformed the face of Christendom. '[When] I grasped the truth that the righteousness of God is that righteousness whereby, through grace and sheer mercy, he justifies us by faith I felt myself to be reborn and to have gone through open doors into paradise.'[5]

One further aspect needs comment, bearing in mind the immense solemnity of the final judgment. What of our anxiety and pain for those who are excluded? The redeemed in Revelation are recorded as *celebrating* the final judgment of God. How can that be, if among those who go away into the 'outer darkness' are people we love, to say nothing of the multitudes of our fellow humans at present unknown to us who are consigned by that judgment to the anguish of an eternal hell?

Several comments are in order. First, *the consigning of individuals to either hell or heaven is simply not our business.* 'The Lord is judge.' From one end of Scripture to the other, judgment is the sole prerogative of deity. There is great relief in that basic fact. In the end we have no certain, infallibly reliable knowledge concerning the destiny of any individual, whether known or unknown. Our family member's or friend's destiny rests with the God who made them and has sustained them and loves them enough to give himself for them on a cross. Our prayers are not unheard, nor our witness unrecorded. The Judge of all is Love, and he will do right by all. But the judgment is his, not ours.

Second, *the requirement*, as we have seen above, *is faith in God's mercy in Christ.* In the Old Testament that was clearly savingly expressed for multitudes who had never heard directly of Jesus since they lived in ages before his incarnation. Their faith, centred on the messianic covenant promises of God, was accordingly accounted as righteousness in anticipation of Jesus' coming. It was not the full, mature conviction of the New Testament period, yet it *was* saving faith, as Hebrews 11 or Romans 4 leave in no doubt.

Jesus likened faith to a grain of mustard seed, 'the smallest of all seeds' (Matt. 13:31–32). The crucified criminal next to Jesus at Golgotha illustrates that vividly. His 'faith' was essentially confined to a cry to Jesus for mercy in the last gasp of his life, but it was sufficient because of the sufficiency of the one to whom it was directed. As even a modicum of knowledge of the human heart (not least of our own) will instantly confirm, no 'faith' is ever perfect. Our believing, in this sense, also has to be justified by Christ. But he who could discern a particle of genuine faith beneath clearly superstitious

---

[5] *Luther's Works,* Weimar ed., vol. 54 (1928), p. 179f.

accretions in the case of a trembling, anonymous woman (Mark 5:25–34) will unfailingly find such wherever it may lurk in her countless sisters and brothers across the ages. Studdart Kennedy catches the spirit of that woman and the dying criminal, as well as their many cousins, in the following poem.

> It is not finished, Lord.
> There is not one thing done,
> There is no battle of my life,
> That I have really won.
> And now I come to tell Thee
> How I fought to fail,
> My human, all too human, tale
> Of weakness and futility.
> And yet there is a faith in me,
> That Thou wilt find in it
> One word that Thou canst take
> And make
> The centre of a sentence
> In Thy book of poetry . . .
> I can but hand it in, and hope
> That Thy great mind, which reads
> The writings of so many lives,
> Will understand this scrawl
> And what it strives
> To say – but leaves unsaid. . .[6]

'One word' was all the criminal could utter, one trembling touch was all the woman could offer, but they sufficed because they were directed to Jesus.

Third, *no-one knows precisely what transpires in a human heart in the final moments of earthly life*. In Puritan times people noted that 'it is a long way from the saddle to the stirrup'. In an age when death would not infrequently be met on horseback, it was a reminder that the final, dying moment could be, in God's mercy, a forgiving moment. I can only bear witness from my years as a pastor to how remarkably often I had the privilege of helping people find Christ literally in the last moments of their lives, as God in great mercy drew near and gave them 'dying grace'.

Fourth, *we cannot forget Paul's hope in Romans 5 that the effect of Christ and the gospel will be 'much more' than the effect of Adam's*

---

[6] G. A. Studdart Kennedy, *The Unutterable Beauty* (Hodder and Stoughton, 1947), pp. 96–97.

transgression (Rom. 5:15–21). We recall also the indicator given to Abraham of the final outcome of God's covenant in terms of the countless stars in the heavens and the numberless grains of sand on the seashore (Gen. 22:17). John Stott, while correctly underlining the Bible's unvarying insistence on salvation only being possible through Jesus Christ, observes, 'We seem to be assured by Paul that many more people will be saved than lost, because Christ's work in causing salvation will be more successful than Adam's in causing ruin, and because God's grace in bringing life will overflow "much more" than Adam's trespass in causing death.'[7]

Dogmatism is plainly out of place here. We cannot forget that Jesus spoke of 'many' on the road that leads to destruction (Matt. 7:13); we dare not lose even for a moment our concern for the spread to every person of the one message which gives sure hope at the end. Our Lord, however, also made repeated mention of surprises at the judgment day. 'The first shall be last, and the last first' is the saying from his teaching most frequently cited in the Gospels. An open-eyed optimism that anticipates delighted surprise on the day of judgment does not therefore appear biblically inappropriate.

Fifth, *the experience of the end will be different.* On that day, we will see things in very different terms from the present. Things which are now dark will then be light, and matters which are of greatest concern now will cease to be such then. That day will also be a day of celebration.

b. The last judgment is a glorious event

The last judgment is a solemn prospect, but we dare not forget that the judgment day is very much more than the banishment of the impenitent. God's judgment means nothing less than the establishing of his just and joyous reign, the putting right of all that has gone wrong, and the liberation of all things from the usurping shadow of evil. It is this perspective that enables the psalmist to *celebrate* God's judgments. 'Let the heavens rejoice, let the earth be glad . . . let the fields be jubilant . . . the trees . . . will sing for joy . . . before the LORD, for he comes . . . to judge the earth . . . and the peoples in his truth' (Ps. 96:11–13).

Our hearts have cried with the people of God throughout the ages:

O that you would rend the heavens and come down! . . . Let God be God! . . . Vindicate your name . . . overthrow the forces of darkness . . . vanquish the devil and remove him . . . bring an end to the long night of wrong and evil; an end to exploitation and sin, and

[7] J. R. W. Stott, *The Contemporary Christian* (IVP, 1992), p. 319.

wickedness in all its forms . . . Come Lord Jesus, take your rightful place upon the throne and reign in your glory . . . Father,
hallowed be your name, your kingdom come, your will be done
on earth as it is in heaven . . . Let there be glory to the Father, and
the Son and the Holy Spirit, one God for ever!

The coming of the judgment day is the answer to these prayers, and
the means of their being answered. It is also therefore a day for
rejoicing. This is the way it is consistently viewed in the book of
Revelation, where the redeemed are regularly exhibited celebrating
the just judgments of God.

> We give thanks to you, Lord God Almighty,
>   the One who is and who was,
> because you have taken your great power
>   and have begun to reign.
> The nations were angry;
>   and your wrath has come.
> The time has come for judging the dead,
>   and for rewarding your servants the prophets,
> and your saints and those who reverence
>   your name,
>   both small and great –
> and for destroying those who destroy the earth . . .
>
> Great and marvellous are your deeds,
>   Lord God Almighty.
> Just and true are your ways,
>   King of the ages.
> Who will not fear you, O Lord,
>   and bring glory to your name?
> For you alone are holy.
> All nations will come
>   and worship before you,
> for your righteous acts have been revealed . . .
>
> You are just in these judgments,
>   you who are and who were,
>   the Holy One,
>   because you have so judged . . .
>
> Yes, Lord God Almighty,
>   true and just are your judgments . . .

Hallelujah!
Salvation and glory and power belong to our God,
    for true and just are his judgments . . .
Hallelujah!

                     (Rev. 11:16–18; 15:3–4; 16:5, 7; 19:1, 3)

Summary

All history is moving to a climax. At the centre of it will be the last judgment. It will occur 'before the throne of God'. It will be universal: every human person from all the ages of history will be there. It will call in evidence all human deeds. The only hope of acquittal will lie in our names being entered in 'the Lamb's book of life'. The alternative, for those not acquitted, is overwhelmingly solemn – being consigned to hell. The last judgment is God's final triumph over all his foes, and therefore a major ground for his praise.

Revelation 21:1 – 22:21
20. The colours of heaven

> He lifts me to the golden doors;
> The flashes come and go;
> All heaven bursts her starry floors,
> And strows her lights below,
> And deepens on and up! the gates
> Roll back, and far within
> For me the heavenly Bridegroom waits,
> To make me pure of sin.
> The sabbaths of eternity,
> One sabbath deep and wide –
> A light upon the shining sea –
> The Bridegroom with his bride!
>
> (Lord Alfred Tennyson, 'St Agnes' Eve')

With the completion of judgment and the removal of the perpetrators of evil, both demonic and human, the true goal of the historic purpose of God is reached – the full and final triumph of the kingdom of God. When we recall the pastoral focus of the book of Revelation, a message of hope to a suffering church, here in essence is what it promises: 'God himself, in the company of those who love him'.[1] The image through which this transcendent reality is portrayed is that of a city. Set within the sweep of the book of Revelation, we can note the brilliant employment of the counterpoint motif. Just as in chapter 13 we were introduced to the anti-trinity of the devil, the beast and the false prophet, who fall before the power and majesty of the Lord, the Lamb and the Spirit (19:1; 17:14 and 19:11–20; 22:17), now, set against 'Babylon the Great', the 'home for demons' (18:2), 'drunk with the blood of the saints' (17:6),

---

[1] G. R. Beasley-Murray, *The Book of Revelation* (Eerdmans, 1974), p. 305.

we behold 'Jerusalem the Golden', the home of God (21:2–3, 18), where the saints reign for ever (22:5).

The account of the city of God begins with an extended description of its salient features (21:1–27), and then moves in climax to consider its glorious deployment (22:1–5). The city is seen by the seer himself (21:1–2), by him 'who was seated on the throne' (21:3–8), and finally by 'one of the seven angels' (21:9–27).

1. The city described (21:1–27)

a. The city as seen by John (21:1–2)

John's first general characterization is of 'a new heaven and a new earth' (v. 1). This phrase picks up the language of Isaiah 65:17 and 66:22, and is also echoed in 2 Peter 3:13. In interpreting this general identification of the new world, we need to hold together the thoughts of *continuity* and *discontinuity*. The latter is underlined immediately: 'The first heaven and the first earth had passed away, and there was no longer any sea' (v. 1). For the ancients the sea was a source of evil. Hence in 13:1 the dragon is set on 'the shore of the sea', from which emerges the blasphemous beast (cf. Dan. 7:3). Accordingly, 'no more sea' means simply no more evil. This discontinuity of the new order from the old is unequivocally stated in 21:5: 'I am making everything new!' Heaven is not simply a polished, enhanced and sanitized version of earth, a different and better tune played on the old, familiar instruments. It will be *new*!

Heaven at hand
Yet the newness is not absolute. 'Earth' is also used to describe it. In the same vein of continuity, we note that the city 'comes down' from God (v. 2). Notions of heaven which see our future destiny as a 'going up' to a distant, purely spiritual realm somewhere in the blue yonder therefore appear to need correction. Heaven is not so much a new world 'up there' as a new world 'down here'. This is the element of validity in the dream of a millennial kingdom of Jesus here on earth. The doubtful dispensationalist schematic to which it is commonly tied should not blind us to the validity of the instinct to see God and his purposes vindicated in some real sense within this very world in which these purposes have been challenged by the incursion of evil.

Another expression of the instinct for continuity is reflected in the name of the city, 'The New Jerusalem'. The new order is in a significant degree linked to that earthly city where occurred the decisive events, the death and rising of the Lamb, by which the entire conflict with evil was finally resolved and the eternal kingdom of God established for the everlasting ages.

Other features follow as John attempts to define the city. We note its *moral purity*. The city is 'Holy' (v. 2). This reflects not simply – and negatively – the absence of sin and evil in all their forms, but the glorious positiveness of the outshining majesty of God in his resplendent otherness, the God who is 'the Holy One', the God in whose presence the 'Holy, holy, holy' ceaselessly sounds (Is. 6:3; Rev. 4:8). Because the city is the dwelling place of such a God, it cannot be other than a holy place. That moral purity is expressed in the setting of *corporate identity*, however, for it is a city (cf. Is. 54:11–17). In keeping with the other biblical symbols, heaven is a social order (cf. Heb. 12:28; Ezek. 40 – 48; Rev. 19:7; Matt. 8:11). Thus the prospect of heaven as a lonely journey to a beatific vision is seriously misleading. Heaven is community, supremely with God, but also with his people. That is entirely as we would expect, for the Creator who is in himself 'community' in the inner life of the Trinity made creatures in his image. As his image-bearers, we are accordingly communal beings for whom being alone was 'not good', even before the incursion of sin (Gen. 2:14). When that community had been disrupted, and the long journey to redemption begun, it should not surprise us to find, at the end of that road, a *city of joy*. Thus the city, which in Genesis 11 in the form of Babel is the symbol of division and antagonism, becomes in the redemptive work of God the location of perfected community and eternal love.

The defining of the city affirms *divine sovereignty*. The city is seen 'coming down out of heaven from God' (v. 2). 'Heaven' is used here in the sense of the invisible realm of God. The point is that the new order is the handiwork of God. Our participation in it is explicable only in terms of his inexplicable grace. The church which will possess heaven, and which will live henceforth at the interface of the unveiled God and his creation, will be there only because it was chosen, justified, regenerated, sanctified and glorified by this same triune God of grace and glory. It is God who organized the wedding, sent out the invitations, came in person as the bridegroom, and then formed and wooed the bride.

There is also about the city, as the last sentence hinted, a *loving intimacy*. John sees a city, but in the delightful freedom of inspired imagery he describes the city as a person, 'a bonny bride'. The beauty of the church needs noting, for, to eyes attuned to the often repulsive disfigurements of the historical church with its countless divisions, chronic unbelief, tepid convictions and pervasive worldliness, the thought of the church being 'beautiful' comes almost as a new idea. Yet nothing less is its destiny. We will, at the last, be 'something beautiful for God' (cf. 1 Thess. 5:23–24). In John's image, the bride is central – not her adornments, but she herself, in her uniqueness and personhood. Here we touch that elemental truth which Victor Frankl celebrated amid the horrors of the Nazi death camps, 'the truth that is set into song by so many poets, proclaimed as the final wisdom by so many thinkers – that love is the ultimate and the highest goal to which humanity can aspire . . . that the salvation of humanity is through love and in love'.[2] Or, biblically, the truth is that God is love (1 John 4:16), and hence we as his creatures are made in love and for love, and we find ourselves in loving and being loved by one another and ultimately by God. The experience of heaven is the bliss of being utterly and eternally loved.

b. The city as stated by God (vv. 3–8)

There now occurs a sacred commentary on these amazing scenes. God himself speaks from the throne (vv. 3, 5). Here is heaven from the perspective of heaven. We focus on four aspects.

i. The city is imbued with God's presence (vv. 3–6a)

'Now the dwelling of God is with human beings, and he will live with them. They will be his people and God himself will be with them and be their God' (v. 3 NIVI). This is surely one of the great statements of the Bible, and among its most triumphant. Here is gathered up the whole range and extent of the purposes of God across the ages of human history. It was for this that God's covenant was made at the first with Abraham and his successors, and at the last with his people in Christ. 'I will put my dwelling-place among you, and I will not abhor you. I will walk among you and be your God, and you will be my people' (Lev. 26:11–12; cf. Jer. 32:38; Ezek. 37:27). It is from this perspective that we encounter God in the Old Testament period searching for a people to be his own, to whom he can reveal himself, and who will respond to him in love and faithfulness. 'It is God's unmistakable purpose to have a people of his own.'[3] Paul expands on this: 'We are the temple of the living God. As God has said: "I will live with them and walk among them, and I will be their God, and they will be my people . . . I will be a Father to you, and you will be my sons and daughters," says the Lord Almighty' (2 Cor. 6:16–18).

---

[2] Victor E. Frankl, *Man's Search for Meaning* (Simon and Schuster, 1963), pp. 58–59.
[3] A. Stibbs, *God's Church* (IVP, 1959), p. 12.

The word 'dwelling' (v. 3) literally means 'tent' and has rich Old Testament associations in terms of the Tent of Meeting (cf. Exod. 33:7), or tabernacle, where sacrifice would be offered, where God would meet with Moses as he interceded for the people of God, and where the visible sign of the divine presence would appear in the pillar of cloud (Exod. 33:9). More generally, the word is etymologically associated with the $š^e k\hat{\imath}n\hat{a}$, the unveiled glory of the Lord, which would periodically be manifested in tabernacle and temple (Exod. 16:7; 24:16; 40:34; Lev. 9:23; Num. 14:10; 16:19, 42; 20:6; 1 Kgs. 8:11; 2 Chr. 5:14; 7:1ff.). John had memorably seized on the term in the prologue to his Gospel, 'The Word became flesh and made his dwelling [lit. 'tabernacled'] among us' (John 1:14). That glory, the outshining of the divine majesty, seen at Sinai and in tabernacle and temple, was now enfleshed in Jesus Christ. The vision of Revelation carries this whole swelling tide of revelation to its final, cascading fullness. 'The dwelling of God', 'God himself', is now with us for ever.

It is in this context that we note the 'coming down' of the bride (v. 2), and the passing away of the first heaven (v. 1), for in the deepest sense the effect of this coming of the end is *the obliteration of the distinction between earth and heaven*. 'Heaven' as the immediate dwelling place of God is now 'on earth'; the new heavens and the new earth are not two places, two levels of reality – 'the two have become one'! The unveiled presence of God is the essence of heaven.[4]

ii. The city is blessed with God's peace (v. 4)

God now speaks of conditions within the city in terms of its exclusions. 'He will wipe every tear from their eyes. There will be no more death or mourning or crying or pain . . .' (v. 4). Here is the blissful *shalom* of Old Testament dream, when 'the ransomed of the LORD will return. They will enter Zion with singing; everlasting joy will crown their heads. Gladness and joy will overtake them, and sorrow and sighing will flee away' (Is. 35:10). It is life in its fullness, the life for which we were created. The falling of the 'last enemy' brings the joy of unbroken and unthreatened relationship; 'we will be with [together with] the Lord for ever' (1 Thess. 4:17). For those who struggle with enduring physical pain and wasting illness, the prospect is wonderfully relevant, as it was for a woman in one of my

---

[4] As Eugene Peterson observes, this may account for today's relative disinterest in heaven, since, 'If we don't want God, or don't want him very near, we can hardly be expected to be very interested in heaven' (*Reversed Thunder* [Harper, 1988], p. 185).

congregations who struggled for years with debilitating chronic pain, and for whom this verse with its promise was her daily lifeline to sanity.

The yielding of these physical and emotional threats also points to a richer cause for thanksgiving. The defeat of death is the defeat of sin, its progenitor, and hence the triumph of God's salvation in the person and work of the last Adam, the Lord Jesus Christ. Verse 4 is in this sense a deeply Christological statement, for all these blessings flow, and can only flow, from him who engaged all our enemies on our behalf in the hell of Calvary, and won there for us an everlasting liberation. The tenderness of the image must not be missed: 'He will wipe every tear from their eyes.' The Glorious Lord of overwhelming *šᵉkînâ* majesty, who dwells among us, is ever *Abba*, Father, caring so personally for his children, and in the uninhibited possibilities of the heavenly order expressing that tender, personal love in even deeper and more heart-touching ways.

iii. The city is secured by God's promise (vv. 5–6)

The city is absolutely impregnable, resting as it does on the word of 'he who [is] seated on the throne' (v. 5). This statement is immediately confirmed by the divine self-testimony, 'These words are trustworthy and true' (v. 5). Its security therefore rests on the character and veracity of the 'God who does not lie' (Titus 1:2; Heb. 6:18). They are, moreover, the words of him who is 'the Alpha and the Omega, the Beginning and the End' (v. 6), and hence the one who holds all time in his hands, who knows 'the end from the beginning' (Is. 46:5).

Lest there be any slightest quiver of remaining uncertainty, he cries, 'It is done' (v. 6). The tense here is everything. It is not a matter of future prospect – he does not say, 'It will be done.' That would be enough in itself, since the speaker is God, but the tense he uses is *past*. It is already accomplished.

iv. The city is possessed by God's people (vv. 6–8)

God describes his people in several ways. First, they are *a thirsty people* (v. 6). A sense of need is the only requirement in those who wish, in this life, to begin to follow the Lamb, but a sense of need continues to be a feature of the relationship with God in heaven. This need is not the need for forgiveness or deliverance from the power of sin, as here on earth. Rather, it is a need fostered by our new closeness to God, and with that our new capacity to desire him. This is why it is spoken of as a 'thirst'. Heaven will both satisfy and dissatisfy us. It will be the completion of all our dreams, the fulfilling of all our longings, the satisfying of all our desires, but in so far as these desires are centred on the infinite God who made and redeemed us, heaven will awaken unimaginable new depths and heights of longing. Having found God, or, better, having been at last so overwhelmingly found by him, we will yearn for him as we never have before. To know God and to thirst to know him more and more is the paradox of heaven. Bernard of Clairvaux wrote:

> We taste Thee, O Thou Living Bread,
> And long to feast upon Thee still;
> We drink of Thee the Fountainhead
> And thirst our souls from Thee to fill.

And fill them we *may*, in fulfilment of the prophecy of Isaiah, 'Come, all you who are thirsty, come to the waters; and you who have no money, come . . .' (Is. 55:1); and fill them we *will*, for God promises to meet that thirst: 'I will give [them] to drink without cost from the spring of the water of life' (v. 6). The source is literally limitless. We will drink, and drink, and drink again. 'Come! Whoever is thirsty, let [them] come, and whoever wishes, let [them] take the free gift of the water of life' (22:17).

Second, they are *an overcoming people*. 'Those who overcome will inherit all this' (v. 7 NIVI). 'Overcoming' summarizes the promises made in the pastoral letters in the early chapters of Revelation (2:7, 11, 17, 26; 3:5, 12, 21). The message of 21:7 is that all the incentives held out to them in the trials in which they found themselves will be theirs at the end – 'the right to eat from the tree of life' (2:7; cf. 22:2), 'not [being] hurt at all by the second death' (2:11; cf. 21:8), to eat of 'the hidden manna' (2:17; cf. 21:14; 7:16), 'authority over the nations' (2:26; cf. 21:24; 22:5), being 'dressed in white' and never having their name blotted 'from the book of life' (3:5; cf. 7:9; 21:27), having written on them 'the name of God' (3:12; cf. 22:4), and 'the right to sit with me on my throne' (3:21; cf. 22:5). We will overcome in the end 'by the blood of the Lamb and by the word of [our] testimony' (12:11), by our testimony that we are his. The true source of our overcoming is the Lamb himself, who will overcome all our enemies and rescue us from all our trials, 'because he is Lord of lords and King of kings' and by grace we are one with him as his 'called, chosen and faithful followers' (17:14).

Third, they are *an inheriting people* (v. 7). The prospect for those who are citizens of the New Jerusalem is almost beyond our ability to conceive. They have a glorious future in every sense of that word. Specifically, they will enjoy a new degree of relationship with God himself; the 'all this' (v. 7) is probably a reference back to the summation of the heavenly life in verse 3 as life with God, 'I will be their God'. But the relationship finds its deepest indication in terms of family – 'They will be my children' (v. 7 NIVI). The linkage between inheritance and family echoes Paul in Romans 8:15–17, 'If we are children, then we are heirs – heirs of God and co-heirs with Christ' (cf. 2 Sam. 7:14). The inheritance to which we travel in our journey to the Holy City is nothing less than the embrace of our *Abba*, Father. Like the prodigal son, arrival at the Father's house in heaven is both the ending of our journey of rebellion in the far country of self-gratification, and at the same moment the beginning of our new journey of discovery of the height, depth, breadth and length of the loving heart of our Father. Heaven is home, and home is above all being buried in our Father's heart.

Fourth, they are *a distinct people*. Not all people are within the city. Despite the often expressed hope that in the end all will be saved, it has to be stated that this universalist dream finds no biblical support. Sin is too serious to be overlooked. Furthermore, the sinful heart will continue to be respected in the exercise of its terrible freedom to refuse to bow the knee to its rightful Lord. And that means hell. Thus there are those within the city and those outside it: 'Let those who do wrong continue to do wrong, let those who are vile continue to be vile.' Correspondingly, 'Let those who do right continue to do right, let those who are holy continue to be holy' (22:11 NIVI). Life goes on, both within the city and outside it; the one locked into the endless pursuit of sin and the anguish of its consequences, the other glorying in the endless, blissful, all-fulfilling pursuit of godliness.

c. The city as shown by the angel (vv. 9–27)

The divine voice ceases; God has spoken concerning the nature of the city. John is now approached by one of the angels associated with the outpoured wrath of God (cf. 16:1ff.); indeed, the language is identical to that in 17:1, and hence we may conclude that the heavenly guide is the same angel who had led John to view the destruction of Babylon. Clearly, for the writer of Revelation, the twin themes of the judgments of God's wrath and the triumphs of his grace are in no sense antithetical in the unfolding of the divine purpose here and hereafter.

We ought not to overlook the reference here to the Holy Spirit – 'He carried me away in the Spirit' (v. 10). Although understandably in this account of the Holy City stress falls on the presence and glory of the Lord Almighty and the Lamb, the third person of the Godhead is not absent. It is his blessed ministry to make all of this available to the people of God over the ages as he inspires the prophetic witness expressed in the book of Revelation. He who brings insight to John continues to work in the hearts of John's readers in every generation, to afford them understanding of these amazing coming glories, and to bear witness with our spirits that these things are true, not least because the heavenly life depicted here has already begun within us, in the presence of the gracious divine indweller, who is 'the Lord, the Spirit'. Turning back to the text, what does the angel guide reveal?

i. The splendour of the city (v. 11)

Since God is resident within the city, there is a holy radiance which emanates from it. 'It shone with the glory of God.' This radiance had a certain fleeting anticipation in the glowing face of Moses after his meetings with God on Sinai (Exod. 34:29–35; 2 Cor. 3:7–18). It had more substantial precedent in the glorious person of the Lord Jesus at the transfiguration (Luke 9:28–36; 2 Pet. 1:16–18). Like Paul before him outside Damascus, John had been completely over-whelmed by the revelation of the glory of the exalted Christ on Patmos (Acts 9:1–9; Rev. 1:12–17). Now that divine glory suffuses the entire city. To live in the city is to live continually in the presence of the unveiled glory of God. John's best analogy is that of the incandescent sparkling of precious stones as light is reflected back and forth by the surfaces deep within the stones (v. 11); or the unique radiance of pure burnished gold gleaming throughout the city (v. 18), especially in the city's 'great street' (v. 21).

ii. The security of the city (vv. 12–14)

Heaven is a place of complete and eternal safety. The symbol of security is the wall which surrounds the city. Of particular note is the presence of the names of the twelve tribes of Israel on the gates. 'The ancient people of God is not forgotten in the final disposition of things.'[5] Each gate has a foundation where the names of the twelve apostles appear. Thus John sees the one people of God united in the culmination of God's age-long purpose.

iii. The size of the city (vv. 15–17)

Twice in the Old Testament the attempt to measure the people of God was negatively viewed. In the case of David it brought the judgment of a plague (2 Sam. 24). In the case of Zechariah an angelic messenger forbids it (Zech. 2:1–5). The reason in both cases was the same – the instinct to measure was the product of hubris, the sinful

---

[5] L. Morris, *The Book of Revelation* (IVP, 1987), p. 249.

pride of achievement which permits no real place for that secret, sovereign work of God which alone explains its growth. Significantly, the only measuring which *is* affirmed is that of the perfect city of Ezekiel 40 – 47, the prototype of the New Jerusalem. Only beyond the purging of the judgment and the arrival of the heavenly Jerusalem is the human heart able to measure the work of God in a manner which gives him his proper honour, for only then will we be able to appreciate how completely the work is his, not ours.

The other striking feature of the size has often been noted: what begins as a square becomes in fact a cube, 'as wide and high as it is long' (v. 16). Obviously, in all of this we are dealing in pictures and hence normal proportionality is hardly to be demanded. The point of the cubic shape is surely that this reflects the proportions of the Holy of Holies in the Jerusalem temple (cf. 1 Kgs. 6:22). Herein lies the explanation of the otherwise astonishing fact of the absence of any temple, 'I did not see a temple in the city' (v. 22). *The whole is temple*! That explanation is wonderful, expressed by the cubic form. To live in heaven is to live in the Holy of Holies. Not only is the curtain torn in two, enabling continual access (Matt. 27:51); the curtain has in fact now entirely disappeared and the walls of the Holy of Holies have been rebuilt to encompass our complete living space. We have set up our home in the Holy Presence of God.

> The new earth will be covered with the knowledge of God as the waters cover the sea, and the truth shall be so inscribed upon the hearts of God's children that they will not need any man to teach them. The night of estrangement will be over, and they shall be at home with God and he will be their Father and Christ Jesus shall be their friend.[6]

One other aspect is worth comment, without overpressing what are necessarily symbols: the multiplication of the 12,000 stadia renders a picture of a city of immense size, 'staggeringly large'.[7] What is accordingly dismissed by this imagery are all narrow, confining anticipations of the heavenly order. Here at last is scope and vastness and space. Away with all grudging and impoverished images! Life in this world is necessarily curtailed in a vast array of ways. Limiting boundaries express the nature of mundane existence. Heaven, by contrast, is the throwing back of these limitations; it is the experience

[6]T. F. Torrance, *The Apocalypse Today* (Jas. Clarke, 1960), pp. 180–181.
[7]Beasley-Murray, *The Book of Revelation*, p. 322.

of freedom in its ultimate terms. Heaven is immeasurably vast.

We may also need to open ourselves to a numerical expansiveness in terms of the population of the city. In the vision of the end in Revelation 7, note is made of 'a great multitude that no-one could count' (v. 9). While we cannot be dogmatic here, and our duty to proclaim the gospel to all remains firmly in place, this expansive anticipation is certainly not out of keeping with the impression conveyed by the astonishingly far-flung dimensions of the heavenly city.

iv. The stones of the city (vv. 18–21)

John now moves to the external appearance. He has already referred to the city's general radiance; he now comes to closer quarters. The radiance is again in view in the reference to the 'wall . . . made of jasper, and the city of pure gold, as pure as glass' (v. 18). The predominance of gold may hark back to the temple of Solomon, which was resplendent with gold in its glorious heyday, especially in the central worship core (1 Kgs. 6:20ff.).

The series of twelve precious stones which John sees studded into the walls has anticipation in Isaiah's prophecy of the coming kingdom of God, 'O afflicted city . . . I will build you with stones of turquoise, your foundations with sapphires. I will make your battlements of rubies, your gates of sparkling jewels, and all your walls of precious stones' (54:11–12).

The stones also have probable connection with the twelve precious stones which were sewn into the breastpiece of the high priest's ephod (Exod. 28:15–21), in indication of his intercessory ministry, carrying the twelve tribes on his heart into the Holy Place. For the citizens of the New Jerusalem, the Great High Priest is now about and among them, and the jewel-strewn walls around the city vividly portray their life as enclosed within the heart of a God for whom each last individual is remembered and every person's concerns are his unceasing care.

v. The shrine of the city (vv. 22–23)

Here we touch that most significant feature of the New Jerusalem, 'I did not see a temple in the city.' The absence of a visible shrine, which would hardly occasion the slightest surprise for a modern, secular urban dweller, would have struck any ancient citizen dumb. Paul's experience in Athens, where temples and idols jostled on every corner (Acts 17:16, 22f.), was not exceptional. A heavenly city containing no overt site for worship would have been the last anticipation, particularly for a Jew. 'For the old Synagogue the future Jerusalem without a temple was an inconceivable idea.

The building of the sanctuary was the most self-evident element of the old Jewish hope of the future.'[8]

It is noteworthy in this regard, as Beasley-Murray observes, that nothing in Jesus' teaching appears to have occasioned greater offence or aroused greater hostility than his announcement of the future destruction and replacement of Herod's temple (Mark 13:2; 14:8). It is the demolition of the temple, 'not one stone here will be left on another' (Mark 13:2), which symbolizes the arrival of the end and the final revelation of the Son of Man, who will claim his place at the centre of the transformed worship of the new era (Mark 13:26–27). That prophecy now reaches its final fulfilment, in the worship of the heavenly community in the New Jerusalem. The temple indeed is no more, but the reason is to hand: 'The Lord God Almighty and the Lamb are its temple' (21:22).

Thus the *šᵉkînâ* of the divine self-manifestation, which was anticipated and discerned at special moments and in limited degrees in ages past, is now the abiding context of the life of God's people. Such is the measure of this splendour that it radiates the city and thereby renders all other light sources irrelevant (v. 23). We will, in a degree probably never contemplated by the prophet, 'walk in the light of the LORD' (Is. 2:5). 'The temple of the New Jerusalem *is* the Lord God Almighty and the Lamb. Everything for which the temple stood is transferred to the life of the city. All is sacred, the *Shekinah* glory fills the entire city, and God is everywhere accessible to the priestly race.'[9] The close identity of the 'Lord God Almighty' and the 'Lamb' should be noted (v. 22). Theologically stated, it is the expression of the full deity of Jesus Christ.

Moreover, 'the Lamb is [the] lamp' of the city (v. 23), rather than 'the sun or the moon'. 'Their splendour is simply put to shame by the glory of God himself',[10] or, more specifically, by the glory of the Lamb. Thus he who was and is 'the light of the world' (John 8:12) is fittingly the light of the new world.

Among the implications of this is the simple reality that, to all the depths of eternity, the atoning mediation of the Lamb of God remains the source of illumination for the life and function of the people of God. In his light we see, and will for ever see, light (cf. Ps. 36:9). It shines, and it will shine for ever, and its beams will embrace the world, for 'the nations will walk by its light' (v. 24).

---

[8] H. L. Strack, P. Billerbeck, *Kommentar zum Neuen Testament aus Talmud und Midrash* (C. H. Beck, 1926), III, p. 852.

[9] Beasley-Murray, *The Book of Revelation*, p. 327.

[10] R. H. Charles, *A Critical and Exegetical Commentary on the Revelation of St John* (T. and T. Clark, 1920), vol. 1, p. 279.

vi. The style of the city (vv. 24–27)

The community is multinational. From the universal creation of Genesis 1, through the promise to Abraham of a blessedness touching all the earth's families and peoples, on by way of the 'psalms of the nations' and Daniel's dream of the Son of Man receiving worldwide worship, on through Jesus' sacrifice, 'lifted up' for all, and his sending of the church to 'all nations', to the universal acclaim of the throne vision of Revelation 7 and, here, the global family amid the heavenly splendour: the people of God are the peoples of the whole wide world.

The nations, however, are not merely represented among its citizenry; in the persons of their leaders they 'bring their splendour into [the city] . . . the glory and honour of the nations will be brought into it' (vv. 24, 26). That John is not lapsing into a universalist thought-mode is immediately clear, as we are reminded again of the distinction between those within and those outside the city (v. 27). Yet without threatening that foundational evangelical insight, in some valid sense the 'glory and honour of the nations' *are* to be preserved for the eternal order.

While mystery will of necessity always cloud our understanding of *how* this will be, it must not rob us of the *fact* that it will be. John is asserting that nothing of ultimate worth from the long history of the nations will be omitted from the heavenly community. Everything which authentically reflects the God of truth, all that is of abiding worth from within the national stories and the cultural inheritance of the world's peoples, will find its place in the New Jerusalem. This will hardly surprise us if we have drunk at the wells of human culture and have experienced the deepening of sensitivity, broadening of understanding and enlargement of heart and mind which such engagement can promote.

The one who is Lord of the whole of life was never going to bring us at the end into an eternal existence of mental constriction, or of emotional and creative impoverishment. Creativity will surely be valued, for such an anticipation must be in keeping with the nature of him who set the morning stars a-singing when he created them at the beginning, and whose joyful, uninhibited cry echoes across the battlements of the new creation: 'See, I am making everything new!'

In other words, the 'glory and honour of the nations' will only provide a starting point. What creative possibilities await us in the unfolding of the eternal ages no present imagination can begin to unravel. And since we are going to a heaven of, among other things, unprecedented cultural creativity, what authentication this gives to the worthwhileness of all such endeavour in the present. In this, too, we may dare to believe, '[our] labour in the Lord is not in vain' (1 Cor. 15:58).

2. The city deployed (22:1–5)

We come finally to John's account of the life of those within the city – their deployment. The dominating reality is again God himself in his glory: 'Now the dwelling of God is with human beings, and he will live with them' (21:3 NIVI); '[The city] shone with the glory of God' (21:11); 'I did not see a temple in the city, because the Lord God Almighty and the Lamb are its temple' (21:22). The life of the city revolves around God, and we can gather up this final paragraph of our chosen passage in terms of the features of his presence which it identifies.

a. God's throne (22:1, 3)

The throne overshadows all else. From the beginning of John's vision in 4:2, 'I looked . . . and there before me was a throne in heaven with someone sitting on it', through to these final scenes of the glories of the eternal city, all is set in the context of God's throne and hence under the authority of the Sovereign Lord of all. The vision of the future is a vision of the throne. No other being can stand before him, and no other power, whether terrestrial or supraterrestrial, whether angelic, demonic or human, can thwart the triumph of his purpose. More specifically, the life of the Holy City and the bliss of the redeemed within it flow directly from the Lord God himself. In all things he presides, and the joys of heaven are the joys that come directly from his hand and heart. Precisely because he is their source, they are joys which will never be in danger of being diluted or brought to an end.

b. God's river (v. 1)

At this point we note the unmistakable allusions to the Garden of Eden in the account of the life of the blessed. 'A river watering the garden flowed from Eden' (Gen. 2:10). Not surprisingly, as God finishes his 'undoing' of the tragic interlude of the fall, we find hints of the Garden repossessed by God's image-bearing creature. The expression of God's blessing as a sparkling, flowing river is a familiar one through Scripture (cf. Pss. 23:1; 46:4; Ezek. 47:1–12), and deeply appropriate to the life of Middle Eastern peoples regularly threatened by drought and barrenness. No biblical character could have failed to experience the racking pangs of thirst, nor the corresponding delight of having that thirst relieved by a gushing stream, whether in desert or mountain.

Ezekiel's vision of a river flowing out from under the threshold of the temple surely lies close to hand (Ezek. 47:1ff.), and Jesus' offer of 'streams of living water' (John 7:38) is of similar import. This latter is all the more appropriate considering John the evangelist's identification of the stream: 'By this he meant the Spirit', who would be given to all who believed in Jesus being 'glorified' (John 7:39). That movement of exaltation, begun in the cross and resurrection, has now found final expression in the eternal reign of the Lamb (Rev. 5:12–13; 22:3). Let the Spirit, who is himself the life of the kingdom, now be given in uninhibited fullness. Let the Spirit come! Let the waters flow!

c. God's tree (v. 2)

Again the Garden of Eden and the visions of Ezekiel hover in the background. Humankind has forfeited access to the tree of life (Gen. 3:22–24). Indeed, the 'flaming sword flashing back and forth to guard it' vividly conveys the terrible consequence of our sin, that it exposes us to the fire of the holy wrath of God; his very presence becomes a threat. Yet, in the unimaginable wonder of his grace, he himself grasped that fiery sword of wrath, plunged it at the cross into his own heart, and extinguished it there. He did this for us, foolish, sinning rebels.

Permanent access to the tree of everlasting life is thus afforded to those in the city. The fruitfulness of the tree (or trees?) of life is underlined. There are 'twelve crops of fruit, yielding its fruit every month' (v. 2), in fulfilment of Ezekiel's dream: 'Fruit trees of all kinds will grow on both banks of the river. Their leaves will not wither, nor will their fruit fail. Every month they will bear, because the water from the sanctuary flows to them. Their fruit will serve for food and their leaves for healing' (Ezek. 47:12).

John's development of the outcome, 'the healing of the nations' (v. 2), is noteworthy. It accords with the global perspective noted earlier (21:24, 26). Thus the undoing of the effects of the fall means the lifting of the curse pronounced in Eden (Gen. 3:14–19) which extended to the whole life of humankind, including the ceaseless warfare with the serpent, the devil and all his minions (Gen. 3:13–15), the pains and struggles of earthly life and its relationships (Gen. 3:16), and the toil and cost involved in hewing out a life within an often resistant and unyielding natural environment (Gen. 3:17–19). All that is no more, for the curse is lifted for a healed humanity.

d. God's service (v. 3)

'His servants will serve him' (v. 3). Here is the essence of the deploy-ment of the city: it will be life in the service of God. The word in the Greek text for 'serve', *latreia*, is also the primary New Testament term for 'worship'. Some earlier translations opted for the latter. 'Serve' is probably to be preferred, bearing in mind the earlier part of the text, 'his servants' (cf. similar ambiguities in Deut. 10:12; Rom. 12:2; Phil. 3:3). The distinction is certainly less than absolute, however, for the highest form of service is worship, and the deepest meaning of worship is service of the living God through our honour-ing and blessing him.

During our earthly lives, the bringing of all of life under God's rule always remains an elusive, distant objective, but in heaven the gulf between aspiration and actuality at last falls away. Now at last, thankfully, and wonderfully, our every breath will be worship, and our every motion will be service to God.

Two other comments are in order. First, the idea of continuing service is worth retaining in that it gives some imaginable content to the heavenly life. Some over the years have expressed disinterest in the prospect of heaven on the grounds of its feared monotony. Sir Walter Scott dreaded for himself 'an eternity of music', and hoped for 'some duty to discharge with the applause of a satisfied con-science'. Lloyd George confessed, 'When I was a boy, the thought of Heaven used to frighten me more than the thought of Hell. I pic-tured Heaven as a place where time would be perpetual Sundays, with perpetual services from which there would be no escape.'[11] We cannot in honesty pretend ignorance of such feelings. At times on this earthly journey, worship can seem dry and burdensome, and the arrival of the closing benediction a welcome relief. The word 'service' in our text, however, entirely dispels such fleeting anxieties and in its way responds to Scott's hope of 'some duty to discharge'. Jesus lends support to this vision in two of his parables. In the case of both the pounds and the talents (Luke 19:11–27; Matt. 25:14–30), the reward at the last for faithful service in this life is further respon-sibilities. Paul has a similar pointer: 'Do you not know that the saints will judge the world? . . . Do you not know that we will judge angels?' (1 Cor. 6:2, 3). Who can even begin to guess to what minis-tries of grace we will be called, what adventures and endeavours in the Spirit, what trophies to be won for our Blessed King and Captain in the aeons of eternity?

[11] Cited W. E. Sangster, *Sangster of Westminster* (Marshall, Morgan and Scott, 1960), p. 99.

The second point to note is that the object of the verb 'serve' in verse 3 is singular. Since both 'God and the Lamb' are referred to, we can affirm with Beasley-Murray that 'God and the Lamb are viewed as a unity in so real a fashion that the singular pronoun alone is suitable to interpret them.'[12] In the heavenly world the three persons of the Trinity will function with a unity and harmony which will afford new occasion for our adoring praise.

e. God's face (v. 4)

To see the face of God, to look into his eyes without shame or trace of fear, is the ultimate height of redemption. The invitation of the writer to the Hebrews on the basis of Christ's perfect sacrifice, 'Let us draw near to God . . .' (Heb. 10:22), finds here its final realization. It also beautifully summarizes the relational achievement of salvation. That seeing of the face of God to which the psalmists had aspired (Pss. 11:7; 27:4; 42:2) and of which the prophets had dreamed (Is. 52:8; 60:2; Zech. 9:14) is now realized. We will live, at last, *coram Deo*, 'before the face of God', as Luther put it.

Helen Keller, after a lifetime of blindness, was once asked what she would do if, for just one day, the power of sight were restored to her. She replied, 'I should call to me all my dear friends and look long into their faces.'[13] What a prospect for every child of God, to be called into the presence of the dearest Friend of our lives, whom we have here known by faith and not by sight, and there to look, and look, for ever.

f. God's seal (v. 4)

'His name will be on their foreheads.' The idea of being 'branded' in this way occurred earlier in the book of Revelation in terms of the seal of ownership by which the servants of God are identified (7:2, 3), in distinction from the seal required by the beast for all who would buy or sell in his anti-kingdom of evil (13:16, 17). The seal is a symbol of yet another blessing of the city, identity as those who belong to God. All other relationships and all other forms of belonging are now secondary to this. We are defined by, and we exist as, the children of this God. That which the Holy Spirit had given in fore-taste (2 Cor. 1:22; 5:5; Eph. 1:14) is now poured out in fullness. The Spirit's indwelling presence as a 'seal' of ownership, and hence a

---

[12] Beasley-Murray, *The Book of Revelation*, p. 332.
[13] Cited J. Macbeath, *The Face of Christ* (Marshall, Morgan and Scott, 1954), p. 15.

'deposit guaranteeing our future redemption', is now brought to its projected realization.

The association immediately noted with light, 'There will be no more night . . . for the Lord God will give them light' (v. 5), may denote an allusion to the Aaronic benediction in Numbers 6:22–26. Its words certainly represent a fitting summary of life in the New Jerusalem for the old and new Israel: 'The LORD bless you and keep you; the LORD make his face shine upon you and be gracious to you; the LORD turn his face towards you and give you peace.' It ends, 'So they will put my name on the Israelites, and I will bless them.' Indeed, he has; indeed, he will.

g. God's reign (v. 5)

'They will reign for ever and ever.' The blessing noted above can hardly be better expressed than in the final characterization of the future destiny of God's people. It is fitting that this final word concerning the people of God should refer to their dominion, for these were precisely the terms of God's purpose in the beginning. 'You shall have dominion' (Gen. 1:28, AV, RSV). 'You made them rulers over the works of your hands; you put everything under their feet' (Ps. 8:5 NIV).

Tragically, humanity failed to fulfil its calling as God's vice-regents. Instead we have tumbled down to the dust from which we were taken and grovelled on the earth instead of reaching to the skies. In the laconic words of the writer to the Hebrews, 'At present we do not see everything subject to him [i.e. humanity]' (Heb. 2:8). Pascal, as no other, plotted humanity's story in these terms when he referred to man as a king who has lost his crown. 'All the miseries of man prove his grandeur; they are the miseries of a dethroned monarch.'

Redemption reverses this tragic abdication. In Christ we have begun again to experience a degree of mastery. In Christ we can even be referred to as 'seated . . . with him in the heavenly realms' (Eph. 2:6). With the coming of the heavenly order the restoration is complete. Humanity will again raise their heads and stand tall in God's presence, and in his world. The wretch will ascend the throne. The rebel will reign. The condemned will be crowned.

To acknowledge the supremacy of God, to be defined as 'his servants' and to live henceforth in a city whose essence consists in his manifest glory, is not to lose ourselves, but for the first time truly to find ourselves. To live to the honour of God is our ennoblement; to obey him is our liberation; to live for him only is our final and all-fulfilling glory. His servants are kings. We shall reign!

Where God is all in all

God's throne, God's river, God's tree, God's service, God's face, God's seal, God's reign: such are the features of the life of the people of God in the coming Holy City. The relationship of all these features to God himself is not accidental. The final thing to be said about life in the city, which is of course simply another way of referring to the life of heaven, is to say that it is life totally centred on God. That is the deepest and most glorious prospect imaginable, for there is no reality comparable to the triune God, the ever-blessed Father, Son and Holy Spirit, who made, upholds and is the goal of all that is. To be consciously with him, to see him 'face to face', to have opened to us even a measure of his infinite depths of love, holiness, compassion, righteousness, faithfulness, sovereignty, mercy, joy and beauty, is a programme of discovery which will afford enough to occupy, entrance, amaze, delight and fulfil us into the endless depths of eternity. In the end we were made by God and made for him, and in knowing him to ever-deepening degrees lies the realization of all our dreams and desires. To that heaven will introduce us, and upon that limitless journey it will set our first steps. The return of the Lord, and the dawning of heaven, is where that journey will begin.

> But the things that began to happen after that were so great and beautiful that I cannot write them. And for us this is the end of all the stories, and we can most truly say that they all lived happily ever after. But for them it was only the beginning of the real story . . . which no-one on earth has read: which goes on for ever: in which every chapter is better than the one before.[14]

3. In the meantime . . . (22:6–21)

So the heavenly glories slowly recede; the distant triumph song of heaven grows fainter; the curtain falls gently back across the stage of time, and the city recedes once more from view. We find ourselves back on earth. The long waiting goes on – but in the meantime there are things to do. John points us to several of them as he concludes his book.

'Unseal the book!' (vv. 6, 7b, 10, 16, 18–19)

The call to John at the conclusion of the vision, 'Do not seal up the words of the prophecy of this book' (v. 10), is highly pertinent as we

---

[14] C. S. Lewis, *The Last Battle* (Penguin, 1956), p. 165.

reach our conclusion. 'Do not seal' means 'do not hide these words and this truth'. For too long the church has shied away from the heavenly hope and become almost embarrassed by its own inheritance. To proclaim the coming triumph of the Lamb is not merely to bring needed encouragement to struggling hearts. It is to honour the Lord himself as the one whose salvation is not to be confined to the trifling changes that may be traceable in our lives here and now, but reaches out to embrace the entire universe and find its apex in the spotless bride of the Lamb. We must not withhold these truths from others; we must not withhold them from ourselves. 'Unseal the book!'

'Trust the Saviour!' (vv. 14, 17)

'Blessed are those who wash their robes, that they may have the right to the tree of life, and may go through the gates into the city' (v. 14). The implications of these truths are incomparably important. Nothing in the end is as necessary for anyone than that they be among those who enter the eternal city. The alternative, an eternity in hell, is so solemn as to be virtually unthinkable. We need not give it a further thought, however, for the gates stand beckoningly open and the invitation continues to be issued.

The glories of heaven are such that to miss out on them is simply inconceivable. John's picture gallery, as we have walked its halls, has surely stirred within us a great longing. Here is life as we have always longed for it; life of which we have caught only the most fleeting of glimpses in our moments of highest human happiness. These glimpses, all too brief as they may have been, have been enough to spoil us for ever for life in the here and now. Glory awaits, and all it offers – how could we let it slip from our grasp? The doors are open, and the invitation falls upon our ears once more, 'The Spirit and the bride say, "Come!" And let those who hear say, "Come!" Let those who are thirsty, come; and let all who wish take the free gift of the water of life' (v. 17 NIVI). It is difficult to think of a biblical invitation which is as winsome and inclusive. Never has the invitation been so generously extended; never has the requirement seemed so readily to hand.

The message is surely plain and accessible, and the terms of the response by this time very clear. Trust the Saviour.

1. Admit your sin to God, and your complete inability to achieve salvation for yourself.
2. See Christ the Lamb of God dying for you.
3. Turn from all your sins, not least your self-reliance, and ask him

now to forgive and save you. 'Lord, wash me, and give me the right to the tree of life, that I may one day go through the gates into your Holy City. In Jesus' name. Amen.'

The last word is, do not delay! The issues are urgent. The Lord is coming. Come now, while you may.

'Live the life!' (vv. 15, 8–9)

The coming of the Holy City has major moral implications. We traced those earlier in studying 2 Peter 3:11, 'Since everything will be destroyed in this way, what kind of people ought you to be?' John is no less insistent. There are those within the city and those outside (v. 15). The distinction between the two groups is expressed once again in the conclusion to the book of Revelation, not only in terms of salvation, 'Blessed are those who wash their robes' (v. 14), but also in moral ones, 'Outside are the dogs, those who practise magic arts, the sexually immoral, the murderers, the idolaters and everyone who loves and practises falsehood' (v. 15). To believe in the coming of the Holy City, and to claim title in Christ to citizenship there, is to come under obligation to reflect its holiness here and now. In particular, it is a summons to worship – 'Worship God!' (v. 9). Our hearts are to be given over in submission to the one who has made all this possible for us, the one who for love of us bore on the cross the sins that would otherwise have destined us for hell. To worship him here is to prepare ourselves for that blessed eternity where we shall worship him with all our hearts and souls and minds. The coming of heaven calls for the heavenly lifestyle now.

'Look for his coming!' (vv. 7, 12, 16, 20)

The last picture of Jesus in the book of Revelation is drawn from deep in the Old Testament. He is 'the Root and the Offspring of David' (cf. Is. 11:1; John 15:1ff.). In him all the historic purposes of God for Israel have found their final fulfilment in the great company of the redeemed, the followers of the Lamb, who occupy the city. He is 'the bright Morning Star' (cf. Num. 24:17), the messianic King whose coming was anciently promised, and who will in the end be seated on the throne of God in the New Jerusalem.

The morning star, Venus, is the star of promise. To glimpse this star is to know beyond any doubting that the day is at hand, and will in time dawn in fullness. It means, truly, 'He is coming!' The Lord who holds the reins of eternal judgment and eternal salvation in his wounded hands is coming. And so for each last one of us, heaven and hell will cease to be the names of two awesome destinies. They will be present realities which have enveloped our lives. The end is sure, and it draws daily nearer. 'He who testifies to these things says, "Yes, I am coming soon"' (v. 20). To which John adds a prayer which echoes from the hearts of God's people in every age: 'Come, Lord Jesus.' End the long, dark night of sin and evil, liberate your people, and above all, exalt your own great name over all your enemies, and over all things, for ever and ever. 'Amen. Come, Lord Jesus' (v. 20).

The last word is of grace – 'The grace of the Lord Jesus be with God's people' (v. 21) – and rightly so, for the story of heaven and hell is the story of grace received and grace resisted. Hell is real because, in the mysterious depths of iniquity, God's creatures may refuse to humble themselves to receive that grace, and choose instead to go on endlessly living in denial of the mercy so gloriously and terribly won for them at the cross. Heaven is real because God, in utter grace, has made a way for his sinful creatures to return to him, and to live with him in everlasting righteousness and joy. So, 'As in revelation, so in history, grace shall have the last word.'[15] Indeed it will, for heaven is simply grace abounding, grace unleashed, grace uninhibited, grace unending, in the land of the Trinity, for ever more.

The grace there, as the grace here, is simply another name for Jesus. So, fittingly, the last word of all is his: 'The grace *of the Lord Jesus* be with God's people. Amen' (v. 21).

There can be only one response: 'Glory be to the Father, and to the Son, and to the Holy Spirit; as it was in the beginning, as it now is, and as it shall be *for ever and ever.*'

---

[15] Beasley-Murray, *The Book of Revelation*, p. 350.

In place of a summary . . .

The Last Enemy

And he who each day
Reveals a new masterpiece of sky
And whose joy
Can be seen in the eyelash of a child
Who when he hears of our smug indifference
Can whisper an ocean into lashing fury
And talk tigers into padding roars
This my God
whose breath is in the wings of eagles
whose power is etched on the crags of mountains
It is he whom I will meet
And in whose Presence I will find tulips and clouds
kneeling martyrs and trees
the whole vast praising of his endless creation
And he will grant the uniqueness which eluded me
in my earthly bartering with Satan
That day when he will erase the painful gasps of my ego
and I will sink my face into the wonder of his glorylove
and I will watch as planets converse with sparrows
On that day
When death is finally dead.

(Stewart Henderson)[16]

Study Guide

PART ONE. THE DAWNING OF DESTINY: HEAVEN AND HELL IN THE OLD TESTAMENT

Introduction (pp. 25–31)

1. Milne gives three reasons for starting at the opening of the Old Testament. What are they (pp. 25–26)?
2. Explain the Hebrew term *Sheol* (p. 27). Contrast this with the view of a 'continuing presence of the deceased in or around the place of burial' (p. 29). What do the views have in common?
3. How did ancestor worship impact the development of a comprehensive view of human destiny (p. 29)?
4. On what basis can speculation concerning the abode of the dead be negated (p. 29)?
5. Summarize the four ways in which the Old Testament anticipated the New Testament's revelation of human destiny (pp. 30–31).

'While the fullest and clearest teachings about the afterlife do certainly come from the lips of Jesus and the apostles in the New Testament, every last one of them was nurtured on the Old Testament' (p. 25).

Genesis 1:1–5, 26–27; 2:14
1. Meeting the Judge and the defendant (pp. 32–52)

1. Reflect on the afterlife. What are your thoughts about it?
2. How does Milne come to the conclusion that there is 'fullness' and 'richness' in the being of God (p. 33)?

3. The author of Genesis 1 talks of two agencies developing the creative action of God. What are they and how do they work together (pp. 33–34)?
4. Note the theme with which Genesis 1 is most concerned (p. 34).
5. Describe the relevance of the use of the word *Yahweh* (p. 35).

'So it becomes clear that creation is not for a moment to be viewed as an end in itself. Creation occurs with a view to covenant. The personal God creates human partners "in his image" (Gen. 1:26) in the anticipation that he can enter into a relationship with them. The created order is formed as a context within which this relationship can be expressed' (p. 35).

---

6. Reflect on the picture of God in Genesis 1. What is he like (p. 35)?
7. Why do we need heaven (p. 36)?
8. 'There was nothing but the Trinity, then there was the triune God plus everything that exists' (p. 37). What is the relevance of creation 'out of nothing' for learning about who God is?
9. In what ways does your church, or one you know, fit the 'deity' in a box? How can a sense of mystery and awe be introduced (p. 38)?
10. 'We are clever. We have the know-how. We are our own little gods. And all the time we live *only by God's power and permission*' (p. 39). Reflect on this statement. To what extent do you think it is true?
11. Compare reverent fear and cringing fear (p. 40). What are the differences?
12. By what means are we dependent on God (p. 41)?
13. Karl Barth says, 'The world simply cannot be absolutely godless, as it would like to be' (p. 43). Define how atheism is technically impossible.
14. Why are we accountable to God, and what obligates us to being responsible (p. 45)?

'Creatureliness means responsibility. In other words, life is not ours to use as we please, to indulge, direct or invest in whatever ways may appeal to us. The creatorhood of God means that life is not ours at all. It is not a possession to consume, it is a gift to invest. Life is not ours' (p. 46).

---

15. How do the parables show that we will be judged, and on what grounds does God judge (p. 47)?

16. Define how the Trinity shows us how to relate as humans (p. 48).
17. 'Many moderns do not believe in God. "Where is he?" they ask. And seemingly they get no answer' (p. 49). Where is God?
18. Give an example of why we should not fear judgment (p. 50).
19. Think about the call of a lover (p. 51). How is that calling similar to that of God?

Genesis 2:16–17; 3:1–24
2. The wages of sin (pp. 53–72)

1. Why is it not possible for God to speak to us in the language of angels (p. 54)?
2. Read Romans 5:12–20. In what way does this story relate to the fall (p. 55)?
3. What are the three reasons given supporting the view that the passage is a myth (p. 55)?
4. Contrast the creation accounts in Genesis and Babylonian mythology. How do they differ (p. 56)?
5. 'He [Jesus] is the Second or Last Adam, undoing *for the entire race* the malignant influence *upon the race* of the first Adam' (p. 57). What is the historical significance of this statement?
6. Explain the consequences of dehistoricizing the fall (p. 58).
7. How do we know the serpent is the devil in disguise (p. 59)?
8. Milne asserts that the origin of sin lies outside ourselves. What is the implication for life in heaven (p. 60)?
9. Clarify the fate of humans who are unrepentant (p. 60).
10. By what means are we assured of the coming of the heavenly order (p. 61)?
11. Reflect on the essence of the first sin. Why was the fruit so attractive to Eve, and what is the root of sin (p. 62)?
12. Interpret 'the wages of sin is death' in terms of what was said by God to Adam and Eve (p. 65). What is the ultimate spiritual tragedy of Adam's and Eve's revolt?

'Because of the fall our immortality is overshadowed by the multiple effects of the incursion of sin and evil into God's good world. We may retain our immortal natures, but they are expressed within an order marked by futility, threatened by human selfishness and brutality, and overshadowed by death' (p. 67).

---

13. Think about or discuss in a group what might have happened if Adam and Eve had been faithful to God's command (p. 66).

14. Give some examples of how we domesticate sin (p. 68).
15. In what way is God gracious to Adam and Eve despite their rejection of him? What is the link with the garments of salvation in Isaiah 61:10 (p. 69)?
16. Define the significant cost implied by the statement 'you will strike his heel' in Genesis 3:15 (p. 70).

Psalm 16
3. The path of life (pp. 73–82)

1. How is David brought closer to God, and what does the cup symbolize (p. 74)?
2. Explain the significance of God being his 'portion' or 'inheritance' (p. 74).
3. 'How often the children of God have learned in the crucible of trial a new and hitherto unreached degree of intimacy with their God – the discovery that in the end he is all we can ever need' (p. 75). To what measure is this statement true in your life?
4. Why can loving God never be separated from loving God's people (p. 77)?
5. Read 1 Corinthians 1:26. In what way is the congregation at Corinth similar to our gatherings today (p. 78)?
6. Define how this psalm links with heavenly hope (p. 78).
7. Taking into account the background of *Sheol* in the Old Testament, how does the psalm show that God is Lord of death (p. 79)?
8. Describe the relationship between the two primary themes of the psalm. How does one form the basis of the other (p. 81)?

'In the face of some specific threat to his life the psalmist clings to God, whom he experiences in the context of the worshipping community. Here he renews his confidence that the God who has been with him and has sustained him through his earthly life will not leave him in the moment of death. Rather, there awaits him beyond the grave a life in which he will experience even more of God and his joyful presence' (p. 82).

Psalm 72
4. Long may he live! (pp. 83–95)

1. Is there a basis for interpreting Psalm 72 as the vehicle of a dream of the future heavenly reign of Jesus the Lord (p. 83)?

2. Why could no earthly monarch match the description of the king in this psalm (p. 84)?
3. How is it possible to know there *will* be a unique and perfect ruler (p. 84)?
4. Define the source of righteousness (p. 85).
5. What is a particular feature of divine kingship and how does it link to the psalm (p. 85)?
6. In what way does Milne describe the heavenly kingdom (p. 86)?

'Each child of God will recognize him- or herself as an infinitely beloved child of God. All need to compete, or to exalt ourselves, or to put others down will have been eliminated. All will know themselves as "the disciple whom Jesus loves" ' (p. 87).

---

7. Look at verses 5 and 7. How long will the Messiah's kingdom last (p. 87)?
8. Why should the reference to dying not be applied literally (p. 87)?
9. Explain the security of heavenly treasures (p. 88).
10. Think about our throw-away culture in the West. How does impermanence affect us psychologically (p. 89)?
11. Milne says of universality: 'This . . . wonderful dimension of the Messiah's reign is all the more impressive in an age of globalism' (p. 90). Why might it be easier to understand the concept of universality now rather than fifty years ago?
12. What thread runs through the Old Testament and New Testament regarding the king's dominion (p. 91)?

'The universality of Christ's reign has the most profound implications for every disciple, as we daily serve the one whose name is Lord, and whose destined inheritance is the whole wide world' (p. 92).

---

13. Describe how Jesus is the ideal king (p. 92).
14. Reflect on verse 6. Allow the words to touch your spirit.

Daniel 7:9–14; 12:1–13
5. Either/or (pp. 96–106)

1. In what way is the book of Daniel different from others (p. 96)?

2. Explain the difference between apocalyptic writing and prophecy (p. 96).
3. 'In Daniel 7 the notion of kingly dominion is carried a stage further.' How (p. 97)?
4. Describe how the vision of Daniel moves us beyond judgment and recompense (p. 98).
5. What other features of the vision call for comment (p. 98)?
6. In Daniel 7:13–14 reference is made to 'one like a son of man, coming with the clouds of heaven'. What information can be gleaned about this enigmatic figure (p. 99)?
7. Why is it unlikely that the 'son of man' is a collective term (p. 101)?
8. 'It appears much wiser . . . to see a more general reference to manifestations of evil right across the ages which will find a special expression towards "the time of the end".' What basis does Milne have for making this statement (p. 102)?
9. List what is noteworthy about verse 12:2 and explain what is significant (p. 103).
10. How should we prepare for the moment of judgment (p. 104)?

'God is utterly fair and just, utterly righteous and holy, and also utterly loving and compassionate. If we trust our destiny to Jesus Christ, we can be assured of eternal life with God in the glory of heaven' (p. 105).

PART TWO. DESTINY DETERMINED: HEAVEN AND HELL IN THE GOSPELS

Mark 1:15; Matthew 13:24–30, 36–43; 25:31–45
6. Your kingdom come! (pp. 109–129)

1. Summarize Jesus' preaching in Mark (p. 109).
2. Where does the root of the biblical notion of God as King lie (p. 110)?
3. Into what tradition did Jesus come and reign (p. 110)?
4. Why would the announcement that the kingdom of God is near be startling (p. 110), and what is the relevance of the use of the term 'Son of Man'?
5. Define what going to heaven actually means (p. 111).
6. According to Milne, what are the parables designed to do (p. 112)?

7. Give the interpretation of the wheat and the weeds (p. 113). What is the thrust of the parable?
8. Describe the possible allusion referred to in Matthew 11:12 (p. 114).
9. How does Matthew 13:30 echo Matthew 3:12 (p. 114)?

'The kingdom has arrived, but the old order has not yet been swept away. Truly it will be eliminated; the sovereign Lord will not tolerate its opposing, usurping presence for ever. But that is not yet. Today the sons of darkness continue to oppose the sons of light' (p. 115).

---

10. In what way does the parable speak into the here and now (p. 115)?
11. 'Everyone in Galilee knew about "harvest home"' (p. 115). What was it?
12. On what basis is our eternal destiny certain (p. 116)?
13. Explain why the coming of our destiny is supernatural (p. 117).
14. 'We are all daily moving closer to a final and overwhelming encounter with our Maker' (p. 121). What are Milne's further two points on the story?
15. How does the author arrive at his conclusion that there are no second chances after judgment (p. 122)?
16. Outline the way in which the story goes further than Daniel 7 (p. 123).
17. Look at verses 25:37–39. Define the criteria for judgment (p. 124). If time permits, think about and discuss the role of faith and works.
18. What is hell and who is it for (p. 125)?
19. Summarize the 'truths concerning heaven' (p. 128).

Mark 12:18–27
7. What about heaven? (pp. 130–143)

'It is Holy Week in Jerusalem, the final week of Jesus' earthly life. He is teaching daily within the great court of the temple, where rabbis met with their disciples to share their insights and to answer questions. The debate which ensues about life after death is one of a series of encounters during that fateful week' (p. 130).

---

1. Name the different groups identified in Mark's account. What do they have in common (p. 130)?

2. The Sadducees have two questions about life. What were they asking and what was their intent (p. 131)?
3. Who were the Sadducees and what were their beliefs concerning life after death (p. 132)?
4. Give Jesus' argument for an afterlife (p. 133).
5. Why was Jesus not content with a defence of the Sadducees' scepticism (p. 134)?
6. 'The acid test of any belief, as my philosophy professor taught me years ago, is the difference the belief makes to our values and choices' (p. 134). To what extent do you agree with Milne's professor?
7. Explain how the Scriptures witness to an afterlife (p. 135).
8. Note the primary way that God demonstrates his omnipotence (p. 136).
9. What clues are there as to what heaven will be like (p. 137)?
10. According to Milne, what will sex in heaven be like (p. 138)?
11. In terms of community life, what will heaven be like (p. 140)?
12. Read the passage again. How does it challenge our culture (p. 141)?

'Something better awaits and beckons us all. We shall be "like the angels", which means not neutered, anaemic spirits, but full, free and liberated persons in whom all the possibilities of our God-given humanity will burst forth in undreamed-of fulfilment' (p. 142).

Mark 9:42–48
8. So what about hell? (pp. 144–161)

1. Outline the setting to Mark 9:42–48 (p. 144).
2. Who are 'these little ones' to whom the passage refers (p. 145)?
3. Why does Jesus put such emphasis on 'causing to stumble' as a sin (p. 146)?
4. 'Jesus now speaks of the fate awaiting such sinners in the most solemn terms' (p. 146). How does he describe hell?
5. Give the context of the passage (p. 148).
6. Explain the reference to 'cutting off' a member of the body (p. 148). What does the Lord's use of dramatic figures of speech say about his love for us?
7. Compare the traditionalist and conditionalist points of view concerning the duration of hell (pp. 150–151).
8. What are the main criticisms of the conditionalist view (p. 155)?

9. Note the common ground of both teachings (p. 154).

'Being "correct" or "enlightened" or "biblical" on the issue of the duration of hell is secondary to the question of whether or not we reflect an attitude towards it which corresponds to that of Jesus. Jesus cannot be Lord if we do not submit to his teaching, and that includes, among other things, his teaching concerning the reality and the awfulness of hell' (p. 156).

---

10. On what basis can we be sure that God will always do right (p. 156)?
11. 'How can language created and shaped by earthly experience be related to heavenly or infernal realities' (p. 158)?
12. Discuss the questions raised by Milne on page 159. For instance, 'What will "eternal" look like after the new order breaks in?' 'What will an "everlasting" existence be experienced as, whether in heaven or hell?'

Luke 23:32–43
9. When heaven begins (pp. 162–173)

1. 'I tell you the truth, today you will be with me in paradise' (Luke 23:43). What are the points to note regarding Jesus' meaning (p. 164)?
2. How is it possible for Jesus to reign from the tree (p. 165)?
3. Why is it amazing that God is gracious to the criminal (p. 165)?
4. What are the wider implications of this story (p. 167)?
5. In what way does the intermediate state not detract from the glory and completeness of the coming victory of Christ (p. 167)?
6. Explain why the intermediate state does not reflect a 'spiritualizing' instinct which denigrates the human body by suggesting that we can have a meaningful, indeed a full and satisfying, relationship with the Lord apart from the body (p. 168)?
7. Show why belief in an intermediate state does not betray a failure to face the judgment represented by human death (p. 169).
8. 'Since time was created by God, it is in principle totally relative' (p. 169). How does the elimination of time help the argument for an intermediate state?
9. What support is there for the idea of purgatory (p. 170)?
10. Summarize the biblical evidence for the notion of the intermediate state (p. 171).

11. How can we best understand the intermediate state as a dimension of Christian hope (p. 172)?

Matthew 27:45–50
10. Hell on earth: the death of Jesus (pp. 174–188)

'Hell is "in" today. "My years in Auschwitz – hell on earth!" "My heart attack was hell on earth!" "My five years of hell with an abusive husband!" " 'It was hell today on the Centre Court' says tennis star." By a strange irony, at a time when the word "hell" has almost entirely dropped from the language of the church, and from its preaching in particular, hell is one of the staples of everyday discourse' (p. 174).

1. In what way was the death of Jesus not just a personal event (p. 176)?
2. Define the term *substitution*. Where does it come from and how does it work (p. 176)?
3. By what means does hell come into play on the cross (p. 178)?
4. 'In Scripture death is never a neutral, amoral phenomenon, a purely natural fate' (p. 178). What is death, in the biblical sense?
5. Milne asserts that the true terror of death is not that in it we escape from God, but precisely that in it we meet him (p. 179). Reflect on this statement and discuss.
6. Read Matthew 27:46. What is Milne's first observation of Jesus' last hours of agony (p. 181)?
7. Explain why the words 'My God, my God, why have you forsaken me?' appear to undermine the strength of the Trinity (p. 181).
8. 'It is not enough to think here only of an abandonment, terrible as that must have been' (p. 182). What does the cup of wrath signify?
9. According to Calvin, what is Jesus' 'descent into hell' (p. 184)?

'. . . if we are to understand "for us" to mean that Christ takes our very place and, in that place of ours, accepts on our behalf entire responsibility for the whole burden of our sins, then we are driven to understand the death of Jesus on the cross in these terms' (p. 184).

10. Why is the duration of hell not of primary importance when looking at hell on the cross (p. 185)?

11. How does Milne describe hell in the light of the cross (p. 186)?

John 20:1–31; 21:1–25
11. Encountering heaven: the risen Jesus (pp. 189–200)

1. By what means can the resurrection of Jesus and the life of heaven be linked (p. 189)?

2. 'The resurrection did not take place in a vacuum. It happened within a specific nation at a particular stage of their national and religious development' (p. 190). What did Jews believe about the resurrection?

3. Define Jewish expectation at the time of Jesus (p. 190). How were they not prepared for his resurrection?

4. Explain how the resurrection of Jesus is heaven on earth (p. 191).

5. In what way does the author conclude that the resurrection created Christianity (p. 192)?

6. Milne asserts that life in the heavenly world will preserve personal identity (p. 194). How is this so?

7. Outline the way in which heavenly life is a Christ-centred life (p. 195).

8. 'The Jesus who meets us in the Gospel records of his earthly life is pre-eminently the liberated human' (p. 197). List some of the possibilities that open up to us in heaven.

'. . . we shall love one another as never before, and shall enjoy in that heavenly world the righteousness of true, pure, committed relationships of absolute love for every one' (p. 199).

---

9. Explore the idea that heavenly life will be embodied (p. 197). How does Milne's theory rest with John 21:4 where the disciples did not recognize Jesus?

10. 'We will become through God's renewing grace all that we were eternally intended to be. That is heaven' (p. 199). What is the effect of this statement on our earthly existence?

PART THREE. DESTINY DECLARED: HEAVEN AND HELL IN THE REST OF THE NEW TESTAMENT

Acts 17:22–34
12. An unpopular perspective (pp. 203–212)

1. Note the setting and background to the apostle Paul's visit to Athens (p. 203).
2. Explain the encounter of two worlds (p. 204).
3. What was Paul's concern and how did it make him feel (p. 204)?
4. Outline the content of his message (pp. 204–205).
5. Name the two schools represented in the Areopagus. Contrast the groups' beliefs (p. 205).
6. Why does Paul deal with their understanding of who God is (p. 205)?
7. Reflect on two or three of the seventeen truths Paul asserts (pp. 205–207). How do they affect you?

'One cannot read this list without astonishment. What Paul gave the Areopagus that day was nothing less than a crash course in basic theology. In particular he taught them a comprehensive doctrine of God' (p. 207).

---

8. Give the reason for Paul preaching Jesus and the resurrection (p. 208).
9. 'People are not out of touch with God prior to hearing about his coming in Jesus' (p. 208). Why not?
10. Define repentance (p. 209).
11. 'The day is coming, every hour brings it closer. He has already chosen it' (p. 210). If the day is predestined, can we affect the coming of the day of judgment with our prayers or actions?
12. In what way does the resurrection prove judgment (p. 210)?
13. Milne lists three possible responses we can make to God (pp. 211–212). Summarize them.

Romans 1:18 – 2:11
13. The revealing of wrath (pp. 213–225)

1. What are the circumstances behind this letter (p. 213)?

2. How does pluralism show itself in our culture (p. 214)?
3. Define the wrath of God (p. 215). Against whom is it directed?
4. According to Milne, what has the wrath of God to do with hell (p. 216)?
5. Describe the clearest indication of God-centredness in the letter to Romans (p. 217).
6. By what means can our response to God be passed under judgment (p. 218)?
7. 'For the apostle there is no such thing, strictly speaking, as a godless man or woman' (p. 219). Why?

'Since God has given us life, we are radically dependent upon him and accountable to him. So we are "without excuse" (1:20), our "consciences also bearing witness, [our] thoughts now accusing, now even defending" (2:15)' (p. 218).

---

8. Explain what is so terrifying about God 'giving over' people to their sin (p. 221).
9. Name the further form of divine wrath in this section of Romans (p. 222). What does Paul say about this form?
10. Outline the hope there is in spite of God's wrath (p. 224).

Romans 8:12–39
14. The privilege of children (pp. 226–243)

1. What assurance does Paul give of our heavenly destiny (p. 226)?
2. 'Those who are led by the Spirit of God are the children of God.' What does being 'led by the Spirit of God' mean and how does the Spirit work (p. 227)?
3. In terms of daring to be holy (p. 227), what things can be noted about the Christian life?
4. 'In the words of Calvin, it is not that Christians are "wholly free from vice", but that they "heartily strive to form their lives in obedience to God"' (p. 229). In what ways does Paul refer to the inner working of the Spirit?

'Being a Christian, then, means being indwelt by God the Holy Spirit in such a manner that his indwelling presence makes a difference in our lives, not least in terms of our concerns, interests and desires; and further that this difference is one of the grounds of our assurance that we will one day share the life of heaven' (p. 230).

---

5. Explain how a step closer to God may also be a step closer to his people (p. 230).
6. Give the reason why adoption was as valid as biological sonship in the Roman world of the first century (p. 231).
7. 'The Spirit's witness is his giving to Christians a persuasion that God has chosen and received them into his family, and that they are henceforth his true sons or daughters' (p. 231). Do you feel you experience this?
8. Outline the five aspects of our heavenly inheritance (pp. 232–234).
9. How does creation work towards the reality of God's triumphant purpose (p. 235)?
10. Paul notes four expressions of how God's purpose is being realized in Christians (p. 237). Make a summary of each.
11. In what ways can our future full salvation be threatened (p. 241)? What hope is there for Christians in the light of these?

1 Corinthians 15:1–58
15. An embodied hope (pp. 244–257)

1. With what issues was the church in Corinth struggling (p. 244)?
2. Describe the errant members' beliefs about the Christian's future. Why did they think this way (p. 245)?

'The assured basis of our hope is the resurrection of Jesus from the dead. The empty tomb of Jesus and his risen life after death (vv. 1–11) demonstrate beyond any question both the reality of a life beyond the grave and the embodied nature of that life' (pp. 245–246).

---

3. Why was it important that the Palestinian Christians had a physical grave-emptying resurrection (p. 246)? In what way were the Corinthians different?
4. Explain the significance of Paul mentioning the five hundred still alive (p. 247).
5. In what way does Paul make an appeal to logic (p. 247), and what are his three arguments to drive his point home (p. 248)?
6. Show why baptism of the dead is inconsistent with a purely spiritual hope (p. 249).
7. Note the arguments Paul uses to support bodily resurrection (p. 250). What is his primary point?
8. How did the Corinthians' beliefs affect the way they lived their lives (p. 252)?

9. According to Paul, what is the goal to which we aspire after the 'end' has arrived (p. 252)?
10. Paul brings five points to light in regard to the way transformation will take place (p. 254). What are they?

'Not only is death due for termination, but also its two henchmen – sin, which gives death its shadowing, destructive right to us, and the law, with its impossible demand for perfect righteousness' (p. 255).

---

11. Describe the effects of the fact of Christ's resurrection and the prospect of our own (p. 255).
12. 'Every kingdom work, whether publicly performed or privately endeavoured . . . everything, literally, which flows out of our faith-relationship with the Ever-Living One, will find its place in the ever-living heavenly order which will dawn at his coming' (p. 257). Spend some time in prayerful reflection.

2 Corinthians 4:16 – 5:6
16. Ministering in hope (pp. 258–268)

1. Despite the residual issues for some of the congregation at Corinth, what is the general context of this letter (p. 259)?
2. Define one secret of a successful ministry (p. 259).
3. Give a modern-day interpretation of treasure in jars in clay (p. 260).
4. 'In the final analysis, ministry is not a matter of human frailty; it is a matter of human finality' (p. 260). How is ministry 'impossible'?
5. Explain how Paul manages to carry on in ministry (p. 261).
6. In what way is the return of the Lord and the heavenly resurrection central for the apostle (p. 262)?
7. Summarize the contrasts Paul makes in 5:1–5 (p. 263).

'To a degree our local church can become a further dimension of "home" for us, and in doing so can be an earthly pointer to the unseen home that awaits us. We cannot enter or possess it while "in the body" (v. 6), by which Paul means, surely, in this present earthly body' (p. 264).

---

8. Outline the ways in which the heavenly hope makes a difference to Christian ministry (p. 265).

1 Peter 1:3–9
17. Suffering in perspective (pp. 269–281)

1. Who are Peter's readers and what was his purpose in writing to them (p. 269)?
2. Compare Peter's benediction with the synagogue form (p. 270). How is it different?
3. Name the three discernible effects of the resurrection (p. 271). What changes do these effects have on our lives?
4. Explain the significance of the use of the word 'inheritance' (p. 272).
5. Define the importance of the phrases 'can never perish', 'can never spoil' and 'can never fade' (pp. 273–274).
6. 'Peter in verse 5 . . . speaks of the coming salvation, our inheritance, as "ready to be revealed"' (p. 275). What will happen when the Saviour appears?
7. By what means do we know that we will be both expected and let in to heaven (pp. 275–276)?

'Peter's message is clear: on the day when you are called to bear any one of these trials, recall the heavenly prospect which lies before you. In the light of that coming inheritance we can take heart: our trials have a purpose; they will be productive; and they will pass' (p. 277).

---

8. 'God works in our trials. They are not accidental' (p. 278). To what extent do you think this is true?
9. Why does faith need to be purified (p. 278)?
10. Reflect on the quote from Desmond Tutu on page 279. How can heavenly hope change situations?
11. Milne asserts that there is someone greater than the triumph over earthly trials (p. 280). What do we lose when we lose sight of Jesus?

2 Peter 3:1–14
18. Why live differently? (pp. 282–294)

1. What is Peter's overriding concern for the health of the churches (p. 282), and what does the letter specifically address?
2. Describe the teaching going on at the time (p. 282).
3. How are the false prophets described (p. 283)?
4. In what ways do they criticize the Christian doctrine (p. 283)? Outline their real motive.

5. Peter appeals first to the Word of God. What is the bedrock of belief (p. 284)?
6. Given Peter's next points on the coming of God, what is the historical precedent for the intervention of God (p. 285)?
7. 'To accuse him of delay is effectively to ignore, even to blaspheme, his sovereignty, and to question his purpose of love' (p. 286). Give your interpretation of this statement.
8. Why will evil not go unpunished for ever (p. 286)?

'How often we excuse ourselves by alluding to the brevity of the action in question, "it happened in an instant", or "the word was out before I could stop it", as if the very intensity of the experience represented some sort of excuse, and since it happened so quickly we are really hardly responsible for it at all' (p. 287).

---

9. Suggest why there is an apparent delay in God's coming (p. 287).
10. How is it sad for those who criticize the delay in judgment (p. 288)?
11. Read the three texts to which Peter alludes in reference to the description of destiny (p. 288). On what basis does Milne come to his conclusions?
12. What are the positive effects of the believer's embrace of future destiny (p. 290)?

Revelation 20:1–15
19. Final judgment (pp. 295–308)

1. Define the book of Revelation. Who wrote it (p. 295) and who is it for?
2. Outline the two themes of the book (p. 296).
3. Why does the throne of God dominate the scene and what is symbolic about the throne itself (p. 297)?

'The judgment applies to all. The church is not excluded. Some distinction between the redeemed and the unredeemed is certainly in order with respect to the final judgment of God, and John will come to that as the vision develops' (p. 298).

---

4. How does Milne conclude that hell is made for the devil and not for humankind (p. 298)?
5. On what basis are we judged (p. 299)? Do you think this is fair?

6. Which volume of the 'books' stands apart and why (p. 300)?
7. Explain the means by which an acquittal is obtained (p. 301).
8. Imagine the 'lake of fire'. What reality does this metaphor hold for those who do not find acquittal (p. 302)?
9. What is the only way to avoid hell (p. 303)?
10. Give examples of ways we can cope, knowing that some of our loved ones may be going to hell (p. 304).
11. Why should we celebrate the last judgment as a glorious event (p. 306)?

Revelation 21:1 – 22:21
20. The colours of heaven (pp. 309–331)

1. Look at the relevant verses in Revelation. How is the image of God portrayed (p. 309)?
2. What is the relevance of continuity and discontinuity in interpreting the general identification of the new world (p. 310)?
3. According to Milne, where is heaven (p. 310)?
4. List some of the ways in which John defines the city (p. 311).

'The bride is central – not her adornments, but she herself, in her uniqueness and personhood. Here we touch that elemental truth which Victor Frankl celebrated amid the horrors of the Nazi death camps, "the truth that is set into song by so many poets, proclaimed as the final wisdom by so many thinkers – that love is the ultimate and the highest goal to which humanity can aspire..."' (p. 312).

---

5. What does heaven look like from the perspective of heaven (p. 312)? Focus on the four aspects drawn out by Milne.
6. How does God describe those who possess the city (p. 314)?
7. Who is the heavenly guide by whom John is approached in verses 9–27 (p. 316)?
8. Summarize what the angel guide reveals (pp. 317ff.). How is it possible for our home to be in the presence of God (p. 318)?
9. Imagine the creative realm in heaven. Spend some time reflecting on this aspect of life there.
10. What are the allusions to the Garden of Eden in 22:1–6 (p. 322)?
11. Define the 'healing of the nations' (p. 323).
12. 'Some over the years have expressed disinterest in the prospect of heaven on the grounds of its feared monotony' (p. 324). What hope can be drawn from verse 3?

13. Think about the face of God. What would you expect to see (p. 325)?
14. How is it fitting that the final word concerning the people of God should refer to their dominion (p. 326)?
15. Where is God in all of this (p. 327)?
16. In what way should we live while we wait for Jesus' return (pp. 327ff.)? Make a summary of Milne's points.

'The last word is of grace . . . and rightly so, for the story of heaven and hell is the story of grace received and grace resisted. Hell is real because, in the mysterious depths of iniquity, God's creatures may refuse to humble themselves to receive that grace . . . Heaven is real because God, in utter grace, has made a way for his sinful creatures to return to him, and to live with him in everlasting righteousness and joy' (p. 330).
